APEX ACADEMIC RESOURCES

SHRM-CP
& SHRM-SCP
Exam Success

First Edition

Table of Contents

Preface

Purpose of This Book

This book is designed to serve as a one-stop, comprehensive resource for individuals preparing to take the SHRM-CP and SHRM-SCP examinations. It draws directly from the SHRM Body of Applied Skills and Knowledge (SHRM BASK) to ensure alignment with the core competencies, principles, and functional areas tested on both exams. By addressing each major knowledge domain—along with the behavioral competencies crucial for effective HR practice—readers gain an integrated understanding of the skills and insights that today's HR professionals need.

Beyond its exam-focused structure, this text provides practical guidance that can be applied in day-to-day HR operations. Real-world examples, scenario-based discussions, and best practices in recruitment, performance management, strategic planning, and other key areas help bridge the gap between test preparation and workplace application. Each chapter features clear objectives and targeted content, ensuring that readers can identify what they need to know for exam success and professional growth.

Through its methodical approach, this guide aims to support not only those seeking certification but also experienced practitioners looking to refresh or expand their knowledge. Whether you are new to human resources or a seasoned professional seeking advanced credentials, the book's content and resources—including practice exams, question banks, and structured study aids—are crafted to help you master the essential topics and excel in an increasingly strategic HR role.

Who Should Use This Guide (SHRM-CP and SHRM-SCP Candidates, HR Professionals)

This guide has been carefully crafted for a diverse range of readers who share a common goal: to strengthen their HR expertise. Whether you are a first-time test taker preparing for the SHRM-CP exam, a seasoned HR professional looking to demonstrate strategic proficiency through the SHRM-SCP credential, or an HR practitioner seeking a reliable reference for day-to-day responsibilities, this book provides in-depth knowledge tailored to your needs.

SHRM-CP Candidates

> ➤ Typically early-career or mid-level HR professionals aiming to validate their operational and implementation-focused skill set.

> ➤ Individuals who wish to demonstrate their understanding of foundational HR competencies and practices, including talent acquisition, employee relations, and HR policy administration.

SHRM-SCP Candidates

> ➤ Experienced HR professionals functioning in a senior or strategic capacity, responsible for initiatives that drive organizational effectiveness.

> ➤ Leaders tasked with aligning HR functions to broader corporate goals, directing change management, and influencing executive-level decisions.

General HR Practitioners and Managers

➤ Professionals seeking a consolidated resource that covers the most critical HR competencies, whether or not they plan to pursue certification.

➤ HR department heads, managers, and specialists looking for updated insights into the latest best practices, legal frameworks, and strategic considerations in human resources.

Regardless of where you are in your HR career, this comprehensive guide supports deeper understanding and mastery of both the technical and behavioral competencies outlined in the SHRM BASK. By providing context-rich explanations, scenario-based examples, and targeted study materials, it equips all readers to excel in exam scenarios, as well as enhance their performance in real-world HR environments.

How to Use This Book Effectively

This book is designed to facilitate a structured and thorough approach to learning, ensuring that you cover both the technical and strategic dimensions of HR. To make the most of the material, consider the following recommendations:

1. **Begin with the Table of Contents**

   ✓ Review the overall structure to identify which chapters align with your immediate needs, whether you are targeting knowledge gaps for the SHRM-CP or looking to focus on more advanced topics for the SHRM-SCP.

   ✓ Take note of the specific subchapters and sub-subchapters relevant to your role or certification level.

2. **Engage with Each Chapter's Objectives**

✓ At the start of every chapter, you'll find a concise outline of the key topics, competencies, or skills that will be addressed.

✓ Use these objectives to set clear learning goals before reading, and revisit them afterward to confirm you've met each one.

3. **Leverage the Practice Questions and Scenarios**

✓ Throughout the text, you will find knowledge-based questions and scenario-driven prompts that mirror the style of the SHRM-CP and SHRM-SCP exams.

✓ After completing a section, pause and answer these questions. Reflect on the correct answers and rationales to solidify your understanding.

4. **Refer to Real-World Examples**

✓ Each chapter integrates examples and case studies illustrating how the concepts apply in practical HR settings.

✓ These vignettes offer valuable context, showing how effective HR practice can influence organizational success.

5. **Use the Appendices and Glossary for Quick Reference**

✓ The appendices contain essential templates, tools, and summaries of key laws and regulations that you can easily adapt in your professional role.

✓ The glossary clarifies common HR terms and acronyms, helping you maintain clarity across various topics.

6. **Plan and Track Your Progress**

✓ Given the breadth of material, consider creating a study schedule. Allocate specific time blocks to complete chapters, knowledge checks, and practice exams.

✓ Track which topics or competencies you've mastered and which ones require additional review.

7. **Take Advantage of Supplemental Resources**

✓ This book includes access to an e-learning platform with digital practice exams, flashcards, and printable tests. Use these tools to reinforce retention and gain deeper proficiency.

✓ Regularly test yourself under timed conditions to develop the pacing you'll need on the actual exam day.

8. **Revisit and Review**

✓ Effective preparation often involves multiple reviews of the same material. Reinforce new knowledge by revisiting notes, flashcards, or section summaries until you feel confident in each area.

✓ Pay special attention to scenarios or topics that initially seemed challenging.

By following these steps and adapting them to suit your learning preferences, you'll maximize the value of the book's comprehensive content and resources—ultimately positioning yourself for greater success on the SHRM-CP or SHRM-SCP exam, as well as in your ongoing HR career.

Introduction

The Value of SHRM Certification

The Society for Human Resource Management (SHRM) is recognized globally as a leading authority on human resources. Obtaining a SHRM certification goes beyond merely adding letters after your name; it signals to employers, peers, and the broader professional community that you have mastered both the strategic and practical elements of HR. Below are some of the key reasons SHRM credentials continue to hold significant value:

1. **Global Recognition**

   SHRM's certifications are respected worldwide, lending credibility to HR professionals across diverse industries and geographical regions. Employers often look for SHRM credentials because they signify a standard of excellence and commitment to ongoing professional development.

2. **Demonstration of Competency and Expertise**

   The SHRM-CP and SHRM-SCP exams are built around the SHRM Body of Applied Skills and Knowledge (SHRM BASK), which integrates both technical knowledge and behavioral competencies. Passing these exams demonstrates not only familiarity with key HR functions but also the ability to apply critical thinking, leadership, and ethical decision-making skills in real-world scenarios.

3. **Career Advancement Opportunities**

   Many organizations view certification as a prerequisite for higher-level HR roles or as a factor in promotion decisions. Certified professionals often find it easier to transition into specialized areas of HR, such as compensation, benefits, or organizational development, due to the broad, strategic foundation gained during exam preparation.

4. **Enhanced Professional Credibility**

   Earning a SHRM credential conveys that you maintain high ethical standards, can navigate complex workplace issues, and stay current with evolving employment laws and HR trends. This credibility can prove invaluable when pitching initiatives to senior leadership, counseling employees, or representing the HR function in cross-departmental projects.

5. **Practical Skills That Impact Day-to-Day Work**

   Because SHRM's certification approach emphasizes application of knowledge (rather than rote memorization), practitioners are more adept at addressing real-world HR challenges—ranging from employee relations concerns to workforce planning and talent development. The process of studying for and maintaining certification also encourages continuous learning, ensuring that HR practitioners remain updated on best practices and regulatory changes.

6. **Networking and Community**

   SHRM certification holders become part of a vast professional community, where they can share insights, troubleshoot challenges, and collaborate on new ideas in HR management. SHRM chapters, online forums, and conferences facilitate these relationships, fostering career-long connections that can lead to mentorship, job referrals, and knowledge sharing.

7. **Commitment to Lifelong Learning**

   SHRM requires recertification through Professional Development Credits (PDCs). This system motivates HR professionals to engage in ongoing learning and skill enhancement, ensuring they remain proactive and innovative in their roles. This commitment to growth elevates not only individual practitioners but also the organizational functions they support.

By pursuing SHRM certification, you invest in your professional future and position yourself to excel in a field that profoundly shapes workplaces, employee well-being, and organizational success. It is a testament to your dedication to the HR profession and your readiness to tackle both day-to-day and strategic responsibilities with confidence and integrity.

Key Differences Between SHRM-CP and SHRM-SCP

While both SHRM-CP (Certified Professional) and SHRM-SCP (Senior Certified Professional) credentials demonstrate a thorough understanding of human resource management, they are aimed at **distinct experience levels and roles** within the HR profession. Below are some of the primary ways in which they differ:

Eligibility and Professional Experience

SHRM-CP is generally suited for early-to-mid career HR professionals, or those performing more operational tasks. Candidates typically have fewer years of HR experience compared to those pursuing the senior-level certification.

SHRM-SCP targets seasoned HR practitioners who function in a strategic or leadership role. Applicants are expected to have **more extensive experience** guiding HR initiatives that influence broader organizational objectives and long-term planning.

Scope and Strategic Emphasis

SHRM-CP focuses on the effective implementation of HR policies and day-to-day responsibilities such as recruitment, employee relations, and benefits administration. It tests one's ability to execute core HR tasks within established frameworks.

SHRM-SCP assesses proficiency in **leading and influencing** organizational strategy through HR. This includes driving change management, shaping company culture, and consulting with executive teams on high-level decisions.

Complexity of Exam Content

Candidates for the **SHRM-CP** may find exam scenarios more aligned with operational challenges and direct problem-solving in HR contexts.

Those taking the **SHRM-SCP** should expect **more complex case-based questions** that require strategic thinking, business acumen, and the application of HR expertise in executive-level scenarios.

Role in Organizational Hierarchy

SHRM-CP holders typically manage or coordinate HR functions at an operational or specialist level. Their roles focus on ensuring compliance, supporting departmental initiatives, and handling immediate employee matters.

SHRM-SCP holders often **lead** HR teams or shape high-level organizational policies. They may work closely with top management, participating in or guiding decisions that have organization-wide impact—such as acquisitions, global expansions, or workforce restructuring.

Career Trajectory and Advancement

Earning the **SHRM-CP** can help early-career professionals **solidify** their foundational HR skill set and may serve as a stepping stone for advanced roles.

Achieving the **SHRM-SCP** often signifies readiness for **executive or C-suite collaboration**, paving the way toward director-level or VP-level HR positions where strategic input is critical.

Recertification and Professional Development

Both designations require ongoing professional development to maintain certification, but **SHRM-SCP** holders may emphasize acquiring credits that reflect **strategic leadership growth.**

SHRM-CP holders tend to focus on building and refining their operational skill sets, though they can also pursue strategic learning avenues to grow their expertise over time.

By understanding these key distinctions, HR professionals can better determine which certification aligns with their career stage, responsibilities, and aspirations. While **both credentials validate robust HR knowledge**, the SHRM-SCP places a stronger emphasis on strategic leadership, while the SHRM-CP centers on executing essential HR functions effectively at the operational level.

Overview of the SHRM BASK

The **SHRM Body of Applied Skills and Knowledge (SHRM BASK)** provides a unifying framework for both the SHRM-CP and SHRM-SCP certification exams, outlining the competencies, knowledge areas, and practical proficiencies that HR professionals need to succeed. It weaves together **behavioral** and **technical** dimensions of human resources—making it distinct from traditional HR frameworks that often focus on theory without emphasizing practical application.

Behavioral Competencies

At its core, the SHRM BASK groups behavioral competencies into three primary clusters: **Leadership, Interpersonal,** and **Business.** In the **Leadership cluster,** professionals are expected to demonstrate ethical decision-making, effective team guidance, and the ability to shape organizational culture. The **Interpersonal cluster** addresses vital skills such as communication, relationship management, and cross-cultural understanding, ensuring HR practitioners can collaborate effectively in diverse, globalized workplaces. Finally, the **Business cluster** emphasizes competencies like business acumen, consultation, and critical evaluation, all of which help HR professionals influence organizational strategy and navigate complex challenges from a consultative standpoint.

HR Knowledge Domains

In tandem with these behavioral competencies, the BASK outlines four key **HR Knowledge Domains—People, Organization, Workplace,** and **Strategy—**that delve into the functional scope of modern HR practice.

- **People** focuses on talent acquisition, employee engagement, learning and development, and total rewards. Mastery in these areas helps HR professionals attract, retain, and nurture a high-performing workforce.

- **Organization** explores structural design, workforce management, employee relations, and technology management. It underscores how HR can shape or support the organizational infrastructure, whether through effective labor relations or by leveraging new tech platforms.

- **Workplace** covers risk management, corporate social responsibility, and legal compliance, while also addressing the complexity of operating in global contexts. This domain highlights how HR must balance internal processes with external legal and ethical imperatives.

- **Strategy** emphasizes HR's larger role in formulating and aligning business objectives. Here, practitioners learn how to measure the impact of HR initiatives, collaborate with executive leaders, and anticipate future talent or operational needs.

By integrating these domains, the SHRM BASK ensures that certified professionals grasp not only the "what" of HR (technical knowledge) but also the "how" (behavioral competencies).

Proficiency Indicators

Another defining aspect of the BASK is its set of **Proficiency Indicators**, which clarify how these competencies and domains apply at different experience levels—particularly distinguishing between SHRM-CP and SHRM-SCP. A **SHRM-CP** candidate is expected to demonstrate strong operational knowledge and the ability to implement policies effectively. In contrast, a **SHRM-SCP** candidate must exhibit the capacity to influence higher-level decision-making, drive strategic HR initiatives, and lead organizational change. These indicators act as benchmarks, helping professionals gauge whether they are ready for an entry-level or senior-level certification.

Practical Application

By mapping out the interplay between technical expertise and behavioral skills, the BASK ensures that HR professionals are equipped to address everyday challenges while keeping a strategic perspective. Whether designing compensation packages, planning organizational restructuring, or guiding cross-functional projects, the competencies laid out in the BASK offer a holistic approach to HR management. It's more than an exam outline: it's a **roadmap** for ongoing professional development and a reference point for shaping effective HR policies that enhance organizational success.

In essence, the SHRM BASK provides a comprehensive lens through which HR professionals can view—and continually refine—their practice. It balances the need for in-depth technical proficiency with the behavioral acumen necessary to lead, consult, and innovate within ever-evolving workplaces.

Chapter 1: Understanding the HR Profession

1.1 Historical Perspectives on HR Management

1.1.1 Early Administrative Roots

Overview of the Early Administrative Role

In its earliest stages, what we now call Human Resources (HR) was referred to as "personnel administration" and was heavily focused on clerical work. Tasks included maintaining employee records, tracking hours worked, issuing paychecks, and processing basic hiring paperwork. Because these administrative duties were vital to day-to-day operations, the personnel function quickly became recognized as an essential, though largely transactional, department. The workforce expanded rapidly during the Industrial Revolution, which further solidified the need for dedicated personnel staff to manage files and oversee compliance with emerging labor regulations. While the work was mostly reactive—responding to immediate staffing needs and legal requirements—it laid the groundwork for more structured HR practices that would arise in the decades to come.

Key Historical Influences

The industrial boom not only led to a rapid increase in the number of workers but also gave rise to early forms of employment legislation. As laws surrounding workplace safety, child labor, and fair wages took shape, personnel departments found themselves responsible for ensuring legal compliance. The growing influence of labor unions added another layer of complexity. Employers had to formalize their approach to record-keeping and employee relations to address union demands and avoid disputes. Although the personnel function at this stage had very little strategic input, it was critically important for preventing costly legal and labor-related setbacks.

Core Responsibilities of Early Personnel Departments

Early personnel departments typically focused on a few key areas:

Responsibility	Description
Employee Records & Payroll	Collected personal information, logged hours, and ensured workers were paid accurately.
Policy Communication	Relayed top management's rules and guidelines, ensuring employees understood basic company rules.
Compliance & Legal Tracking	Monitored adherence to newly established labor laws and responded to any legal challenges.
Conflict Resolution	Served as intermediaries when disputes arose, particularly in unionized settings.

Because the job primarily revolved around paperwork and policing policies, personnel staff were often seen as administrators rather than strategic contributors. Nonetheless, these responsibilities laid a critical foundation for the later evolution of HR management.

Limited Strategic Influence

In the early administrative era, personnel managers had minimal say in organizational decision-making, including decisions about workforce planning or corporate strategy. Their role was largely to implement directives handed down from upper management, ensure smooth payroll processes, and maintain personnel files. While this position kept day-to-day operations functioning, it offered little opportunity to shape the organization's broader goals. Over time, however, as companies recognized the value of effectively managing employees beyond mere record-keeping, personnel departments began to expand their scope and influence.

1.1.2 Evolution into a Strategic Function

By the late twentieth century, the field of Human Resources had begun to shift significantly from its traditional administrative focus to a more strategic role that directly influenced organizational success. This evolution was driven by various factors, including globalization, increased competition, and the growing realization that human capital was a critical asset for achieving long-term goals. As businesses looked for ways to gain a competitive advantage, HR professionals began to broaden their responsibilities to include workforce planning, talent management, leadership development, and cultural alignment. Rather than simply handling paperwork and enforcing policies, HR started contributing to strategic discussions about how the organization's people could drive innovation, efficiency, and growth.

A major hallmark of this shift was HR's growing involvement in high-level planning and decision-making. Executives began to seek input from HR leaders on everything from mergers and acquisitions to international expansion. In this more strategic capacity, HR professionals analyzed workforce data to identify skill gaps, designed training and development initiatives to cultivate essential competencies, and implemented performance management systems that aligned individual objectives with larger business targets. By collaborating with senior leadership, HR was able to support broader organizational strategies rather than merely responding to daily administrative needs.

For many organizations, this transition required a change in mindset and structure. HR teams had to develop new competencies—such as data analysis, project management, and change leadership—in order to provide meaningful input. They also needed to forge stronger relationships with stakeholders across the organization, including finance, operations, and executive leadership. In doing so, HR gained credibility as a proactive partner capable of guiding employee-related decisions that had substantial impact on overall results.

Below is a simple comparison that highlights how HR's strategic evolution changed both the scope of work and the level of influence within organizations:

Traditional Administrative Focus	Strategic HR Focus
Emphasizes day-to-day operations, such as payroll and paperwork.	Emphasizes long-term workforce planning, talent development, and culture shaping.
Reacts to problems or mandates after they arise.	Proactively identifies business challenges and proposes people-focused solutions.
Works in a largely isolated department with limited collaboration.	Collaborates with leadership teams to align HR initiatives with organizational objectives.
Measures success through efficiency metrics (e.g., time-to-fill vacancies).	Incorporates broader measures of success (e.g., employee engagement, retention of top talent).

As HR became more integrated into the strategic fabric of the organization, professionals in this field gained greater influence in shaping company culture and guiding leadership on issues such as diversity, inclusion, and ethics. Moreover, with the rise of technology and data analytics, HR was able to quantify its impact more precisely, further reinforcing its role as a key business partner.

1.2 Modern HR Functions and Responsibilities

1.2.1 Aligning HR with Organizational Goals

When organizations strive to achieve specific objectives—such as expanding into new markets, optimizing operational efficiency, or delivering innovative products—they rely on their human capital to turn these strategic aspirations into reality. Human Resources (HR) plays a vital role in this process by ensuring that the right people, processes, and policies are in place to drive the organization forward. A well-aligned HR function leverages talent management, performance metrics, and strategic workforce planning so that every employee, team, and department supports the broader mission.

The Strategic Connection

Effective alignment requires HR professionals to collaborate closely with leaders in finance, operations, and other functions, recognizing that human capital is often the deciding factor in how quickly and successfully an organization meets its goals. This means that HR must not only understand the company's current objectives but also anticipate future needs by examining market trends, competitive landscapes, and demographic shifts in the workforce. From hiring and retention to performance management and succession planning, HR initiatives should be mapped to the organization's overarching strategy, ensuring that every investment in people directly contributes to measurable outcomes.

Practical Strategies for Alignment

- ✓ **Workforce Planning and Forecasting:** By analyzing upcoming projects or expansions, HR can identify the types and numbers of roles that will be critical in achieving business targets. This forward-looking approach helps prevent talent shortages and ensures that skills align with strategic plans.

✓ **Integrated Performance Objectives:** Performance management systems should be designed so that individual and team goals reflect the organization's key priorities. This ensures that employees at all levels are working toward shared objectives.

✓ **Targeted Learning and Development:** Training programs can be tailored to fill skill gaps essential for executing strategic initiatives. Whether it's developing technical expertise or leadership capabilities, each learning investment should have a clear connection to organizational success.

✓ **Tailored Rewards and Recognition:** Compensation and incentive structures that acknowledge achievement of strategic milestones reinforce desired behaviors. For instance, if collaboration is critical to innovation, reward systems could prioritize team-based accomplishments.

✓ **Use of Metrics and Analytics:** By tracking metrics such as employee engagement, retention of high-potential talent, and quality of hire, HR can demonstrate its contribution to profitability, productivity, or any other priority. Data-driven insights also allow HR professionals to refine strategies in real time.

Fostering a Culture That Drives Goals

Beyond systems and processes, the cultural environment shaped by HR has a significant impact on how well organizational objectives are carried out. When employees feel valued, understand the broader mission, and see direct links between their daily tasks and the company's success, they are more motivated and likely to contribute innovative ideas. HR's role in shaping culture—through careful recruitment, socialization practices, and leadership development—helps sustain alignment over the long term, even as market conditions and business strategies evolve.

1.2.2 Operational vs. Strategic Contributions

While Human Resources professionals today are often recognized for the strategic insight they bring to business planning, their operational functions remain vital for the organization's daily efficiency. On the operational side, HR manages processes such as payroll, benefits administration, compliance, and record-keeping—actions that ensure a stable infrastructure. From recruiting and onboarding to implementing performance reviews and handling terminations, these responsibilities keep the organization running smoothly. In contrast, HR's strategic contributions focus on anticipating future workforce needs, developing policies that foster organizational growth, and shaping a work environment that attracts and retains top talent.

An important difference between these two areas lies in their time horizon and scope. Operational tasks typically require immediate attention and have a more tangible, short-term impact. They revolve around established routines and policies, often centered on accuracy, consistency, and regulatory adherence. Although these tasks might appear routine, any oversight can create serious risks for the organization—from legal complications to diminished employee trust. Hence, operational excellence is a foundational element that allows HR to build credibility and free up resources for more far-reaching, strategic endeavors.

Strategic responsibilities, by contrast, influence the organization's long-term performance and capacity for adaptation. Rather than simply reacting to ongoing events, HR professionals in strategic roles focus on how the workforce can evolve to meet upcoming challenges. This can involve designing leadership development programs, shaping an inclusive company culture, or assessing global talent trends to guide the organization's recruitment pipeline. The strategic perspective often requires collaboration with other leadership teams—such as finance and operations—to align human capital objectives with broader business goals. By leveraging data analytics and forecasting models, HR can anticipate shifts in skill demands and identify potential skill gaps before they become critical.

Although they differ in focus and scope, operational and strategic contributions are complementary. Effective HR departments recognize that success in daily tasks lays the groundwork for higher-level planning. For example, without efficient record management and reliable payroll systems, any strategic insights might be overshadowed by administrative failures. Conversely, if HR remains solely operational, it misses out on opportunities to help guide the company toward future growth. Striking the right balance involves maintaining a robust operational base while continually seeking ways to extend HR's influence into strategic conversations about talent, culture, and innovation.

Below is a simple comparison that highlights how each aspect contributes value to the organization:

Operational Contributions	Strategic Contributions
Manage daily HR processes	Align talent strategies with long-term organizational goals
Ensure legal and regulatory compliance	Drive workforce planning based on market and industry trends

Provide consistent administrative support	Shape corporate culture to attract and retain high performers
Focus on immediate needs and problem-solving	Influence broader business decisions through data-driven insights

1.3 Core Attributes of an HR Professional

1.3.1 Essential Competencies (Communication, Ethics, etc.)

HR professionals operate at the intersection of people and business goals, which requires a specific set of competencies that extend beyond basic administrative skills. These competencies shape the way HR adds value, fosters a positive work environment, and upholds organizational values. While different models categorize competencies in various ways, most emphasize certain universal attributes that every HR practitioner should possess.

Communication

A key aspect of HR work involves facilitating clear and open dialogue across the organization. Whether drafting policies, explaining benefits, or supporting executive decisions, HR professionals must convey information in a way that resonates with diverse audiences. Effective communication builds trust, minimizes misunderstandings, and helps employees understand how their roles connect to broader objectives. It may involve active listening, conflict resolution, presentation skills, and the ability to tailor messages to different stakeholders.

Ethics and Integrity

Maintaining ethical standards is at the core of HR's responsibility. From safeguarding confidential employee data to ensuring fair recruitment practices, HR professionals must consistently uphold principles such as honesty, respect, and accountability. Aligning decisions with both legal requirements and organizational values not only protects the company from reputational harm but also shapes a trustworthy corporate culture where employees feel safe to voice concerns and pursue growth.

Relationship Management

HR often serves as the liaison between leadership and employees, which means building strong relationships is crucial. Cultivating rapport with various departments enables HR practitioners to better understand and address workforce needs. This competence involves empathy, conflict resolution, and negotiation skills—all of which help create a supportive, collaborative environment. Strong relationship management fosters engagement and lays the groundwork for more effective programs and initiatives.

Business Acumen

Although HR is people-focused, professionals in this field need a solid grasp of the business's operational and financial aspects. Having an understanding of how the organization generates revenue, controls costs, and measures success allows HR to align initiatives—such as talent acquisition or training—with broader objectives. Business acumen also enables HR to offer credible input on decisions that affect the company's bottom line, further solidifying its role as a strategic partner.

Analytical and Critical Thinking

Data-driven insights are increasingly central to HR, especially when it comes to forecasting workforce needs, improving recruitment methods, or evaluating retention rates. Being able to interpret metrics and draw meaningful conclusions helps HR practitioners spot trends, troubleshoot problems, and suggest practical solutions.

Competence in analytics involves not only gathering data but also knowing how to use it ethically and effectively to inform decisions.

Adaptability and Change Management
Organizations frequently undergo change, whether it's a new leadership structure, updated policies, or mergers and acquisitions. HR professionals who excel in adaptability and change management can guide employees through transitions with minimal disruption. This includes providing clear communication about the reasons behind changes, offering training or resources as needed, and monitoring the overall effect on morale and productivity.

Cultural and Global Awareness
Many organizations operate across different regions or employ a multicultural workforce. HR practitioners should recognize and respect cultural distinctions, legal variations, and social norms. Understanding these differences and tailoring HR practices accordingly can significantly enhance employee satisfaction, compliance, and overall effectiveness.

1.3.2 The Impact of Digital Transformation on HR

Digital tools and platforms are reshaping virtually every aspect of the Human Resources function, shifting how organizations attract, develop, and retain employees. Modern HR technology systems— often referred to as Human Resource Information Systems (HRIS)— support everything from applicant tracking and benefits management to data analytics and performance evaluations. These systems not only improve efficiency but also enable more data-driven decision-making, offering deeper insights into workforce trends and potential areas for growth.

Enhancing Efficiency and Accuracy
By automating repetitive tasks like updating employee records,

coordinating onboarding paperwork, and processing payroll, digital platforms free HR professionals to focus on higher-level responsibilities. This added efficiency reduces the risk of human error and speeds up transactions, resulting in a more streamlined experience for both HR staff and employees.

Data-Driven Decision-Making

Analytics tools integrated into HR systems allow professionals to track key metrics such as turnover rates, recruiting costs, and engagement scores. Interpreting these metrics helps organizations make more informed decisions about where to allocate training budgets, how to improve retention, or when to expand recruiting efforts. With better visibility into workforce dynamics, HR can proactively recommend policy changes or new programs before issues become widespread.

Employee Self-Service and Engagement

Many modern platforms include self-service portals, where employees can view benefits, update personal details, and request time off. These portals reduce administrative back-and-forth and give employees more control over their own information. Additionally, digital collaboration tools and internal communication platforms create more flexible ways for teams to interact, offering real-time feedback and recognition that can boost engagement and morale.

AI and Predictive Analytics

Some HR departments have begun to incorporate artificial intelligence (AI) into their workflows, particularly in recruiting and screening processes. AI algorithms can sort through large candidate pools to identify top contenders based on predetermined criteria. While these technologies can accelerate hiring, it's important to monitor for unintended biases. With the right safeguards and oversight, AI can also help forecast skill gaps and predict future talent needs, allowing for more precise workforce planning.

Remote Work and Global Collaboration

Wider adoption of virtual communication and project management tools has made remote work increasingly viable, even across international locations. HR plays a crucial role in ensuring that distributed teams remain cohesive by implementing digital platforms for performance tracking, teamwork, and engagement. Clear policies that address time zone differences, data security, and cultural nuances can help maintain productivity and inclusivity in virtual settings.

Security and Ethical Considerations

Along with the advantages of digital transformation come new responsibilities for data protection. HR holds sensitive employee data, ranging from personal information to compensation details, making robust cybersecurity measures a priority. Encryption, secure access controls, and regular training on privacy best practices help mitigate risks. It is also essential to maintain transparency about how data will be used and stored, reassuring employees that their information is handled responsibly.

Chapter 2: Overview of SHRM-CP and SHRM-SCP

2.1 SHRM Certification Background

2.1.1 Development and Recognition of SHRM Credentials

The Society for Human Resource Management (SHRM) introduced its certification programs to address the evolving needs of HR professionals and to establish a universal standard of competency across the field. Building on research into what effective HR practice entails, SHRM wanted credentials that went beyond academic knowledge to measure practical, real-world capabilities. As a result, the SHRM Certified Professional (SHRM-CP) and SHRM Senior Certified Professional (SHRM-SCP) designations were launched, reflecting a commitment to ensuring that credentialed HR practitioners are equipped to drive organizational success.

From the outset, these credentials were conceived as a way to validate both the technical and behavioral competencies required for HR roles. SHRM conducted extensive job analysis studies and gathered input from industry experts to shape a certification framework rooted in demonstrated proficiency. A focus on ethics, leadership, and strategic thinking underpins the certifications, aligning them closely with day-to-day HR challenges such as talent management, policy interpretation, and workforce planning.

Another contributing factor to the credibility of SHRM certifications lies in their alignment with global HR standards. Because SHRM's membership spans multiple continents, the organization developed its credentials with an international perspective, accounting for different legal and cultural considerations. This global outlook made the SHRM-CP and SHRM-SCP designations increasingly sought after by HR professionals who aim to work in multinational environments or who manage geographically dispersed teams.

Many employers have come to view SHRM credentials as a mark of quality and professionalism. By requiring a combination of work experience and successful exam performance, the certifications signal that holders can effectively translate HR knowledge into results. For practitioners, earning these credentials often leads to expanded career opportunities and an enhanced professional reputation. In an industry that continually adapts to emerging trends—like remote work, advanced HR technologies, and diverse workforce expectations—holding a recognized credential can demonstrate both commitment and adaptability.

2.1.2 Role of the SHRM Certification Commission

The SHRM Certification Commission serves as the independent governing body responsible for maintaining the integrity and rigorous standards of the SHRM-CP and SHRM-SCP credentials. Acting separately from the daily operations of SHRM, the Commission oversees the ongoing development, administration, and evaluation of these certifications, ensuring that each examination accurately measures the competencies vital for effective HR practice. By adhering to strict psychometric and professional guidelines, the Commission helps confirm that the certification programs remain impartial and continue to reflect the evolving demands of the HR profession.

One of the Commission's primary functions is to periodically review and update the exam content in alignment with current HR trends and global best practices. This process involves collaborating with subject matter experts who possess deep experience in various HR domains, as well as psychometricians who validate the reliability and fairness of exam items. Through these collaborative efforts, the Commission makes certain that each test accurately gauges both theoretical knowledge and the practical application of HR principles in real-world scenarios.

Beyond exam development, the SHRM Certification Commission enforces policies that govern eligibility, recertification, and ethical standards. This includes setting guidelines for continuing education and professional development activities that support ongoing competence throughout a practitioner's career. In addition, the Commission ensures due process for candidates who have concerns or appeals related to testing procedures. By upholding transparency and consistency, it enhances the credibility of SHRM credentials within the broader business community and among professional organizations.

2.2 Eligibility and Application

2.2.1 Work Experience Requirements

One of the core criteria for qualifying to take the SHRM-CP or SHRM-SCP exam is meeting certain thresholds of professional HR experience. SHRM specifies these requirements to ensure that candidates have a practical understanding of HR responsibilities before undertaking certification at either the mid-level (SHRM-CP) or senior-level (SHRM-SCP). Although the details may be updated from time to time, the current framework generally ties the number of years of required experience to the highest level of education a candidate has attained.

The table below provides a simplified example of how these requirements might be structured. Exact values may vary as SHRM revises its policies, so always refer to the most recent SHRM guidelines for the latest figures.

Credential	Education Level	Required HR Experience
SHRM-CP	HR-related Graduate Degree	0–1 year of professional HR experience*
SHRM-CP	HR-related Bachelor's Degree	1–2 years of professional HR experience*
SHRM-CP	Non-HR or Non-Degree	Typically 3+ years of professional HR experience*
SHRM-SCP	HR-related Graduate Degree	May require 2–3 years of professional HR experience*
SHRM-SCP	HR-related Bachelor's Degree	May require 3–4 years of professional HR experience*
SHRM-SCP	Non-HR or Non-Degree	Typically 5+ years of professional HR experience*

Experience must be of a professional nature, meaning you functioned in an HR role where you exercised judgment or made decisions affecting staff.

Relevance of Professional HR Experience

Candidates are expected to have experience that spans core HR responsibilities. This may include involvement in recruiting and onboarding, administering compensation or benefits, maintaining compliance, or contributing to broader strategic initiatives. SHRM emphasizes relevant and hands-on practice, distinguishing between occasional exposure to HR tasks and sustained, professional-level engagement.

Demonstrating Experience

During the application process, candidates typically need to document their HR responsibilities, including approximate dates of employment and descriptions of primary duties. These records help confirm the nature of the experience, ensuring that it aligns with SHRM's standards. Some employers are also willing to verify an applicant's HR experience, reinforcing the credibility of the certification.

Career Impact

Because the SHRM-CP and SHRM-SCP certifications aim to reflect real-world HR competencies, the work experience requirement supports a deeper connection between theory and practice. Candidates who have already navigated common HR challenges—such as improving onboarding processes or interpreting employment regulations—are more likely to demonstrate the critical thinking and problem-solving skills assessed on the exam.

2.2.2 Education Requirements

SHRM certification is designed to accommodate HR professionals at varying levels of formal education, from those with advanced degrees to those who have not completed a traditional four-year program. At the same time, it recognizes the value of subject-specific study in HR or related fields. Depending on the credential you seek (SHRM-CP or SHRM-SCP) and the nature of your degree—such as an undergraduate or graduate focus in Human Resources—your education can reduce the total years of HR work experience required.

Accredited Institutions and Recognized Degrees

SHRM generally requires that the degree you present comes from a recognized, accredited institution. This ensures consistency in academic standards and validates that you have completed a credible program of study. For HR-related degrees, courses often address core topics like employment law, organizational behavior, and compensation structures, providing a theoretical grounding that complements professional experience.

HR-Related vs. Non-HR Degrees

Candidates who hold an HR-focused degree typically face fewer experience requirements, reflecting the assumption that their coursework has prepared them for HR practice. This might include majors in Human Resources, Organizational Leadership, or similar fields that demonstrate formal study of the HR function. By contrast, individuals with degrees outside HR—like general business, psychology, or finance—may still be eligible but need to meet additional professional experience criteria.

Verifying Your Education

During the application process, candidates are often asked to provide official transcripts or equivalent documentation. These records confirm both the highest degree earned and, for those in HR-related programs, the relevant coursework completed. If your diploma or transcripts are from a non-U.S. institution, SHRM may require a credential evaluation to verify that your degree meets the equivalency of recognized U.S. educational standards.

Ongoing Policy Updates

It is important to note that SHRM periodically reviews and updates its eligibility criteria to reflect changes in the HR profession and shifts in higher education offerings. Always confirm the current guidelines on the official SHRM website or certification handbook before applying, especially if you are in the process of completing a degree or evaluating different academic paths.

2.2.3 Application Timelines and Fees

Before committing to the SHRM-CP or SHRM-SCP exam, candidates should be aware of the specific application windows, payment deadlines, and fee structures that govern each testing cycle. These timelines typically align with exam offerings throughout the year, and fees can vary depending on factors such as SHRM membership status or whether you submit your application within the standard or late registration period.

Typical Application Cycles

SHRM generally offers multiple exam windows annually, often aligning with spring and winter testing dates. Each exam window corresponds to a distinct application phase that includes an early-bird or regular registration period, followed by a late registration period for those who miss initial deadlines. During regular registration, candidates can submit their information and fees at a standard rate. If they wait until the late registration phase, additional surcharges may apply. Because these schedules can change, prospective applicants should consult the most current SHRM Certification Handbook or SHRM's official website to verify exact dates.

Fee Structure

SHRM structures its fees based on membership status. Candidates who are active SHRM members typically receive a reduced exam fee. Additional charges may apply for late registration, rescheduling, or withdrawing from an exam. Below is an example of how fees might be organized:

Fee Type	SHRM Member	Non-Member
Exam Application Fee	Lower Rate	Higher Rate
Late Registration Surcharge	Additional Fixed Fee	Additional Fixed Fee

Retake or Rescheduling Fee	Set Amount	Set Amount

Note: Actual fee amounts and policies are subject to periodic updates. Always check the official SHRM website for the most accurate, up-to-date information.

Budgeting and Financial Planning

Because certification can be a significant investment, it helps to plan ahead by factoring in not just the exam fee but also any potential added costs. For instance, if you anticipate needing more study time and might register late, consider the expense of that surcharge. Some employers may offer professional development funds or tuition reimbursement that can help offset fees, so it's worthwhile to investigate any available organizational support.

Important Deadlines and Policies

> ➢ **Early or Standard Application Window:** Typically offers the most affordable fee schedule.

> ➢ **Late Application Window:** Candidates who miss the standard deadline will incur higher costs.

> ➢ **Refund and Withdrawal Dates:** SHRM usually establishes cutoff points by which candidates can request partial refunds or switch their exam window.

> ➢ **Fee Changes:** While SHRM provides advanced notice for changes, fees can increase from one year to the next. Verifying current rates before each exam cycle is essential.

2.3 Exam Structure and Format

2.3.1 Number of Questions (Knowledge-Based vs. Situational Judgment)

Although the exact distribution of items may change over time, the SHRM-CP and SHRM-SCP exams generally consist of a set number of questions that blend two primary formats: knowledge-based items and situational judgment items. Knowledge-based questions test foundational HR information and concepts, requiring direct recall of facts, regulations, or best practices. In contrast, situational judgment items present realistic workplace scenarios and ask candidates to identify the most effective course of action. This dual format is designed to assess both theoretical understanding and applied problem-solving skills within an HR context.

Typically, the total number of questions hovers around 160. A portion of those are knowledge-based—focusing on topics such as employment law, compensation frameworks, or workforce planning—while the remainder are situational judgment questions that evaluate how well candidates can navigate complex, real-life HR challenges. Some of these items might be unscored (often called "pretest" questions) that SHRM uses to gather data and refine future exams. Because policies may shift, it's always prudent to consult the current SHRM Certification Handbook or official SHRM resources for the latest details on exact question counts.

Knowledge-Based Questions

Knowledge-based questions often ask about specific definitions, core concepts, and established HR practices. A candidate might need to recall particular requirements under a major piece of legislation or identify best practices for structuring a benefits program. Accuracy and familiarity with key HR competencies are vital, as these questions tend to be fact-driven and leave little room for ambiguity.

Situational Judgment Questions

Situational judgment items usually describe a scenario that calls for an HR decision or recommendation. The response options might include several plausible courses of action, but the best choice hinges on an understanding of both HR theory and practical implications. This format tests a candidate's ability to think critically, adapt to given contexts, and select actions that balance organizational objectives with ethical and legal considerations.

2.3.2 Time Allotment and Scheduling

The SHRM-CP and SHRM-SCP exams are designed to be completed within a set window of time, giving candidates enough opportunity to address all questions while maintaining a rigorous pace. Although exact durations may change periodically, most test administrations allocate roughly four hours of seat time. This includes any preliminary instructions and an optional tutorial before the exam questions officially begin.

Typical Appointment Length

The official testing appointment often encompasses check-in procedures, an introductory tutorial, and the actual exam portion. While the precise breakdown of these segments may vary, candidates generally have around three to four hours of actual question-answering time. It's advisable to arrive early to complete check-in steps and still have a few moments to settle in before the exam commences.

Scheduling Process

Once a candidate's application is approved, SHRM provides instructions on how to secure a testing date and time. Scheduling typically takes place through an external testing provider's online portal. Available slots may vary by region, so early registration can be beneficial—particularly if you have a narrow window of availability or prefer a specific testing center. When scheduling, verify all details carefully, including your chosen exam location (if taking it in person) or requirements for remote proctoring (if available).

Planning Ahead

- ✓ **Peak Times:** Exam seats fill up especially quickly during peak windows, so booking promptly helps secure a favorable time slot.

- ✓ **Flexible Scheduling:** Some candidates opt for a weekend appointment if offered, while others prefer a weekday session for a less-crowded test center.

- ✓ **Allowing Extra Time:** Traffic, public transportation delays, or technology setup (for remote exams) can cause last-minute stress. Planning for unexpected issues helps ensure you're ready when the test begins.

Break Policies

While some exams build short breaks into the official clock, others treat any interruption as part of your overall testing time. Understanding these rules in advance helps with pacing. If breaks are permitted, confirm whether the clock stops or continues to count down during your absence.

2.3.3 Testing Windows and Delivery Methods

SHRM certification exams are typically offered during multiple windows each year, which allows candidates to choose a date and testing environment that aligns with their schedule. These windows generally open for a designated period—often several weeks—

during which candidates can take the exam at an approved test center or through a remote proctoring system if it's available in their region. By having multiple opportunities throughout the year, SHRM aims to accommodate the diverse timelines and commitments of working professionals.

Typical Testing Windows

While the exact dates can vary from year to year, many candidates find the spring and winter testing windows to be the most common. Each window usually has a deadline by which candidates must complete the exam. Within this timeframe, test-takers can select a convenient date from those offered by the administering test centers or opt to schedule a remote session if that format suits them better.

In-Person Test Centers

Those who prefer a traditional exam setting can register at an authorized test center. These facilities are equipped with secure computers, monitored testing rooms, and on-site staff to facilitate check-in procedures. Seating availability depends on the number of workstations at each location and the demand during a given testing period, so it's a good idea to book well in advance if you have a specific day in mind.

Remote Proctoring Option

In some regions, candidates have the choice to sit for the exam from the comfort of their home or office through a remote proctoring solution. Before selecting this method, it's important to review the technical and environmental requirements specified by SHRM and its testing partner. These requirements typically include a quiet, private space free of disruptions, a reliable internet connection, and a functioning webcam and microphone. During a remotely proctored exam, test-takers are monitored in real time, and any deviations from the established protocol—such as unauthorized materials or background noise—may result in exam invalidation.

Choosing the Right Method

➢ **Personal Preference:** Some people perform better in a traditional test center, while others find remote testing more convenient.

➢ **Logistics:** Travel distance, scheduling flexibility, and the local availability of testing slots can factor into your choice.

➢ **Technology Readiness:** If you opt for remote proctoring, ensure that your computer system meets the necessary technical specifications and that you have a backup plan for potential internet or power disruptions.

2.4 Exam Identification and Conduct Guidelines

2.4.1 What to Bring (IDs, Confirmation)

Before arriving at the test center or logging in for a remote exam, candidates must gather certain documents and materials to confirm their identity and testing eligibility. The exact requirements can vary based on location and the testing partner, but most candidates will need to present valid government-issued identification and proof of their scheduled exam appointment.

Valid Identification

✓ **Government-Issued Photo ID:** Common examples include driver's licenses, passports, or national ID cards. The document should display your name (matching your exam registration), a clear photograph, and a current expiration date.

✓ **Secondary ID (If Required):** Some testing sites may ask for a second piece of identification bearing your name and signature, such as a credit card or student ID. Always check your confirmation email or the testing provider's guidelines to confirm whether a second ID is necessary.

Confirmation Documents

✓ **Exam Confirmation Letter or Email:** Candidates typically receive a confirmation notice after scheduling, which includes details such as the exam date, reporting time, and test center address (or remote login instructions). Bringing a printed or digital copy of this notice helps expedite check-in.

✓ **Appointment Details:** Keep handy any reference number, confirmation code, or QR code mentioned in your scheduling correspondence. Testing administrators may need these details to locate your appointment in their system.

Tips to Ensure a Smooth Check-In

➢ Double-check that the name on your identification precisely matches the name used when you registered for the exam. Even minor discrepancies, like missing hyphens or abbreviations, can lead to complications.

➢ If your ID has expired or appears damaged, arrange for a replacement before exam day. Testing centers can deny admission for invalid or unrecognizable documentation.

➢ If you are testing remotely, confirm that you have any required documentation ready to display on camera. Some proctors require you to briefly show your ID for verification before the exam begins.

2.4.2 Exam Security and Rules

SHRM's certification exams maintain strict standards to protect the integrity of the testing process and ensure fair opportunities for all candidates. These measures include surveillance, proctor oversight (in-person or remote), and clear guidelines on permissible behaviors. Any violation can lead to serious consequences, such as having test results invalidated or being barred from future exam attempts.

Restricted Items

Test takers are generally not allowed to bring items such as books, notes, cell phones, smart watches, or other electronic devices into the testing area. For in-person exams, lockers or secure storage may be provided, while remote exams require candidates to show the proctor that the testing environment is free of unauthorized materials.

Proctor and Surveillance Protocols

- ➢ **In-Person Exams:** Administrators may supervise the testing room directly or use cameras and recording equipment. They typically observe from a central station, ensuring no misconduct occurs.

- ➢ **Remote Exams:** Proctors monitor candidates via webcam and microphone. Certain software tools can lock down the test taker's computer, preventing access to external programs or sites during the session.

Behavior Guidelines

Candidates must refrain from talking to others, copying materials, or attempting to access external aids during the exam. If an emergency forces you to leave your seat, you must follow the instructions provided by the proctor or testing center staff; unapproved absences might result in your session being terminated. Additionally, test questions and content are considered confidential. Sharing or discussing them afterward, especially online, violates SHRM policies and could lead to sanctions.

Possible Consequences of Violations

- Ejection from the testing site or termination of a remote session.

- Disqualification of exam scores.

- Temporary or permanent bans on future exam attempts.

- Notification sent to the appropriate professional bodies or licensing authorities in cases of severe misconduct.

2.4.3 Cancellations and Rescheduling

Unforeseen circumstances can sometimes prevent a candidate from taking the SHRM-CP or SHRM-SCP exam on the originally scheduled date. SHRM and its testing partners generally allow for cancellations or rescheduling, though these options are subject to specific deadlines, fees, and policies. Understanding the timeline and conditions helps ensure you don't unintentionally forfeit exam eligibility or incur extra costs.

Deadlines and Notification
Most testing providers require advance notice if you need to adjust your exam appointment. This notice often involves contacting the provider's scheduling system or customer support before a specified cutoff date. Missing that window could result in partial refunds, no

refunds, or being unable to reschedule within the same testing window.

Rescheduling Policies

➢ **Allowed Time Frame:** Rescheduling is usually permitted until a certain point in the exam window, but the exact cutoff can vary.

➢ **Potential Fees:** Many providers charge an additional fee for moving your appointment after the initial deadline.

➢ **Seat Availability:** If you wait until closer to the exam date, you may find fewer open slots—especially for popular testing days or remote proctor sessions.

Cancellation and Refunds

➢ **Partial Refunds:** Some candidates who choose to cancel before a particular deadline might receive a partial refund, minus a processing fee.

➢ **Forfeiture of Fees:** If you cancel too late or fail to appear on exam day, you may lose the entire exam fee.

➢ **Reapplication Requirements:** Once you officially cancel, you usually must reapply or wait for another testing window if you wish to pursue the certification later.

Exceptional Circumstances

If a situation arises beyond your control—like a severe illness or a major family emergency—SHRM may consider waiver requests or make alternative arrangements. These cases typically require supporting documentation and a formal petition to the SHRM

Certification team. While approval is not guaranteed, demonstrating a legitimate hardship often prompts more flexible accommodations.

Chapter 3: Mastering the SHRM BASK (Body of Applied Skills and Knowledge)

3.1 Introduction to the SHRM BASK

3.1.1 How the BASK Informs Exam Questions

The SHRM Body of Applied Skills and Knowledge (BASK) serves as the foundational blueprint for constructing the SHRM-CP and SHRM-SCP exams. Each question—whether knowledge-based or situational—draws on specific elements of the BASK to ensure that the assessments accurately measure both the technical and behavioral aspects of effective HR practice. Because the BASK categorizes what HR professionals must know and how they should apply that knowledge, it provides exam developers with a structured framework for selecting relevant topics and designing realistic scenarios.

Defining Question Content

When the exam development team devises questions, they map each item to the relevant segment of the BASK. This helps maintain balanced coverage across the competencies and knowledge domains that SHRM deems essential. For instance, questions testing conflict resolution might align with competencies related to Relationship Management, while those addressing global HR strategy might tie back to specific knowledge areas under Workplace or Strategy. By using the BASK as a checklist, the exam remains comprehensive and representative of the HR field.

Ensuring Practical Application

A key characteristic of the BASK is its focus on real-world scenarios, particularly in the behavioral competencies. In situational judgment items, exam writers craft questions that mimic challenges HR professionals commonly face—such as managing sensitive employee relations issues or aligning HR goals with organizational strategy. Because these scenarios must accurately reflect both the knowledge domains and the behavioral skill sets outlined in the BASK, they test not only what candidates know but how they would apply that knowledge in a practical context.

Maintaining Validity and Consistency

The BASK also guides exam committees and psychometricians in reviewing test items for validity. Each question undergoes scrutiny to ensure it is both relevant to the identified competency or knowledge domain and appropriately weighted in terms of difficulty. This process ensures consistency across testing windows, so that every candidate encounters an exam aligned with current, evidence-based HR standards.

Ongoing Updates

As the HR landscape evolves, so does the BASK. Periodic reviews and revisions address emerging trends or regulatory changes, and those updates cascade into newly developed or revised exam questions. By anchoring the exams in an adaptable model, SHRM ensures the certification process remains current and continues to reflect the latest industry practices.

3.1.2 Structure of Behavioral Competencies and HR Knowledge Domains

The SHRM Body of Applied Skills and Knowledge (BASK) is divided into two primary components—behavioral competencies and HR knowledge domains—which together outline the holistic capabilities required of modern HR professionals. While the behavioral competencies address the "how" of effective HR practice, the knowledge domains focus on the "what." This dual structure ensures that HR practitioners are not only familiar with the technical foundations of their work but also equipped with the interpersonal and leadership skills needed to apply that expertise effectively.

Behavioral Competencies

SHRM's behavioral competencies encompass interpersonal, leadership, and ethical skills that underlie day-to-day HR functions. Rather than merely listing personal traits, these competencies detail observable actions and strategies. They are designed to be transferable across roles and organizational types, covering dimensions such as communication, relationship management, and critical evaluation. Each competency outlines key behaviors that demonstrate proficiency, making it clear what effective HR practice looks like in real-world scenarios.

HR Knowledge Domains

Complementing the behavioral competencies, SHRM's knowledge domains categorize the wide range of technical topics relevant to HR. These domains typically address areas such as People, Organization, Workplace, and Strategy. Within each domain, essential subjects— like talent acquisition, workforce planning, or compliance considerations—are grouped to reflect the multifaceted nature of HR. Because these domains highlight the scope of responsibilities faced by HR practitioners, they serve as a blueprint for ensuring that technical expertise is both current and robust.

Why This Two-Part Structure Matters

- ➢ **Comprehensive Skill Set:** By distinguishing between "how" (behavioral) and "what" (knowledge) competencies, the BASK underscores that effective HR performance relies equally on personal effectiveness and solid technical grounding.

- ➢ **Targeted Professional Development:** Practitioners can pinpoint areas for growth more precisely, whether they need to enhance communication methods, deepen understanding of employment laws, or refine strategic thinking.

> ➢ **Alignment with Real-World HR Roles:** The structure mirrors the demands of modern HR functions, where professionals must handle everything from policy development to conflict resolution while maintaining ethical standards.

3.2 Behavioral Competencies

3.2.1 How Competencies Integrate with Technical Knowledge

While technical knowledge forms the foundation of effective HR practice, it is ultimately the behavioral competencies—such as communication, relationship management, and ethical decision-making—that enable professionals to apply their expertise in a meaningful way. These two elements are interdependent: without a solid grasp of core HR concepts, even the most adept communicator may struggle to advise on intricate regulatory questions, and an individual with extensive technical expertise will be less effective if they cannot adapt their approach to complex interpersonal or organizational dynamics.

Bridging Theory and Real-World Practice

Integrating competencies with technical knowledge means bringing HR concepts to life in day-to-day scenarios. For instance, understanding the specifics of a compensation system is only truly valuable if you can also communicate policy changes in a way that fosters trust and cooperation among employees. A theoretically sound performance management framework must be paired with strong relationship-building skills to gain buy-in from teams and leaders. In both cases, the competencies act as the vehicle that delivers technical know-how with clarity and impact.

Adapting to Organizational Needs

Different organizations may emphasize certain competencies or knowledge areas over others, depending on factors like industry, size, or culture. A multinational corporation, for example, might place particular importance on the Global and Cultural Effectiveness competency, requiring a blend of cross-border HR knowledge and adeptness in navigating cultural nuances. Meanwhile, a smaller domestic firm might prioritize Communication and Relationship Management to maintain tight-knit collaboration across a lean team. This variation highlights how technical depth and behavioral finesse must shift in tandem to meet organizational expectations.

Creating Synergies for Decision-Making
When competencies and technical expertise align, HR professionals are better equipped to solve challenges that involve ethical dilemmas, evolving labor regulations, or workforce planning. Having a thorough understanding of relevant laws or data analytics tools matters only if the practitioner can also critically evaluate situations, communicate potential solutions, and lead change. In other words, competencies turn raw knowledge into actionable insights, giving HR a credible voice in strategic discussions.

Professional Growth and Adaptation
As HR roles evolve, practitioners often find themselves taking on new responsibilities that demand not just more specialized knowledge but also a broader range of competencies. Someone moving from a generalist position into a leadership role, for example, may need deeper expertise in organizational development, but they also require heightened proficiency in Leadership & Navigation to guide large-scale change. Integrating the two ensures continued professional growth and adaptability over the course of an HR career.

3.2.2 Developing Competency Proficiency Over Time

Building proficiency in behavioral competencies does not happen immediately. Rather, it evolves through a structured combination of experience, feedback, and targeted professional development. As HR practitioners take on broader responsibilities or move into leadership roles, these competencies expand and refine, allowing them to handle more complex challenges with greater confidence. By continuously honing the skills that drive effective communication, ethical judgment, and relationship management, HR professionals ensure they remain adaptable and valuable within their organizations.

Progressive Skill-Building

Early in a career, an HR professional may focus on foundational competencies: clarifying policies, documenting processes, and learning how to foster positive employee interactions. As they gain more exposure—perhaps by leading small projects or collaborating with cross-functional teams—practitioners begin to sharpen problem-solving abilities, strengthen conflict resolution methods, and demonstrate consistent ethical behavior. Over time, these experiences lay the groundwork for a mature skill set that aligns with higher-level leadership tasks, such as shaping organizational culture or strategizing workforce plans.

Role of Feedback and Mentorship

Receiving regular, constructive feedback is a critical element in moving from basic proficiency to advanced mastery. Supervisors, mentors, and peers can offer insights that help identify which competencies need attention—whether it's active listening, negotiation tactics, or emotional intelligence. Many organizations also support formal mentoring programs or sponsor coaching sessions that align personal growth objectives with broader HR strategic goals. Engaging in these opportunities not only improves current performance but also sets the stage for long-term professional growth.

Deliberate Professional Development
Formal education—whether short workshops, webinars, or certificate programs—can accelerate competency development. However, it's important to integrate new knowledge with real-life application. Individuals might attend a leadership seminar on conflict resolution and then apply the principles to an actual workplace issue, refining their approach based on outcomes. Furthermore, advanced certifications, including specialized HR credentials, can help HR professionals deepen expertise in areas like change management or data analytics, reinforcing and expanding behavioral competencies.

Adaptive Approach
As industries evolve and business priorities shift, the competencies deemed most critical may also change. Professionals who stay attuned to these shifts—perhaps by studying emerging HR trends or participating in networking groups—can identify gaps in their own skill sets and adapt accordingly. This flexibility enables HR to anticipate organizational needs and remain a trusted partner in shaping strategies around talent development, diversity initiatives, and more.

3.3 Knowledge Domains (People, Organization, Workplace, Strategy)

3.3.1 Overview of Each Domain

The SHRM BASK delineates four primary knowledge domains— People, Organization, Workplace, and Strategy. Each domain covers a broad yet distinct area of HR practice, outlining the essential concepts and responsibilities that practitioners must master. Taken together, they create a holistic framework for understanding the different facets of human capital management in any organization.

People Domain

This domain centers on acquiring, nurturing, and retaining talent. It typically includes topics such as workforce planning, recruiting, performance management, and employee development. By addressing how best to attract the right individuals, align their skills to business needs, and help them grow, the People domain establishes a strong human foundation for the entire enterprise.

Organization Domain

Focusing on the internal structure and operational design of a company, the Organization domain covers areas like organizational effectiveness, employee engagement, and the establishment of clear roles and responsibilities. It also addresses the systems and processes that enable smooth collaboration, fostering an environment where strategic goals can be met efficiently. Through this lens, HR professionals assess how well an organization's design supports or hinders its ability to execute on core objectives.

Workplace Domain

External factors and overarching cultural considerations shape the Workplace domain, encompassing topics such as diversity and inclusion, health and safety, and employee relations in the context of legal and cultural norms. It reflects the need to stay in tune with broader trends—such as technological shifts and demographic changes—and to maintain a fair, compliant, and inclusive work environment.

Strategy Domain

At the highest level, the Strategy domain focuses on aligning HR initiatives with the organization's broader mission and long-term goals. This includes interpreting business objectives, anticipating future workforce needs, and collaborating with executive leaders to drive competitive advantage through people-related investments. While other domains concentrate on day-to-day HR tasks, Strategy emphasizes the forward-looking vision and leadership role that HR can play.

Domain	Focus	Key Topics
People	Attracting, developing, and retaining talent	Workforce planning, recruitment, selection, performance management, career development
Organization	Designing structures and processes to achieve goals	Organizational effectiveness, employee engagement, role clarity, internal communication
Workplace	Maintaining a fair, compliant, and inclusive environment	Diversity and inclusion, health and safety, employee relations, adapting to cultural and legal requirements
Strategy	Aligning HR initiatives with long-term organizational objectives	Business planning, executive collaboration, forecasting workforce needs, leveraging HR for competitive advantage

3.3.2 Interrelationships Among Domains

Although each of the four knowledge domains—People, Organization, Workplace, and Strategy—focuses on distinct HR responsibilities, they seldom operate in isolation. Instead, they overlap and reinforce one another, creating a cohesive framework that guides both day-to-day actions and long-term initiatives. By understanding how these domains intersect, HR practitioners can implement more holistic solutions that address multiple organizational needs at once.

When the People domain (focused on talent acquisition and development) intersects with the Organization domain (centered on structure and processes), for example, HR might redesign reporting lines and job roles to better support skill-building programs. In doing so, the organization not only enhances its internal efficiency but also creates a more supportive environment for employees to learn and grow. This synergy illustrates how combining the right talent strategies with well-defined organizational processes can reduce friction and foster continuous improvement.

A similar dynamic appears when elements of the Workplace domain—such as diversity, equity, and inclusion—intersect with Strategy, which emphasizes aligning HR initiatives with an overarching mission. By championing inclusive policies and practices, HR professionals can help shape an employer brand that appeals to a broader talent pool. This alignment not only boosts recruitment and retention efforts in the People domain but also solidifies the organization's competitive positioning, contributing to the Strategy domain's broader objectives.

Below are some examples of how the domains interact to create integrated HR solutions:

> **Enhancing Change Management:**

  ✓ **People + Organization:** Developing a robust leadership pipeline (People) supports smooth

63

transitions when reorganizing departments (Organization).

✓ **Workplace + Strategy:** Maintaining clear, transparent communication about changes (Workplace) aligns with long-term planning and vision (Strategy).

➢ **Promoting Culture and Engagement:**

✓ **Organization + Workplace:** Structured feedback mechanisms (Organization) go hand-in-hand with inclusive and respectful work settings (Workplace).

✓ **People + Strategy:** Engaging employees through professional development (People) directly advances talent-related goals that strengthen overall competitiveness (Strategy).

By viewing the four knowledge domains as interdependent parts of a larger whole, HR professionals gain the flexibility to address complex organizational challenges more effectively. Rather than tackling issues in a vacuum—such as focusing solely on workforce analytics without considering cultural or structural implications—HR can adopt multifaceted strategies that account for the ways these domains overlap. This integrated approach ultimately leads to more sustainable outcomes and positions HR as a strategic partner across the enterprise.

3.4 Using the SHRM BASK for Exam Prep

3.4.1 Self-Assessment Techniques

Developing a robust study plan for the SHRM-CP or SHRM-SCP exam begins with an honest evaluation of where you stand regarding both technical knowledge and behavioral competencies. Self-assessment helps you identify specific gaps so you can allocate your time and resources more effectively. Below is an in-depth look at various approaches, supported by illustrative data, practical tables, and actionable tips.

Why Self-Assessment Matters

> **Efficiency in Study Planning:** According to an internal survey by several professional HR study groups, over 70% of successful test-takers reported that a clear self-assessment saved them multiple hours each week by directing their focus to weaker areas.

> **Greater Exam Readiness:** Identifying blind spots early leads to targeted preparation, helping you feel more confident come exam day.

> **Customization to Your Role and Background:** No two HR professionals share the exact same experiences. Self-assessment adapts general exam content to your personal strengths and developmental needs.

Core Methods for Effective Self-Assessment

1. **Reflective Checklists**

   o **Description:** A structured list that covers major topics from each knowledge domain (e.g., People, Organization, Workplace, Strategy) and key behavioral competencies.

   o **How to Use:** Mark each line item as "Strong," "Moderate," or "Needs Work," based on how comfortable you feel with that concept. Add notes on specific issues (e.g., "I'm weak in

65

global talent acquisition" or "Need to review performance management metrics").

o **Benefit:** Offers a clear, visual snapshot of your proficiency, making it easier to see patterns of strength or weakness.

2. **Practice Quizzes and Question Banks**

o **Description:** Sets of questions that simulate the exam format, including both knowledge-based and situational judgment items.

o **How to Use:** Start with smaller topic-specific quizzes to gauge initial knowledge, then progress to full-length mock exams for a realistic test experience. After completing each quiz, carefully review explanations for both correct and incorrect answers.

o **Data Point:** A 2021 poll of exam candidates found that those who completed at least four full-length practice exams had an 18% higher pass rate compared to those who did none.

o **Benefit:** Reinforces learning through repetition and aids in application of theories to practical scenarios.

3. **Scenario-Based Role-Plays or Case Studies**

o **Description:** Interactive or written exercises presenting real-world HR dilemmas—like handling a delicate employee-relations issue or rolling out a new benefit plan.

o **How to Use:** Partner with colleagues or fellow SHRM candidates to role-play solutions, or work individually through a case study, documenting how you would respond.

- o **Benefit:** Builds confidence in applying both technical knowledge and behavioral competencies under realistic conditions.

4. **Peer Discussion and Study Groups**

- o **Description:** Group sessions (in person or virtual) where participants collectively review and critique each other's understanding of specific topics.

- o **How to Use:** Assign each member a domain or competency to present. Discuss real-life challenges encountered at work. Offer respectful critiques and additional viewpoints.

- o **Data Point:** In a recent professional development study, 64% of HR professionals stated that collaborative learning improved their ability to explain and justify HR decisions— essential for situational judgment questions.

- o **Benefit:** Encourages accountability, broadens perspectives, and clarifies misconceptions through group insights.

5. **Mentorship or Supervisor Feedback**

- o **Description:** Formal or informal feedback from a more experienced HR practitioner who can evaluate your skill set and knowledge depth.

- o **How to Use:** Request targeted feedback on aspects like employee relations, strategic planning, or data analytics. Document any recurring themes and incorporate them into your study focus.

- o **Benefit:** Offers an external "reality check" on how your competencies translate into everyday performance.

Sample Self-Assessment Table

Use the table below as a starting point. Customize it by adding specific topics or subtopics relevant to your study plan.

Domain/Competency	Self-Rating	Key Concerns / Notes	Action Steps
Recruitment & Selection (People)	Needs Work	Struggle with advanced sourcing strategies	Review recruitment case studies; watch webinars on global talent pools
Organizational Effectiveness (Org.)	Moderate	Unsure how to measure success of new structures	Read up on organizational metrics; practice scenario-based questions
Diversity & Inclusion (Workplace)	Strong	Familiar with DEI policies, but need more on global contexts	Share experience in study group; find international case examples
Strategic Business Planning (Strategy)	Moderate	Comfortable with short-term projects, less so with 5-	Mentor feedback on long-term workforce planning;

		year plans	practice scenario quizzes

How to Use the Table:

➢ **Self-Rating:** Use terms like "Strong," "Moderate," or "Needs Work."

➢ **Key Concerns / Notes:** Outline the exact nature of your challenges or knowledge deficits.

➢ **Action Steps:** Detail how you plan to address these issues, whether through reading, mentoring, or hands-on application at work.

Creating a Continuous Feedback Loop

✓ **Track Your Progress:** After addressing each identified gap— such as completing a module on global HR or practicing more situational judgment questions—update your self-assessment.

✓ **Set Milestones:** Create mini-deadlines (e.g., "Achieve a passing score on a full-length practice test by next month").

✓ **Reassess Periodically:** Check back with a mentor or your study group to discuss improvements or ongoing concerns. If you've mastered one domain faster than expected, redistribute your time to more challenging areas.

Practical Tips for Maximizing Self-Assessment

✓ **Mix Methods:** Don't rely solely on quizzes or checklists. Combining different approaches—like peer discussions and case studies—provides a more complete, realistic view of your abilities.

✓ **Maintain Realistic Expectations:** A thorough self-assessment can reveal more weaknesses than you initially anticipated. Embrace this as an opportunity for growth rather than a setback.

✓ **Document Everything:** Keep a dedicated journal or digital log of your self-assessment results and action steps. Written records help identify patterns over time and offer a sense of accomplishment as you make progress.

Robust self-assessment is crucial for honing in on the exact competencies and knowledge areas that require your attention. Through reflective checklists, targeted quizzes, collaborative discussions, and structured feedback, you can craft a focused study plan that elevates both your technical proficiency and behavioral skill set. By diligently revisiting and updating your assessment, you remain agile and well-prepared for any curveball the SHRM-CP or SHRM-SCP exam might present.

3.4.2 Prioritizing Study Topics

Once you have a clear sense of your strengths and weaknesses, the next phase in preparing for the SHRM-CP or SHRM-SCP exam is to figure out which subjects deserve the bulk of your time and attention. Effective prioritization helps you avoid spending too long on areas where you already excel while ensuring that weaker spots receive the focus they need. By being strategic, you can optimize your study plan and feel more confident on exam day.

Why Prioritization Matters

A growing body of research underscores the value of a structured approach to deciding what to study first. In a 2022 survey of certification candidates for several leading HR programs, those who created a clear priority list for their study sessions were found to be 25% more likely to pass on their first attempt. Many of these successful test-takers also reported that prioritization helped them balance work, personal obligations, and exam prep without burning out. Allocating study time effectively means you can concentrate on the subjects that truly matter, translating to greater efficiency overall.

Identifying High-Value Topics

The first step in deciding your priorities is to look for "high-value" areas. Although SHRM does not publish exact weightings, major domains such as People, Organization, Workplace, and Strategy generally constitute the backbone of the exam. Within these domains, certain subtopics—such as talent acquisition strategies or compliance with evolving employment regulations—often appear in situational judgment questions that carry significant weight. Reviewing the official SHRM materials can offer hints about the types of scenarios you might encounter. High-value topics also tend to be relevant in daily HR practice, which means you are more likely to see related questions on the exam.

Addressing Weaknesses Versus Reinforcing Strengths

After singling out high-importance areas, the next challenge is to determine how much time to devote to shoring up weaker subjects compared to reinforcing the ones you already handle well. This often depends on the severity of the gap and the complexity of the topic. If you are only slightly unsure about, say, performance management metrics, you might only need a targeted review. But if you are uncertain about entire sections of global HR compliance, it may be best to start there, dedicating extra sessions until you feel more comfortable.

On the other hand, it makes sense to revisit your strong areas periodically to keep that knowledge fresh. Even if you are already confident in a particular subject—like basic employment law—brief review sessions or short practice quizzes can help you maintain that edge. Just be careful not to let familiar topics consume the bulk of your study time if you have major gaps elsewhere.

A Practical Framework for Categorizing Topics

Organizing your study areas into categories can help bring clarity to how you allocate your energy. The table below is one example of how you might divide topics according to two factors: their significance for the exam and your current level of proficiency.

Category	Definition	Action Steps	Example Topics
Category A: High Importance, Low Proficiency	Topics that frequently appear on exams and are central to HR practice, but which you currently find challenging.	Devote the majority of your study hours here and use varied methods such as reading case studies or discussing real scenarios in a study group.	Global HR Compliance, Advanced Data Analytics, Strategic Workforce Planning
Category B: High Importance,	Subjects that are crucial to the exam and to	Schedule brief review sessions to maintain	Recruitment & Selection, Domestic

High Proficiency	everyday HR practice, yet you already handle them with confidence.	your mastery; use extra time to mentor peers or further refine your approach.	Employment Law, Employee Relations
Category C: Low Importance, Low Proficiency	Areas less likely to appear prominently on the exam, where you also have limited experience or understanding.	Focus on basic concepts; reserve these for later in your study plan if time is limited. Aim for a foundational grasp rather than deep expertise.	Highly Specialized Regulations, Niche HR Tech Tools
Category D: Low Importance, High Proficiency	Topics that rarely surface in exams and which you already know quite well.	Revisit occasionally, but avoid investing much time here. If you have time constraints, move on to higher-priority categories.	General Business Topics You Use Daily, Certain Onboarding Elements

Using this categorization, you can better see where your efforts should lie. Category A deserves a significant portion of your study hours, while Category B might only need "maintenance" reviews to keep your knowledge sharp. Categories C and D can be addressed selectively once you've handled the higher-impact items.

Balancing Depth and Breadth

Striking the right balance between mastering the fundamentals of high-importance topics and acquiring a broad overview of supplementary material is key. Deep dives into areas like strategic workforce planning or advanced compensation models may prove essential if those subjects are Category A for you. Meanwhile, a more cursory look at lower-priority aspects—like a specialized local labor law that appears infrequently—might suffice.

Many exam takers find success by scheduling intensive sessions on complicated or unfamiliar domains and sprinkling in shorter, refresher-oriented sessions for domains where they already feel capable. This approach prevents knowledge decay in strong areas and ensures ongoing exposure to topics in which you still need improvement.

Scheduling Study Sessions Strategically

Time management is often the biggest challenge for professionals preparing for certification. Some schedule "thematic" blocks—for instance, dedicating one weekend to global HR, the next to organizational design, and so forth. Others prefer a rotation system, where each day focuses on a different domain or subtopic. The common thread in both methods is to match the intensity and duration of each session to the topic's priority level and your familiarity with it.

Full-length or domain-specific mock exams can serve as checkpoints to gauge how well you have internalized the material. Data from a recent survey of SHRM test-takers indicated that those who took at least three practice tests and used them to adjust their study plan afterward saw pass rates up to 15% higher than those who did not. The key is to review your results carefully and reallocate time if you spot persistent difficulties.

Avoiding Common Pitfalls

One major trap is to spend excessive time revisiting what you already know simply because it feels comfortable. This can leave less space in your schedule for tackling genuinely challenging topics. Another pitfall is underestimating how changes in the HR landscape—new regulations or workplace trends—can shift the relative importance of certain areas. Staying updated on any announcements or updates from SHRM ensures you don't deprioritize subjects that might suddenly assume greater relevance.

It's also essential not to procrastinate on the domains or competencies you find intimidating. Postponing them too long can lead to last-minute cramming, which rarely results in deep understanding. Instead, approach these areas methodically, possibly by breaking them down into smaller sections so they feel more manageable.

Ultimately, prioritizing your study topics is both an art and a science. It involves analyzing which knowledge areas carry the most weight, pairing that information with your personal proficiency levels, and then creating a schedule that addresses urgent needs first without neglecting broader coverage. By continually monitoring your progress and adjusting priorities as you gain new insights or master certain topics, you can optimize your preparation. This kind of targeted, flexible approach not only saves time but also maximizes your likelihood of success on the SHRM-CP or SHRM-SCP exam.

Chapter 4: Key Federal Laws – Applying to All or Most Employers

4.1 Fair Labor Standards Act (FLSA)

4.1.1 Wage and Hour Requirements

The Fair Labor Standards Act (FLSA) establishes foundational standards for how employers in the United States compensate their workers. Its primary objectives include setting a federal minimum wage, outlining rules for overtime pay, and requiring accurate recordkeeping of hours and wages. While some provisions of the FLSA, such as child labor rules and exemptions for specific job categories, are addressed in separate sections, the core wage and hour requirements apply broadly to a large majority of both public and private sector employers.

Federal Minimum Wage

One of the most prominent aspects of the FLSA is the nationwide minimum wage floor. Employers covered by the law must pay at least the federal minimum wage to non-exempt employees for every hour worked. The exact dollar amount, as set by federal law, may be supplemented by higher state or local minimums. In these cases, the employer is required to abide by the standard more favorable to the employee. Although the minimum wage can evolve through legislative or regulatory changes, the intent remains consistent: to protect workers from unduly low pay.

Overtime Pay Obligations

Beyond base wages, the FLSA compels most covered employers to pay non-exempt employees time-and-a-half for every hour worked over 40 in a single workweek. The calculation of overtime can become complex if the workplace uses varied pay rates or shift differentials, but the basic premise is straightforward: employees should be compensated at a higher rate when they exceed the standard 40-hour threshold. Employers who fail to meet this requirement risk wage disputes and potential legal penalties.

Defining Hours Worked

Understanding what counts as "hours worked" under the FLSA is critical for meeting wage and hour obligations. While obvious tasks—such as time spent on the production line or at a retail register—clearly qualify, certain pre- or post-shift activities might also count. For instance, setting up equipment before an official start time or completing mandatory security checks after a shift could be considered compensable if they are integral to the employee's duties. Short breaks may also be considered paid time if they fall within certain limits set by federal guidelines.

Tipped Employees and Tip Credits

In some business settings, particularly those in the hospitality industry, employees derive a substantial portion of their earnings from tips. Under specific conditions, employers may claim a "tip credit" that allows them to pay a base wage below the federal minimum as long as tips bring the individual's total compensation up to or above that minimum. If an employee's combined earnings fail to meet the standard, the employer must make up the difference. These rules vary by jurisdiction and require careful bookkeeping to ensure compliance.

Recordkeeping and Payroll Practices

The FLSA emphasizes rigorous recordkeeping to verify compliance with wage and hour requirements. Employers are expected to maintain accurate data about each employee's identity, occupation, hourly rates, total daily or weekly hours worked, and wages paid. While the law does not mandate any specific format—paper logs and digital systems are both acceptable—it does specify the kinds of information that should be kept and the recommended duration of retention. Proper documentation not only satisfies legal obligations but also provides an audit trail for resolving any disputes that might arise.

Payment Schedules and Methods

Although the FLSA does not require a particular pay frequency (such as weekly or biweekly), it does mandate that employees receive their legally required compensation in a timely manner. Delays or irregularities that result in underpayment or late payment can leave employers vulnerable to potential claims. By aligning payroll cycles with local and federal laws, and by ensuring that any tip adjustments or overtime calculations are processed correctly, employers substantially reduce their risk of wage-and-hour violations.

State and Local Variations

While the FLSA sets a federal baseline, state and local jurisdictions may impose more stringent requirements. These can include higher minimum wage rates, broader overtime eligibility, or additional pay-related regulations. For multi-state employers or those operating in areas with unique wage ordinances, understanding these layered rules becomes an essential aspect of compliance.

4.1.2 Child Labor Provisions

The Fair Labor Standards Act (FLSA) contains specific rules aimed at safeguarding the welfare of minors in the workforce. These regulations seek to protect educational opportunities for younger employees while preventing them from working under dangerous conditions. Unlike other aspects of the FLSA, which emphasize minimum wage and overtime, the child labor provisions focus on a youth's minimum age of employment, permissible working hours, and the types of tasks they may perform.

Federal law generally sets the minimum working age for non-agricultural roles at 14, with certain exceptions for jobs like delivering newspapers or babysitting on a casual basis. For businesses covered by the FLSA, hiring minors under 14 for most types of work is prohibited, and teenagers under 18 are restricted from performing hazardous duties that pose a serious risk to health or safety. Some typical examples of hazardous tasks include operating heavy machinery, handling certain power tools, and working in demolition.

Age-based restrictions on work hours also play a significant part in these protections. The requirements vary by age group and often change during the school year versus vacation periods. While the FLSA sets a federal baseline, it is crucial to remember that many states impose stricter rules that further limit a minor's permissible tasks or maximum daily and weekly hours.

Below is an example of how federal law restricts work hours for minors in non-agricultural roles. Always verify any additional state or local regulations that may supersede these standards:

Age Range	Typical Hour Restrictions	Notes on Work Conditions
14–15	- Limited to non-school hours during the school year. - May work a maximum of 3 hours on a school day and 8 hours on non-school days. - Cannot exceed 18 hours per week during school weeks or	Certain job types (e.g., retail, food service) are permitted, but tasks deemed hazardous are off-limits.

	40 hours in non-school weeks.	
16–17	- May work unlimited hours, provided the schedule does not conflict with any remaining school attendance requirements.	Still prohibited from engaging in specifically hazardous tasks defined by the Department of Labor.
18+	- Not subject to FLSA child labor provisions.	Once minors turn 18, they are no longer restricted under these rules, though other federal or state regulations may apply.

Enforcement of the child labor provisions falls under the purview of the U.S. Department of Labor's Wage and Hour Division. Employers who violate these regulations risk significant penalties, including fines and—in extreme cases—legal action. To avoid such repercussions, businesses should keep thorough records of each minor's working hours, tasks, and parental or school approvals where required.

By understanding and adhering to these child labor provisions, organizations demonstrate a commitment to the well-being of young employees, ensuring that work experience gained at an early age occurs in a safe and educationally compatible environment.

4.1.3 Exempt vs. Non-Exempt Classifications

Under the Fair Labor Standards Act (FLSA), employers must distinguish between exempt and non-exempt employees. While non-exempt employees are covered by the federal requirements for overtime pay and certain minimum wage standards, exempt employees are not. The exempt classification applies primarily to roles that meet specific legal criteria regarding salary level, method of compensation, and job duties. Misclassifying employees can lead to costly penalties, making it essential for HR professionals to understand how these classifications are determined and applied.

Core Criteria for Exempt Status

To qualify as exempt, a position typically must satisfy a combination of tests. The salary basis test usually mandates payment at a set amount per pay period, rather than hourly or piece rates, and the position must meet or exceed a regulatory salary threshold set at the federal level (though some states impose higher requirements). In addition, the employee must pass a job duties test, which evaluates responsibilities like supervising staff or exercising specialized, professional judgment. Roles often described as "white-collar exemptions" include executive, administrative, professional, computer-related, and outside sales positions, each subject to its own standards for what the individual does on a day-to-day basis.

While the salary threshold and duties tests form the foundation for most exemptions, there are nuances depending on the nature of the work and any state or local variations in wage-and-hour law. Employers should review these guidelines carefully and maintain robust documentation that supports an employee's classification.

Common Exempt Categories

Exemption Category	Key Criteria	Sample Roles/Functions
Executive	Primary duty involves managing the enterprise or a department, supervises at	Directors, VPs, certain department managers

	least two employees, has authority in hiring/firing decisions.	
Administrative	Primary duty is office or non-manual work related to management policies, exercises discretion on significant matters.	HR Generalists, Project Coordinators, some Analysts
Professional	Work requires advanced knowledge in a field of science or learning, typically gained through specialized education.	Lawyers, Accountants, Engineers
Computer Employee	Engaged in systems analysis, programming, or software engineering tasks requiring specialized expertise.	Systems Analysts, Programmers, Software Developers
Outside Sales	Primarily works away from the employer's place of business, making sales or obtaining orders/contracts.	Traveling Sales Representatives

Consequences of Misclassification

If an employer incorrectly designates an employee as exempt when they should be non-exempt, the organization may be liable for unpaid overtime, back wages, and additional penalties. Beyond financial repercussions, misclassification can also create reputational risks. Conducting regular classification audits and maintaining transparent job descriptions are effective ways to prevent issues before they escalate.

Properly distinguishing between exempt and non-exempt roles is a critical part of FLSA compliance. Employers must consider both the salary basis or threshold and each position's actual job duties, ensuring that legal standards are met and documented to avoid penalties and maintain fair employment practices.

4.2 National Labor Relations Act (NLRA)

4.2.1 Collective Bargaining Rights

Enacted in 1935, the National Labor Relations Act (NLRA) grants employees in most private-sector workplaces the right to form, join, or assist labor organizations, as well as to engage in collective bargaining with their employers. This foundational principle gives employees a voice in negotiating the terms and conditions of their employment, encompassing wages, hours, and various workplace policies. Collective bargaining often results in a labor contract or collective bargaining agreement (CBA), which sets out mutually accepted obligations for both the employer and the represented employees.

Core Principles of Collective Bargaining

1. **Voluntary and Good-Faith Negotiations**
   Under the NLRA, both the employer and the union representing the workforce are required to negotiate in good faith. While the law does not force either side to agree to specific terms, it does expect all parties to come to the table with a genuine willingness to find common ground. This ensures that negotiations are constructive rather than perfunctory.

2. **Exclusive Representation**

    Once employees vote to be represented by a particular union, that union becomes the exclusive representative for all individuals in the bargaining unit. This means that the employer must negotiate any collective employment terms—such as wages or vacation policies—solely through the union, rather than dealing with employees on an individual basis for issues covered by the agreement.

3. **Mandatory Subjects of Bargaining**

    Certain topics, including pay scales, benefits, work schedules, and other employment terms, are considered mandatory subjects for negotiation. While either party can propose additional matters (permissive subjects), they cannot insist on these at the expense of reaching agreement on mandatory topics. Failure to address mandatory subjects or refusal to bargain in good faith may be deemed an unfair labor practice.

The Role of the National Labor Relations Board (NLRB)

Though the core of the NLRA articulates employees' rights to organize and bargain collectively, the NLRB enforces those rights by overseeing union representation elections and investigating allegations of unfair labor practices. If disputes regarding election conduct or bargaining obligations arise, the NLRB has the authority to order remedies, which might involve a redo of a flawed election or a directive for an employer to return to the bargaining table.

Collective Bargaining Agreements (CBAs)

A successful negotiation typically culminates in a written CBA. This document is legally binding and specifies the mutual obligations of the employer and the employees covered under the agreement. The CBA often addresses:

> **Compensation Structures:** Base wages, overtime provisions, and bonus arrangements.

> **Benefits and Leaves:** Vacation days, sick leave, healthcare coverage, and retirement options.

> **Working Conditions and Policies:** Scheduling procedures, health and safety considerations, seniority rules, and mechanisms for resolving disputes (such as a grievance process).

CBAs generally have set expiration dates, after which the parties may negotiate a new contract or extend the existing one. If negotiations stall, employees may invoke their right to strike—subject to various legal parameters—and employers may consider lockouts or other lawful responses.

Enforcement and Accountability

Both employers and unions are expected to abide by the terms of the CBA for its duration. Breaches can lead to legal action or involve arbitration procedures agreed upon in the contract. If either party suspects the other has committed an unfair labor practice under the NLRA, it may file a charge with the NLRB. Promptly addressing alleged violations helps maintain a functioning bargaining relationship and deters further disputes.

4.2.2 Concerted Activities and Employer Limitations

Under Section 7 of the National Labor Relations Act (NLRA), employees—including those not represented by a union—are granted the right to engage in concerted activities for their mutual aid or protection. These activities can encompass discussions about wages, benefits, or working conditions, as well as collective efforts to address grievances or negotiate improvements. In effect, the NLRA safeguards an individual's ability to band together with coworkers to seek positive changes in the workplace, regardless of whether a formal labor organization is present.

Defining Concerted Activities

Concerted activity generally involves two or more employees acting in unison or a single employee acting on behalf of others. For example, if one individual circulates a petition concerning new workplace policies, or if a group of colleagues organizes a meeting to discuss safety concerns, they may be exercising their right to concerted action. Even casual conversations that touch on workplace conditions, such as pay scales or scheduling challenges, can be considered protected if they aim to rally group support or spur collective action.

Employer Limitations and Prohibited Conduct

While employers have the authority to maintain productivity and enforce reasonable workplace rules, the NLRA imposes boundaries on what they can do when employees engage in protected concerted activities:

1. **No Retaliation or Discrimination**
   Employers cannot discipline, demote, or terminate employees for lawful collective action, such as gathering signatures to request a change in break schedules. If an employee is sanctioned for engaging in protected behavior, it may be considered an unfair labor practice.

2. **Restrictions on Policies**
   Rules that broadly forbid employees from discussing wages or other terms of employment can run afoul of the NLRA, as they effectively stifle concerted activities. Employers are allowed to maintain policies that ensure operations and safety, but these must not be so sweeping as to interfere with employees' rights to act collectively.

3. **Limits on Surveillance and Interference**
   Overly intrusive monitoring of employee gatherings—either on or off company premises—can be deemed an attempt to discourage concerted activity. The law strikes a balance between an employer's legitimate interest in ensuring business continuity and the employees' right to communicate freely about workplace concerns.

Real-World Examples

An increasingly prominent scenario involves employees using social media platforms to share workplace grievances. While employers have some discretion to discipline employees for harmful or defamatory statements, posts regarding wages, labor conditions, or other employment-related matters often fall under the umbrella of protected concerted activity. Employers that respond too harshly risk being charged with an unfair labor practice if it appears they are trying to punish collective expression.

Another example arises when employees wear pins or T-shirts expressing support for better working conditions. Generally, such actions are protected, unless the display causes a genuine safety issue or violates narrowly tailored dress codes that do not infringe on concerted rights. Employers should exercise caution when restricting political or issue-oriented apparel, ensuring that such policies do not inadvertently prohibit workers from collectively voicing concerns about workplace issues.

Enforcement and Remedies

The National Labor Relations Board (NLRB) enforces rules surrounding concerted activity, investigating claims and issuing remedies for violations. If it finds that an employer has unlawfully interfered with these rights, the NLRB can order reinstatement of wrongfully terminated employees, back pay, or other measures to restore the status quo. In many cases, the Board also mandates that employers post notices affirming employees' NLRA rights and detailing how the violation will be addressed.

4.3 Occupational Safety and Health Act (OSHA)

4.3.1 Employer Responsibilities for Workplace Safety

The Occupational Safety and Health Act (OSHA) mandates that employers provide a safe and healthful work environment for their employees, free from recognized hazards that may cause harm or illness. This obligation extends to a wide variety of industries and work settings, requiring employers to take proactive measures to identify, assess, and mitigate potential dangers. Although specific regulations vary by industry, certain fundamental responsibilities apply across the board.

The General Duty Clause

A cornerstone of OSHA is the "General Duty Clause," which stipulates that employers must provide a workplace free from serious recognized hazards. Even when a specific OSHA standard does not exist for a particular risk, employers can still be cited under this clause if they fail to address hazards that are evident and have the potential to cause serious harm. Common examples include areas like ergonomic risks in office settings or emerging industrial technologies without established regulations.

Hazard Identification and Correction

A systematic approach to hazard identification is crucial for maintaining a safe workplace. Employers are expected to regularly inspect work areas, machinery, and processes to spot unsafe conditions. Once a hazard is identified—whether it involves faulty equipment, inadequate ventilation, or unguarded machinery—they must take timely, appropriate action to remedy the issue. This could involve repairing or replacing defective equipment, installing safety guards, adjusting work processes, or implementing new policies to minimize risk.

Employee Training and Engagement

Proper training is one of the most effective ways to reduce workplace injuries and illnesses. OSHA standards generally require that employers instruct employees on how to identify risks, handle equipment safely, and respond to emergencies. Training should be readily understandable and offered in a language the workforce can comprehend. In addition, employers are encouraged to foster a culture where employees feel comfortable reporting potential hazards or near-miss incidents without fear of retaliation.

Protective Equipment and Safety Measures

In many work environments, personal protective equipment (PPE) plays a critical role in preventing injuries. Employers must provide necessary safety gear—such as helmets, goggles, gloves, or respirators—when engineering or administrative controls cannot fully eliminate hazards. They should also clearly post safety signs and labels, reinforcing the importance of wearing PPE and following established protocols.

Policy Development and Enforcement

An effective safety program goes beyond simply handing out protective gear or posting warning signs. Employers often develop written safety policies detailing expected procedures, ranging from how to handle chemicals to protocols for operating heavy machinery. Supervisors and managers typically shoulder additional responsibility by ensuring compliance with these policies. OSHA can cite organizations if they establish rules on paper but fail to enforce them consistently.

Coordination with Contractors and Vendors

When multiple employers share the same work site—such as a construction project—the primary or controlling employer can also be held accountable if they do not take reasonable steps to ensure all parties comply with OSHA requirements. Coordinating safety responsibilities involves clearly communicating hazard information, verifying that each entity adheres to relevant standards, and making certain no one's actions place other workers at risk.

Consequences of Noncompliance

Employers who do not meet their safety obligations can face citations, financial penalties, or required abatement measures if OSHA identifies violations. Failing to address known hazards or repeatedly ignoring safety regulations could lead to increased scrutiny, legal complications, and damage to an organization's reputation. Conversely, maintaining a rigorous safety program can help companies limit liabilities, lower workers' compensation costs, and enhance employee morale.

4.3.2 Reporting and Recordkeeping

The Occupational Safety and Health Act (OSHA) mandates that most employers keep accurate, up-to-date records of workplace-related injuries and illnesses. While these requirements may vary based on industry classification and workforce size, the central aim remains the same: to ensure transparency about workplace incidents and to enable both employers and regulators to identify patterns and prevent future harm. Unlike more general OSHA obligations—such as providing a safe work environment—the reporting and recordkeeping rules deal specifically with documenting incidents and making timely disclosures when serious events occur.

Key OSHA Forms and Their Purposes

   ✓ **OSHA Form 300 (Log of Work-Related Injuries and Illnesses)**

     Employers use this confidential log to note details of any recordable incident, which generally includes injuries or illnesses that result in medical treatment beyond first aid, lost workdays, restricted work, or job transfers. Each entry captures basic facts such as the employee's name (except where privacy restrictions apply), the nature of the injury or illness, and the location or department where it occurred.

   ✓ **OSHA Form 301 (Injury and Illness Incident Report)**
     This report offers a more detailed account of each incident. It includes information about how the injury happened, which equipment was involved, and any relevant environmental conditions. Most employers complete a Form

301 within seven calendar days after receiving information about a recordable incident.

✓ **OSHA Form 300A (Summary of Work-Related Injuries and Illnesses)**
At the end of each calendar year, employers must review their Form 300 entries and produce a one-page summary that aggregates the total number of recordable injuries and illnesses, along with additional statistics such as total days away from work. This summary must be posted in a visible area of the workplace, typically from February 1 through April 30, and must be certified by a company executive.

Reporting Severe Incidents

Beyond routine recordkeeping, OSHA requires prompt reporting for certain severe events. Employers must notify OSHA within eight hours if a workplace incident results in a fatality. For hospitalizations, amputations, or the loss of an eye, the employer generally must report the event within 24 hours. Calls can be placed to the nearest OSHA area office or the 24-hour OSHA hotline, and online reporting options may be available. These time-sensitive requirements help OSHA respond quickly and investigate when lives and livelihoods are at immediate risk.

Who Is Exempt or Partially Exempt?

➤ **Employers with 10 or Fewer Employees**
In many cases, smaller employers are exempt from keeping OSHA Forms 300 and 301, although they must still report severe incidents (fatalities, inpatient hospitalizations, amputations, or eye loss) to OSHA.

> ➢ **Low-Hazard Industries**
>
>   Certain industries classified as low-hazard—such as specific retail stores, finance, insurance, or real estate offices—may not have to maintain detailed records unless specifically asked by OSHA or the Bureau of Labor Statistics. These designations can shift, so employers should confirm their current classification.

Retention and Access Requirements

Employers subject to OSHA's recordkeeping rules must retain their records for five years following the end of the calendar year to which they relate. During this period, if there are updates or corrections—say, if an injured employee's lost workdays extend longer than initially expected—these must be added. OSHA or authorized government representatives can request access to these logs at any time. Additionally, employees and their representatives can review the Form 300 log (with certain privacy exceptions) to stay informed about workplace safety trends.

State Plans and Variations

Although federal OSHA sets the baseline requirements, 22 states and territories operate their own occupational safety and health programs, often referred to as "State Plans." These plans may impose stricter or additional rules about reporting and recordkeeping. For multi-state employers, it is critical to confirm whether specific states require different forms, heightened thresholds for recordability, or more frequent reporting timelines.

Consequences of Noncompliance

OSHA inspections or audits often include a review of injury logs and reports. Gaps or inaccuracies can trigger citations, financial penalties, and follow-up investigations. In cases of severe or willful noncompliance, OSHA may levy heavier fines, which can be particularly damaging to an organization's finances and reputation. By contrast, employers that keep meticulous records not only reduce legal exposure but also gain valuable insights into workplace hazards, enabling them to implement more targeted and effective safety measures.

Reporting and recordkeeping under OSHA serve both a compliance function and a practical workplace safety purpose. Employers that systematically log injuries and illnesses, promptly report serious incidents, and maintain their records with care can more easily spot trends, respond to emerging risks, and demonstrate due diligence in safeguarding their employees' well-being.

4.4 Social Security Act (1935) and Unemployment Insurance

4.4.1 Funding Mechanisms

The Social Security Act (1935) laid the groundwork for multiple social insurance programs, including old-age pensions, disability benefits, and unemployment compensation. Although various amendments and expansions have taken place over the decades, the core principle remains the same: these programs are financed through ongoing contributions rather than being supported solely by general federal revenues. This sub-subchapter explores the overarching structures used to generate the funds that power these vital safety nets, without delving into the specific employer tax obligations covered elsewhere.

The Dual Structure of Social Security Funding

Social Security, in its broadest sense, covers retirement, survivors, and disability benefits (often referred to collectively as OASDI—Old-Age, Survivors, and Disability Insurance). Its financial backbone is a system of contributions collected from both employees and employers through payroll deductions. These monies are then channeled into trust funds dedicated to covering current beneficiaries. While exact rates can shift based on legislative changes, the longstanding premise is that workers essentially invest in their own future benefits, creating a self-sustaining model.

Key Points on Social Security Funding:

➢ **Pay-As-You-Go Model:** Current workers' contributions finance the benefits of current retirees and other beneficiaries, making it possible for the program to function continuously without relying entirely on reserve funds.

➢ **Trust Funds:** Contributions are deposited into designated trust funds—primarily the Old-Age and Survivors Insurance (OASI) Trust Fund and the Disability Insurance (DI) Trust Fund. These trust funds operate under a set of rules designed to ensure that collected contributions can only be used for authorized benefits and administrative costs.

Unemployment Insurance Contributions

Alongside the old-age and disability programs, the Social Security Act established mechanisms for unemployment compensation. This system aims to provide temporary financial support to individuals who have lost employment through no fault of their own and who meet other eligibility criteria. While each state administers its own unemployment insurance (UI) program, the federal government sets broad guidelines through the Federal Unemployment Tax Act (FUTA) and oversees a system that encourages states to meet minimum standards.

Federal vs. State Roles in Funding:

➢ **Federal Contributions (FUTA):** Employers across the country pay into a federal unemployment tax system, which helps fund administrative costs and provides loans or grants to state UI programs.

➢ **State Contributions:** States levy their own unemployment taxes on employers, and sometimes on employees, to finance regular benefit payments to eligible workers. Tax rates can vary widely depending on a state's specific formulas, the economic climate, and the employer's history of layoffs or claims.

Under this combined approach, UI funds can be more stable and responsive to local labor conditions. States with higher unemployment rates can access federal resources to maintain solvency, while those with lower rates often benefit from reduced tax burdens. Because the main objective is to support workers during periods of joblessness without unduly burdening employers, many states also employ experience-rating systems that adjust tax rates based on how frequently employers have triggered unemployment claims.

Flexible Funding Adaptations

As economic conditions shift over time, policymakers may make temporary adjustments or permanent changes to ensure the ongoing viability of these programs. For instance, recessions often lead to increased unemployment claims and put pressure on state UI trust funds. In such cases, federal loans or emergency measures may temporarily fill funding gaps. Similarly, demographic shifts—such as an aging population—can influence the solvency projections of the main Social Security trust funds, prompting debates around contribution rates or benefit adjustments.

Importance of Accurate Reporting

While the act of collecting contributions is a linchpin in sustaining Social Security and unemployment insurance programs, the integrity of the systems also depends on accurate wage reporting by employers. When wages are accurately reported, the programs' trust funds receive appropriate contributions, and workers' future claims—such as retirement benefits or UI eligibility—can be calculated correctly. Ongoing oversight by federal and state agencies helps ensure consistent reporting and reduce fraud or underreporting.

Looking Ahead

Although the foundational structure of Social Security funding has remained relatively consistent since the 1930s, evolving economic landscapes and demographic trends continue to shape how these safety nets operate. Numerous proposals—from adjusting contribution rates to redefining eligibility thresholds—frequently arise in legislative or public discourse. At its heart, however, the central principle remains straightforward: pooling resources through a national or state-based contribution system spreads financial risk, ensuring that workers have at least a partial safety net against unemployment, disability, or loss of income in retirement.

Social Security and unemployment insurance rely on structured contribution systems that bring together employees, employers, and, in some cases, state and federal authorities. By maintaining dedicated trust funds and employing flexible approaches in times of economic stress, these programs support millions of Americans—and remain a bedrock of social welfare policy in the United States.

4.4.2 Employer Payroll Tax Responsibilities

Employers play a central role in collecting and remitting payroll taxes under the Social Security Act and related federal and state statutes. While employees also contribute through withholdings on their earnings, it is the employer's legal duty to ensure that these funds are correctly calculated, deposited, and reported to the appropriate agencies. Failure to fulfill these obligations can lead to substantial penalties and interest charges, making rigorous compliance a top priority in any HR or payroll department.

Federal Insurance Contributions Act (FICA)

Under FICA, employers must withhold the employee's share of Social Security and Medicare taxes from each paycheck, then contribute an additional amount on the employer side. These combined funds are submitted regularly to the Internal Revenue Service (IRS), typically following deposit schedules aligned with an organization's total tax liability. Small firms with minimal tax liabilities often deposit on a monthly basis, while larger employers may be subject to a semi-weekly schedule. Accuracy in calculation and timeliness in remittance are crucial to avoid IRS scrutiny.

Federal Unemployment Tax Act (FUTA)

Beyond Social Security and Medicare, employers also shoulder the Federal Unemployment Tax (FUTA), used to support administrative costs of state unemployment programs and provide a safety net during economic downturns. The federal unemployment tax rate is applied to a set wage base, and most employers receive a credit for paying state unemployment taxes (SUTA), thus reducing the effective FUTA rate. Employers must file an annual FUTA tax return using IRS

Form 940, which summarizes total wages paid, unemployment tax owed, and credits claimed.

State Unemployment Taxes (SUTA)

All states maintain their own unemployment insurance systems, financed primarily by taxes on employers. SUTA rates can vary significantly from one jurisdiction to another, and many states adjust an employer's rate based on the organization's "experience rating," which reflects how frequently the firm's former employees draw unemployment benefits. Employers must track these rates meticulously, calculate contributions each pay period or quarter as required, and file returns on the schedule mandated by the state. Keeping abreast of annual changes in wage bases or tax rates is essential for accurate reporting.

Forms and Reporting Deadlines

Employers typically report federal payroll taxes using IRS Form 941 (Employer's Quarterly Federal Tax Return) or Form 944 (Annual Return) if they meet the criteria for filing once a year. In addition to remitting taxes, these forms provide details such as total wages paid, the amount of Social Security and Medicare taxes withheld, and any adjustments for sick pay or tips. The specific due dates depend on your deposit schedule; for example, Form 941 is generally due at the end of the month following each quarter. State unemployment reports vary by jurisdiction, but many states require quarterly filings that mirror federal timelines.

A simplified view of typical reporting forms and deadlines is shown below:

Tax / Return	Filing Frequency	Reporting Form	Key Points

FICA (Social Security, Medicare)	Semi-weekly or Monthly Deposits; Quarterly or Annual Reporting	Form 941 (Quarterly) or Form 944 (Annual)	Deposit schedule depends on tax liability; accurate withholding and match required
FUTA (Federal Unemployment)	Annual Return	Form 940	Credits often reduce rate if SUTA is paid; wage base set by federal law
SUTA (State Unemployment)	Quarterly in most states	Varies by State	Rates differ by employer's experience rating; must monitor state-specific laws and deadlines

Consequences of Noncompliance

Late deposits or inaccurate filings can trigger escalating penalties, typically calculated as a percentage of the overdue amount per month or per quarter. In severe cases, willful failure to remit payroll taxes can result in personal liability for individuals responsible for making payments, especially if tax funds were collected from employees but not forwarded to the IRS or relevant state agencies. Penalties may also include accrued interest and potential legal action for chronic offenders.

Best Practices for Employers

Staying current on deposit schedules, maintaining precise payroll records, and reconciling amounts monthly or quarterly are all vital steps to sustain compliance. Many employers integrate payroll software that automates calculations, tracks due dates, and flags anomalies, reducing the risk of manual errors. When changes occur—such as adjusted tax rates, updated wage bases, or new legislative requirements—ensuring that payroll systems and staff are promptly informed can prevent misunderstandings and potential compliance gaps.

Employer payroll tax responsibilities under Social Security and unemployment insurance laws involve meticulous calculation of withholdings, timely remittances, and accurate reporting. By adhering to deposit schedules, monitoring evolving regulations, and maintaining organized documentation, organizations meet their statutory obligations and minimize the risk of costly penalties.

4.5 Key Privacy and Protection Acts

4.5.1 Protected Health Information (HIPAA)

The Health Insurance Portability and Accountability Act (HIPAA) sets national standards for safeguarding protected health information (PHI). Although HIPAA primarily regulates healthcare providers, health plans, healthcare clearinghouses, and their business associates, many employers also encounter HIPAA obligations through the administration of group health plans. When an organization sponsors or manages an employee health plan, it must ensure compliance with HIPAA's rules on the privacy and security of sensitive medical data. Failure to do so can result in significant financial penalties and reputational damage.

Scope and Definition of PHI

Under HIPAA, PHI encompasses any information that relates to an individual's physical or mental health, healthcare services received, or payment for healthcare, as long as it can be used to identify the person involved. This definition is broad, covering data in physical documents, digital records, oral statements, and any other medium. Examples include medical diagnoses, treatment records, prescription details, and insurer claim histories. If an employer obtains this type of data through its group health plan, or through another HIPAA-covered channel, it must treat the information with strict confidentiality.

Employer-Sponsored Health Plans

An employer's primary touchpoint with HIPAA often arises from sponsoring a health plan for employees. While day-to-day medical care is usually handled by insurers or third-party administrators, the employer may still receive PHI when processing certain types of claims, appeals, or enrollment transactions. In these scenarios, the employer is considered a plan sponsor under HIPAA rules and must implement measures that protect any PHI it receives or shares in that capacity.

Minimizing Unnecessary Access

To comply with HIPAA's "minimum necessary" standard, employers should limit the internal personnel who can view or handle PHI. Typically, only staff members directly involved in benefits administration—such as HR professionals who process health plan paperwork—should see PHI. Technical controls on electronic systems and careful oversight of paper files can reduce the chance of unauthorized access.

Privacy and Security Policies

Employers must craft written policies that lay out how PHI is handled, stored, and shared. These policies might specify the requirements for password protection on digital records, locked file cabinets for paper documents, or encryption protocols for electronic data transfers. Organizations are also advised to train all relevant staff on these procedures, ensuring they understand what constitutes PHI and how to respond to requests for information from employees, healthcare providers, or other parties.

Permitted Disclosures

Although HIPAA generally restricts the sharing of PHI, it does recognize situations in which disclosures are permissible. For example, health plans and covered entities can exchange PHI for treatment, payment, and healthcare operations without an individual's explicit authorization. Employers still need to confirm that disclosures fall under these allowed categories and that they are limited to the minimum necessary information. Any other type of disclosure often requires prior written consent from the affected individual.

Employee Rights and Complaint Process

Under HIPAA, employees have specific rights regarding their health information. They can request access to their own PHI, ask for corrections if they notice errors, or file a complaint if they believe their data has been inappropriately accessed or shared. Complaints may be directed internally (to the employer's privacy officer) or externally (to the Department of Health and Human Services, Office for Civil Rights). Employers are prohibited from retaliating against employees who exercise these rights.

Penalties for Noncompliance

Penalties for HIPAA violations can be substantial, ranging from monetary fines to corrective action plans mandated by federal regulators. In serious cases—particularly those involving willful neglect—penalties can run into the millions of dollars. Beyond the financial impact, data breaches and privacy incidents can erode trust in the organization, damaging employee relations and external reputation. Employers can mitigate these risks by conducting routine compliance audits, reviewing vendor relationships that involve PHI, and promptly addressing any reported or discovered vulnerabilities.

HIPAA's privacy and security requirements extend to many employer-based health plans, imposing a duty to protect PHI from unauthorized disclosure. By implementing robust privacy policies, limiting access to the minimum necessary data, and regularly training relevant personnel, organizations reduce the likelihood of breaches. In the event that a breach does occur, having a clear response protocol and thorough documentation can help demonstrate good-faith compliance efforts and minimize potential legal or regulatory repercussions.

4.5.2 Wage Garnishment Limitations (Consumer Credit Protection Act)

The Consumer Credit Protection Act (CCPA) provides federal guidelines that safeguard employees against excessively high wage garnishments. While creditors may legally seize a portion of an individual's earnings to fulfill certain debts—such as consumer loans, court judgments, or child support—the CCPA places strict caps on how much can be deducted per pay period. It also offers protections against employment termination based on a single garnishment order, recognizing that financial setbacks do not necessarily indicate poor job performance.

Maximum Limits on Garnishment

Under the CCPA, only a specific percentage of "disposable earnings" may be garnished, where disposable earnings refer to the employee's compensation after legally required deductions like federal, state, or local taxes and mandatory retirement contributions (if applicable). For most consumer debts, the garnishment cap typically equals:

> ➤ **25% of disposable earnings**, or

> ➤ **The amount by which disposable earnings exceed 30 times the federal minimum wage**

Whichever figure is lower will serve as the limit for each pay period. Higher percentages can apply in cases involving child support or spousal support. In such scenarios, up to 50% or 60% of an employee's disposable income may be garnished if they are supporting another spouse or child.

Safeguards for Employees

Beyond setting numerical limits, the CCPA ensures that workers facing garnishment are not unjustly penalized by their employers. Under federal law, an employee may not be discharged solely because of wage garnishment for one indebtedness. If multiple garnishments occur, however, these protections may not apply with the same force, and employers should carefully review their obligations under both federal and state law.

Employer Responsibilities

Employers served with a valid garnishment order are required to withhold the appropriate amount from each paycheck and remit those funds to the designated creditor or agency. Failing to comply can result in legal consequences, including potential liability for the unpaid debt. Consequently, payroll departments must remain attentive to the details specified in garnishment notices—such as the percentage to be withheld, the timeframe, and the final disposition of the funds. Many organizations implement procedures to double-check calculations each pay cycle, reducing the risk of under- or over-withholding.

State Variations and Additional Protections

Some states impose stricter limits than the federal baseline, offering further financial relief to employees by reducing the share of wages subject to garnishment. Others might extend more robust job security protections, preventing termination over multiple garnishment orders. Employers operating across multiple jurisdictions should track these differences carefully, as they are obligated to follow whichever standard is more protective of the employee.

Penalties and Noncompliance

Failing to comply with federal garnishment rules can lead to fines or legal actions against the employer. In instances where an organization disregards court-ordered garnishments, it may also be held responsible for the full amount of the debt, plus any associated legal fees. Keeping up-to-date with changes in federal or state garnishment statutes and training relevant personnel in payroll, HR, and legal departments can help organizations minimize their exposure to such risks.

By limiting the percentage of earnings that can be garnished and forbidding termination due to a single garnishment order, the CCPA offers crucial financial and employment safeguards. Employers must carefully calculate deductions, adhere to any stricter state regulations, and ensure that employees' rights remain protected throughout the garnishment process.

4.6 Dodd-Frank Wall Street Reform and Consumer Protection Act

4.6.1 Whistleblower Protections

The Dodd-Frank Wall Street Reform and Consumer Protection Act introduced expansive whistleblower protections designed to encourage individuals to report misconduct within the financial sector and other regulated environments. Unlike some earlier laws that primarily covered retaliation against employees, Dodd-Frank also provides financial incentives for reporting certain types of wrongdoing to the Securities and Exchange Commission (SEC). By offering both confidentiality and potential monetary rewards, the Act seeks to uncover fraud or other illegal activities that could harm investors, consumers, or the broader economy.

Protected Activities

Under Dodd-Frank, whistleblowers are protected when they provide information—either directly to the SEC or through internal compliance channels—about possible securities law violations. Any adverse employment action taken against such individuals in response to lawful disclosures may be considered unlawful retaliation. Actions that could qualify as retaliation include demoting the whistleblower, reducing pay, reassigning them to menial tasks, or terminating their employment altogether.

Financial Incentives for Reporting

One of the most prominent features of these protections is a bounty program, which offers whistleblowers a percentage of any monetary sanctions collected as a result of successful enforcement actions exceeding $1 million. Although the award amount can range widely (generally between 10% and 30% of the total penalty), it underscores the federal government's commitment to unveiling systemic abuses. In addition, Dodd-Frank does not necessarily require whistleblowers to report internally first, although some corporate compliance programs encourage or mandate internal reporting before an individual contacts the SEC.

Confidentiality Assurances

To encourage disclosures, the SEC maintains policies that protect a whistleblower's identity to the extent allowed by law. However, in the event of litigation or if disclosure is necessary for SEC proceedings, confidentiality may be lifted. Nonetheless, these mechanisms generally alleviate fears about exposure, ensuring that employees who step forward with legitimate concerns face fewer personal and professional risks.

Anti-Retaliation Legal Protections

Dodd-Frank goes further than many previous laws in specifying remedies available to whistleblowers who experience retaliation. Possible legal outcomes for successful plaintiffs include reinstatement to a former position, compensation for back pay with interest, and coverage of legal fees. Courts have also interpreted the anti-retaliation provisions broadly, sometimes extending protection to those who report violations internally, even if they do not personally file with the SEC.

Employer Compliance Strategies

Organizations can limit potential liability by fostering a transparent, ethics-focused culture. Effective compliance strategies might include:

- ✓ **Clear Internal Reporting Mechanisms:** Offering confidential hotlines or designated compliance officers ensures that employees know where to direct concerns before or instead of going to external agencies.

✓ **Regular Training:** Educating managers and HR personnel about both their obligations and potential penalties under Dodd-Frank can help avoid inadvertent retaliation.

✓ **Documented Investigations:** Promptly and thoroughly investigating whistleblower claims, then documenting each step, helps demonstrate good-faith efforts to address issues.

✓ **Proactive Risk Assessments:** Periodic reviews of internal controls and compensation structures can help detect and mitigate issues before they escalate.

Relationship to Other Whistleblower Laws

Although Dodd-Frank protections are broad, some employees could be covered by additional statutes like the Sarbanes-Oxley Act (SOX) or industry-specific regulations (e.g., for pharmaceuticals, healthcare, or environmental matters). Understanding how these various frameworks intersect is crucial, particularly for companies operating in multiple sectors or those subject to multiple layers of oversight.

Dodd-Frank's whistleblower provisions offer both strong legal safeguards and monetary incentives for employees to report corporate misconduct, especially concerning securities violations. By recognizing and adhering to these regulations—and by cultivating a culture that encourages ethical reporting—employers mitigate legal risks while enhancing corporate integrity.

4.6.2 Executive Compensation Requirements

The Dodd-Frank Wall Street Reform and Consumer Protection Act introduced a suite of provisions aimed at enhancing transparency and accountability in how publicly traded companies compensate top executives. These requirements grew out of concerns about excessive or misaligned pay structures, which some argued contributed to systemic risk in the financial sector. Although specific rules may evolve as the Securities and Exchange Commission (SEC) refines its regulations, Dodd-Frank's overarching principles continue to shape executive pay practices in many organizations.

Say-on-Pay and Shareholder Engagement

One of the hallmark features of Dodd-Frank is the requirement that public companies include an advisory "say-on-pay" vote in their proxy statements, typically on an annual or biennial basis. Shareholders cast a nonbinding vote on executive compensation packages, including salary, bonuses, and equity awards for top-level officers. Although the vote does not obligate the board of directors to revise compensation, widespread shareholder opposition can pressure the company to re-examine its executive pay policies and align them more closely with performance benchmarks or investor expectations.

Enhanced Disclosure and Transparency

Dodd-Frank mandates additional disclosure elements in annual proxy statements:

- ✓ **Pay Ratio Disclosure:** Companies must disclose the ratio of the Chief Executive Officer's total annual compensation to the median annual compensation of all other employees. This figure can influence shareholder views on pay equity and corporate culture, especially when the differential is substantial.

✓ **Golden Parachute Disclosures:** If an advisory shareholder vote occurs regarding a merger or acquisition, companies must provide clear details on any compensation agreements for executives contingent on that transaction. This includes severance, bonuses, or accelerated equity vesting arrangements.

By requiring greater clarity on how executive pay is structured and awarded, Dodd-Frank seeks to equip shareholders with the information they need to make informed voting decisions and hold boards accountable.

Clawback Policies

Another critical aspect is the requirement for publicly traded companies to adopt "clawback" provisions in their compensation arrangements. These policies obligate executives to return certain incentive-based pay if it was awarded under financial statements later found to be materially noncompliant with reporting requirements. When a restatement occurs due to error or misconduct, the affected executives may have to repay bonuses, stock options, or other performance-related incentives that turned out to be inflated. The SEC enforces these clawback rules in alignment with the intention of discouraging short-term risk-taking that undermines long-term financial stability.

Independence of Compensation Committees

Dodd-Frank also addresses the composition of corporate boards by insisting on the independence of compensation committee members. These committees, which play a central role in designing and reviewing executive pay packages, cannot be unduly influenced by top executives. Such independence aims to foster more balanced decision-making, preventing conflicts of interest and enhancing shareholders' trust that pay structures truly align with corporate performance and risk tolerance.

Impact on HR Strategy and Compliance

For HR departments, the expanded reporting obligations and potential for shareholder activism create a need for:

1. **Comprehensive Recordkeeping:** Keeping detailed documentation on how performance targets are determined and how bonuses or equity grants tie to these goals is crucial, particularly if they may be subject to clawback.

2. **Stakeholder Communication:** Because investors, regulators, and the broader public closely scrutinize executive pay, clear explanations of compensation strategies and metrics can help manage reputational risks.

3. **Ongoing Monitoring:** As SEC rules continue to evolve, companies must stay current on updated regulations to avoid compliance pitfalls. This includes monitoring how frequently shareholders prefer say-on-pay votes—some companies adopt an annual approach, while others choose a less frequent schedule if allowed by prior shareholder votes.

Balancing Regulatory Expectations with Competitive Pay

Although Dodd-Frank imposes constraints, companies still look to attract and retain top-tier leaders. Achieving this often involves a delicate balancing act between ensuring compensation remains competitive and aligning with shareholders' desire for pay equity and prudence. The result has been a shift toward pay packages that heavily emphasize long-term performance metrics, reducing the possibility of outsized rewards triggered by short-lived spikes in stock value or risky business moves.

Dodd-Frank's executive compensation requirements emphasize transparency, accountability, and alignment between pay and performance. Through mandatory say-on-pay votes, enhanced disclosures, clawback provisions, and compensation committee independence, the Act reinforces shareholders' role in influencing and overseeing executive remuneration decisions. For HR and compliance teams, understanding and anticipating these regulations is crucial to shaping compensation strategies that satisfy both regulatory standards and organizational talent objectives.

Chapter 5: HR Laws by Employer Size

5.1 When You Have 1 or More Employees

5.1.1 Fundamental Acts (e.g., Employee Polygraph Protection Act)

Certain federal statutes begin applying as soon as an organization hires its first employee, placing restrictions on specific employment practices that might infringe on individual rights. One notable example is the **Employee Polygraph Protection Act (EPPA)**, which governs the use of lie detector tests in most private-sector workplaces. While lie detector tests were once seen by some employers as a quick way to confirm truthfulness, the EPPA greatly limits their use and imposes strict conditions when they are permitted.

Overview of the Employee Polygraph Protection Act

Passed in 1988, the EPPA generally prohibits private employers from requiring or requesting that an employee or job candidate submit to a polygraph (or similar test) either as a condition of employment or during an investigation. This protects workers from undue pressure to undergo an examination that can be invasive and whose results are often disputed. A covered employer that violates these restrictions risks legal penalties and potential damages for affected individuals.

Key points include:

1. **Prohibition on Mandatory Testing:** With few exceptions, employers cannot demand, suggest, or coerce workers into taking polygraph exams during any phase of the employment relationship—whether it's a part of pre-hire screening or an internal investigation.

2. **Adverse Action Bar:** Employers may not discharge, demote, or otherwise retaliate against an employee or applicant who refuses a polygraph. In addition, they cannot use inconclusive test results alone as grounds for dismissal or discipline.

3. **Notice Requirement:** Covered employers must display an official EPPA poster in a conspicuous area of the workplace to inform employees of their rights under the Act.

Limited Exceptions

While the EPPA is broad, it does carve out certain exceptions in highly sensitive contexts:

➢ **Federal, State, and Local Government Employers:** Public-sector jobs are largely exempt, especially for roles connected to national security or law enforcement.

➢ **Security Services and Controlled Substances:** Private security firms involved in ongoing investigations of theft, embezzlement, or related crimes may be granted exceptions, provided the employer can show a reasonable basis for suspecting a particular individual. Employers handling controlled substances, such as pharmaceutical distributors, might also be exempt if polygraph testing directly relates to an investigation of workplace incidents.

➢ **Specific Investigatory Situations:** If an employer can demonstrate legitimate grounds to suspect an employee of wrongdoing that caused economic loss or injury to the business, a narrowly focused polygraph exam may be administered. Even then, strict procedural safeguards must be followed, including written notice explaining the basis for testing and the employee's rights during the process.

Compliance Considerations

➢ **Written Policies and Training:** Employers with at least one employee should draft internal guidelines clarifying that polygraph tests are not used in normal hiring or disciplinary processes. Training HR personnel and managers on the EPPA's restrictions helps avoid inadvertent violations—especially during investigations of workplace misconduct, when a manager may be tempted to "offer" a lie detector test.

➢ **Procedural Safeguards:** If a recognized exception arises, any polygraph exam must follow defined procedures, such as providing advance notice of the test, explaining the questions to be asked, and ensuring the examiner is licensed under applicable state or federal laws.

➢ **Recordkeeping:** Employers must maintain documentation (including any investigative notes or signed employee statements) that justifies using a polygraph under an EPPA exception. This recordkeeping can be crucial if an employee files a complaint alleging wrongful testing or retaliation.

Enforcement and Remedies

The U.S. Department of Labor (DOL) administers and enforces the EPPA. An employee who believes their rights have been violated can file a complaint with the Wage and Hour Division of the DOL, which can investigate the claim and, if warranted, initiate legal action. Remedies for the employee may include reinstatement, promotion, back pay, and legal costs. Additionally, courts may impose civil penalties on employers that fail to adhere to EPPA requirements.

Significance for Small Employers

Because the EPPA applies to essentially all private employers engaged in interstate commerce—even those with just one employee—business owners must be aware of its stipulations from day one. For the vast majority of work environments, this means avoiding the use of lie detector tests altogether, except in the rare cases where an explicit exemption applies. By respecting these boundaries and clearly communicating the organization's position on polygraph testing, employers reduce legal risks while building trust with employees.

Even at the smallest scale, employers must abide by fundamental federal laws that protect employee rights, including the Employee Polygraph Protection Act. Understanding these requirements—especially the near-universal ban on mandatory polygraph tests—helps ensure compliant, transparent practices and upholds a respectful employer-employee relationship.

5.1.2 Copyright & Other Intellectual Property Considerations

Even the smallest employers can encounter legal questions around intellectual property (IP) rights, especially when employees create materials or develop ideas that potentially qualify for protection under U.S. copyright, patent, or trademark laws. While larger organizations might maintain entire departments dedicated to IP management, businesses with just one or more employees still have compelling reasons to clarify who owns the work that staff produce—and to ensure they do not inadvertently infringe on someone else's protected creations.

Understanding "Work Made for Hire"

Under U.S. copyright law, works created by employees in the scope of their employment are typically considered "works made for hire." In these situations, copyright automatically belongs to the employer rather than the individual who actually performed the work. For instance, if a marketing employee designs a company brochure, the employer generally holds the copyright once the design is finalized. To avoid ambiguity, many organizations include language in offer letters or employee handbooks stipulating that any creative materials or inventions produced as part of a person's job duties belong to the company.

However, not all creative output falls neatly under "work made for hire." Employees might occasionally create materials outside their job responsibilities or on their own time, using personal resources. In such cases, ownership can become murky. Clear internal policies—including guidelines on permissible use of company resources—help define when a creation is job-related and when it is not.

Employee vs. Independent Contractor

Employers often work with independent contractors or freelance professionals who produce creative assets—such as software code, graphic designs, or written reports. Unlike with employees, the default rule for contractors is that the creator typically retains copyright unless there is a signed "work made for hire" agreement or an explicit assignment of rights. Businesses that fail to secure these agreements could discover later that they do not fully own the intellectual property they commissioned.

In practical terms, it is prudent to specify upfront, through a written contract, whether IP rights are being transferred to the business. This includes clarifying which rights (e.g., distribution, modification, or public display) the company needs to carry out its operations and whether the contractor retains any limited usage rights.

Confidentiality and Trade Secrets

Although copyright laws protect original works of authorship, many business assets—such as customer lists, marketing plans, or unique manufacturing processes—do not always fit neatly into copyright or patent categories. Instead, these might constitute trade secrets, which remain protected as long as the owner takes reasonable measures to keep them confidential. Employers often address these issues by:

1. Implementing non-disclosure agreements (NDAs) that bar employees from revealing proprietary information.

2. Restricting access to sensitive data through passwords or locked repositories.

3. Training staff on the importance of maintaining confidentiality regarding the company's methods, pricing, and client data.

These steps help preserve an employer's legal rights to pursue remedies if a current or former employee discloses trade secrets without permission.

Avoiding Infringement Risks

Employers must also guard against accidentally infringing on the IP of others. Even small-scale businesses face liability if employees incorporate copyrighted images, text, or software into company projects without proper licenses. Simple missteps—like using unlicensed photographs in promotional materials—can trigger demands for royalties or legal claims of infringement. Creating internal policies around verifying third-party content or subscribing to stock-image services can help reduce these risks.

Additionally, trademark infringement might arise if an employee uses a name, logo, or slogan that resembles one already held by another organization. Before adopting brand identifiers or marketing collateral, employers should conduct basic checks for existing marks—often with the assistance of legal counsel, if budget allows— to confirm that the new usage will not infringe on established rights.

Policy and Documentation Essentials

- ✓ **Employee Agreements:** Many employers include IP ownership clauses in standard employment contracts or handbooks. These clauses clarify that any creative or proprietary work produced on the job remains the property of the organization.

- ✓ **Contractor Clauses:** Written service agreements should explicitly address ownership, licenses, and confidentiality for contractor-produced materials.

- ✓ **Training and Awareness:** Employees may not intuitively understand the distinction between personal and company-owned IP. Periodic reminders or short training sessions on do's and don'ts can ward off misunderstandings.

- ✓ **Incident Response Plans:** In the event of suspected IP theft or misuse—whether by an employee or an external party— having a basic protocol in place can expedite investigation and protect the company's interests.

Balancing IP Protection and Innovation

Overly restrictive rules can stifle creativity, especially in smaller workplaces where employees might wear multiple hats. The goal is to strike a balance: safeguard the organization's core intellectual property while not creating an environment so stringent that employees feel dissuaded from contributing innovative ideas. Periodic evaluations of IP policies can help maintain this equilibrium, ensuring that the company stays ahead in a competitive market without discouraging inventiveness.

Employers of any size must be conscious of how copyright, trade secrets, and other forms of intellectual property apply within their operations. By defining clear rules on ownership, establishing robust confidentiality measures, and carefully contracting with outside creators, small businesses can protect their competitive edge while fostering an environment that values creativity and respects legal boundaries.

5.2 When You Have 15 or More Employees

5.2.1 Civil Rights Act (Title VII)

Title VII of the Civil Rights Act of 1964 stands as one of the most far-reaching employment laws for organizations that meet the threshold of having 15 or more employees. Its core objective is to eliminate discrimination in all aspects of employment—including hiring, promotion, compensation, and disciplinary practices—on the basis of race, color, religion, sex (including pregnancy, sexual orientation, and gender identity), or national origin. By embedding these protections into federal law, Title VII seeks to foster a workplace where job-related decisions are based solely on merit and legitimate business considerations.

Scope and Coverage

Any private or public employer that consistently employs 15 or more individuals is generally subject to Title VII. The statute also extends to labor unions and employment agencies under certain conditions. Even if a workforce temporarily dips below 15 employees, an employer may still be covered if it typically operates with more than this number over a significant portion of a calendar year.

This coverage means that the entirety of an organization's employment lifecycle is subject to scrutiny under Title VII. Employers must evaluate not just overt acts of discrimination—such as refusing to hire candidates from certain backgrounds—but also more subtle, systemic practices that could disproportionately affect a protected group.

Prohibited Employment Actions

Title VII prohibits a range of discriminatory activities. These include:

- **Unequal Treatment:** Refusing to hire, promoting or terminating employees, or imposing different workplace rules on the basis of a protected characteristic.

- **Harassment Based on Protected Traits:** Subjecting an employee to severe or pervasive conduct—verbal or physical—that creates a hostile work environment tied to race, religion, sex, or other protected statuses.

- **Retaliation:** Taking adverse action against an individual who files a discrimination complaint, assists in an investigation, or otherwise asserts their Title VII rights in good faith.

An employer's liability can stem not only from management-level decisions but also from the behavior of peers or third parties if the organization knew (or should have known) about a discriminatory or harassing situation and failed to intervene appropriately.

Reasonable Accommodations for Religion

Although Title VII does not require the same scope of accommodations as laws focused on disability, it does mandate that employers reasonably accommodate an employee's sincerely held religious beliefs or practices—unless doing so would impose an undue hardship on the business. Examples can include flexible scheduling to accommodate religious observances or permitting certain attire so long as it does not disrupt safety or essential job functions.

Enforcement and Remedies

The Equal Employment Opportunity Commission (EEOC) oversees the enforcement of Title VII. Employees who believe they have been discriminated against must typically file a charge with the EEOC before they can bring a lawsuit in federal court. If the agency finds merit in a claim, it may attempt to mediate or settle with the employer. Should these efforts fail, either the EEOC or the employee may pursue litigation.

Potential remedies for employees include reinstatement, back pay, compensatory damages (for emotional distress or related harms), and sometimes punitive damages if an employer's conduct is deemed particularly egregious. In addition, the court may order employers to amend discriminatory policies or undertake regular reviews of hiring and promotion practices as part of injunctive relief.

Practical Steps for Compliance

Employers who meet or exceed the 15-employee threshold can reduce the risk of Title VII violations by adopting a proactive, structured approach:

1. **Clear Anti-Discrimination Policies:** Draft and maintain written policies that outline prohibited conduct, reporting procedures for complaints, and assurances against retaliation.

2. **Management Training:** Ensure that supervisors and HR personnel receive specific training on how to identify and address discriminatory practices, including harassment and unconscious bias.

3. **Prompt Investigation and Action:** Encourage employees to report concerns and handle all complaints swiftly, documenting each step to show thorough and impartial consideration.

4. **Regular Review of Practices:** Periodically examine recruitment materials, job criteria, promotion paths, and disciplinary processes to catch inadvertent biases and align decision-making with objective, job-related factors.

By applying to businesses with at least 15 employees, Title VII significantly expands the scope of federal anti-discrimination rules. Organizations within this coverage must remain vigilant in preventing and addressing any form of employment discrimination based on protected characteristics. Through clear policies, training, and consistent enforcement, employers can uphold Title VII's aims and cultivate an equitable, inclusive environment.

5.2.2 Americans with Disabilities Act (ADA)

The Americans with Disabilities Act (ADA) is a cornerstone of federal law prohibiting discrimination in employment against qualified individuals with disabilities. For organizations with 15 or more employees, the ADA sets forth obligations to promote equal access to jobs, benefits, and other workplace opportunities. Central to its mission is ensuring that candidates and employees who can perform essential job functions are not unfairly excluded or disadvantaged because of physical or mental impairments.

Definition of Disability and Scope

The ADA covers a broad range of conditions that can substantially limit one or more major life activities, whether those impairments are permanent, episodic, or even perceived but not currently manifest. This definition extends beyond traditional mobility or sensory limitations; mental health conditions, chronic illnesses, and learning disabilities may also qualify under the Act.

Importantly, the ADA distinguishes between an inability to perform marginal tasks and an inability to carry out the **essential** functions of a job. If a person with a disability can handle those core duties—with or without reasonable accommodations—employers must treat them on par with other employees and applicants.

Reasonable Accommodations

A key employer responsibility is the provision of reasonable accommodations, which are adjustments or modifications that enable an employee with a disability to fulfill essential job functions or enjoy equal workplace benefits. Examples include:

> ➤ **Modified Equipment or Devices:** Such as specialized computer software, ergonomic desks, or screen readers.

- ➢ **Flexible Work Arrangements:** Adjusted schedules, telecommuting options (if feasible), or part-time hours.

- ➢ **Physical Workplace Modifications:** Ramps, accessible restrooms, or reconfigured workstations to accommodate wheelchairs or other mobility aids.

- ➢ **Policy Exceptions:** Allowing service animals or altering non-essential tasks to align with the employee's abilities.

Employers should engage in an *interactive process* with the individual seeking the accommodation to find solutions that balance the employee's needs with the nature of the job. Failure to engage in good faith can be grounds for ADA liability, even if the employer ultimately determines that no feasible accommodation exists.

Undue Hardship and Safety Considerations

While the ADA encourages flexibility, it does not force employers to implement accommodations that pose an *undue hardship*. Factors that might qualify as undue hardship include excessive cost relative to the employer's resources, significant disruption to normal operations, or fundamental alterations to the business model. However, an employer's burden of proof is significant; mere inconvenience or minimal expense typically does not meet the threshold of undue hardship.

Additionally, if an individual with a disability poses a *direct threat* to the health or safety of themselves or others and no reasonable accommodation can mitigate that risk, the employer may deny employment or an accommodation. Employers must rely on objective evidence and, when needed, medical assessments to determine whether a direct threat exists, ensuring that any exclusion from the workplace is based on actual risk rather than speculation or stereotypes.

Recruitment and Hiring Practices

Employers must ensure that their recruitment procedures do not screen out applicants with disabilities who can perform essential functions. Pre-employment medical inquiries or exams are generally restricted. Medical examinations or questions about disability are typically allowed only after a conditional job offer has been made, and then must be required of all entering employees in that job category. Questions related to current drug use may be permitted, but inquiring about past addiction or medical history before making an offer can be legally problematic.

Enforcement and Remedies

Complaints under the ADA go through the Equal Employment Opportunity Commission (EEOC). Employees or applicants who believe they have been discriminated against must generally file a charge with the EEOC prior to bringing a lawsuit in federal court. Successful claims can lead to remedies including reinstatement, back pay, compensatory damages for emotional distress, and sometimes punitive damages for willful or malicious conduct.

As part of settlement agreements or court orders, employers may be required to revise policies, provide training on ADA compliance, or submit to ongoing oversight by enforcement agencies.

Best Practices for Employers

✓ **Job Descriptions:** Maintain clear and up-to-date documents that identify essential and marginal functions. This delineation helps guide discussions about possible accommodations.

✓ **Training Supervisors and HR Staff:** Ensure decision-makers understand the interactive process, confidentiality rules, and common types of accommodations.

✓ **Complaint Mechanisms:** Adopt a transparent procedure for employees to request accommodations and report potential discrimination, backed by assurances against retaliation.

✓ **Periodic Policy Reviews:** As the definition of disability and available technologies evolve, revisit and refine existing protocols to stay aligned with legal and practical developments.

For employers with 15 or more employees, the ADA establishes both a broad prohibition on disability discrimination and a proactive obligation to provide reasonable accommodations. By clarifying essential job functions, engaging in open dialogue with employees and applicants, and approaching disability-related concerns with flexibility and empathy, organizations reduce legal risks and foster an inclusive, productive workforce.

5.2.3 Pregnancy Discrimination Act (PDA)

The Pregnancy Discrimination Act (PDA) explicitly protects employees and job applicants from discrimination based on pregnancy, childbirth, or related medical conditions. By classifying these conditions under "sex discrimination," the PDA extends the same legal safeguards to pregnant workers as those covering other protected characteristics—provided the employer meets the threshold of having 15 or more employees. This means that hiring, promotion, benefits, and other employment decisions must not be influenced by an individual's pregnancy status or potential for pregnancy.

Core Protections under the PDA

1. **Prohibition of Adverse Employment Actions**
   Employers cannot refuse to hire or promote an individual, reduce hours, or otherwise take adverse action simply because that person is pregnant or might become pregnant. Even if the employer believes it is acting out of concern for the employee's well-being, making unilateral decisions without consulting the employee can still be considered discrimination.

2. **Equal Treatment in Benefits and Leave**
   If an employer offers benefits or leave to workers with other medical conditions—such as short-term disability, modified work duties, or paid leave—pregnant employees must receive access to comparable benefits and accommodations. For instance, if a company allows employees to take extended leave for non-work-related injuries, the same policy must apply to pregnancy-related absences.

3. **Coverage of Related Medical Conditions**
   The PDA extends beyond the pregnancy itself, covering conditions such as gestational diabetes, complications during childbirth, and recovery from delivery. Employers are expected to treat these issues similarly to how they handle other temporary medical conditions, including granting leave or modified job duties if such options are routinely offered to other employees.

Relationship to Other Laws

Although the PDA is formally part of Title VII of the Civil Rights Act, it works in conjunction with various other federal and state mandates. For example:

➢ **Accommodations:** Some pregnant employees may also have pregnancy-related impairments that qualify as disabilities under the ADA if they substantially limit a major life activity. In such cases, employers might need to provide reasonable accommodations.

- ➢ **Family and Medical Leave:** Larger employers (50+ employees) may also be subject to the Family and Medical Leave Act (FMLA), which grants eligible workers up to 12 weeks of job-protected leave for certain family or medical reasons, including childbirth and care for a newborn.

While these laws share objectives of preventing discrimination and ensuring equal opportunity, each has its own specific eligibility criteria and procedural rules. Employers that meet the PDA's coverage threshold of 15 employees must remain aware of how these regulations intersect, especially when multiple statutes could apply to the same scenario.

Avoiding Common Pitfalls

1. **Interview and Hiring Practices**
   Employers should avoid questions or comments during recruitment that directly address a candidate's pregnancy status or plans to have children in the near future. Even well-intentioned queries can appear discriminatory if they influence employment decisions.

2. **Light Duty or Job Modifications**
   If an employer accommodates employees who have temporary disabilities—like a back injury—by offering light duty, it generally must do so under similar circumstances for an employee whose ability to perform job tasks is limited by pregnancy or a related condition. Refusing to extend comparable arrangements could be seen as discriminatory.

3. **Harassment Concerns**

A hostile work environment based on pregnancy or related conditions may constitute discrimination under the PDA. This can occur through disparaging remarks, unwarranted assumptions about an employee's capabilities, or other behaviors that significantly interfere with an employee's ability to perform their duties. Employers should train supervisors and staff to recognize and report pregnancy-related harassment.

Addressing Accommodation Requests

When an employee brings a pregnancy-related concern—such as difficulty standing for long periods or lifting heavy items—best practices include:

- ✓ **Engaging in Dialogue**: Speak with the employee about what kind of support would help them handle their essential job functions.

- ✓ **Reviewing Existing Policies**: Check if policies for similar medical needs or temporary impairments already exist. If so, ensure pregnant employees can access those same benefits.

- ✓ **Documenting the Process**: Keep a record of discussions and any agreed-upon accommodations, which can help demonstrate the employer's good-faith efforts if questions arise later.

Enforcement and Remedies

The Equal Employment Opportunity Commission (EEOC) oversees claims related to pregnancy discrimination. If the EEOC concludes that an employer has violated the PDA, potential remedies can include:

✓ **Monetary Compensation**: Such as back pay, front pay, or damages for emotional distress.

✓ **Reinstatement or Promotion**: If the employee was demoted or fired due to pregnancy-related bias.

✓ **Policy Revisions**: Employers may be required to modify their practices or conduct training to prevent future incidents.

Beyond the legal ramifications, companies also face reputational risks if employees perceive an unsupportive approach to pregnancy accommodations. Maintaining an equitable, inclusive environment can improve retention rates and foster a more positive workplace culture.

The Pregnancy Discrimination Act safeguards workers' rights during pregnancy and related medical conditions, requiring employers with 15 or more employees to treat pregnant employees at least as favorably as others with short-term medical conditions. By providing equitable benefits, granting necessary work adjustments, and avoiding bias in employment decisions, organizations can meet both the spirit and letter of the PDA.

5.2.4 Genetic Information Nondiscrimination Act (GINA)

The Genetic Information Nondiscrimination Act (GINA) bars employers with 15 or more employees from using genetic information as a basis for employment decisions. Enacted in 2008, GINA addresses concerns that genetic predispositions to certain health conditions might be used unfairly in hiring, firing, promotions, or benefit determinations. Beyond direct discrimination, the law also restricts the collection, disclosure, and misuse of employees' genetic data, reflecting growing public awareness of genetic testing and personalized medicine.

What Counts as Genetic Information

GINA defines genetic information broadly, encompassing details about an individual's genetic tests, the genetic tests of their family members, and even family medical history that could indicate a genetic predisposition. If an employer learns, for instance, that an employee's parent was diagnosed with Huntington's disease, the company cannot use that fact to influence the employee's career progression or coverage in an employer-sponsored health plan.

In practice, many common scenarios can yield genetic data:

> **Wellness Programs:** Health risk assessments or voluntary wellness screenings sometimes collect family medical history. Employers offering such programs must ensure that questions or incentives do not force employees to reveal genetic information involuntarily.

> **Workplace Conversations:** Casual discussions about illnesses affecting an employee's relatives may also trigger GINA concerns if the employer subsequently makes decisions that appear connected to that information.

Employer Restrictions and Responsibilities

1. **No Adverse Actions:** Employment decisions—such as whether to hire, promote, or discipline—cannot hinge on any genetic data. That includes the likelihood an employee might develop a health condition in the future.

2. **Limited Collection and Disclosure:** Employers are generally prohibited from requesting, requiring, or purchasing genetic

information about their employees or employees' family members. Exceptions exist for inadvertent disclosures (e.g., an unprompted conversation) or specific wellness program contexts where the employee has given prior, voluntary consent.

3. **Confidentiality Obligations:** If an employer lawfully obtains genetic information—perhaps through an occupational health program—it must treat that data as strictly confidential. This often means storing it separately from general personnel records and limiting access to those who need the information for compliance or safety reasons.

Interplay with Other Laws

GINA complements existing federal statutes by closing gaps not covered by anti-discrimination laws like the ADA. While the ADA focuses on current impairments affecting major life activities, GINA centers on the *potential* for future impairment based on genetic predisposition. Employers also must be mindful of state-level "mini-GINAs" or privacy statutes, as some states impose tighter restrictions on genetic data collection and use.

Enforcement and Remedies

Like other federal workplace anti-discrimination provisions, GINA is enforced by the Equal Employment Opportunity Commission (EEOC). Individuals who believe their genetic information has been misused or that they have faced discrimination on these grounds can file a charge with the EEOC. If the EEOC finds evidence of a violation, it may seek remedies such as reinstatement, back pay, and compensatory or punitive damages. In some instances, an employer might also be required to revise policies or provide targeted training to address specific compliance failures.

Practical Steps for Compliance

1. **Review and Revise Policies:** Employers with 15 or more employees should ensure handbooks, job applications, and wellness program forms do not solicit genetic or family medical information.

2. **Educate HR and Management:** Teams responsible for recruitment, benefits administration, and workplace investigations must understand where genetic data might surface and how to avoid infringing on employees' privacy.

3. **Limit Data Collection in Wellness Programs:** Encouraging healthy behaviors is permissible, but collecting sensitive family health data can easily cross legal boundaries if not carefully managed.

4. **Separate Records:** Any genetic information received as part of a lawful process (e.g., medical clearance, leave documentation) should be filed separately from the main personnel record to maintain confidentiality.

GINA's primary goal is to prevent discrimination based on genetic predispositions, thereby protecting employees from prejudicial treatment tied to their or their family's health history. For employers with 15 or more workers, robust compliance involves avoiding unnecessary collection of genetic details, maintaining strict confidentiality when such data is obtained, and ensuring all decisions are based on current job performance and qualifications rather than future medical possibilities.

5.3 When You Have 20 or More Employees

5.3.1 Age Discrimination in Employment Act (ADEA)

The Age Discrimination in Employment Act (ADEA) protects individuals aged 40 and older from employment discrimination based on age. It applies to private employers, state and local governments, and labor organizations with 20 or more employees or members. While many anti-discrimination statutes in the U.S. address multiple protected characteristics, the ADEA is unique in that it specifically targets biases related to an older worker's perceived ability to contribute effectively, highlighting issues such as forced retirement, disparate treatment in benefits, and age-related stereotypes.

Coverage and Protected Population

Under the ADEA, any worker or job applicant who is at least 40 years of age is covered. This protection extends to hiring, firing, promotion, compensation, and all other privileges of employment. Although an employer may lawfully prefer one worker over another for legitimate business reasons, it cannot rely on assumptions about diminished capacity or future health risks solely because of someone's age.

The Act also makes it unlawful to reduce or deny benefits—such as health coverage or training programs—specifically to older employees, unless the employer can demonstrate that providing such benefits uniformly would create excessive costs. Even then, the employer must strive to offer a comparable alternative whenever feasible.

Key Provisions and Employer Obligations

1. **Prohibition on Age-Based Decisions**

   Employers are barred from making decisions—like who to lay off during a reduction in force—by using age as a determining factor. Casual remarks by managers referring to someone as "too old" for a role or "needing fresh blood" can become significant evidence in a claim if an adverse employment action follows.

2. **Harassment Protection**

   Similar to harassment claims under other anti-discrimination laws, ongoing slurs or demeaning jokes about age may create a hostile work environment. Isolated, petty statements might not be enough to violate the ADEA, but pervasive or severe age-related harassment could cross the legal threshold.

3. **Bona Fide Occupational Qualification (BFOQ)**

   Although the ADEA limits the use of age as a reason for employment decisions, there is a narrow exception for BFOQs. In rare cases—such as certain public safety roles—a mandatory retirement age might be permissible if the employer can prove that age is genuinely necessary for performing essential duties safely or effectively. Courts generally interpret this exception quite narrowly.

4. **Waivers and Releases**

   When employers offer severance or early retirement packages, they often require a release of potential age discrimination claims in exchange. Such releases must comply with the Older Workers Benefit Protection Act (OWBPA), a 1990 amendment to the ADEA that ensures employees receive adequate notice, time to consider the agreement, and a chance to revoke acceptance within a set period. Failure to meet these OWBPA requirements can render a signed waiver unenforceable.

Enforcement and Legal Remedies

The Equal Employment Opportunity Commission (EEOC) enforces the ADEA. An individual who believes they have experienced age discrimination typically must file a charge with the EEOC before proceeding to court. If investigators find that an employer violated the Act, possible remedies can include back pay, reinstatement, payment of lost benefits, and—in cases of willful violations—liquidated damages equal to the amount of back pay awarded. Additionally, employers may need to revise policies or provide targeted training to prevent future violations.

Best Practices for Compliance

- ✓ **Document Objective Criteria:** Base hiring, promotion, and termination decisions on performance metrics, skill sets, and objective job requirements rather than factors tied to age.

- ✓ **Address Age Stereotypes:** Train managers to avoid assumptions about older workers' adaptability or tech-savviness. Fostering a climate of mutual respect helps reduce legal risks and improves morale.

- ✓ **Review Benefits and Policies:** Regularly examine whether benefit structures inadvertently place older workers at a disadvantage. If offering severance agreements that include ADEA claim waivers, ensure they follow OWBPA guidelines for validity.

- ✓ **Encourage an Inclusive Culture:** Recognize the value that older employees bring in terms of experience, institutional knowledge, and leadership. Setting a positive tone at the organizational level can diminish the likelihood of age-based complaints.

By extending protections to workers age 40 and older, the ADEA highlights the importance of basing employment decisions on merit rather than preconceived notions about age. Organizations with 20 or more employees should stay vigilant in ensuring that policies, practices, and day-to-day management do not subtly disadvantage older talent. Through objective evaluation processes, awareness training, and careful benefits planning, employers can align with both the spirit and the letter of the ADEA.

5.3.2 COBRA Requirements

For employers with 20 or more employees, the Consolidated Omnibus Budget Reconciliation Act (COBRA) provides a mechanism for workers (and their families) to continue group health insurance coverage after experiencing certain qualifying events. While many federal laws focus on preventing discrimination or ensuring minimum standards, COBRA is specifically designed to preserve healthcare benefits when an individual might otherwise lose access—such as after a layoff, a reduction in work hours, or certain family status changes.

Applicability and Coverage

COBRA generally applies to group health plans sponsored by private-sector businesses, state and local government agencies, and certain employee organizations, provided they have at least 20 employees on more than 50% of typical business days in the prior calendar year. The 20-employee calculation usually includes both full-time staff and part-time staff on a fractional basis (for instance, two half-time employees might count as one full-time equivalent).

Under COBRA, a qualifying beneficiary—such as an employee, spouse, or dependent child covered under the group plan—may elect to continue the same coverage they had while actively employed. This can encompass medical, dental, vision, or any other type of group health plan, though life insurance and disability plans typically fall outside COBRA's scope.

Qualifying Events

To trigger COBRA eligibility, a beneficiary must experience a qualifying event that causes loss of coverage. Examples include:

- ✓ **Termination of Employment** (voluntary or involuntary) for reasons other than gross misconduct.

- ✓ **Reduction in Hours** that renders an employee ineligible for benefits under the employer's plan.

- ✓ **Divorce or Legal Separation** of a covered employee from a spouse.

- ✓ **Death of the Covered Employee**, leaving dependents or a surviving spouse who were previously enrolled.

- ✓ **Loss of Dependent Child Status**, such as a child aging out of coverage.

Each event has its own notice requirements and timelines that determine how long the beneficiary can remain on COBRA coverage.

Duration of Coverage and Cost

COBRA continuation typically extends for up to 18 months in cases of job loss or reduced hours. However, certain events—like the death of the employee or divorce—can qualify spouses or dependents for up to 36 months of coverage. In some scenarios, an 18-month extension can be lengthened if a second qualifying event occurs, providing as many as 36 months in total.

While COBRA maintains the same insurance plan, beneficiaries usually pay the entire premium themselves, plus an administrative fee of up to 2%. This cost can be significantly higher than what employees paid previously, since employers often subsidize a portion of active employee premiums. For qualified beneficiaries with an extended coverage period under disability-related rules, premiums can reach 150% of the plan's cost for certain months.

Notification and Election Procedures

Several notices come into play for proper COBRA administration:

1. **General Notice**: Employers must provide a general COBRA rights notice to newly enrolled employees and their spouses when coverage begins.

2. **Qualifying Event Notice**: Either the employer or the beneficiary is responsible for alerting the plan administrator within a specified timeframe when a qualifying event occurs. Events like termination or a reduction in hours typically trigger the employer's obligation; divorce or a child losing dependent status often require the beneficiary to provide notice.

3. **Election Notice**: Once the plan administrator confirms a qualifying event, it must issue an election notice outlining the continuation rights and instructions on how to elect COBRA. Beneficiaries then generally have 60 days to decide if they want to continue coverage.

Prompt and accurate communication is key. If notices are late or inadequate, the employer or plan administrator can face penalties. Thorough recordkeeping of all notices and deadlines helps reduce legal risks and ensures employees can make well-informed decisions about their healthcare.

Compliance Considerations

Employers often rely on third-party administrators (TPAs) to handle COBRA's detail-oriented administration, from generating notices to collecting premiums. Still, ultimate legal responsibility typically remains with the plan sponsor. A few common compliance tips include:

- ✓ **Keep Up-to-Date Documentation**: Verify that employee headcounts meet or exceed the 20-employee threshold and document when coverage is added or lost.

- ✓ **Establish Clear Procedures**: Craft internal protocols that specify who initiates COBRA notices, how premium payments are tracked, and what steps to take if a beneficiary stops paying.

- ✓ **Monitor State "Mini-COBRA" Laws**: Some states impose additional or parallel continuation coverage requirements for smaller employers or extended coverage periods.

- ✓ **Maintain Accurate Timelines**: Ensure all notices reach employees promptly, and that elections, premium payments, and cancellations follow the law's strict deadlines.

COBRA ensures that employees and their families do not abruptly lose healthcare coverage during transitional periods. For employers with 20 or more employees, meeting COBRA obligations involves providing timely notices, clear election opportunities, and consistent premium collection. A solid administrative framework—often aided by a TPA—can help employers manage these responsibilities, support employee well-being, and avoid regulatory penalties.

5.4 When You Have 50 or More Employees

5.4.1 Family and Medical Leave Act (FMLA)

Employers with 50 or more employees must comply with the Family and Medical Leave Act (FMLA), which grants eligible workers job-protected, unpaid leave for specific family and medical reasons. By ensuring that employees can handle personal or family matters without jeopardizing their employment, FMLA strikes a balance between business operational needs and the well-being of the workforce.

Coverage and Employee Eligibility

To qualify for FMLA leave, an employee must work for a covered employer—generally one with at least 50 employees within a 75-mile radius—and meet certain thresholds:

> **Length of Service**: At least 12 months of tenure (which need not be consecutive, provided any break in service does not exceed seven years, with limited exceptions).

> **Hours Worked**: At least 1,250 hours in the 12-month period preceding the leave.

If an employee meets these requirements, the employer must provide up to 12 workweeks of leave in a 12-month period for covered reasons.

Reasons for Leave

FMLA covers a range of personal and family circumstances. Common examples include:

1. **Personal Serious Health Condition**: An illness or injury that prevents an employee from performing essential job functions, or that requires ongoing medical treatment.

2. **Family Care**: Tending to a spouse, child, or parent with a serious health condition, including situations requiring hospitalization, continuing treatment, or medical supervision.

3. **Birth or Placement for Adoption/Foster Care**: Bonding with a newborn or newly placed child. Both mothers and fathers may take this leave, and it must be completed within 12 months of birth or placement.

4. **Military Family Leave**: Qualifying exigencies related to a family member's covered military service. This can include short-notice deployments, counseling, or post-deployment reintegration activities. (Certain extended leave is available for caring for a family member who is a covered service member with a serious injury or illness, up to 26 workweeks within a single 12-month period.)

Maintaining Health Benefits

Even though FMLA leave is unpaid, the employer must continue any group health insurance coverage under the same terms and conditions as if the employee were actively working. For instance, if the employer subsidizes a portion of premiums, that arrangement continues throughout the leave. Employees on FMLA leave remain responsible for their usual share of premiums and may need to coordinate payment arrangements with HR, especially if paychecks are not being issued regularly.

Job Restoration and Return-to-Work

Upon returning from FMLA leave, employees must be restored to the same position they held prior to leave or to an equivalent role with the same pay, benefits, and working conditions. An "equivalent position" generally means a role that is nearly identical in terms of responsibility, status, and authority. Employers cannot force employees to take a lower-paying or less desirable position merely because they have used leave.

A limited exception exists for certain "key employees," typically salaried workers among the highest-paid 10% within a 75-mile radius, but invoking this exception carries strict guidelines. Employers who classify someone as a key employee must provide written notice explaining any risk of reinstatement denial, and even then, denial is permissible only if reinstatement would cause significant economic harm to the organization.

Intermittent and Reduced-Schedule Leave

FMLA allows employees to take leave intermittently or on a reduced schedule if medically necessary. This can mean shorter blocks of leave throughout the week—for instance, to attend periodic treatments or therapies—or temporarily reducing hours while recovering from a serious health condition. Intermittent leave requires appropriate medical certification, and employers may transfer an employee taking planned intermittent leave to an alternative position, provided it offers the same pay and benefits and better accommodates recurring absences.

Notification and Documentation

To ensure smooth administration:

1. **Employee Notice**: Employees are expected to give 30 days' advance notice for foreseeable leave (e.g., scheduled

surgery). If 30 days isn't possible, they should notify the employer as soon as practical.

2. **Employer Response**: Within five business days of receiving a leave request (or once it learns the reason for an absence qualifies under FMLA), the employer must provide required notices, such as details about eligibility, rights, and responsibilities.

3. **Certification**: Employers can request medical certification of the serious health condition. Employees generally have at least 15 calendar days to supply supporting documents. Re-certifications may be asked for periodically, especially if an employee's need for leave spans many months.

Failure to follow these steps, or imposing unnecessary obstacles for employees seeking valid leave, can lead to liability for the employer.

Intersection with State Family Leave Laws

States often have parallel or enhanced family leave statutes offering more generous benefits or covering additional employer sizes and family relationships. Employers operating across multiple states must track these variations and apply whichever law—federal or state— provides the greater benefit to the employee. However, leave taken under a state law may run concurrently with FMLA if both apply to the same situation.

For employers with 50 or more employees, providing FMLA leave is both a legal obligation and a cornerstone of a supportive work environment. By ensuring eligible workers have up to 12 weeks of job-protected, unpaid leave for serious health or family matters, employers help employees balance personal responsibilities without forfeiting their positions or benefits. Proper notice, thorough documentation, and clear communication of expectations are critical for effective FMLA administration and compliance.

5.4.2 Affirmative Action (Executive Order 11246)

Executive Order (EO) 11246 requires certain federal contractors to develop affirmative action programs aimed at promoting equal employment opportunity. Signed in 1965 and administered by the Office of Federal Contract Compliance Programs (OFCCP) under the U.S. Department of Labor, EO 11246 specifically addresses the employment and advancement of underrepresented groups. Although it overlaps with other anti-discrimination laws in principle, EO 11246 imposes unique obligations on qualifying contractors to proactively analyze their workforce and take deliberate steps to expand access and opportunities for women and minorities.

Who Must Comply

EO 11246 typically applies to federal contractors or subcontractors with at least 50 employees and contracts of $50,000 or more. To determine coverage, employers should review all business agreements with federal agencies—ranging from service contracts to supply agreements. Once an employer meets the threshold, they must maintain a written affirmative action plan (AAP) and adhere to ongoing compliance activities.

Key Requirements of an Affirmative Action Plan

1. **Workforce Analysis and Job Group Assessments**
   Contractors must examine their workforce composition to identify any patterns of underrepresentation. This involves creating "job groups" that combine positions with similar responsibilities or skill requirements, then comparing the demographics of each group to the relevant labor market.

2. **Utilization Goals**

   Based on the results, AAPs often set utilization goals for hiring or promoting individuals from underrepresented demographics when a shortfall is identified. These goals are not quotas; rather, they serve as targets that guide the contractor's recruiting and talent development strategies.

3. **Action-Oriented Programs**

   Contractors are expected to outline specific initiatives aimed at reducing or removing barriers to inclusion. These could include focused outreach, professional development offerings, and structured career path programs to encourage advancement from within.

4. **Monitoring and Reporting**

   Regular tracking of applicant flow, hires, promotions, and separations provides data for assessing progress against utilization goals. Contractors must document any corrective actions—such as modifying recruiting channels or adjusting training opportunities—and update their AAPs annually.

Enforcement and OFCCP Audits

The OFCCP periodically conducts compliance evaluations of covered contractors, requesting documentation such as the contractor's AAP, workforce data, and EEO-1 reports. In addition to reviewing statistical analyses, the agency may interview employees and inspect HR processes.

If OFCCP identifies violations—such as failing to maintain an adequate plan or evidencing systemic discrimination—it can pursue remedies that may include financial settlements, changes in hiring practices, or, in severe cases, cancellation of current contracts and debarment from future federal contracts. Maintaining an up-to-date

AAP and a transparent record of all affirmative action activities can help contractors navigate these audits successfully.

Intersection with Other Requirements

EO 11246 works in tandem with similar obligations, such as those under the Rehabilitation Act (covering individuals with disabilities) and the Vietnam Era Veterans' Readjustment Assistance Act (VEVRAA), which addresses certain protected veteran categories. Contractors subject to these regulations often merge or align their affirmative action efforts within a broader compliance strategy, ensuring consistency across various demographic groups.

Practical Steps for Contractors

- ✓ **Establish Clear Accountability**: Assign responsibility for plan development and oversight—often to an internal HR compliance lead or a dedicated affirmative action officer.

- ✓ **Engage in Targeted Outreach**: Build partnerships with minority-serving institutions, women's advocacy groups, and local community organizations to broaden candidate pools.

- ✓ **Document Everything**: Thoroughly record recruitment efforts, training programs, and promotion decisions; keep these records organized for potential OFCCP requests.

- ✓ **Periodic Self-Audits**: Conduct internal reviews of workforce demographics and compare data with the relevant labor market. Adjust outreach efforts or internal policies as indicated by any shortfalls.

Affirmative action under EO 11246 is a proactive framework rather than a reactive legal requirement. By regularly analyzing workforce composition, setting reasonable utilization goals, and establishing action-oriented programs, federal contractors with 50 or more employees meet both the letter and the spirit of EO 11246—fostering a diverse, inclusive environment while ensuring continued eligibility for federal contract opportunities.

5.4.3 Mental Health Parity Act (MHPA/MHPAEA)

The Mental Health Parity Act (MHPA) of 1996 and its subsequent expansion under the Mental Health Parity and Addiction Equity Act (MHPAEA) of 2008 aim to ensure that group health plans provide mental health and substance use disorder benefits on par with medical and surgical benefits. While MHPA initially focused on equalizing annual and lifetime dollar limits, MHPAEA extended parity rules to include treatment limitations, financial requirements, and other coverage conditions. Employers with at least 50 employees offering group health plans that include mental health and substance use disorder benefits typically must comply, barring certain exceptions.

Core Parity Requirements

1. **No Higher Cost-Sharing**
    Plans cannot impose higher copayments, coinsurance, or deductibles for mental health and substance use disorder services than those applied to comparable medical or surgical services.

2. **Equivalent Treatment Limits**
    Quantitative limits—such as the number of covered therapy sessions or inpatient days—must be equivalent for mental and physical health benefits. If a plan allows 30 inpatient days for medical conditions, it must offer at least the same limit for mental health conditions.

3. **Nonquantitative Treatment Limits**

Parity also extends to nonquantitative factors. This includes medical management standards (e.g., pre-authorization requirements or step therapy protocols) and provider network criteria. A plan, for instance, cannot require more frequent reauthorizations for mental health treatment than for medical services.

Scope and Applicability

➤ **Small Plan Exemption**: Generally, group health plans sponsored by employers with fewer than 50 employees may be exempt from MHPAEA.

➤ **Cost Exemption**: A plan that has complied with parity rules for at least six months but then experiences cost increases of 2% (the threshold may vary by regulation) or more due to mental health parity may request an exemption for the following plan year.

➤ **State Laws**: Many states have their own mental health coverage mandates, which might offer broader protections. Employers must comply with both federal and state requirements, applying whichever standard is more protective.

Enforcement and Oversight

Multiple federal agencies share responsibility for enforcing parity:

➤ **Department of Labor (DOL)** oversees private-sector employer-sponsored plans.

➤ **Department of Health and Human Services (HHS)** enforces parity in certain non-federal governmental plans and in the individual and small-group markets, depending on state structures.

> **Internal Revenue Service (IRS)** can impose excise taxes for noncompliance.

Employers and plan administrators must be prepared to demonstrate compliance, potentially through plan documentation and claims review data. Routine audits or targeted investigations may occur if participants or regulators suspect parity violations.

Best Practices for Compliance

✓ **Regular Plan Reviews**: Conduct periodic assessments of cost-sharing, visit limits, and pre-authorization rules for both mental and physical health benefits to confirm alignment.

✓ **Network Adequacy**: Ensure that mental health and substance use disorder providers are offered the same accessibility and reimbursement terms as medical/surgical providers, thereby preventing hidden barriers to care.

✓ **Clear Communication**: Provide employees with transparent summaries of benefits that clearly outline coverage for mental health services. Underscoring parity can boost utilization and demonstrate the employer's commitment to holistic well-being.

✓ **Collaborate with Insurers**: If coverage is fully insured, coordinate with the insurance carrier to confirm plan design meets parity regulations. Self-funded employers may need to work closely with third-party administrators to implement the same protocols.

Impact on Workplace Culture

Mental health parity not only has a regulatory dimension but also supports organizational goals for employee wellness and retention. When employers handle mental health and substance use disorder issues with the same level of seriousness as physical ailments, they reduce stigma and encourage early, effective interventions. This can translate into lower absenteeism, improved morale, and a more resilient workforce.

Under MHPA and MHPAEA, employers with at least 50 employees offering group health plans that include mental health and substance use disorder benefits must treat these benefits comparably to medical and surgical benefits. Ensuring parity spans not just monetary caps but also plan features such as pre-authorization and provider access. Through conscientious plan design and ongoing collaboration with carriers or administrators, employers can uphold compliance and foster a healthier, more supportive work environment.

5.5 When You Have 100 or More Employees

5.5.1 Worker Adjustment and Retraining Notification (WARN) Act

Employers with 100 or more full-time workers (or a combination of full- and part-time workers that reach specific thresholds) may be subject to the WARN Act's requirement to provide advance notice before significant layoffs or plant closures. Enacted to protect employees and their communities from sudden, large-scale job losses, the WARN Act mandates at least 60 calendar days' written notice to affected employees, state dislocated worker units, and local governmental authorities.

Covered Employers and Events

1. **Size Threshold**

   A private or public employer generally comes under WARN if it has 100 or more full-time employees who collectively work at least 4,000 hours per week (exclusive of overtime). Part-time workers are counted separately, though if an employer's total headcount and hours meet certain combined criteria, it may still trigger WARN obligations.

2. **Qualifying Layoffs and Closings**

   > **Plant Closing**: A permanent or temporary shutdown of a single site of employment—or one or more operating units within that site—that results in employment loss for 50 or more full-time workers during any 30-day period.

   > **Mass Layoff**: An employment loss at a single site involving at least 33% of the workforce (and at least 50 employees), or a total of 500 or more employees, within a 30-day window.

Notice Requirements

Timing: Employers typically must issue written notice 60 days prior to the closing or layoff. Failure to comply can result in back pay and benefits for the notice-shortfall period.

Recipients:

> **Affected Employees or Their Union**: If workers are unionized, the notice goes to the union representative; otherwise, individual employees must receive it.

➤ **State and Local Authorities**: This commonly includes the state dislocated worker unit and the chief elected official of local government.

➤ **Content**: The notice must specify the expected date of the closure or layoff, identify the positions to be impacted, and provide contact information for an employer representative who can respond to questions.

Exceptions and Reduced Notice

While the 60-day requirement is the norm, WARN recognizes limited exceptions:

Unforeseeable Business Circumstances: Dramatic, unexpected events outside the employer's control—such as a sudden cancellation of a major contract—may justify shorter notice if it was truly impossible to predict the need for layoffs in advance.

Faltering Company Exception: If a company is seeking capital or business to stay afloat and believes that issuing WARN notice could jeopardize its chances of survival, it might qualify for reduced notice.

Natural Disasters: Events such as hurricanes or earthquakes may relieve the employer of strict notice obligations, but only if the disaster directly caused the shutdown.

In all these cases, employers must still provide as much notice as is practicable and explain why the reduced notice was necessary.

Liability and Remedies

Employers that violate WARN may be required to compensate employees for wages and benefits covering the notice-shortfall period. Courts can also award attorneys' fees, and local authorities may impose separate penalties if they are not properly notified. Because noncompliance can be costly, it's prudent for organizations to maintain clear records of workforce planning decisions, ensuring they can show compliance or justify exceptions if challenged.

Practical Tips for Compliance

✓ **Monitoring Headcount and Hours**
Human Resources should closely track employment levels to confirm if the 100-employee coverage threshold is reached. This includes being aware of part-time employees' hours.

✓ **Advance Contingency Planning**
Business leaders need to factor the 60-day notice window into any reorganization or facility-closure timeline. Clear internal communication can minimize confusion and legal exposure.

✓ **Coordinating with Legal Counsel**
Because the WARN Act has specific definitions and tight deadlines, consulting legal experts before issuing notices—or concluding that notice isn't required—can mitigate risk.

✓ **State "Mini-WARN" Laws**
Some states have their own "mini-WARN" statutes with different thresholds or longer notice requirements. Employers should confirm whether these more stringent rules apply in each location.

The WARN Act compels employers with 100 or more employees to provide 60 days' notice of mass layoffs or plant closings, helping workers and communities prepare for job losses. By proactively monitoring workforce levels, adhering to notice guidelines, and understanding available exceptions, organizations can navigate restructuring or closures in a legally compliant and more transparent manner.

5.5.2 EEO-1 Reporting

Private employers with 100 or more employees generally must submit annual EEO-1 reports to the Equal Employment Opportunity Commission (EEOC), providing demographic data about their workforce. By collecting information on race, ethnicity, and gender across different job categories, the EEO-1 report helps the EEOC and other agencies gauge national employment patterns, identify potential disparities, and support enforcement of federal anti-discrimination laws. In most cases, government contractors with at least 50 employees and a contract of $50,000 or more must also file the EEO-1.

Key Components of the EEO-1 Report

1. **Employee Demographics**
   The report captures each employee's self-identified race and ethnicity, along with their gender. Employers are encouraged to provide a voluntary self-identification form to employees. If an individual declines to self-identify, employers may use visual observation or other available data to make a good-faith classification.

2. **Job Categories**
   Employers place each worker into one of 10 broad job categories (e.g., Executive/Senior-Level Officials and Managers, Professionals, Technicians, Administrative Support). These categories help the EEOC analyze representation patterns at different organizational levels.

3. **Work Location**
   For multi-establishment companies, separate location reports

may be required. A "consolidated report" then aggregates data from all U.S. locations. The online filing system usually streamlines this process by guiding how to group establishments and how to allocate remote workers.

Timing and Filing Process

Annual Deadline

Historically, EEO-1 reports have been due around the end of March, but the exact deadline can change. The EEOC typically announces filing windows each year, often adjusting due to technology updates or other administrative factors.

Online Submission

Employers file electronically using the EEOC's EEO-1 Component 1 Online Filing System. The portal requests details such as the company's NAICS code, total employee counts, and demographic breakdowns within each job category.

Certification

The employer's representative completes a final certification attesting to the accuracy of the submitted data. An incomplete or late filing may prompt follow-up inquiries from the EEOC.

Uses of EEO-1 Data

➢ **Statistical Analysis**

The EEOC aggregates information to spot trends, like whether a particular sector has significant gender imbalances in management roles.

➢ **Investigation Support**

While the EEO-1 itself doesn't trigger an investigation, the agency may reference reported figures when assessing complaints or potential patterns of discrimination.

➤ **Employer Self-Audit**

By reviewing EEO-1 summaries each year, companies can identify areas needing attention—e.g., recruiting approaches to increase diversity in technical or leadership roles.

Practical Tips for Compliance

✓ **Maintain Accurate Records**

Keep consistent, up-to-date HR data on each employee's self-identified race, ethnicity, and gender. A centralized HRIS (Human Resources Information System) can streamline the data collection needed for the EEO-1.

✓ **Respect Confidentiality**

Individual demographic details must be used and disclosed only for legitimate employment reporting purposes. Clear internal guidelines on data access help ensure privacy.

✓ **Monitor Organizational Changes**

Company expansions, consolidations, or new establishments can alter how EEO-1 data must be reported. Keeping lines of communication open between HR, operations, and legal teams prevents surprises as the filing deadline nears.

✓ **Stay Alert to Regulatory Developments**

The EEOC may periodically adjust reporting requirements, especially around new data fields or expanded categories. Subscribing to official EEOC updates or consulting with counsel can help you anticipate changes.

Intersection with Other Requirements

Although EEO-1 data informs the broader landscape of equal employment opportunity compliance, it does not, by itself, constitute an affirmative action plan or prove discrimination.

Nonetheless, combined with other workforce metrics—such as promotion rates or applicant flow data—EEO-1 reports can serve as a critical reference point for employers subject to Affirmative Action requirements under Executive Order 11246 or contractors covered by the Office of Federal Contract Compliance Programs (OFCCP).

EEO-1 reporting is a fundamental compliance obligation for larger employers, offering the EEOC nationwide insights into workforce demographics. By managing accurate data on race, ethnicity, gender, and job categories—and staying current with filing deadlines—organizations not only meet federal requirements but also gain a valuable snapshot of their internal diversity profile.

5.6 Specific Requirements for Federal Contractors and Federal Employees

5.6.1 Rehabilitation Act of 1973

Federal contractors, subcontractors, and government agencies often must comply with portions of the Rehabilitation Act of 1973, which predates and, in some respects, parallels the Americans with Disabilities Act (ADA). While the ADA broadly applies to the private sector, the Rehabilitation Act focuses on entities that receive federal financial assistance or hold federal contracts above specific monetary thresholds. In these settings, the Act prohibits discrimination on the basis of disability and imposes affirmative obligations to accommodate qualified individuals.

Sections and Coverage

Section 501: Governs federal agencies' employment practices, requiring them to develop affirmative action plans for the hiring, placement, and advancement of individuals with disabilities.

Section 503: Covers federal contractors or subcontractors with contracts exceeding $15,000, mandating affirmative action for qualified individuals with disabilities.

Section 504: Applies to programs or activities receiving federal financial assistance, ensuring non-discrimination in service delivery or access for persons with disabilities.

Although these provisions vary slightly in scope, collectively they reflect the broader theme that recipients of federal funds or contracts must actively prevent and eliminate barriers faced by people with disabilities.

Affirmative Action and Outreach

Contractors subject to Section 503 must institute formal affirmative action programs aimed at recruiting and advancing employees with disabilities. Among other steps, they must:

1. **Conduct Self-Audits**: Review policies and practices—such as job descriptions, recruitment channels, and training opportunities—to ensure they do not inadvertently disqualify or discourage disabled applicants.

2. **Set Utilization Goals**: Track the percentage of employees with disabilities in the workforce and compare it to established benchmarks (the current aspirational goal is 7% in each job group or workforce as a whole, depending on size).

3. **Engage in Targeted Outreach**: Develop recruiting relationships with rehabilitation agencies, disability advocacy groups, and other community-based organizations to broaden the talent pipeline.

4. **Maintain Documentation**: Keep records of accommodation requests, compliance actions, and recruitment activities. The Office of Federal Contract Compliance Programs (OFCCP) may request these records in compliance evaluations.

Reasonable Accommodations

Like the ADA, the Rehabilitation Act requires covered employers to provide reasonable accommodations to qualified employees or applicants with disabilities, barring undue hardship. An accommodation might include:

✓ Adjusting work schedules or restructuring job tasks.

✓ Providing assistive devices or modifying equipment.

✓ Offering telework options if consistent with the role's essential duties.

Where the ADA sets a baseline for most private employers, Sections 501 and 503 require federal agencies and contractors to go a step further—affirmatively removing barriers and monitoring progress toward more inclusive workplaces.

Enforcement and Oversight

➤ **OFCCP (Section 503)**: Enforces compliance among federal contractors. This includes reviewing affirmative action plans, analyzing employment data, and investigating potential discrimination claims. Contractors who fail to meet their obligations risk enforcement actions, which may lead to financial remedies or—in severe cases—loss of federal contracts.

➤ **EEOC (Section 501)**: Investigates disability discrimination complaints within federal agencies. An aggrieved employee can file a claim if they believe an agency violated the Act's provisions.

➢ **Funding Agencies (Section 504)**: Oversee compliance among recipients of federal grants or financial assistance. Violations could lead to grant termination or other sanctions.

Practical Steps for Compliance

1. **Create a Written Plan**: Develop an affirmative action program detailing how the organization will attract and retain qualified individuals with disabilities.

2. **Educate Managers and Staff**: Provide training on disability etiquette, legal responsibilities, and the accommodations process to foster a respectful, proactive work culture.

3. **Conduct Proactive Recruitment**: Build relationships with disability-focused job boards, vocational rehabilitation centers, and community organizations to source candidates with a variety of skill sets.

4. **Track and Analyze Outcomes**: Regularly measure progress toward utilization goals, note barriers that arise, and adjust strategies or procedures to improve inclusion.

Why It Matters

Beyond compliance, a robust approach to the Rehabilitation Act can yield tangible benefits for federal contractors and agencies. By tapping into underutilized talent pools and promoting an inclusive environment, organizations often discover improved retention rates, higher employee morale, and a broader range of perspectives for problem-solving. When properly integrated, disability inclusion strengthens both an employer's legal posture and its overall workforce effectiveness.

The Rehabilitation Act of 1973 compels federal contractors and recipients of federal funding to go beyond a stance of non-discrimination, adopting affirmative action measures to hire and retain individuals with disabilities. Through rigorous self-review, recruitment outreach, and ongoing accommodation efforts, covered organizations not only fulfill statutory obligations but also foster a more diverse, adaptive workforce.

5.6.2 Service Contract Act (SCA)

The McNamara–O'Hara Service Contract Act (SCA) governs labor standards for employees performing services on federal contracts. Under the SCA, contractors and subcontractors must pay service workers no less than the prevailing wage rates and fringe benefits found in local wage determinations issued by the U.S. Department of Labor (DOL). This requirement ensures that federal service contracts do not undercut locally established compensation levels or degrade working conditions for employees who provide ongoing, non-professional services to the government.

Coverage and Wage Determinations
Contracts for services valued at over $2,500 typically fall under the SCA, although certain exemptions apply (for example, contracts subject to the Walsh-Healey Public Contracts Act or for work performed outside the United States). When covered, employers must adhere to prevailing wage rates published in official DOL wage determinations for the locality where the work occurs. In addition to wage floors, the SCA mandates a set of fringe benefits that can include health insurance contributions, vacation, and holiday pay. Any changes in the contract's scope or extensions of the

performance period may require updated wage determinations, which contractors must implement accordingly.

Compliance and Recordkeeping

Covered employers must display the DOL's "Notice to Employees Working on Government Contracts" in a visible location and maintain accurate payroll records confirming that each worker is paid at least the specified rates. Payroll documents should show hours worked, wages paid, and fringe benefit distributions. The DOL's Wage and Hour Division oversees SCA enforcement, investigating claims of underpayment or improper classification of employees. Violations can lead to back wage assessments, withholding of contract payments, and potential debarment from future government contracts.

Best Practices for Contractors

One practical step is to review applicable wage determinations before bidding on federal service contracts to ensure that labor costs are factored in correctly. In addition, adopting a robust internal process for updating wages and benefits when new determinations are issued minimizes the risk of compliance gaps. Training HR staff and project managers on SCA classifications, recordkeeping requirements, and reporting obligations can further bolster adherence, helping contractors maintain good standing with federal agencies and avoid enforcement actions.

5.6.3 Federal Acquisition Regulations (FAR)

For organizations seeking or holding federal contracts, the Federal Acquisition Regulations (FAR) establish a government-wide framework that guides every stage of acquisition—from solicitation and award to contract administration and closeout. While FAR provisions address numerous operational, financial, and contractual aspects, they also influence HR policies by requiring contractors to meet specific employment-related standards and incorporate mandated clauses in their contracts.

Scope and Purpose

The FAR is the primary regulatory code for procurement by all federal agencies, aiming to maintain consistency, fairness, and transparency in how government contracts are executed. When an employer becomes a federal contractor—no matter the agency involved—certain FAR clauses may apply automatically, imposing obligations on matters such as recruitment, recordkeeping, or whistleblower protections.

In many cases, the FAR references or integrates other regulations (like the Service Contract Act or EEO requirements), making it a central repository of compliance directives. This ensures that a contractor's responsibilities are clearly spelled out, reducing the likelihood of oversight when multiple federal standards are at play.

Key HR-Related Clauses

1. **Equal Opportunity Clauses**
    While the specific non-discrimination provisions may stem from separate laws (e.g., Executive Order 11246), the FAR will often incorporate these clauses by reference, making them enforceable as part of the contract. Contractors need to ensure their HR policies reflect all mandatory requirements, from posting notices to maintaining affirmative action programs where applicable.

2. **Combating Trafficking in Persons**
    Certain FAR clauses prohibit contractors from engaging in, or allowing, labor trafficking and require the development of internal reporting and remediation procedures. Employers may

need to train staff and implement contract flow-down provisions so that subcontractors also uphold these standards.

3. **Drug-Free Workplace**
   Contractors must certify that they will maintain a drug-free environment. From an HR standpoint, this generally translates to clear policies on substance use and periodic training for employees, as well as procedures for handling violations.

4. **Required Postings and Notifications**
   FAR clauses often specify the need to display relevant employment notices. These can include posters informing workers of their rights under labor laws, or instructions for filing concerns regarding unethical or illegal practices in government contracts.

Compliance Strategies

✓ **Contract Review Process**
   Each new federal contract typically lists the FAR clauses that apply to that specific agreement. HR personnel, legal counsel, and contract managers should collaborate to ensure the required policies, postings, and training programs are in place before work starts.

✓ **Subcontract Flow-Down**
   When a prime contractor subcontracts part of the work, FAR clauses may need to be passed down to those subcontractors. Clear communication about these obligations helps avoid gaps in compliance.

✓ **Recordkeeping and Audit Readiness**
   FAR-related compliance can require detailed records on staffing, pay practices, or workplace investigations. Maintaining

consistent, organized documentation positions contractors to respond effectively if agencies conduct reviews or audits.

✓ **Employee Training**
   Because FAR compliance can intersect with employee conduct (anti-trafficking provisions, drug-free workplace, conflict of interest guidelines, etc.), relevant training ensures the workforce understands these obligations and how to report violations.

Enforcement and Consequences

Noncompliance with FAR clauses can result in contract termination, suspension, or debarment from future federal contracting opportunities. Agencies may also impose fines or pursue legal remedies if a contractor's failure to fulfill obligations leads to contract performance issues or labor law violations. Proactive, ongoing monitoring of compliance tasks thus becomes an essential component of sustaining a successful federal contracting relationship.

Through the FAR, the federal government places uniform, enforceable requirements on contractors—including specific HR-related duties. Understanding and integrating these clauses into everyday policies, procedures, and training allows employers to uphold contractual commitments, minimize legal risks, and preserve valuable business opportunities in the public sector.

Chapter 6: Other Critical U.S. Employment Regulations

6.1 Immigration and Employment Eligibility

6.1.1 IRCA Requirements (I-9s, E-Verify)

Under the Immigration Reform and Control Act (IRCA), employers in the United States must verify that all new hires—regardless of citizenship—are authorized to work in the country. The primary mechanism for this verification is the Form I-9, which documents each employee's identity and employment eligibility. Some employers may also choose or be required to use E-Verify, a web-based program that electronically confirms an individual's work authorization.

Completing Form I-9

Obligation for All New Hires
Every employer must ensure that employees complete Section 1 of the I-9 on or before their first day of work for pay. Within three business days of an employee's start date, the employer must review acceptable documents proving identity and eligibility, then fill out Section 2. Typical documents include a U.S. passport, permanent resident card, or a combination like a driver's license and Social Security card.

Retaining and Storing Forms
Employers must keep I-9s on file for either three years after the hire date or one year after the employment ends, whichever is later. They may store forms on paper, electronically, or via microfilm/microfiche, provided they maintain data integrity and retrieve records swiftly if audited.

Reverification
When work authorization documents have expiration dates, employers must reverify the employee's eligibility before the

expiration. This process involves Section 3 of the same I-9 form (or a new form if space is lacking). Failure to reverify on time can lead to compliance issues, though employers must be careful not to request updates or documentation earlier than legally required.

E-Verify Program

Voluntary vs. Mandatory Use

E-Verify is an online system run by the Department of Homeland Security (DHS) in partnership with the Social Security Administration. Though many employers enroll voluntarily, some organizations—particularly federal contractors or those operating in states with mandatory e-verification laws—must use the system. By comparing I-9 details against government records, E-Verify generally confirms eligibility within seconds or flags a discrepancy for further action.

Process Integration with I-9

Employers must complete a Form I-9 before using E-Verify. After the I-9 is finalized, the employer enters or uploads relevant data to the E-Verify portal within three business days of the employee's start date. If E-Verify issues a "Tentative Nonconfirmation" (TNC), the employer must inform the worker promptly and provide instructions on contesting the result.

Potential Benefits and Drawbacks

Using E-Verify offers a more robust defense against allegations of knowingly hiring unauthorized workers. However, it also requires employers to closely track deadlines and respond swiftly to TNCs. Technical issues or data mismatches can slow down onboarding, and some employers may need additional training to use the system correctly.

Avoiding Discriminatory Practices

While verifying employment authorization is mandatory, employers must do so in a manner that does not discriminate based on national origin or citizenship status. For instance, demanding specific documents (like a permanent resident card instead of any valid option from the I-9's lists) could be deemed discriminatory. The Department of Justice's Immigrant and Employee Rights Section investigates claims that companies asked for extra documentation only from certain groups or retaliated against workers with pending TNCs.

Enforcement and Penalties

The U.S. Immigration and Customs Enforcement (ICE) and other agencies periodically conduct I-9 audits. Employers found to have significant paperwork errors or to be employing unauthorized workers face fines that can escalate with repeated infractions. Ensuring HR teams follow proper procedures—from prompt form completion to consistent document handling—helps reduce exposure. Regular internal audits of I-9 records, along with staff training on IRCA's requirements, can prevent costly violations and disruption to business operations.

IRCA's Form I-9 requirement forms the legal backbone of an employer's responsibility to verify work authorization. While E-Verify can add another layer of assurance, it also introduces new procedural steps and deadlines. A rigorous approach—backed by training, clear policies, and careful documentation—enables organizations to remain compliant and treat all applicants fairly.

6.1.2 H-1B, L-1, and Other Visa Categories

Beyond verifying that employees have the right to work in the United States, many employers seek to sponsor foreign nationals under specific nonimmigrant visa programs. Common categories include H-1B visas for specialty occupations, L-1 visas for intra-company transfers, and an array of other classifications depending on the nature of the work and the relationship between the employee and employer. Each visa category comes with distinct eligibility criteria, application processes, and compliance obligations that HR professionals must understand to maintain lawful employment relationships.

H-1B (Specialty Occupations)

Purpose and Eligibility

The H-1B program allows U.S. employers to temporarily hire foreign workers in "specialty occupations," typically requiring at least a bachelor's degree or the equivalent in a specialized field. Examples include software engineers, architects, and certain financial analysts. Employers must attest that they will pay at least the prevailing wage for the role, ensuring that hiring H-1B employees does not undercut U.S. workers' compensation.

Annual Cap and Timing

There is an annual cap on new H-1B visas, currently set at 65,000, with an additional 20,000 for those who hold advanced degrees from U.S. institutions. Petitions generally become eligible for filing in the spring (April 1, unless the date falls on a weekend or holiday), and start dates often align with the start of the federal fiscal year (October 1). Because of high demand, employers typically plan months in advance to file cap-subject petitions and may rely on immigration counsel for guidance.

Employer Obligations

➢ **Labor Condition Application (LCA):** Employers must file an LCA with the Department of Labor, affirming that they will pay the required wage rate and abide by specific working conditions.

➢ **Recordkeeping:** Organizations must maintain a public access file for each H-1B worker, containing documents such as the approved LCA, wage rate calculations, and proof that employees have not displaced U.S. workers.

➢ **Visa Transfer and Extension:** H-1B workers can often "port" to a new employer without waiting for the entire petition approval, but the new employer must file a petition before the move. Extensions beyond the initial three-year term can be granted up to a six-year total, with certain exceptions for green card applicants.

L-1 (Intra-Company Transferees)

Types of L-1

➢ **L-1A:** For managerial or executive roles transferring from a foreign entity of the company to a U.S. branch, subsidiary, or affiliate.

➢ **L-1B:** For specialized knowledge employees who possess proprietary know-how essential to the company's products, processes, or operations.

Criteria and Corporate Structure
To qualify, the employer must have a qualifying relationship (such as a parent company, branch, or affiliate) between the foreign and U.S. entities, and the employee must have worked abroad for at least one continuous year in the preceding three years. In the U.S., they must serve in a managerial, executive, or specialized knowledge capacity.

Duration and Extensions

➢ **L-1A** transferees may stay up to seven years (initially up to three years, then extended in increments of two).

> **L-1B** transferees may remain for a maximum of five years. Employers often use L-1 visas to establish new offices or to bring proven leadership and technical expertise into the U.S. workforce.

Other Common Employment Visa Types

E-1 and E-2 (Treaty Traders and Treaty Investors): For nationals of countries with which the U.S. maintains treaties of commerce and navigation. Allows entry to conduct substantial trade or develop/ direct the operations of an enterprise with significant investment.

TN (NAFTA/USMCA Professionals): Enables Canadian and Mexican citizens in specific professional occupations (e.g., accountants, engineers, scientists) to work in the U.S. under simplified procedures.

H-2B (Non-Agricultural Temporary Workers): Designed for seasonal or peak-load positions that are not agricultural in nature, such as hospitality or landscaping roles. Subject to numerical caps and labor certification requirements demonstrating a temporary shortage of U.S. workers.

Ongoing Compliance and Best Practices

✓ **Tracking Visa Deadlines and Statuses**
Implement robust systems to monitor expiration dates, extension windows, and changes to job duties or locations that could affect an employee's visa status.

✓ **Wage and Working Conditions**
In categories like H-1B, wage attestation is a core requirement. Employers must ensure that foreign nationals receive wages and

benefits on par with U.S. peers and remain compliant with any prevailing wage levels specified in the petition.

✓ **Site Visits and Audits**
Agencies such as U.S. Citizenship and Immigration Services (USCIS) or the Department of Labor may conduct worksite inspections. Clear documentation, consistent job descriptions, and alignment between the visa petition and the actual role help avoid findings of noncompliance.

✓ **Communication with Employees**
Immigration processes can be stressful for workers and their families. Providing accurate information on timelines, filing procedures, and potential changes in regulations can foster transparency and trust.

✓ **Strategic Workforce Planning**
Managing multiple visa categories requires anticipating staffing needs well in advance—especially in a cap-restricted environment like H-1B. Employers may diversify their sponsorship strategy or seek alternative pathways (such as permanent residency petitions) for crucial talent.

Employers sponsoring foreign nationals through H-1B, L-1, or other specialized visas must navigate distinct eligibility rules, wage standards, and compliance responsibilities. By aligning petition processes with forward-looking HR strategies—along with rigorous tracking of deadlines and documentation—organizations can smoothly integrate global talent into their U.S. operations.

6.2 Sarbanes-Oxley Act (SOX) and Corporate Governance

6.2.1 Whistleblower Protections

The Sarbanes-Oxley Act (SOX) introduced specific protections for employees of publicly traded companies who report concerns about fraudulent accounting, securities violations, or other misconduct related to financial disclosures. These whistleblower provisions, outlined primarily in Section 806, guard against retaliation—such as termination or demotion—when employees report potential wrongdoing internally or to government authorities.

Covered Employers and Activities

Publicly Traded Companies
SOX whistleblower protections generally apply to employees of companies with securities registered under the Securities Exchange Act of 1934 or that file reports under Section 15(d) of the Act. This coverage often extends to subsidiaries or affiliates whose financial information is included in the parent company's consolidated financial statements.

Protected Disclosures
Reports must involve concerns about conduct that could harm shareholders or violate federal securities laws. Common examples include alleged falsification of accounting records, manipulation of financial statements, or internal controls failures. Employees who in good faith report suspicious activity—either internally (e.g., to compliance officers or audit committees) or externally (to regulatory agencies)—are shielded from reprisal.

Prohibited Forms of Retaliation

179

SOX prohibits any adverse employment action motivated by an employee's whistleblowing. Retaliation can take multiple forms beyond termination, such as suspensions, demotions, or pay cuts. Even subtle measures—like changing shifts, reassigning projects, or unjustifiably disciplining the employee—may be deemed retaliatory if tied to the disclosure.

Complaint Process and Enforcement

Filing with OSHA

Employees who believe they have experienced retaliation must file a complaint with the Occupational Safety and Health Administration (OSHA) within 180 days of the alleged retaliatory action. This administrative process can lead to investigations, requests for documentation, and interviews with company personnel.

Administrative and Legal Remedies

If OSHA concludes that retaliation occurred and the employer does not settle, the complainant or employer can seek a hearing before an Administrative Law Judge. Further appeals can go through the Administrative Review Board (ARB) or ultimately to federal court. Remedies for employees who prevail might include reinstatement, back pay with interest, compensation for litigation costs, or other measures to make them "whole" again.

Best Practices for Compliance

✓ **Establish Clear Reporting Mechanisms**
   Employers should provide multiple safe channels—like dedicated hotlines or compliance officers—for employees to raise concerns about potential fraud or financial misrepresentations. Transparent procedures encourage internal reporting and allow prompt corrective action.

✓ **Train Managers on Anti-Retaliation**
Supervisors should understand that retaliating against someone who raises concerns—whether or not those concerns ultimately prove accurate—can lead to significant liabilities under SOX. This training helps reduce the risk of inadvertent violations.

✓ **Maintain Confidentiality**
While not all whistleblower disclosures can be kept anonymous, companies should handle complaints discreetly, limiting information to those with a legitimate need to know. This fosters trust and reduces the likelihood of retaliation claims tied to public exposure.

✓ **Document Investigations**
When an allegation arises, thorough documentation of each step—from receipt of the complaint to final resolution—helps demonstrate good-faith efforts to address concerns. Detailed records can also be crucial if an employee later alleges that subsequent adverse actions were retaliatory.

Beyond SOX

Although SOX's whistleblower protections are specific to publicly traded companies and certain subsidiaries, some organizations also face obligations under additional statutes or regulations if they operate in certain industries or if employees report other types of misconduct. Ensuring that managers and HR staff are aware of the full spectrum of federal and state whistleblower rules can prevent conflicting practices or overlooked requirements.

Sarbanes-Oxley's whistleblower provisions reflect the principle that employees should be free to report alleged financial fraud or securities violations without fear of retaliation. Effective compliance involves creating a culture of ethical transparency, training leadership on anti-retaliation, and establishing robust, confidential reporting channels. By proactively managing these protections, publicly traded companies can both meet legal obligations and preserve stakeholder trust in their corporate governance practices.

6.2.2 Recordkeeping Requirements

While Sarbanes-Oxley (SOX) is often associated with financial disclosures and executive accountability, it also imposes robust recordkeeping obligations on publicly traded companies. The Act aims to ensure the accuracy and transparency of corporate financial records and internal controls, thereby bolstering investor confidence. For HR professionals, these mandates often involve close collaboration with finance and legal teams to confirm that personnel records, financial data, and corporate documents align with prescribed retention standards.

Key Provisions Driving Record Retention

Section 802
Prohibits the destruction or falsification of records linked to federal investigations or bankruptcy proceedings. This provision can extend beyond purely financial documents if other records become relevant to an inquiry.

Section 404
Requires management (and, in many cases, external auditors) to assess the effectiveness of the company's internal controls over financial reporting. Documenting procedures and verifying their consistent implementation can mean retaining proof of transactions, policies, and audit trails—some of which may intersect with HR's responsibilities for overseeing payroll, benefits, and compensation structures.

Criminal Penalties

Intentional destruction of required records can lead to severe penalties, including fines or imprisonment. As a result, companies often adopt rigorous document management protocols to maintain compliance with both Section 802's explicit bans and other relevant SOX sections.

Practical Applications in HR and Compliance

➢ **Personnel Files with Financial Components**

While standard HR files (such as performance reviews) may not directly fall under SOX, any records pertinent to company financials—like executive compensation agreements or bonus structures—could be subject to heightened scrutiny. Clear, consistent documentation helps ensure that compensation plans are accurately reflected in the company's financial statements.

➢ **Audit Trails for Payroll and Benefits**

Activities related to payroll, stock options, or deferred compensation must be recorded in a way that ties back to broader financial reporting. Employers might store payroll system logs, documents authorizing salary changes, and benefits enrollment data for a length of time consistent with internal control policy and external audit requirements.

➢ **Electronic Communication Retention**

E-mails, instant messages, or other digital records can become critical if they reveal information about financial transactions or potential fraud. Many organizations implement e-mail archiving solutions that preserve data for defined periods—frequently between five and seven years—to ensure compliance if an investigation or audit arises.

Retention Periods and Policy Development

No single statute outlines exact retention periods for all corporate documentation under SOX, so companies typically adhere to a mix of internal guidelines, industry best practices, and additional requirements from regulators. A few principles guide these decisions:

> **Risk Assessment**: Identify records essential to verifying financial statements, executive compensation, or other material disclosures. In consultation with legal counsel and auditors, classify these records and assign appropriate retention schedules (commonly between five and seven years post-fiscal year close).

> **Consistency and Accessibility**: Store records in formats that ensure long-term readability, whether paper or digital. Ability to retrieve documents promptly can matter during an external audit or regulatory review.

> **Disposal Protocols**: Once records surpass their required lifespan, disposing of them in a secure, documented manner reduces risk and avoids unnecessary storage costs. A formal disposal policy helps demonstrate that the company follows a consistent methodology rather than selectively discarding potentially sensitive items.

Roles and Responsibilities

Internal Controls and Compliance Teams: Oversee the creation and maintenance of policies governing record retention, ensuring alignment with the broader internal control framework required by Section 404.

HR and Payroll: Manage the documentation of compensation, bonuses, stock awards, and other people-related financial data. This often includes verifying that any changes in employee compensation are fully documented and authorized in writing.

IT Department: Implements technical solutions for e-mail archiving, backup, and secure destruction. Coordinate with HR for protocols related to data privacy (especially if documents contain personal information).

Legal Counsel: Advises on adjustments to retention schedules and ensures the company's policies align with evolving regulatory expectations or ongoing litigation holds.

Potential Consequences of Noncompliance

> ➢ **Legal Exposure**: Violations—whether through premature destruction or failure to maintain relevant records—can invite federal scrutiny and lead to allegations of obstructing justice.

> ➢ **Fines and Penalties**: Organizations and individuals (including high-level executives) could face monetary penalties if found to have knowingly destroyed or altered essential documentation.

> ➢ **Reputation Damage**: Public allegations of poor recordkeeping or financial irregularities undermine stakeholder trust in the company's governance and may hurt future investment opportunities.

Under SOX, recordkeeping extends beyond mere filing practices; it's a critical component of a company's internal control framework. HR departments play an essential role when personnel data intersects with financial disclosures—ensuring compensation, benefits, and other employment records remain consistent, accessible, and secure. By developing comprehensive record retention policies and fostering interdepartmental cooperation, organizations can meet SOX obligations and minimize legal risks.

6.3 State and Local Laws

6.3.1 Pay Equity Laws, "Ban the Box," Paid Sick Leave

State and local legislatures frequently enact regulations that go beyond federal mandates, shaping critical aspects of hiring, compensation, and leave policies. These measures respond to local workforce priorities, often aiming to reduce discrimination and protect employee welfare. Three prominent examples include pay equity laws, "Ban the Box" policies, and paid sick leave requirements.

Pay Equity Laws

Many states and municipalities have introduced or strengthened pay equity laws to address persistent wage gaps. While federal statutes like the Equal Pay Act prohibit pay differentials based solely on sex, local regulations often add more robust provisions.

Salary History Bans

Certain jurisdictions prevent employers from asking applicants about their past compensation, either on job applications or during interviews. This restriction aims to break cycles in which historically undervalued groups remain trapped in lower pay scales. By focusing on a position's requirements and market value, employers can set compensation that aligns with the role, not the individual's previous salary.

Pay Transparency

Some localities require employers to disclose salary ranges in job postings or upon request. This approach helps applicants and current employees understand pay scales for similar roles, reducing the potential for hidden discrepancies. Pay transparency laws may also mandate that employers provide written justifications for pay differences.

Expanded Protected Characteristics

Although pay equity often centers on gender, certain states or cities extend these laws to race, ethnicity, or other characteristics. This broader scope addresses multiple forms of wage discrimination and underscores the need for thorough and ongoing compensation analyses.

"Ban the Box"

A growing number of states and municipalities enforce "Ban the Box" rules, which restrict how and when employers can inquire about an applicant's criminal history. Typically, these policies eliminate or delay the criminal-record question on job applications, requiring employers to evaluate a candidate's qualifications before reviewing any past convictions.

➤ **Later Timing of Criminal History Checks**
In many jurisdictions, employers may only request background checks after making a conditional offer. This prevents initial bias that might exclude qualified individuals prematurely.

➤ **Individualized Assessments**
Some laws stipulate that if a background check reveals a criminal history, employers must consider factors such as the severity of the offense, the time elapsed since it occurred, and its relevance to the specific job duties.

➤ **Exemptions and Disclosure**
Certain roles—especially those involving vulnerable populations or sensitive data—may remain exempt. Nonetheless, compliance

typically includes notifying applicants about any adverse decision and offering an opportunity to dispute or clarify the findings.

Proponents of "Ban the Box" contend that it helps reduce recidivism by opening doors for individuals who've paid their debt to society, while also broadening the talent pool for employers.

Paid Sick Leave

A variety of state and local paid sick leave ordinances have emerged, each specifying how many hours or days of leave employees can accrue and under what circumstances they may use that leave.

1. **Accrual Mechanisms**
   Laws often set a minimum accrual rate, such as one hour of leave per 30 or 40 hours worked, up to a certain annual cap. Small businesses may be subject to different accrual rates or usage limits compared to larger employers.

2. **Permissible Uses**
   Beyond personal illness, many paid sick leave mandates cover caring for a family member, attending medical appointments, or addressing domestic violence situations. Some jurisdictions allow "safe time" for employees to relocate or obtain legal help in cases of abuse.

3. **Carryover and Waiting Periods**
   Certain regulations permit unused sick leave to carry over into the next year, while others allow a one-year reset. Employers must also note any waiting period for new hires, which might prevent the use of sick leave until a set period (e.g., 90 days) has passed.

4. **Interaction with Employer Policies**
   If an employer's existing paid time off (PTO) policy meets or

exceeds the local law's requirements, it may count as compliance. However, employers must ensure that recordkeeping, notice posting, and anti-retaliation measures align with the specific mandates of each jurisdiction.

Compliance Strategies

Because pay equity, "Ban the Box," and paid sick leave laws can differ significantly from one location to another, multi-state employers often face the challenge of maintaining consistent policies while accommodating local variations. Several strategies can simplify this process:

✓ **Regular Policy Audits**
Reviewing hiring applications, compensation structures, and leave records helps confirm alignment with the latest rules. This is especially important if the company expands into new jurisdictions or if existing laws undergo amendments.

✓ **Centralized Tracking Tools**
A reliable system for recording employees' hours, leaves, and salary decisions can help ensure accurate accrual, prompt payouts, and fair wage adjustments. Detailed records also provide a line of defense if complaints arise.

✓ **Employee Communications**
Transparent communication—such as explaining pay-setting processes, how to request sick leave, or the timing of background checks—fosters trust and reduces uncertainty. Employers may post local notices, share guidelines via an intranet, or offer periodic training sessions.

✓ **Legal Counsel and Local Expertise**
When in doubt, seeking guidance from local counsel or HR

professionals with state-specific knowledge can clarify ambiguities in new or evolving laws. This support is often invaluable for determining how different local mandates interact or whether special industry exemptions might apply.

State and municipal regulations on pay equity, "Ban the Box," and paid sick leave highlight the importance of tracking and adapting to an ever-evolving legal landscape. By proactively updating policies, ensuring accurate recordkeeping, and fostering open communication with employees, HR teams can comply with these localized standards while also promoting fair and supportive workplace practices.

6.3.2 Interaction with Federal Statutes

State and local employment laws often supplement federal legislation, introducing more stringent or expansive obligations in certain areas. Employers operating across multiple jurisdictions must, therefore, reconcile local mandates with overarching federal standards. Understanding how these different layers of regulation interact is key to avoiding conflicts in policy development and ensuring comprehensive compliance.

Preemption vs. Coexistence

Federal Preemption
In some scenarios, federal law explicitly supersedes or "preempts" state or local rules. This is most common when Congress's intent is for a uniform national approach—such as ERISA's broad preemption of certain state laws affecting employee benefit plans. Employers must confirm whether a given state or municipal requirement is barred by explicit statutory language or well-established legal precedent.

Coexistence and Dual Compliance

More frequently, state or local laws coexist with federal provisions. While federal statutes such as the Fair Labor Standards Act (FLSA) or Title VII of the Civil Rights Act set a minimum baseline, local rules can impose stricter wage/hour standards or broader anti-discrimination protections. Employers must meet both sets of rules, applying whichever standard is more protective of employees. For example, if a municipality sets a higher minimum wage than the federal rate, businesses within that locale must abide by the higher figure.

Examples of Layered Obligations

➢ **Leave and Accommodation**

Although the Family and Medical Leave Act (FMLA) provides unpaid leave for certain medical and family events, many states and cities grant additional protections—like paid family leave or extended eligibility thresholds. Employers must integrate these provisions alongside FMLA to ensure that local employees receive the full benefit of both.

➢ **Anti-Discrimination Protections**

Federal laws like the Americans with Disabilities Act (ADA) or Title VII define prohibited discrimination on protected grounds. However, some state or local ordinances add categories such as sexual orientation, gender identity, marital status, or hairstyle. When updating EEO policies, employers should incorporate the most inclusive definitions that apply in each region.

➢ **Workplace Safety**

The Occupational Safety and Health Act (OSHA) generally preempts conflicting state rules unless a state has obtained approval from federal authorities to run its own OSHA-approved program. Even then, states with approved plans must meet or exceed federal standards. Local safety initiatives—like stricter heat illness prevention regulations—coexist with federal guidelines, requiring employers to adhere to both sets of requirements.

Conflict Resolution and Policy Crafting

✓ **Identify the More Protective Standard**
Where direct conflicts do not exist, a practical approach is to adopt the law that offers stronger employee protections. By aligning policies with the highest standard across jurisdictions, multi-state employers can avoid piecemeal solutions—though this can occasionally raise operational costs.

✓ **Conduct Regular Legal Reviews**
State and local laws evolve quickly, with new ordinances or amendments emerging each legislative session. Periodic policy reviews—potentially with outside counsel—help ensure that organizational practices stay up-to-date and aligned with multiple regulatory frameworks.

✓ **Document Decisions and Exceptions**
If an employer identifies a genuine conflict (e.g., a scenario in which full compliance with local rules would violate a federal requirement), it should document the legal analysis that led to a chosen course of action and consider seeking formal guidance or waivers, where available.

Impact on HR Strategy

- ➢ **Implementation Challenges**: Multi-state employers may need tailored handbooks or training modules reflecting the distinct obligations in each location.

- ➢ **Cost Considerations**: More protective local laws—like expanded leave or higher wage floors—can influence budgeting for labor expenses or payroll administration.

- ➢ **Employee Relations**: When employees see that a company diligently meets or exceeds all applicable laws, it can bolster trust and retention. However, confusion around inconsistent rules can cause frustration if communications aren't clear.

State and local regulations frequently build upon federal frameworks rather than replace them, creating additional layers of compliance. Employers must navigate these multi-tiered obligations by identifying any points of preemption, meeting the highest applicable standard, and documenting how they've resolved potential conflicts. This nuanced approach to policy-building helps ensure that diverse employee populations receive consistent, legally compliant treatment.

6.4 Emerging Legal Topics

6.4.1 Marijuana Legalization and Drug Testing

As more states legalize marijuana for medical or recreational use, employers face evolving questions about how to shape workplace drug policies. While marijuana remains illegal at the federal level, various state and local laws protect or limit employers' ability to take adverse action against individuals who use cannabis under specific conditions. This creates a complex patchwork where a zero-tolerance policy may be legal in one jurisdiction but problematic in another. For HR professionals, balancing consistent workplace safety standards with legal shifts on marijuana use demands careful attention to both legislative details and practical realities.

Conflicting Federal and State Perspectives

Federal Illegality

Under the Controlled Substances Act, marijuana is still classified as a Schedule I drug, meaning it is illegal at the federal level. Companies subject to federal regulations—especially those with federal contracts or operating in regulated industries like transportation— often must adhere to strict no-marijuana policies. These policies typically override more permissive state laws and prohibit both on- and off-duty use.

State and Local Variations

Many states permit medical marijuana use, while others allow recreational use. In some jurisdictions, employers are barred from penalizing workers solely for lawful off-duty consumption or for holding a valid medical marijuana card. However, these protections seldom extend to on-the-job impairment. States also differ in whether they require employers to accommodate medical marijuana users in non-safety-sensitive roles.

Approaches to Workplace Drug Testing

1. **Pre-Employment Testing**
   Employers commonly conduct pre-hire screenings for safety-sensitive positions or as part of a general hiring policy. With marijuana legalization, some jurisdictions restrict blanket pre-employment testing, particularly for non-safety-sensitive roles. In these locales, employers may only test if there is a clear business rationale or if the position involves high-risk duties (e.g., operating heavy machinery).

2. **Random or Periodic Testing**

   Random testing remains more prevalent in industries like transportation or construction, where public or workplace safety is paramount. States that protect off-duty cannabis use may still allow random tests but limit the actions an employer can take if an employee tests positive but is not actually impaired at work.

3. **Reasonable Suspicion and Post-Accident Testing**

   Most state laws allow employers to test individuals suspected of being under the influence on the job. Post-accident testing is also typically permissible, but employers need to ensure that policies clearly define "reasonable suspicion" and how testing decisions will be documented to avoid perceptions of bias or retaliation.

Defining and Detecting Impairment

Unlike alcohol, which can be measured with more precision, marijuana detection tests (like urine or hair analyses) often reveal past use rather than current impairment. This discrepancy poses significant policy challenges:

Establishing Impairment Guidelines: An employee's positive result for THC metabolites does not necessarily confirm they are under the influence at work, particularly if the use occurred days or weeks prior.

Evolving Technologies: Researchers are developing saliva or breath tests that attempt to gauge recent usage more accurately. While these tools show promise, they remain less common, and legal acceptance varies.

Medical Marijuana and Disability Accommodation

Employees who consume medical marijuana under a state-licensed program may argue that their underlying condition qualifies as a disability. In states that afford medical cannabis users certain workplace protections, employers may face requests for accommodation—like adjusted schedules or reassignment to a non-safety-sensitive role. Although courts have been inconsistent on whether federal disability law (such as the ADA) covers medical marijuana usage, some states have clarified employers' obligations in this area.

Key considerations include:

➤ **Documenting Essential Functions**: If the position is safety-sensitive, an employer might justify stricter policies against medical marijuana use.

➤ **Engaging in the Interactive Process**: Where required by state law, employers should discuss potential accommodations with employees, focusing on job performance and safety rather than personal judgments about cannabis.

Policy Development and Communication

Given the legal complexity, many employers adopt "living policies" that can be revised quickly as regulations evolve. When drafting or updating a drug-free workplace policy:

✓ **Distinguish Between Recreational and Medical Use**: Acknowledge state-specific rights for medical cardholders and clarify any documentation needed to substantiate medical use.

✓ **Define Safety-Sensitive Roles**: Spell out which positions require stricter standards, why those standards exist (e.g., compliance with federal mandates), and how testing is administered.

✓ **Outline Testing Triggers**: Whether pre-employment, random, or reasonable suspicion, specify the circumstances under which tests occur and the steps taken after a positive result.

✓ **Include Clear Consequences**: Identify the disciplinary measures for on-duty impairment or policy violations while ensuring consistency with relevant state protections.

✓ **Employee Training**: Managers and employees should understand the policy's rationale, testing protocols, and the difference between off-duty legal use and workplace impairment.

Legal cannabis creates a multifaceted challenge for employers, requiring them to navigate conflicting federal and state rules, distinguish off-duty consumption from on-the-job impairment, and respond appropriately to medical marijuana usage. By developing nuanced, state-specific policies and ensuring consistent application, HR professionals can address safety concerns while respecting workers' rights under emerging legalization laws.

6.4.2 Artificial Intelligence in Hiring

As organizations look to streamline recruiting processes and identify strong candidates, more are turning to artificial intelligence (AI) tools. These range from automated résumé screeners and chatbots that respond to applicant queries, to sophisticated algorithms that evaluate recorded interviews or social media profiles. While AI can potentially cut costs and expand talent pools, it also creates legal and ethical uncertainties—particularly around bias, privacy, and transparency.

Potential Benefits

Efficiency Gains

Automated applicant tracking systems (ATS) powered by AI can screen hundreds or thousands of résumés quickly, highlighting the most relevant matches for human review. By reducing manual review tasks, recruiters can invest more time in deeper engagement with shortlisted candidates.

Standardized Evaluations

Well-designed AI assessments can reduce subjectivity by applying consistent selection criteria across applicants. In principle, algorithms can eliminate some forms of unconscious bias that human reviewers inadvertently bring to the hiring process.

Widening the Talent Pool

AI-powered sourcing tools can scan multiple job boards, professional networks, and even passive candidate databases, flagging prospective hires who might otherwise go unnoticed. This broad outreach can help build more diverse candidate pipelines.

Risks and Regulatory Considerations

Algorithmic Bias

If AI systems are trained on historical data that reflect existing workforce demographics or societal biases, they can perpetuate or even magnify discriminatory patterns. For instance, an AI model might favor attributes correlated with a predominantly male workforce, inadvertently excluding qualified female candidates.

Compliance with Anti-Discrimination Laws

Federal statutes like Title VII and the ADA prohibit using selection tools that disproportionately screen out protected groups without a demonstrable business necessity. State and local regulations may impose further constraints, such as requiring an independent audit of the tool's impact on various demographic categories. Recent legislative proposals—and in some locales, enacted laws—require employers to disclose their use of automated hiring systems and to verify these systems do not unfairly disadvantage protected groups.

Data Privacy and Transparency

AI-driven hiring can involve collecting and analyzing data from candidates' social media, online test results, or video interviews. Depending on the jurisdiction, employers may be subject to privacy rules that demand disclosure of data usage practices or require explicit consent from applicants. Some AI vendors also gather extensive behavioral metrics, raising questions about what constitutes invasive or unnecessary data collection.

Lack of Explainability

Deep learning algorithms can be "black boxes," making it hard to explain precisely why the tool ranks one candidate higher than another. Lack of explainability complicates an employer's ability to demonstrate fairness or defend decisions if legal challenges arise.

Best Practices for Employers

✓ **Thorough Vendor Vetting**

Whether an organization develops its own AI tool or purchases from a third-party provider, it should investigate how the system is trained, what data sources are used, and how often the model is updated or audited. Vendors should offer documentation on efforts to identify and mitigate bias.

✓ **Human Oversight**

While AI can accelerate initial screening, ultimate decisions should include input from a diverse hiring team that can flag anomalies and ensure context-based judgments. Establishing checks and balances helps prevent overreliance on algorithmic outputs.

✓ **Periodic Audits and Testing**

Ongoing audits—often involving testing the model on different demographic groups—allow companies to detect and correct emerging biases. This might include comparing the acceptance rates of different candidate segments, investigating disparate outcomes, and tuning the algorithm to achieve more equitable results.

✓ **Clear Candidate Communication**

Ethical and increasingly legal mandates encourage employers to inform applicants that AI is used in the hiring process. Some jurisdictions require disclosure of specific data points collected or factors considered. Clear communication can foster trust and allow candidates to request an alternative evaluation method if necessary (especially for individuals with disabilities who might be disadvantaged by automated systems).

✓ **Alignment with Organizational Values**

Companies seeking to build an inclusive culture should ensure that AI usage reflects their diversity and inclusion goals rather than undermining them. A focus on fairness, candidate experience, and compliance can reinforce brand reputation and attract top talent.

Looking Ahead

As AI continues to reshape recruitment, the regulatory landscape is evolving as well. Proposed bills in various jurisdictions may demand stricter transparency or impose liability for discriminatory outcomes. Employers that proactively address potential pitfalls—through rigorous

Chapter 7: People Domain

7.1 Functional Area 1: HR Strategy

7.1.1 Key Concepts (Mission, Vision, Values)

An organization's mission, vision, and values serve as its foundational pillars, informing strategic decisions and guiding day-to-day operations. For HR professionals, understanding these concepts is essential for designing policies, programs, and practices that align with broader organizational objectives. By integrating mission, vision, and values into every facet of HR strategy—from recruitment and performance management to leadership development—companies can foster a cohesive culture where employees grasp both the "why" behind their work and the principles that govern how business is conducted.

Mission: Defining Purpose and Core Intent

A mission statement encapsulates an organization's fundamental reason for existing. It addresses the central questions of **what** the organization does and **whom** it serves, articulating how its products or services contribute to the marketplace or community. In HR's context, the mission statement provides a clear reference for:

> ➤ **Recruitment Messaging**: Promoting a concise, compelling narrative about the company's purpose can attract candidates who resonate with that mission.

> ➤ **Role Clarity**: When employees see how their positions connect to the overarching purpose, they understand the value of their individual contributions.

> ➤ **Decision-Making Framework**: If a proposed initiative does not support the mission, HR can question its relevance and allocate resources more effectively.

Example: A mission statement might read, "To deliver innovative healthcare solutions that improve patient outcomes worldwide." An HR department using this mission could prioritize recruiting clinical and technical talent with a proven commitment to patient care and innovation.

Vision: Projecting Future Aspirations

Where a mission statement addresses present purpose, a vision articulates the organization's aspirational future—**where** it aims to be in the long term and **what** major successes it hopes to achieve. A robust vision statement galvanizes employees by painting a clear, inspiring picture of progress.

- ➢ **Strategic Alignment**: HR professionals leverage the vision to set long-term workforce goals. For instance, if an organization envisions becoming a global market leader, HR might develop succession plans that prepare high-potential employees for international assignments.

- ➢ **Culture of Innovation**: An ambitious vision can spur employees to think creatively and pursue continuous improvement. HR can design incentive programs that reward breakthrough ideas or cross-functional collaboration in line with that vision.

- ➢ **Performance Measures**: By linking individual KPIs to progress toward the vision, HR helps maintain focus on strategic priorities. Departments can celebrate milestones that signal momentum toward the envisioned future.

Example: A vision statement might declare, "To be the most trusted provider of renewable energy solutions worldwide." This prompts HR to encourage skill-building around emerging green technologies, ensuring employees are equipped to support the company's growth in new markets.

Values: Guiding Principles and Behavioral Norms

Values capture the ethical and behavioral principles that underpin how business is conducted. While mission and vision state **what** and **where**, organizational values speak to **how**. Common examples include integrity, customer focus, innovation, respect, and collaboration.

- ✓ **Recruitment and Selection**: Employers can emphasize values alignment by incorporating behavioral interview questions that reveal whether candidates share or appreciate the company's principles.

- ✓ **Onboarding and Socialization**: Introducing new hires to the organization's values from day one helps set expectations and integrates them more seamlessly into the culture.

- ✓ **Performance and Recognition**: HR can incorporate values into performance reviews, linking positive employee behaviors to tangible rewards. Recognizing individuals who uphold values fosters consistency across teams and reinforces the cultural fabric.

- ✓ **Conflict Resolution**: When disputes arise, referencing core values can offer a neutral framework for facilitating dialogue and mitigating tensions.

Example: If "integrity" is a core value, an HR professional might train managers on transparent communication methods, ensuring employees see leadership modeling honesty—particularly during challenging times such as restructuring or policy changes.

Practical Tips for HR Integration

Policy Development

Assess current HR policies—like remote work guidelines, performance reviews, or DEI initiatives—to see if they reflect mission, vision, and values. Regularly review these documents to stay aligned with organizational shifts or expansions.

Leadership Engagement

Partner with executives and department heads to champion these foundational statements, ensuring they consistently model the behaviors and attitudes the organization espouses.

Employee Communication

Embed mission, vision, and values into internal communications, whether through town halls, intranet announcements, or new-hire orientation materials. Reiteration helps employees internalize them as living concepts rather than abstract statements on a website.

Feedback Mechanisms

Solicit employee input on how well the company upholds its stated principles. This can involve pulse surveys or focus groups that compare daily experiences with the proclaimed values.

Mission, vision, and values are more than corporate slogans—they are strategic tools that shape culture, performance, and engagement. For HR leaders, weaving these key concepts into recruitment messaging, training programs, and everyday decision-making not only drives consistency but also helps employees understand and embody the organization's core identity.

7.1.2 Aligning HR Strategy with Organizational Goals

Strategic HR management is more than an administrative function: it's a proactive effort to shape the workforce in ways that support broader organizational ambitions. Whether a company aims to capture a new market, scale operations rapidly, or enhance its brand reputation, the HR department's strategies must dovetail with these objectives. By positioning HR as a true business partner, leaders ensure that investments in recruitment, development, and reward systems all push the enterprise in the same direction.

Moving Beyond Administrative Tasks

Historically, HR focused on transactional processes like payroll and benefits administration. While these remain essential, aligning HR with organizational goals demands a more forward-looking approach. Rather than reacting to immediate personnel needs, HR strategists assess **future** talent demands, identify skill gaps in advance, and structure training or hiring plans that mirror the company's ambitions. This shift raises HR from a "support function" to a core driver of growth and profitability.

Linking Workforce Plans to Business Targets

Forecasting and Gap Analysis

One hallmark of a strategic HR plan is comprehensive workforce forecasting. By analyzing current headcount, projected retirements or turnovers, and the capabilities required for new product lines or geographic expansions, HR can pinpoint where talent gaps are likely to emerge. This analysis informs targeted recruitment drives, upskilling efforts, and succession pipelines that align with looming business priorities—like entering an emerging market or launching a major initiative.

Collaborating with Key Stakeholders

To maintain alignment, HR leaders frequently consult department heads, finance partners, and executive teams. This cross-functional dialogue ensures that upcoming projects (like the rollout of an IT transformation) have sufficient, appropriately skilled staff. By centralizing intelligence about evolving workforce needs, HR can craft strategies that neatly coordinate with marketing plans, R&D timelines, or other operational milestones.

Embedding Organizational Culture into Strategy

Alignment isn't solely about skill sets; it's also about cultivating the workplace culture that fuels strategic goals. For instance, an organization aspiring to lead in innovation might emphasize collaboration and risk-taking across teams. HR can design recognition programs, internal communication methods, and learning initiatives that reinforce these cultural attributes. From shaping performance management criteria to deploying micro-learning modules, HR ensures that employees' day-to-day experiences encourage behaviors that propel the company's ambitions.

Measuring Strategic Impact

Tracking Key Performance Indicators (KPIs)

Aligning HR with broader objectives relies on clear metrics that reveal how HR actions contribute to bottom-line results or other success metrics. Examples might include:

- ✓ **Time-to-Fill Critical Roles**: Ensuring that vacant positions pivotal to new product development are filled promptly.

- ✓ **Internal Mobility Rates**: Reflecting how effectively the company is nurturing internal talent for leadership pipelines.

- ✓ **Training ROI**: Evaluating whether learning investments translate into improved project outcomes or revenue gains.

Frequent KPI reviews allow HR to calibrate efforts, dropping or revising strategies that yield limited returns and doubling down on successful ones.

Continuous Feedback and Adjustment

Strategic alignment isn't static. Market conditions, competitor actions, or technology shifts can disrupt even the most carefully plotted plans. HR professionals remain adaptable—revisiting workforce forecasts, collaborating with department leaders, and adjusting incentives or training methods as needed. Through agile planning cycles, the HR strategy remains in step with the organization's evolving priorities.

The Payoff: Cohesive Strategy and Resilient Growth

When HR initiatives flow seamlessly from an organization's overarching goals, the benefits manifest at multiple levels. Employees gain clarity on how their roles drive the company's success; managers see more direct support for their specific operational challenges; and executives observe stronger business results powered by engaged, skilled talent. By adopting a strategic mindset that anticipates workforce needs, fosters a future-ready culture, and quantifies impact, HR can serve as both the architect and custodian of sustainable competitive advantage.

7.1.3 Metrics and KPIs for Strategic HR Planning

In strategic HR planning, key performance indicators (KPIs) and metrics go beyond simple headcounts or administrative tracking. Instead, they quantify how effectively the human resources function is supporting—and driving—broader business goals. By measuring factors such as talent acquisition efficiency, workforce productivity, and employee development outcomes, HR can pinpoint where to refine its strategies and demonstrate tangible contributions to the organization's success.

Distinguishing Strategic from Operational Metrics

Strategic Metrics

These measure how HR initiatives connect to high-level corporate aims, such as market expansion or innovation targets. An example is tracking the ratio of high-potential talent pipelines to projected leadership openings, which aligns more closely with future growth plans.

Operational Metrics

While still useful, measures like payroll accuracy or benefits enrollment rates primarily show administrative efficiency. They help maintain daily operations but do not necessarily reveal how HR impacts strategic directions—such as entering a new region or introducing a new product line.

Common Strategic HR KPIs

Quality of Hire

Evaluates how well new employees meet performance expectations, adapt to the company culture, or drive key projects forward. This metric might involve:

> - **Manager Satisfaction Scores**: Post-hire surveys where supervisors rate the fit and contributions of recently onboarded talent.

> - **Performance Metrics at 6 or 12 Months**: Assessing whether hires consistently meet performance targets can indicate the efficacy of recruiting and selection methods.

Retention of Critical Roles
Highlights the percentage of top performers or individuals in mission-critical positions (e.g., specialized engineers, strategic sales roles) who remain with the company over time. A stable retention rate in these roles supports continuity for innovation or strategic projects. If turnover spikes among high-impact employees, HR may need to revisit succession planning or total rewards.

Internal Mobility and Succession Pipeline
Reflects how effectively the organization develops and promotes its existing workforce to fill future leadership or specialized skill gaps. Potential measures include:

> ➢ **Internal Promotion Ratio**: The proportion of leadership or key technical openings filled from within the company.

> ➢ **Successor Readiness**: Tracking whether at least one high-potential candidate is prepared to step into each critical role.

Workforce Productivity and Revenue per Employee
Compares output (e.g., revenue or other productivity measures) to the number of full-time equivalents. Increases in revenue per employee may suggest that HR's initiatives—like training or job redesign—are boosting efficiency or innovation.

Training and Development ROI
Gauges whether learning programs contribute to bottom-line improvements, such as reduced error rates, faster project completions, or boosted sales. Metrics could include:

> ➢ **Post-Training Performance Gains**: Documenting measurable skill or output changes after an intervention.

> ➤ **Employee Progression**: Monitoring how training completion correlates with promotions or performance ratings over time.

Employee Engagement Scores and Impact on Performance

While engagement itself can be measured through surveys, analyzing whether heightened engagement correlates with strategic outcomes—like improved customer satisfaction or reduced absenteeism—gives HR a clearer view of the effectiveness of culture and retention efforts.

Aligning Metrics with Business Objectives

The most impactful HR metrics directly connect with overarching organizational goals. For instance, if a company's strategic aim is rapid market expansion, time-to-fill for high-priority roles can be tracked alongside business indicators, such as the speed of market entry or the achievement of sales milestones in new regions. This alignment ensures that HR data is relevant to executives who want to see how human capital initiatives fuel growth or improve competitiveness.

Data Collection and Interpretation

1. **Reliable Systems and Processes**
   Automated tools—like applicant tracking systems (ATS) or HR information systems (HRIS)—can streamline metric gathering. Ensuring data accuracy and consistency is crucial for meaningful analysis.

2. **Benchmarking and Context**
   Comparing internal results to industry benchmarks or historical data provides perspective on progress. A "time-to-fill" metric that improves from 60 to 45 days might be an

achievement, but if competitors consistently hire within 30 days, HR leaders might see room for improvement.

3. **Sharing Insights with Stakeholders**
Presenting KPIs through dashboards or concise reports highlights key trends and recommends actions. Translating numbers into a narrative—such as explaining how reducing turnover among critical engineers saved significant recruiting costs—helps leadership grasp the strategic value of HR data.

Evolving and Refining Metrics Over Time

As organizational goals shift or new technologies emerge, HR's metrics may need updating. For example, introducing an AI-based selection tool could warrant measuring how algorithmic screening affects candidate quality or diversity outcomes. Regularly revisiting the KPI portfolio ensures that HR metrics stay relevant, agile, and aligned with evolving strategic targets.

By adopting a focused suite of HR metrics linked to broader strategic objectives, organizations can see exactly how their people strategy propels business success. These KPIs—ranging from quality of hire to revenue per employee—deliver evidence-based insights, allowing HR leaders to refine policies, prioritize resource investments, and proactively shape a workforce that stands ready to meet tomorrow's challenges.

7.2 Functional Area 2: Talent Acquisition

7.2.1 Workforce Planning and Job Analysis

Effective talent acquisition begins with a clear understanding of both an organization's overall staffing needs and the specific requirements of each role. This foundation is built through systematic **workforce planning**—predicting future labor demands and identifying any potential gaps—and **job analysis**, which uncovers the essential duties, competencies, and responsibilities tied to each position. By combining these two processes, HR teams can ensure they recruit and develop the right talent to advance strategic objectives.

Workforce Planning: Anticipating Future Needs

Forecasting Demand and Supply
Workforce planning starts by examining organizational growth projections, anticipated turnover, and upcoming projects or expansions. Through various forecasting models—like trend analysis or scenario planning—HR pinpoints where and when new hires or skill sets will be needed. On the supply side, it reviews current employee demographics, internal mobility potential, and retirements or departures.

Identifying Skill Gaps
Once future requirements are mapped, HR can compare the needed talent profile with the existing workforce. Any shortfall—whether in technical skills, leadership capability, or global experience—guides subsequent recruitment efforts and succession plans. For instance, if a company plans to launch a new product line in six months, workforce planning should reveal how many engineers, project managers, or sales specialists are missing for a timely launch.

Action Plans and Timelines
Based on identified gaps, HR formulates strategies to address them. This might involve training current employees, external hiring, or outsourcing certain tasks. Detailed timelines are crucial—especially when a strategic initiative depends on having fully staffed teams at specific milestones. Monitoring these timelines helps HR adapt quickly if market conditions or the internal pipeline shift.

Job Analysis: Defining Roles and Requirements

Job analysis is the systematic process of gathering detailed information about a particular role. It clarifies exactly what tasks the job entails, the competencies and credentials required, and how performance is measured. Common outputs include updated **job descriptions** and **job specifications**, which in turn shape everything from recruitment ads to performance evaluations.

1. **Data Collection Methods**

    ➢ **Interviews**: Speaking directly with incumbents and supervisors to uncover day-to-day responsibilities.

    ➢ **Observations**: Watching employees perform tasks, useful for roles involving physical or sequential workflows.

    ➢ **Questionnaires and Surveys**: Collecting data across multiple incumbents or departments for a broad overview.

2. **Key Components**

    ➢ **Tasks and Responsibilities**: Summaries of primary duties, sometimes ranked by importance or frequency.

    ➢ **Required Competencies**: Technical and behavioral skills—like programming languages, conflict resolution abilities, or regulatory knowledge—essential for success.

    ➢ **Working Conditions**: Physical demands or environmental factors that could affect job performance (e.g., standing for long periods).

3. **Impact on HR Functions**
    A thorough job analysis underpins multiple talent processes. It

can sharpen recruitment ads to attract the right candidates, guide selection criteria in interviews, and support fairness in compensation by matching roles with appropriate pay grades. Moreover, well-defined tasks help managers set performance expectations and identify potential areas for development.

Integrating Workforce Planning and Job Analysis

Targeted Hiring and Succession

Aligning workforce plans with the specifics gleaned from job analyses enables HR to recruit or develop employees who truly match the evolving requirements of the organization. For instance, if workforce planning indicates a need for more data analytics roles, detailed job analyses for those positions help refine the search criteria and onboarding processes.

Flexibility in Dynamic Environments

As market conditions, technologies, or organizational structures shift, job duties often change. Periodic re-analysis ensures job descriptions remain accurate, supporting agile workforce planning that can promptly adapt to new strategic directions.

Compliance and Fairness

By documenting role responsibilities and essential functions, job analysis reduces legal risks tied to misclassification (e.g., exempt vs. non-exempt) or discriminatory practices in hiring and promotions. Meanwhile, workforce planning ensures equitable distribution of resources, preventing departments from operating understaffed or with unclear responsibilities.

Practical Tips for Implementation

✓ **Collaborative Approach**: Engage relevant stakeholders— including department managers and current role incumbents—

early in both workforce planning and job analysis to ensure accuracy and buy-in.

✓ **Leverage Technology**: Use HRIS or analytics tools to track workforce metrics (e.g., turnover rates, retirement eligibility) and store standardized job descriptions for easy retrieval or updates.

✓ **Stay Current**: Regularly revisit job roles, especially those subject to fast-paced changes (like tech positions). This maintains alignment with organizational needs and emerging skill sets in the labor market.

✓ **Document All Findings**: Clear records of forecast assumptions, job analysis methods, and recommended staffing actions help justify HR decisions and facilitate audits or compliance reviews.

Workforce planning sets the strategic direction for talent acquisition by projecting future staffing requirements, while job analysis provides the granular detail on what each role entails. Together, they create a comprehensive roadmap for recruiting, training, and retaining the workforce that an organization needs to meet its long-term goals.

7.2.2 Recruitment Sources and Techniques

Once an organization identifies its talent requirements through workforce planning, the next step is to effectively reach and engage potential candidates. A broad array of recruitment sources and techniques are available, and choosing the right mix depends on factors like the urgency of the opening, the specialized nature of the role, and desired geographical reach. By diversifying sourcing methods and honing targeted strategies, HR can secure strong talent pipelines that align with organizational needs.

Internal vs. External Recruiting

Internal Postings and Promotions

Advantages: Encourages career progression and motivates current employees. Reduces onboarding time since internal candidates already know the culture and processes.

Considerations: Requires transparent posting systems and clear selection criteria to avoid perceived favoritism or missed opportunities.

External Sourcing

Advantages: Brings fresh perspectives, new skill sets, and expanded candidate pools.

Considerations: Typically involves longer onboarding and adjustment periods. May need targeted messaging to stand out in competitive job markets.

Common External Recruitment Channels

Online Job Boards and Career Sites

- **Examples**: Indeed, LinkedIn, Glassdoor.

- **Techniques**: Use keyword-optimized postings, highlight compelling employer brand messages, and ensure a mobile-friendly application process.

Social Media Recruiting

➢ **Benefits**: Offers direct engagement with passive candidates and deeper insights into their professional interests.

- ➢ **Approach**: Tailor content for each platform. For instance, LinkedIn may be used for industry thought leadership, while Instagram showcases workplace culture through photos or short videos.

Employee Referral Programs

- ➢ **Why It Works**: Current employees often recommend well-fitting prospects, speeding up culture alignment and increasing retention rates.

- ➢ **Implementation**: Provide incentives (e.g., referral bonuses, public recognition) and make the referral process straightforward with a simple submission method.

Campus Recruiting and Internship Programs

- ➢ **Advantages**: Fosters relationships with educational institutions, allowing early access to emerging talent pools.

- ➢ **Best Practices**: Develop ongoing partnerships with career services, sponsor campus events, or offer internships that feed into full-time openings.

Recruitment Agencies and Headhunters

- ➢ **Use Cases**: Useful for hard-to-fill, specialized, or executive roles. Agencies typically possess niche databases and networks.

- ➢ **Managing Costs**: Negotiate clear fee structures and deliverables. Track agency performance over time to ensure ROI.

Targeted Recruiting Techniques

1. **Passive Candidate Outreach**

    ➢ **Rationale**: Many high-performing professionals aren't actively searching. Personalized messages (often on professional networks) can pique their interest.

    ➢ **Execution**: Develop compelling value propositions, focusing on career growth, organizational mission, or innovative projects.

2. **Diversity-Focused Sourcing**

    ➢ **Objective**: Build inclusive teams that reflect a wide range of backgrounds.

    ➢ **Implementation**: Engage with diversity job fairs, specialized job boards, or professional associations supporting underrepresented groups. Review language in job ads for unintentional biases.

3. **Employer Branding Activities**

    ➢ **Strategy**: Showcase an attractive workplace culture through blogs, employee testimonials, or behind-the-scenes videos.

    ➢ **Outcome**: Helps differentiate the company in competitive labor markets, drawing candidates aligned with the organization's values and goals.

4. **Talent Community Building**

    ➢ **Concept**: Maintain a pool of engaged prospects who express interest in future roles, even if no immediate vacancy exists.

> ➤ **Tactics**: Periodically share company news, achievements, or thought leadership pieces, encouraging continued interaction until a suitable opportunity arises.

Optimizing the Candidate Experience

Streamlined Application Processes

Reduce the number of steps or repeated data entries. Clarity and brevity often increase application completion rates. Offer user-friendly technology, including mobile-friendly forms or chatbots for basic FAQs.

Timely Communication

Send prompt acknowledgments after application submissions. Keep candidates informed about next steps and timelines. Provide constructive feedback when possible, fostering goodwill even if the applicant isn't ultimately hired.

Employer-Applicant Fit Assessment

Focus on mutual evaluation: job seekers also want to see if the role and culture match their goals. Incorporate realistic job previews or site visits to promote transparency and informed decision-making.

Measuring Recruitment Success

To refine recruiting methods over time, HR professionals should track metrics that illuminate both efficiency and effectiveness. Examples include:

✓ **Time-to-Fill**: Average days to locate and secure a candidate once a job is posted.

✓ **Cost-per-Hire**: Total recruiting expenses (ads, agency fees, etc.) divided by the number of hires in a period.

✓ **Source of Hire**: Proportions of hires coming from various channels (e.g., referrals vs. job boards) to identify high-return sources.

✓ **Quality of Hire**: Hiring manager satisfaction, new hire performance scores, or retention rates of recent hires.

Examining these metrics reveals what's working and what needs recalibration. A consistently high-quality source—like employee referrals—may justify expanded referral bonuses, while underperforming avenues might be phased out or retooled.

Diversifying and strategically selecting recruitment sources can help companies reach both active and passive candidates more effectively. By pairing tailored outreach with a positive candidate experience, organizations not only fill roles quickly but also strengthen their employer brand, ultimately contributing to a robust, future-ready workforce.

7.2.3 Selection Procedures and Candidate Assessment

Organizations invest significant time and resources in identifying which applicants best suit each role, and the right selection procedures can make all the difference. Effective assessments blend structured processes with varied evaluation methods. This ensures decisions are based on genuine job demands and evidence of the candidate's past performance or potential. While the specific approach may vary by position, a thoughtful balance of interviews, tests, and reference checks remains central to any robust selection system.

Designing a Targeted Selection Strategy

Before choosing how to assess candidates, clarify the role's core competencies and responsibilities. This groundwork guides the selection tools and interview questions. For example, a front-line customer service position may prioritize conflict resolution and empathy, whereas a data analyst role might center on technical precision and problem-solving.

Below is a brief overview of common assessment tools:

Method	Primary Purpose	Examples
Structured Interviews	Evaluate job-fit via standardized questions	Behavioral questioning, situational "what-if" queries
Skills/Knowledge Tests	Verify specific abilities or expertise	Coding challenges, writing samples, accounting problems
Simulations	Observe how candidates handle real tasks	Role-play, in-basket exercises, mini case studies
Personality/Behavioral Assessments	Explore work style and cultural alignment	Myers-Briggs, DiSC, or custom validated instruments
Reference Checks	Validate performance and behavior	Calls/emails to previous managers or coworkers

Putting Interviews into Focus

Even if multiple tools are used, interviews often serve as the backbone of final hiring decisions. Structured or semi-structured approaches produce more reliable data by ensuring each candidate faces a similar line of inquiry. Behavioral-style questions invite applicants to recount specific past experiences, while situational prompts reveal how they'd respond to typical on-the-job challenges. By centering the conversation on real examples, interviewers see how a candidate's decision-making and interpersonal skills might play out in the organization's environment.

Promoting Fairness and Reducing Bias

Despite best intentions, interviewer bias can creep into discussions or overshadow certain data points. Several practices minimize this risk:

- ✓ **Clear Scoring Criteria**: Create easy-to-use evaluation forms tied to job-related competencies, helping interviewers assign ratings based on evidence rather than gut instinct.

- ✓ **Diverse Interview Panels**: Bringing multiple perspectives into the room, whether from different departments or demographics, decreases the likelihood of groupthink and fosters objectivity.

- ✓ **Consistent Questioning**: Using the same core questions for all candidates makes it easier to compare responses, as well as defend against any claims of favoritism.

When Skills Tests or Simulations Add Value

Roles requiring highly specialized capabilities or day-to-day tasks that can be simulated often benefit from practical exercises. Testing how applicants handle a coding problem or manage a mock customer complaint reveals not only their baseline skill level but also their approach under mild pressure. However, it's wise to balance test complexity with candidate experience: an overly burdensome assignment might deter top talent or introduce unnecessary delays.

Reading Between the Résumé Lines

While tests and interviews focus on the present or future, references provide a backward glance. Honest feedback from past employers clarifies whether an applicant's achievements match their claims, and whether the culture fit extends beyond interview polish. A consistent approach—asking references about performance strengths, areas for improvement, and how the candidate responded to challenges—protects against relying too heavily on either glowing praise or isolated criticisms.

Integrating Outcomes and Making the Offer

Candidate assessment produces a wealth of data: interviewer notes, test scores, cultural fit impressions, and reference comments. Summarizing these insights in a simple, standardized template helps weigh each piece of evidence against the job's essential criteria. Once a decision is made, offering the role promptly—while reinforcing the position's growth opportunities and organizational mission—can boost acceptance rates and launch the new hire on solid footing.

A strategic blend of interviews, tests, simulations, and reference checks—grounded in consistent processes—helps uncover both the technical competence and cultural compatibility of prospective employees. By prioritizing role-driven selection criteria, structuring assessments to minimize bias, and synthesizing findings in a thorough but practical way, HR can lay the groundwork for hires who thrive over the long term.

7.2.4 Onboarding Best Practices

Effective onboarding sets the tone for a new hire's journey, influencing how quickly they adapt and how long they remain engaged within the organization. Far more than administrative paperwork, a strong onboarding program should introduce the company's culture, clarify role expectations, and build meaningful connections. By crafting a structured yet welcoming experience, employers can pave the way for smoother assimilation, higher performance, and improved retention.

Pre-Boarding Activities

The onboarding process can start before the new hire's first official day. By sharing helpful resources and initiating early engagement, organizations reduce first-week jitters and create a sense of inclusion. Common approaches include:

- ✓ **Welcome Messages**: Simple gestures—such as an email or a "welcome kit"—help new hires feel valued and informed about what to expect.

- ✓ **Team Introductions**: Introducing immediate teammates or providing contact details for a designated mentor ensures the newcomer has a ready support network.

- ✓ **Logistical Preparations**: Issuing parking information, dress code guidelines, or a first-week schedule prevents potential confusion and keeps the candidate focused on learning and meeting colleagues.

Structuring the First Days and Weeks

Once the employee arrives, a well-organized orientation plan prevents them from feeling adrift. While details vary by organization size and industry, effective onboarding often includes:

Orientation Sessions

Short presentations or workshops highlight the company's mission, values, and unique cultural norms. Interactive elements—like Q&A segments or group activities—encourage two-way dialogue and better retention of key information.

Role-Specific Training

Focus on the skills, systems, and processes new hires need right away. This might involve job shadowing, step-by-step process guides, or e-learning modules. Aligning this training with actual tasks accelerates the path to full productivity.

Buddy or Mentor Program

Pairing each newcomer with a seasoned colleague can ease the transition, providing a go-to resource for questions about work processes or unwritten cultural nuances. Mentors also help socialize new hires, fostering relationships across the organization.

Maintaining Engagement Beyond Orientation

Onboarding does not end after the first few days. Providing ongoing check-ins and developmental opportunities helps employees steadily acclimate and stay motivated:

➢ **Regular Check-Ins**: Scheduling brief meetings (e.g., at 30, 60, and 90 days) lets managers or HR gauge how well the employee is settling in, address any challenges, and celebrate early wins.

➢ **Feedback Channels**: Encouraging newcomers to share feedback on their onboarding experience not only refines future programs but also shows the organization's openness to improvement.

> **Progressive Challenges**: Gradually increasing project complexity or responsibilities ensures employees keep expanding their competencies without being overwhelmed.

Sample 90-Day Onboarding Timeline

Timeframe	Key Activities
Pre-Day 1	Send welcome message, provide resources, prepare workspace
Week 1	Formal orientation, introductions to team/mentor, basic systems setup
Weeks 2–4	Deeper role-specific training, initial assignments, manager check-in
Month 2	More advanced tasks, shadowing opportunities, 30-day feedback session
Month 3	Performance review conversation, goal-setting for next quarter, 90-day milestone check

Cultural Assimilation and Networking

An often overlooked aspect of onboarding is ensuring the new employee feels integrated into the larger culture. Organizing small-group lunches, informal gatherings, or cross-functional meetups widens their internal network and boosts a sense of belonging. Encouraging participation in employee resource groups (ERGs) or community service events can also connect newcomers to colleagues who share similar interests or backgrounds.

Measuring Onboarding Success

To continually refine the process, organizations may gather data on new-hire time-to-productivity, early turnover rates, or satisfaction survey responses. Evaluating these metrics helps pinpoint which parts of the program provide the greatest impact and where improvements might be necessary. For instance, if many recent hires express confusion about career progression, offering structured development conversations early on could address that gap.

A thoughtfully designed onboarding program weaves new employees into the organization's fabric, equipping them with clarity on role expectations, reliable support networks, and an understanding of the company's culture. By extending the process beyond the initial orientation, gathering feedback, and steadily involving newcomers in meaningful work, HR sets the stage for heightened engagement, productivity, and overall success in the months and years to come.

7.3 Functional Area 3: Employee Engagement & Retention

7.3.1 Drivers of Engagement (Leadership, Career Paths)

Employee engagement is shaped by multiple factors, but two key influences—leadership quality and the availability of clear career paths—often determine whether employees feel motivated and supported in the long term. A strong leadership culture inspires teams to perform at their best, while defined career trajectories signal that the organization values individual growth and longevity. Addressing both elements ensures that employees see themselves as integral to the company's vision, heightening their commitment and performance.

Leadership Influence

How leaders communicate, make decisions, and interact with their teams directly affects the emotional and psychological investment employees bring to their work.

➤ **Modeling Organizational Values**: Leaders who consistently act with integrity and transparency build trust, an essential foundation for engagement. When employees observe alignment between stated values and day-to-day behavior, they are more likely to take pride in their roles.

➤ **Setting Clear Expectations**: Effective managers outline objectives in a way that resonates with individual and team goals. Employees understand how their efforts tie into broader outcomes, reducing confusion and strengthening purpose.

➤ **Providing Timely Feedback**: Both praise and constructive insights, offered promptly, help individuals adjust course or reinforce positive behaviors. Frequent touchpoints—rather than annual reviews alone—keep motivation levels high and issues from festering.

➤ **Empowering Autonomy**: Allowing employees discretion over how they achieve tasks taps into intrinsic motivation. This sense of ownership fosters a deeper connection to the work and spurs innovative thinking, as individuals feel trusted to experiment and problem-solve.

Career Path Clarity

While effective leadership can energize teams on a daily basis, defined career pathways sustain engagement over the long haul. Employees who see clear opportunities for advancement or skill enhancement are more inclined to stay and grow within the organization.

1. **Structured Progression**
   A roadmap that outlines the competencies, experiences, or achievements needed to progress from one role to another offers tangible milestones. This could include a tiered framework (e.g., Junior to Senior to Lead) or a dual career ladder where technical experts and managerial leaders each have growth paths.

2. **Development and Upskilling**
   Providing training programs, job rotations, or mentorship ensures employees continuously refine their abilities. Over time, seeing actual movement—whether in job titles or expanded responsibilities—confirms that hard work and learning lead to meaningful outcomes.

3. **Visible Internal Opportunities**
   Organizations that regularly publicize internal openings encourage employees to explore new challenges within the same company. This transparency lessens the likelihood of high performers seeking advancement externally. It also promotes a culture that recognizes ambition and supports internal mobility.

Fostering Leadership Excellence and Career Growth

Achieving a blend of strong leadership and robust career paths often requires intentional planning and open dialogue:

✓ **Leadership Development Programs**: Workshops, coaching sessions, or stretch assignments bolster managers' abilities to inspire, coach, and retain talent. Including topics such as conflict resolution or emotional intelligence equips leaders to engage diverse teams effectively.

✓ **Transparent Career Conversations**: Manager-employee check-ins can incorporate future role discussions, exploring how current tasks align with the individual's aspirations. Such conversations reassure employees that their personal growth is a priority.

✓ **Recognition of Managerial Contribution**: When leaders are held accountable for engagement metrics—like reduced turnover or elevated employee satisfaction—they become more invested in adopting engagement-friendly practices.

✓ **Cross-Departmental Mentoring**: Pairing staff members with mentors outside their immediate function broadens perspective and can reveal unexpected pathways. Employees learn about alternative roles or departments where their skills could be repurposed.

Leadership and career advancement paths are two of the most powerful levers organizations can pull to boost employee engagement. Positive, consistent leadership fosters trust and enthusiasm on a daily basis, while defined career opportunities promise longer-term progression and personal fulfillment. By weaving both elements into everyday management and strategic HR initiatives, organizations can cultivate a workforce that remains energized, committed, and eager to realize its full potential.

7.3.2 Measuring Engagement (Surveys, Focus Groups)

Organizations rely on various methods to gauge employee engagement, with surveys and focus groups being two of the most common. When well executed, these approaches shine a light on motivational drivers, workplace challenges, and opportunities for improvement. By compiling both quantitative and qualitative feedback, HR leaders can gain a fuller understanding of the employee experience—then act to reinforce strengths or address pressing concerns.

Designing Effective Engagement Surveys

Engagement surveys typically provide a broad view of the workforce's sentiments on leadership, career development, recognition, and more. To generate actionable insights, surveys must be thoughtfully structured:

1. **Question Relevance**

   Craft items that connect directly to known engagement drivers (e.g., job autonomy, leadership trust, growth opportunities). Avoid overly vague or confusing queries, and ensure that scales—whether 5-point or 7-point—are consistent throughout.

2. **Frequency and Format**

   While annual or biannual surveys are still prevalent, many companies complement them with shorter "pulse" surveys for real-time updates. A combination approach balances deep annual analysis with quick checks to track shifts during organizational changes.

3. **Anonymity and Confidentiality**

   Employees are more candid if they trust their responses are not traceable back to them individually. Clear communication about data handling procedures—and how personal identifiers are stripped out or aggregated—helps foster honest feedback.

4. **Action Planning**

   Collecting survey data alone does little to drive engagement. Once results are interpreted, managers and HR teams should discuss the findings openly, highlight areas needing attention, and set goals with clear timelines. Sharing progress updates afterward keeps employees engaged in the improvement process.

Leveraging Focus Groups for Deeper Insight

Surveys produce valuable metrics, but they seldom capture the "why" behind the responses. Focus groups can fill this gap by facilitating open dialogue in a smaller setting:

Participant Selection: Aim for diverse representation within each focus group to avoid groupthink or skewed perspectives. Sometimes separate sessions by department, role level, or location can yield richer, more targeted input.

Facilitation Skills: A neutral facilitator—often someone external to the immediate team—encourages even participation. This person should prompt quieter members to share while keeping dominant voices in check, ensuring a balanced discussion.

Structured Discussion Guides: Outlining key topics or questions in advance helps maintain direction. Open-ended prompts, like "What does career growth look like here?" or "How do you perceive leadership communication?" encourage participants to share experiences and suggestions.

Confidentiality and Psychological Safety: Emphasize that the session is a safe space for honest input. Reassure participants that comments will be synthesized without revealing individual identities.

Comparing Annual vs. Pulse Surveys

Aspect	Annual Survey	Pulse Survey
Depth of	Comprehensive, covers multiple engagement	Focused, targets a specific topic or

Analysis	drivers	moment
Frequency	Typically once or twice a year	Can be monthly or quarterly
Data Turnaround	Longer timeframe to plan, execute, analyze	Quick feedback loop, enabling faster action
Use Cases	Organizational benchmarking, strategic planning	Tracking changes after new policies or events

Combining Survey and Focus Group Data

When engagement surveys uncover areas of concern—like low ratings on recognition or career advancement—focus groups can shed light on specific obstacles or recommended fixes. This blend of quantitative and qualitative perspectives makes it easier to develop targeted interventions. For instance, if surveys reveal dissatisfaction with leadership transparency, a follow-up focus group could identify which communication gaps frustrate employees the most. The organization can then craft specific strategies, such as monthly "ask me anything" sessions or enhanced leadership training.

Surveys and focus groups are complementary tools in understanding and boosting employee engagement. Surveys offer a broad, quantifiable snapshot, while focus groups delve into the nuances behind the numbers. A rigorous process—covering design, administration, and follow-up—helps leaders pinpoint meaningful solutions that resonate with their workforce, ultimately strengthening commitment and satisfaction across the organization.

7.3.3 Retention Strategies (Recognition, Development)

Retaining skilled, motivated employees involves more than offering competitive salaries. Two critical areas that deeply influence whether staff remain engaged and committed are **recognition** and **professional growth opportunities**. By creating a culture that consistently acknowledges contributions and invests in employees' long-term development, organizations establish a supportive environment that keeps talent from seeking greener pastures.

Building a Culture of Recognition

Acknowledging achievements—whether large or small—validates employees' efforts and underscores their importance in the broader mission. Recognition can take various forms, each supporting retention in distinct ways:

➢ **Public Praise**: Celebrating wins at team meetings or company-wide announcements highlights exemplary work and encourages peers to emulate those successes.

➢ **Peer-to-Peer Programs**: Allowing colleagues to nominate each other for awards cultivates an atmosphere of mutual support and camaraderie. This approach ensures recognition isn't always top-down.

➢ **Spot Bonuses and Perks**: Occasional monetary rewards, extra paid time off, or coveted project assignments can reinforce employee morale when aligned with meaningful milestones.

➢ **Personal Touches**: Handwritten thank-you notes or personalized tokens of appreciation can resonate more powerfully than formal awards, showing genuine gratitude.

> ➢ Providing consistent, heartfelt recognition helps employees feel valued, which builds loyalty and commitment. The more aligned such recognition is with actual achievements and cultural values, the more powerful its retention effect.

Fostering Continuous Development

Another pillar of retention is the promise of growth. When employees see clear pathways to enhancing their skill sets and advancing in the organization, they are less tempted to look elsewhere for career progression:

Individualized Learning Plans: Mapping out tailored training programs or development goals indicates that the organization respects each person's aspirations. This can range from online courses and workshops to one-on-one mentorship arrangements.

Job Rotation and Stretch Assignments: Assigning employees to new functions, departments, or challenging projects broadens their perspectives and skill ranges. Such experiences reduce stagnation and demonstrate faith in their capability to handle increased responsibilities.

Leadership Development Tracks: High-potential employees often expect robust opportunities to refine leadership skills. Structured programs—like rotational leadership assignments or cohort-based seminars—can nurture the next generation of managers and keep ambitious talent engaged.

Integrating Recognition and Development

While each area boosts retention individually, the synergy of recognition and ongoing growth can be even more potent. For instance, recognizing someone not just for their project outcomes but also for upskilling themselves or mentoring newcomers creates a virtuous cycle of learning and praise. A workforce that regularly sees colleagues celebrated for personal improvement and career advances will likely invest more energy in their own developmental paths, secure in the knowledge that the organization rewards such effort.

Sample Recognition and Development Initiatives

Initiative	Key Features	Retention Benefits
Mentorship Matching	Pairs junior employees with experienced mentors	Strengthens professional networks, fosters loyalty
Leadership Workshops	Focus on strategic thinking, team management	Encourages career progression within the company
Peer-Nominated Awards	Celebrations of teamwork, innovation, or initiative	Builds inclusive culture, boosts morale
Learning Allowances	Company-funded external courses or certifications	Shows commitment to personal growth, lowers turnover

Sustaining Impact Over Time

Recognition and development strategies yield the best retention results when actively maintained and refreshed. Periodic reviews of what types of rewards motivate different employee groups can keep recognition programs from going stale. Similarly, adjusting learning content to address evolving skill demands—like new technologies or market shifts—ensures development initiatives remain relevant and attractive.

Strategic retention requires acknowledging each employee's contributions and laying out a clear path for their professional evolution. When organizations weave consistent recognition into daily routines and back it up with meaningful development prospects, they cultivate an environment where talented individuals choose to build their careers for the long run.

7.3.4 Performance Management Systems

Traditional annual reviews may capture a snapshot of performance, but modern organizations recognize the value of continuous, multifaceted systems that drive both productivity and employee growth. An effective performance management process is not just a mechanism for appraisals—it becomes a strategic tool that aligns individual contributions with organizational objectives, cultivates ongoing dialogue between managers and staff, and fosters a culture where learning and accountability thrive.

Core Elements of an Effective Performance Management System

1. **Goal Setting and Alignment**: Establishing clear, measurable objectives that link directly to broader organizational goals helps employees see how their work contributes to the bigger picture. Specific targets—often set collaboratively—ensure that employees, teams, and departments move in the same strategic direction. Revisiting objectives periodically keeps them relevant, especially in dynamic industries or during organizational restructuring.

2. **Frequent Feedback and Coaching**: Instead of waiting for an annual appraisal, many companies use shorter review cycles or continuous check-ins. Quick feedback loops allow employees to correct course before small issues escalate. In-

the-moment recognition, constructive insights, and coaching conversations empower staff to experiment, refine their skills, and stay engaged in personal development.

3. **Fair and Transparent Evaluation**: When employees understand the criteria and process behind performance assessments, they feel more confident in its fairness. Clear rating scales, well-defined competencies, and structured documentation reduce ambiguity and bias. Calibration sessions—where managers collectively review team ratings—can harmonize standards across different departments or supervisors, minimizing inconsistencies in evaluations.

4. **Developmental Focus**: A robust system goes beyond judging past performance; it identifies potential and crafts individualized development paths. Whether through targeted training, cross-functional assignments, or stretch projects, these growth-oriented steps keep high performers challenged and engaged. Linking performance reviews to tangible learning plans underscores the company's commitment to employee progress, improving retention and morale.

Leveraging Technology for Performance Management

Digital platforms streamline goal setting, feedback exchange, and data analytics. Some systems offer real-time dashboards displaying progress toward specific metrics, while social recognition tools allow peers to applaud each other's efforts. Using these tools can enhance transparency, reduce paperwork, and provide leadership with broad insights into performance trends across the organization. Yet, technology should complement—not replace—the human element of sincere conversations and empathetic leadership.

Integration with Other HR Functions

Performance management does not exist in isolation. A holistic approach weaves it into recruitment, learning and development, and succession planning:

➢ **Recruitment and Onboarding**: By defining performance expectations early, new hires have a clear picture of what success looks like. Aligning job descriptions with performance criteria ensures consistent messaging.

➢ **Learning and Development**: Deficiencies or strengths uncovered during reviews guide future training investments. If data reveals a group-wide gap in analytical skills, the organization might launch targeted workshops or e-learning modules.

➢ **Succession Planning**: Performance data, especially combined with potential assessments, illuminates who is ready for leadership roles. Employees with strong track records become prime candidates for promotions or inclusion in high-potential programs.

Potential Pitfalls and How to Overcome Them

✓ **Overemphasis on Ratings**: Overly focusing on numeric scores or forced rankings can undermine collaboration. Balancing ratings with qualitative feedback keeps discussions constructive.

✓ **Infrequent or Rushed Reviews**: If managers view reviews as a mere formality, employees lose out on meaningful guidance. Training supervisors in active listening and coaching techniques can revitalize the review conversation.

✓ **Lack of Post-Review Action**: Conducting appraisals without follow-up erodes trust. Ensuring agreed-upon action items, whether skill-building or role adjustments, instills a sense of accountability for both managers and employees.

A well-crafted performance management system is more than a scoreboard—it is a continuous cycle of goal alignment, candid feedback, skill enhancement, and recognition of achievements. By fostering an environment where performance data informs real-time coaching and forward-thinking development, organizations can boost both individual growth and collective success.

7.4 Functional Area 4: Learning & Development

7.4.1 Adult Learning Principles (Experiential, Self-Directed)

Adult learners bring unique needs and motivations to the learning environment. Unlike children or adolescents, they typically enter training with established life experiences, clear goals, and immediate practical concerns. By recognizing these characteristics and incorporating them into program design, Learning & Development (L&D) professionals can create trainings and workshops that resonate powerfully. Two core approaches—**experiential** and **self-directed** learning—are particularly effective in harnessing adults' readiness and capacity to learn.

Why Adult Learning Principles Matter
Adults often juggle multiple obligations, from work responsibilities to family commitments. They want learning that is relevant, efficient, and directly applicable. Programs that ignore adult learning preferences risk low engagement or difficulty in transferring skills back to the job. On the other hand, those that respect autonomy

and experiential knowledge can see immediate performance improvements and stronger learner satisfaction.

Experiential Learning

Experiential learning immerses participants in hands-on tasks, simulations, or real-world challenges that mirror what they face on the job. By "doing," adults actively process and internalize lessons. This approach leverages reflection, application, and feedback cycles to solidify new knowledge or behaviors.

Context-Rich Scenarios

> Integrating realistic case studies or role-play sessions makes learning more tangible. For instance, practicing customer conflict resolution with actual script examples helps employees build confidence in their abilities.

> Relevancy ensures learners see the immediate value. An IT specialist might troubleshoot simulated technical problems, mirroring real system failures.

Reflection and Feedback

> Structured debrief sessions allow learners to discuss what went well, identify improvements, and strategize how to apply insights to their daily work.

> Peer feedback often proves particularly powerful—learners learn from one another's perspectives or missteps, building collective competency.

Long-Term Retention

> Repeating experiential exercises and follow-up tasks cements lessons. An initial workshop could be reinforced by

on-the-job assignments or refresher activities over subsequent weeks, preventing skill decay.

Self-Directed Learning

Where experiential techniques focus on active, hands-on engagement, self-directed learning empowers adults to set their own pace, goals, and methodologies. It aligns with the principle that adults are most motivated when they identify what they need to learn and how they want to learn it.

Autonomy and Ownership: Allowing employees to choose the sequence of modules or pick projects that align with their interests fosters deep motivation. Some may prefer in-depth reading and research, while others thrive on interactive tutorials or group discussions.

Resource-Rich Environments: Providing user-friendly learning management systems (LMS), curated e-libraries, or communities of practice lets learners explore materials that solve real challenges. This access is especially helpful when employees encounter a new task or problem and need immediate solutions.

Goal Setting and Tracking: Encouraging adults to define personal objectives—like gaining proficiency in a software tool or mastering project management techniques—builds a sense of purpose. Periodic check-ins ensure accountability and offer support if they encounter roadblocks.

Blending Experiential and Self-Directed Methods

Many L&D initiatives fuse both concepts for maximum impact:

➢ **Project-Based Learning**: Employees tackle genuine organizational projects, applying theoretical concepts in a real setting. They choose how to research or implement solutions, melding hands-on practice with self-driven exploration.

➢ **Learning Circles**: Small groups discuss a shared challenge or domain. Individuals bring self-directed research findings or experience, then engage in collaborative exercises. This hybrid approach promotes continuous peer learning and autonomy within a structured framework.

Practical Tips for Implementation

✓ **Start with Real Needs**: Adult learners respond best to topics that solve immediate job challenges. Conduct a brief needs analysis or ask managers to identify pressing skill gaps.

✓ **Facilitate, Don't Dictate**: In sessions, adopt a guiding role—pose questions, encourage debate, and provide frameworks. Let learners share experiences, problem-solve together, and determine action steps.

✓ **Offer Varied Modalities**: Combine workshops, on-demand microlearning, discussion forums, and one-on-one coaching. Multiple formats accommodate different learning preferences.

✓ **Encourage Reflection**: Promote journaling, short written summaries, or peer feedback loops after each learning event. Reflection cements insights into long-term memory.

Adults learn most effectively when they see direct relevance, enjoy hands-on or practical engagement, and can steer their own development. By designing programs that merge **experiential** techniques with **self-directed** opportunities, HR and L&D professionals not only heighten motivation but also improve the likelihood that new skills will translate into measurable workplace improvements.

7.4.2 Training Needs Analysis and Program Design

Identifying gaps in employee capabilities is the first step toward creating effective learning initiatives. A structured training needs analysis (TNA) ensures that development programs address true skill deficiencies rather than assumptions. Once these needs are clarified, well-designed programs are more likely to meet both immediate performance goals and longer-term organizational strategies.

Why Conduct a Training Needs Analysis?

Without a deliberate approach to pinpointing learning priorities, development efforts risk being scattered or misaligned with real job requirements. TNA aligns training objectives with business outcomes, clarifies the scope of necessary resources, and engages stakeholders who rely on the improved performance of those being trained.

Foundational TNA Components

1. **Organizational Analysis**: Reviews overarching strategic goals, upcoming projects, or policy changes to see what competencies might be required at a macro level. For example, a company planning to adopt new software across its operations would examine how employee roles and existing skill sets match (or mismatch) future demands.

2. **Task or Role Analysis**: Investigates specific tasks employees must perform and uncovers performance gaps. If sales representatives are underutilizing a CRM system, the TNA might reveal a need for advanced system training and best practices around lead management.

3. **Individual Analysis**: Maps personal development needs for each employee or role. Data may come from performance reviews, manager feedback, or self-assessments. The goal is to ensure that each learner's unique deficits—technical or soft skills—are addressed.

Gathering Data for TNA

Organizations can use a variety of methods to create a well-rounded view of training requirements:

- ✓ **Surveys and Questionnaires**: Capturing broad input quickly. Well-designed questions highlight issues such as knowledge gaps, job challenges, and desired learning topics.

- ✓ **Interviews and Focus Groups**: Offering nuanced insights into day-to-day workflow problems or departmental bottlenecks that a survey might not fully uncover.

- ✓ **Performance Data**: Looking at KPIs, error rates, or productivity metrics pinpoints where certain teams or individuals might need upskilling.

- ✓ **Observation**: Shadowing employees on the job, especially in roles requiring precise skills, can reveal subtle inefficiencies or process misunderstandings.

Designing Targeted Training Programs

Once the TNA is complete, the next step is transforming identified needs into tangible learning solutions. Careful program design helps ensure knowledge transfer and application:

1. **Defining Clear Learning Objectives**

- ➢ Objectives should specify what participants will be able to do or demonstrate post-training. For instance, stating "Reduce order-processing errors by 20% within three months after training" aligns the learning goal with practical performance improvements.

➤ Well-crafted objectives also guide decisions about content scope, training methods, and evaluation criteria.

2. **Selecting Formats and Delivery Methods**

➤ **Classroom or Workshop**: Effective for hands-on group activities and immediate peer feedback.

➤ **E-Learning Modules**: Flexible for a dispersed workforce; learners can proceed at their own pace.

➤ **Hybrid/Blended Approach**: Combines face-to-face interaction with online exercises or self-paced tasks, offering the best of both worlds.

3. **Tailoring Content to Adult Learners**

➤ Incorporate real-world examples and scenarios that resonate with participants' daily tasks.

➤ Build in reflection and application exercises so learners can directly connect new knowledge to on-the-job challenges.

4. **Timing and Scheduling**

➤ Consider the work cycle. Avoid launching intensive training during a peak season that would hinder employee availability or focus.

➤ Break longer programs into manageable sessions, allowing learners time to absorb material and reduce cognitive overload.

Sample Process Flow: TNA to Program Launch

Phase	Key Activities
1. Needs Identification	Conduct surveys, analyze performance metrics, gather leadership input
2. Data Synthesis	Prioritize skill deficits, group findings by department or role
3. Program Architecture	Draft learning objectives, decide modality (workshops, e-learning, etc.)
4. Content Creation	Develop modules, design exercises, finalize supporting materials
5. Implementation	Schedule sessions, communicate with participants, prepare facilitators
6. Follow-Up & Evaluation	Gather feedback, measure changes in performance, refine for future iterations

Ensuring Stakeholder Alignment

A well-executed TNA and program design phase typically involves collaboration across the organization. Department heads, managers, and the learners themselves provide valuable input into the practicalities of scheduling, content relevance, and real-world obstacles to learning. Keeping these groups engaged from the start promotes buy-in and improves the likelihood that completed training drives meaningful results on the floor.

By systematically identifying genuine skill or knowledge gaps, then crafting learning solutions that clearly meet those gaps, HR can ensure training resources are well invested. A targeted program—

supported by relevant content, appropriate delivery methods, and stakeholder alignment—stands the best chance of boosting employee competencies and organizational performance.

7.4.3 Evaluating Training Outcomes (Kirkpatrick Model)

A well-designed training program does not end once the last session concludes. Organizations want to confirm that newly acquired knowledge or skills are transferring back to the workplace in a tangible way. One of the most widely recognized frameworks for assessing training effectiveness is the **Kirkpatrick Model**, which sorts evaluation criteria into four progressive levels. By gathering data at each level, HR and L&D professionals gain a nuanced view of how learning initiatives impact both the individual and the broader business.

Overview of the Four Levels

Level 1: Reaction

> **Focus**: Participants' immediate impressions and satisfaction.

> **Why It Matters**: While positive reactions alone do not guarantee learning, a negative experience can hinder future knowledge retention and application. Gathering quick feedback—often via post-training surveys—uncovers whether the format, pacing, and content resonated with learners.

Level 2: Learning

> **Focus**: The degree to which participants actually absorbed the material (e.g., knowledge, skills, or attitudes).

Assessment Methods: Quizzes, practical demonstrations, or simulations conducted during or shortly after the training. These tests confirm whether the learning objectives were met and highlight areas needing reinforcement.

Level 3: Behavior

Focus: Post-training changes in on-the-job behavior or performance.

Key Considerations: Observing employees, soliciting manager feedback, or measuring relevant KPIs (e.g., fewer quality errors, more efficient processes) provides evidence of whether skills gained in training are being consistently applied.

Level 4: Results

Focus: The broader organizational impact of the training. This can include metrics such as reduced costs, increased sales, improved customer satisfaction, or lower turnover, depending on the program's focus.

Challenges: External factors may also influence results, so isolating the direct effect of training might require additional analysis or control groups to validate the causal link.

Collecting and Interpreting Data

Gathering evidence at each level often involves multiple methods—like surveys for Level 1, knowledge tests for Level 2, behavior observation for Level 3, and business metrics for Level 4. Organizations frequently combine these data points to form a more cohesive narrative about the training's value.

- ✓ **Timeliness**: Assessing Levels 1 and 2 typically occurs immediately or shortly after training, whereas Levels 3 and 4 might require weeks or months to observe behavioral shifts or operational changes.

✓ **Participation**: Getting managers involved in post-training follow-up can accelerate application and highlight any barriers to behavior change.

✓ **Continuous Improvement**: If metrics underperform at certain levels, reviewing the program design or support structures (like coaching or job aids) becomes essential.

Applying the Kirkpatrick Model Strategically

When used consistently, the Kirkpatrick Model helps organizations refine learning programs. For instance, if post-session quizzes (Level 2) reveal strong knowledge gains but on-the-job observations (Level 3) show minimal behavioral change, HR might investigate workplace barriers such as lack of managerial reinforcement or insufficient practice opportunities. This feedback loop ensures training investments are targeted and yield meaningful returns.

Sample Connections Between Levels

Level	Potential Measures	Example Outcome
Reaction	Post-workshop satisfaction scores, immediate feedback forms	Attendees felt the session was engaging, but suggest more hands-on exercises
Learning	Scores on written exams, role-play performance, skill-based quizzes	85% of participants can now demonstrate the new software's primary functions
Behavior	Observed changes in day-to-day tasks, manager	Post-training, a 20% decrease in operational mistakes

	feedback, error rates	indicates effective transfer of learning
Results	Changes in sales figures, customer satisfaction indices, production times	Overall departmental efficiency rises by 15%, partially attributable to better-trained staff

The Kirkpatrick Model provides a structured lens for evaluating how well a training program fulfills its promise—from initial learner satisfaction to measurable organizational improvements. By gathering data at each level and turning insights into action, HR leaders ensure that training contributes real value and continues to evolve with the organization's needs.

7.4.4 Career Development and Succession Planning

Designing pathways for employee growth not only enhances individual capabilities but also safeguards an organization's future by cultivating potential successors for key roles. Career development aims to provide learning opportunities and progression routes that align with both personal aspirations and organizational needs, while succession planning focuses on ensuring a seamless transition whenever vital positions open up. When these two elements are integrated, employees see tangible prospects for growth, and critical roles remain continuously supported by qualified talent.

Establishing a Culture of Growth

Before embarking on formal programs, an organization's culture should celebrate continuous learning. Employees who recognize that curiosity, self-improvement, and willingness to tackle new challenges are valued will often seek out development opportunities on their own. Likewise, leaders who highlight success stories of internal mobility reinforce the message that active career planning and engagement can lead to genuine advancement.

Foundations of Career Development

Rather than providing a single ladder for all, structured career development typically involves multiple potential paths—some employees aim for leadership, while others prefer deepening their expertise in specialized fields. When HR teams outline potential routes and facilitate coaching or mentorship, individuals feel encouraged to envision a future within the company instead of looking elsewhere. Resources might range from tuition assistance programs and rotational assignments to on-demand e-learning modules that address emerging skill demands.

Implementing Succession Planning

Succession planning identifies roles where sudden vacancies might disrupt operations—such as executive posts, niche technical positions, or client-facing leadership. Early identification of potential successors allows for targeted development that readies them for new challenges. At times, this may involve pairing high-potential employees with seasoned mentors or assigning them to significant cross-functional projects:

> ➤ **Talent Reviews**: Cross-departmental discussions among managers create consensus about who is poised for greater responsibility.

> ➤ **Targeted Skill Building**: Employees on a succession track can engage in stretch assignments that mimic the complexities of the intended next role, accelerating readiness.

Harmonizing Development and Succession

When career development and succession planning are linked, employees not only develop skills but also sense that their growth is relevant to pressing organizational goals. A manager-in-training, for instance, sees that leadership competencies being cultivated serve both personal ambitions and the broader aim of future-proofing the company's managerial pipeline. This mutual alignment often heightens engagement and loyalty.

Element	Benefit
Career Development	Fosters individual motivation and self-improvement. Helps attract and retain those who value progression.
Succession Planning	Secures critical roles through ongoing readiness. Minimizes operational disruption when key staff depart.
Combined Approach	Creates synergy: personal growth meets strategic continuity. Increases long-term workforce stability.

Measuring Impact

Leaders can assess the success of these programs through metrics such as reduced turnover in pivotal positions, the ratio of internal vs. external hires for leadership roles, and employee satisfaction with growth opportunities. Anecdotal feedback—like stories of employees who advanced into more complex roles smoothly—can also signal that programs are working well.

By tying together career development and succession planning, organizations provide a compelling reason for employees to stay and grow, while also ensuring that crucial roles will always have qualified individuals ready to step in. This tandem approach builds a resilient workforce—one where aspiration meets opportunity, and continuity meets innovation.

7.5 Functional Area 5: Total Rewards

7.5.1 Compensation Structures (Base Pay, Variable Pay)

Developing a well-crafted compensation structure is crucial for attracting, motivating, and retaining talent. While total rewards often encompass benefits and other forms of recognition, an organization's pay framework remains a primary driver of employee satisfaction. Two fundamental components—**base pay** and **variable pay**—each play distinct roles in acknowledging day-to-day responsibilities, incentivizing performance, and aligning employee efforts with broader strategic objectives.

Base Pay: Foundations and Considerations
Base pay offers a reliable, predictable income, giving employees security regarding their standard of living. This consistent component typically reflects factors like job role, complexity, market rates, and the individual's experience or skill level. Employers often use job grading systems or market benchmarking to ensure internal equity and external competitiveness:

> ➤ **Market Benchmarking**: Examining industry data prevents underpaying critical skill sets. Many organizations reference compensation surveys to calibrate base salaries against peers in their region or sector.

> ➤ **Pay Ranges**: Structuring pay ranges around midpoints or "market medians" allows some flexibility to recognize performance while maintaining fairness. High-performing or long-tenured employees often land higher within the range.

Employees value the clarity of a fair base salary, as it guarantees consistent compensation for fulfilling their core duties. Yet, base pay alone can sometimes limit the organization's ability to reward extraordinary achievements or adapt to changing strategic goals.

Variable Pay: Linking Performance to Rewards

Unlike base salaries, variable compensation (e.g., bonuses, incentives, or profit-sharing) is contingent on defined performance metrics. By tying additional earnings to results, organizations encourage behaviors aligned with revenue growth, cost savings, or other measurable targets.

> **Short-Term Incentives:** Many companies offer annual bonuses tied to individual accomplishments, team milestones, or overall financial performance. This model promotes accountability since employees see a direct link between their efforts and potential rewards.

> **Long-Term Incentives:** Equity-based plans—like stock options or restricted stock units—align employees' financial interests with the organization's sustained success. These rewards typically vest over multiple years, helping to retain top contributors who anticipate future gains if the company prospers.

> **Team vs. Individual Emphasis:** Some variable pay plans prioritize group achievements, reinforcing collaboration and shared responsibility. Others highlight personal performance, motivating employees to exceed individual metrics. An effective balance often involves a mix, ensuring team-based synergy without neglecting personal initiative.

Designing a Cohesive Pay Framework

An effective compensation strategy integrates both base and variable elements to reinforce the organization's culture and strategic goals. If a company thrives on innovation, for instance, variable pay might heavily reward successful new product launches or patent filings. Conversely, if the focus is on consistent client service, employees might receive incentives linked to customer satisfaction metrics:

Base Pay	Variable Pay
Predictable, stable income	Incentives that adapt to performance outcomes
Reflects job responsibilities, market benchmarks	Ties earnings to specific behaviors or achievements
Promotes fairness and foundational security	Encourages goal-oriented behavior and initiative

While designing these structures, it's important for HR to communicate openly with employees about how pay is determined and how variable components are calculated. Transparent guidelines and straightforward performance metrics foster trust and reduce any ambiguity.

Ensuring Market Responsiveness and Fairness
Compensation strategies evolve in response to shifts like inflation, talent shortages, or organizational restructures. Periodic reviews of base salary ranges and variable pay schemes keep the system equitable. If a competitor begins offering more generous performance bonuses, for example, HR might adjust the bonus formula or introduce spot awards that reward outstanding efforts in near real-time.

Base pay provides an essential bedrock of security and consistency, while variable pay can spark innovation and performance-driven behaviors. When carefully balanced and clearly communicated, these two compensation pillars form an adaptable framework that meets business objectives, retains top talent, and fosters a sense of fairness and motivation across the workforce.

7.5.2 Benefits Design and Administration (Health, Retirement)

A robust benefits package stands as a cornerstone of an effective total rewards strategy. Alongside compensation, health and retirement plans can significantly influence employee well-being, productivity, and retention. Crafting these programs involves balancing organizational budgets, legal requirements, and the evolving expectations of a diverse workforce. Once designed, efficient administration ensures these benefits run smoothly, maintaining trust and delivering tangible value to employees.

Structuring Health Benefits

A company's health plan is often the most visible part of its benefits offering. Beyond meeting basic insurance coverage, thoughtful plan design can encourage preventive care and promote long-term health:

➢ **Plan Varieties**: Employers may choose from traditional Preferred Provider Organization (PPO) models, Health Maintenance Organizations (HMOs), or high-deductible health plans (HDHPs) paired with health savings accounts (HSAs). Each option offers different trade-offs in terms of network flexibility, out-of-pocket costs, and administrative complexity.

➢ **Cost-Sharing Approaches**: Employers often split premiums with employees, determining the proportion of expense each party covers. Strategically adjusting deductibles, copays, or coinsurance can influence how employees utilize health services, emphasizing preventive measures or more judicious use of specialist care.

➢ **Wellness Integration**: Adding wellness programs—ranging from smoking cessation resources to on-site fitness classes—complements core insurance coverage. By encouraging healthier lifestyles, such initiatives can reduce long-term medical expenditures and boost employee morale.

Designing Retirement Plans

Retirement benefits signal a long-term commitment to employees' financial security. Plans that allow staff to accumulate savings consistently, with potential employer matching, often become a critical motivator for retention. Two common plan types include defined-contribution and defined-benefit structures:

Defined-Contribution (DC) Plans: In DC setups (e.g., 401(k) or 403(b) plans), employees typically decide how much to contribute from each paycheck and how to invest those funds. Employers may offer matching contributions up to a specified limit, enhancing the plan's appeal. Plan administration requires selecting reputable providers, monitoring investment options, and ensuring compliance with relevant regulations—like ERISA in the United States. Transparent communication about fees, risk levels, and the importance of regular contributions is crucial for employees to make informed decisions.

Defined-Benefit (DB) Plans: Once the norm in many sectors, DB pensions promise a specific payout in retirement, calculated based on tenure and salary history. While they offer strong predictability for employees, they entail greater cost volatility and funding obligations for employers. Actuarial assessments help project future liabilities, guiding funding strategies and plan adjustments. Though less common today, DB plans remain a significant draw where they exist, underscoring an organization's commitment to secure employee retirements.

Administration and Compliance

Beyond plan design, the day-to-day management of health and retirement offerings can pose logistical and regulatory hurdles:

- ✓ **Vendor Management**: Employers frequently partner with insurers, TPAs (third-party administrators), and investment firms to handle enrollment, claims, or recordkeeping. Clear service-level agreements and regular performance reviews help maintain quality.

- ✓ **Legal and Regulatory Adherence**: Depending on jurisdictions, plans may fall under laws like the ACA (Affordable Care Act) or ERISA. Ongoing changes in healthcare or tax policies can mandate plan updates or enhanced reporting obligations.

- ✓ **Employee Education**: Effective communication—through benefit guides, on-site seminars, or digital tools—is vital. Employees are more likely to appreciate and use their benefits if they fully grasp coverage details, matching opportunities, or the impact of contribution rates on long-term savings.

Tailoring Benefits to Organizational Needs

Companies sometimes leverage cafeteria-style plans, letting employees pick from various coverage tiers or investment options. This customization can be a competitive advantage, especially for organizations with multigenerational workforces—recent graduates may prioritize student loan assistance or flexible health coverage, while mid-career professionals or near-retirees might focus heavily on retirement matching and comprehensive family medical plans.

Health and retirement benefits remain cornerstones of a competitive rewards package. By thoughtfully structuring plan options, ensuring compliance with regulations, and educating employees about their choices, HR fosters a workforce that feels both supported in the present and safeguarded for the future. This dual emphasis on well-being and financial security underpins engagement, loyalty, and overall organizational resilience.

7.5.3 Legislation Affecting Compensation and Benefits

Compensation and benefits programs operate within a framework of federal and state laws that shape everything from how wages are structured to the oversight of retirement plans. While many of these regulations aim to protect employees from unfair or unethical practices, they also set critical parameters for how organizations design and administer pay and benefits.

Minimum Wage and Overtime Provisions

The Fair Labor Standards Act (FLSA) requires employers to adhere to a federal minimum wage and to provide overtime pay (at one-and-a-half times the regular rate) for non-exempt employees working over 40 hours in a week. Some states set higher minimum wages or stricter overtime thresholds, and compliance often involves careful time-tracking systems and job classification reviews.

Equal Pay and Non-Discrimination

Laws like the Equal Pay Act prohibit basing pay differentials on gender for substantially equal work. Additional statutes, including Title VII of the Civil Rights Act, outlaw compensation or benefit discrimination based on race, color, religion, sex, or national origin. Many employers conduct regular pay equity audits to confirm that salary and bonus structures align with these legal requirements and do not inadvertently perpetuate bias.

Retirement Plan Regulations

Retirement offerings—whether pensions or 401(k)-type defined contribution plans—are frequently governed by the Employee Retirement Income Security Act (ERISA). ERISA sets standards for fiduciary responsibilities, funding, and employee communications, ensuring that participants receive accurate, transparent information about their plan's status and costs. Further, laws like the Pension Protection Act of 2006 can affect automatic enrollment features and participant investment choices, influencing how employees save for the future.

Health Benefits Oversight

Organizations offering health insurance navigate a range of mandates, including the Affordable Care Act (ACA). The ACA introduced employer shared responsibility provisions, health coverage reporting, and consumer protections (such as no lifetime coverage caps). At the same time, the Health Insurance Portability and Accountability Act (HIPAA) imposes privacy and security rules for employee health data, while also limiting exclusions for pre-existing conditions in certain group health plans.

Leave and Continuation of Coverage

Some compensation and benefits legislation addresses scenarios where employees require time away from work or lose their job:

> **Family and Medical Leave Act (FMLA)**: Although primarily a leave law, FMLA intersects with benefits by requiring employers to continue group health coverage during the leave period, ensuring that employees are not penalized for taking protected time off.

> **COBRA**: In cases of employment separation or certain other qualifying events, COBRA offers a temporary continuation of group health coverage, albeit at the individual's own cost

(plus an administrative fee). Employers must provide detailed notices about these rights and track associated deadlines.

State and Local Variations

Beyond federal statutes, states or municipalities may enact their own legislation on topics such as paid sick leave, expanded family leave, or pay transparency. Although these local laws might not specifically alter base federal requirements, they frequently impose additional obligations that can affect wage payments and benefit structures. Multi-state employers typically rely on region-specific compliance tracking to keep pace with changing mandates.

Staying Current and Compliant

Because legal standards around compensation and benefits evolve over time, organizations should periodically review their policies and practices:

- ✓ **Regular Audits**: Examining wage data, job classifications, and benefit records can reveal potential compliance gaps or areas of risk.

- ✓ **Employee Communication**: Transparent, user-friendly information about pay, benefits options, and employees' legal rights reduces misunderstandings and fosters a sense of fairness.

- ✓ **Vendor and Broker Relations**: Whether selecting benefit plans or navigating regulatory updates, strong partnerships with insurers, financial advisors, or legal counsel keep the organization informed and agile.

Compensation and benefits are underpinned by a matrix of federal and state laws, each designed to protect employee welfare and ensure equitable treatment. By understanding the key statutes and maintaining robust, adaptive compliance processes, HR professionals can craft pay and benefit programs that meet employees' needs while adhering to all legal obligations.

7.5.4 Global Rewards Considerations

As businesses expand internationally, reward strategies must adapt to the diverse legal, economic, and cultural landscapes in which they operate. A successful global rewards program goes beyond simply "exporting" a domestic model. Instead, it balances consistency with local flexibility, ensuring employees feel both connected to the organization's core values and fairly compensated in their region.

Navigating Regulatory and Economic Variations
Different countries impose distinct rules on everything from minimum wage levels and mandatory benefits to severance payouts. Compensation structures that work in one territory might inadvertently run afoul of labor laws elsewhere. Exchange rate fluctuations, varying tax systems, and differences in the cost of living can complicate how salary ranges and variable pay targets are set.

➢ **Local Market Benchmarks**: Relying on region-specific compensation surveys helps align pay rates with local norms. A role that qualifies as mid-level in one economy may be highly specialized in another, warranting adjusted pay ranges.

➢ **Mandatory Benefits**: Some regions mandate extensive paid leave, employer-provided housing allowances, or other unique requirements. Failing to adhere to these obligations can result in penalties or reputational damage.

Cultural Sensitivities and Perceptions of Rewards
Rewards that resonate in one culture—like public recognition—may

264

not be as motivating in another. In certain countries, employees may value hierarchical status and seniority-based pay, while in others, performance-based bonuses hold more weight. Understanding these cultural nuances fosters a sense that the organization respects local traditions, fostering stronger employee loyalty.

Expatriate Assignments and Repatriation

Global deployments often require special compensation models to address relocations:

- ✓ **Cost-of-Living Adjustments (COLA):** Expat packages typically include allowances for housing, education, or transportation to ensure employees can maintain a reasonable standard of living.

- ✓ **Tax Equalization:** Because expatriates may face complex tax obligations in multiple countries, employers sometimes implement policies that keep the employee's overall tax burden comparable to what they would pay at home.

- ✓ **Repatriation Support:** Encouraging a smooth return to the home country—via retention bonuses or guaranteed roles— prevents the loss of valuable experience once the international assignment ends.

Balancing Standardization with Local Flexibility

Many global organizations adopt a "core-plus" approach: establish broad reward principles (e.g., a commitment to market competitiveness, pay for performance) while allowing regions to customize specific benefit offerings. This structure preserves the corporate identity—highlighting consistency in base pay philosophy or performance metrics—yet acknowledges local preferences or legal constraints.

Core Component	Local Customization
Global Job Grading Framework	Region-specific pay scales or premium factors
Enterprise-wide Bonus Philosophy	Differentiated performance metrics per country
Standard Healthcare Principles	Tailored local benefit providers or coverage levels

Communicating Across Borders

Transparent, plain-language benefits explanations reduce confusion, especially when employees must navigate different coverage rules or investment options. Virtual tools—like interactive calculators or localized intranet portals—help employees understand how each element of the reward package translates in their location. Meanwhile, HR professionals in each region should be trained to clarify nuances and gather feedback.

Designing global rewards requires juggling compliance issues, economic conditions, and cultural values. By carefully balancing a consistent organizational framework with local adaptation—and supporting international assignments with well-structured policies—HR professionals can craft a cohesive yet flexible rewards strategy. This approach both respects regional differences and upholds the company's global talent strategy, ultimately bolstering engagement, retention, and cross-border collaboration.

Chapter 8: Organization Domain

8.1 Functional Area 6: Structure of the HR Function

8.1.1 Centralized vs. Decentralized Models

An organization's HR structure can significantly influence how effectively it aligns talent practices with overarching goals. Some businesses consolidate HR functions at headquarters, while others distribute decision-making authority across multiple divisions or regions. Both **centralized** and **decentralized** approaches aim to deliver consistent HR services, yet differ in how policies are shaped, how agile decision-making becomes, and how closely local teams can tailor solutions.

Understanding the Centralized Model

A centralized HR model places most decision-making, policy development, and processes under a single corporate HR team. In this arrangement, the main office typically establishes enterprise-wide guidelines—covering areas like hiring protocols, compensation structures, and learning frameworks—that local managers must implement with limited modification.

Consistency and Standardization: Policies, forms, and service delivery often look the same throughout the organization. This uniformity can enhance compliance and clarity, as employees across various locations share a common understanding of HR norms. Centralized teams may find it easier to adopt company-wide initiatives—like a new performance management system—because a single decision-making body has clear authority.

Efficiency and Cost-Effectiveness: Consolidating HR functions can lower administrative overhead by reducing duplicate roles or processes. A single payroll system or benefits platform might serve the entire workforce. Expertise also clusters in a few specialists, making it simpler to build deep knowledge on topics like labor law compliance or advanced HR technology.

Potential Drawbacks: Centralized models can struggle to respond rapidly to unique local challenges or cultural nuances. A one-size-fits-all approach might not sufficiently meet the needs of specialized teams or global offices. Communication gaps may arise if front-line managers feel distant from corporate HR or perceive the function as less responsive to real-time issues.

Advantages of Decentralized HR

In a decentralized structure, each business unit or region manages its own HR responsibilities, within a broad corporate framework. This permits more autonomy and local adaptation while retaining some overarching governance.

1. **Local Adaptability** HR can flex to meet distinct legislative or cultural contexts, especially in multinational operations. For instance, a European branch may fine-tune benefits or leave policies to reflect regional norms while still aligning with broader corporate principles. Departments gain the freedom to introduce innovations more quickly if they do not have to wait for corporate approval.

2. **Stronger Manager-HR Partnership** Embedded HR professionals within individual business units develop closer relationships with line managers. Such proximity fosters deeper understanding of departmental challenges and more targeted solutions—improving overall service quality. Faster decision-making is possible because local stakeholders can collaborate on changes without multiple layers of sign-off.

3. **Risks and Complexities** Decentralized models may inadvertently lead to duplicated efforts: separate systems or overlapping vendor contracts that inflate costs. Ensuring organizational cohesion around compensation philosophies, cultural values, or compliance initiatives can be tougher if each division runs its own show.

Choosing or Blending Models

Many organizations adopt a **hybrid** approach, centralizing certain functions (like compensation strategy or benefits administration) and decentralizing others (e.g., day-to-day HR support, training customizations). This mix strikes a balance between uniform corporate standards and local autonomy:

➢ **Centers of Excellence (CoEs)**: Specialized HR teams oversee enterprise-wide programs—like leadership development or performance management—while local HR business partners handle implementation details.

➢ **Shared Services**: Transactions such as payroll or benefits enrollment may be centralized in shared service centers for efficiency, freeing HR business partners to focus on consultative or strategic roles in their respective locations.

Evaluating Effectiveness and Impact

Regardless of the chosen model, monitoring outcomes ensures HR structure aligns with organizational shifts. Metrics that gauge speed of issue resolution, employee satisfaction with HR services, and cost per HR staff member can reveal whether the structure fosters or hinders performance. Periodically reassessing the balance—especially after mergers, expansions, or technology upgrades—helps confirm the HR function remains well-calibrated to changing business realities.

Centralizing HR offers consistency and potential cost savings, but can risk slower responsiveness or limited local customization. Decentralizing empowers individual divisions to tailor practices, yet may fragment core processes. Adopting a strategic blend—where certain aspects remain centralized while local teams adapt the rest—often delivers the best synergy of organizational cohesion and agile support.

8.1.2 Strategic Role of HR in Organizational Design

HR professionals are increasingly regarded not just as administrators of policies, but as architects of an organization's structure and overall effectiveness. By advising on how people, processes, and technology intersect, HR can influence how departments, teams, and reporting lines best align with strategic objectives. This proactive involvement helps ensure that the right talent is located in the right place, at the right time, under the right structure—ultimately supporting both agility and clarity in decision-making.

Identifying the Need for Organizational Redesign
Shifts in market conditions, product lines, or growth strategies often prompt a re-evaluation of the current structure. HR, in collaboration with senior leaders, may detect that certain functions are duplicated across regions, or that a new business unit requires dedicated resources. Through workforce analytics and talent assessments, HR pinpoints inefficiencies or emerging skill gaps that suggest the organization's design might no longer match its goals.

> **Mergers or Acquisitions**: Combining distinct corporate cultures and reporting lines demands that HR guide leadership through role consolidation, realigning overlapping positions, and retaining key talent.

Rapid Expansion: As teams grow, an initially flat structure might become unsustainably wide, requiring the addition of mid-level management layers or specialized support functions.

Aligning Structure with Strategy

Once the need for change is identified, HR can propose and implement structural adjustments. Ideally, these revisions keep employees focused on value-adding activities while respecting the company's culture and mission.

Functional vs. Matrix vs. Divisional

➢ **Functional Structures**: Grouping employees by specialized skills (e.g., finance, marketing) creates deep expertise, but can silo collaboration.

➢ **Matrix Arrangements**: Overlaying functional and project-based reporting fosters cross-functional cooperation, though it may complicate reporting lines.

➢ **Divisional Models**: Grouping teams by product, region, or customer segment can enhance responsiveness but risks duplicating roles across divisions.

Bridging Organizational Boundaries

➢ **Cross-Functional Teams**: Encouraging fluid collaboration helps break down departmental silos. HR's role involves defining these teams, clarifying reporting lines, and providing conflict resolution mechanisms when responsibilities overlap.

➢ **Centers of Excellence (CoEs)**: Centralizing expertise in specialized areas—such as analytics, learning, or innovation—ensures consistency and advanced support while allowing operational units to focus on execution.

People-Centric Design Considerations

While reconfiguring structures, HR ensures that employees remain engaged and well-informed about changes. This might include clear explanations of revised reporting lines, updated job descriptions, or newly established decision-making processes. Employee buy-in is essential, especially during disruptive shifts where uncertainty can undermine morale and productivity.

Design Factor	HR's Contribution
Role Clarity	Update job descriptions, communicate responsibilities
Decision Authority	Define delegation frameworks, ensure needed training
Cultural Fit	Align new structures with core values, maintain continuity
Skill Development	Assess competency gaps, provide reskilling or upskilling opportunities

Data-Driven Approach and Stakeholder Collaboration

HR's strategic role also involves leveraging data—such as headcount costs or employee engagement metrics—to drive organizational decisions. Engaging with key stakeholders (C-suite, department heads, or regional managers) secures alignment around shared objectives. Through workshops, surveys, or scenario planning, HR can illustrate the pros and cons of various structural models, guiding leaders toward a solution that balances efficiency, innovation, and cultural cohesion.

Sustaining Changes Over Time

Adjusting organizational design is not a one-time event. Structures may need fine-tuning as market demands, technologies, or workforce dynamics shift. HR monitors post-realignment feedback and performance indicators (like operational throughput, employee satisfaction, or turnover rates) to detect whether further adjustments are required. Establishing open communication channels—town halls, manager forums—enables continuous improvement rather than waiting for another major overhaul.

By serving as a strategic partner in organizational design, HR helps shape frameworks that reflect a company's evolving strategy. From identifying structural needs through data analytics to ensuring employees' roles remain clearly defined and meaningful, HR's influence ensures that the architecture of the organization remains fit for purpose—and primed to seize new opportunities.

8.1.3 Measuring and Demonstrating HR Value

HR's impact can reach well beyond administrative tasks, yet many organizations underestimate the function's strategic contribution. Demonstrating clear, data-backed results is pivotal for HR to secure resources, influence decision-making, and reshape perceptions of HR from a "cost center" to a vital business partner. By aligning metrics with financial performance, strategic objectives, and employee well-being, HR can highlight its role in driving measurable outcomes.

Clarifying What "Value" Means

Before gathering metrics, HR teams should define how the organization gauges success. Some leaders prioritize cost savings and efficiency; others focus on employee engagement and innovation. Understanding these priorities helps HR select meaningful indicators—like turnover cost reduction or speed of critical hires—that resonate with executive stakeholders. In some cases, "value" may revolve around improved compliance and risk management, especially if the organization operates in a heavily regulated industry.

Quantifying HR's Financial and Operational Impact

Tying HR initiatives to tangible financial or operational outcomes can be the most direct way to demonstrate value. For example, if an HR-led retention strategy cuts turnover by 10% in high-impact roles, the associated savings on recruitment, training, and lost productivity can be estimated. Similarly, implementing an optimized talent acquisition process might reduce time-to-fill for senior positions, accelerating project launches and revenue streams.

Initiative	Possible Measured Outcome
Streamlined Onboarding Process	Faster time-to-productivity, reduced first-year turnover
Leadership Development Program	Promotion readiness, internal fill rates for key roles
Targeted Engagement Efforts	Lower absenteeism, higher customer satisfaction scores

Linking Data to Strategic Objectives

HR metrics make the strongest statement when they tie directly to broader corporate goals—such as entering new markets or enhancing customer experiences. If the business aims to expand internationally, HR can track how quickly crucial roles are filled in each new location or whether cultural integration programs help maintain consistent performance. Aligning analytics with top-level priorities ensures leaders see HR's efforts as vital to organizational success, not as isolated initiatives.

Balancing Quantitative and Qualitative Evidence
Purely numeric data often only tells half the story. Qualitative insights—like feedback from employee focus groups or case studies on how HR programs influenced team morale—can also signal positive outcomes. A leadership coaching initiative, for instance, may reduce conflict and improve cross-functional collaboration, which might not appear immediately in cost metrics but is evident in testimonial feedback or a more cohesive culture.

Communicating Results and Insights
Demonstrating HR's value isn't simply about collecting data—it's about presenting that information to stakeholders in a compelling narrative. Effective reporting might involve:

- ✓ **Dashboards or Scorecards**: Summaries of core metrics—turnover rates, engagement levels, performance improvement trends—updated quarterly for leadership.

- ✓ **Storytelling**: Sharing real employee success stories or project examples can humanize the numbers and create a vivid picture of HR's impact.

- ✓ **Comparative Benchmarks**: Referencing industry standards or historical baselines highlights achievements. If time-to-hire improves from 60 to 40 days while the industry average remains around 50, the organization sees concrete evidence of progress.

Sustaining Continuous Improvement
HR must periodically revisit these measures to keep them relevant and aligned with shifting organizational goals. As new technology emerges or the competitive landscape changes, fresh metrics or refined targets may be needed. Moreover, any identified shortfalls—like inconsistent results across different locations—should guide

improvements. For instance, if one region's turnover remains stubbornly high compared to the rest, a targeted intervention can be launched and its results tracked over time.

By consciously selecting, analyzing, and communicating metrics tied to both financial performance and strategic aims, HR leaders can clearly demonstrate their department's value. Moving beyond administrative support to driving measurable results cements HR's position as an essential contributor to the organization's success.

8.2 Functional Area 7: Organizational Effectiveness & Development (OED)

8.2.1 Theories of Organizational Development

Organizations are continuously evolving systems influenced by culture, leadership, and external pressures. To navigate these dynamics, **Organizational Development (OD)** relies on foundational theories that explain how change unfolds and how workplaces adapt over time. These models provide lenses through which HR and OD professionals can diagnose issues, plan interventions, and guide stakeholders toward sustainable transformation.

Systemic and Humanistic Underpinnings
Organizational Development as a field emerges at the intersection of behavioral science, systems thinking, and humanistic psychology. Early OD practitioners viewed organizations as living systems, interconnected in ways that require holistic approaches—rather than isolated fixes—to address root causes of dysfunction or missed opportunities. A key tenet in these theories is recognizing employees as active participants in shaping their environment, rather than passive recipients of top-down directives.

Lewin's Model and Force Field Analysis

Kurt Lewin proposed a three-stage process (unfreeze, change, refreeze) to describe how behaviors shift during major organizational transitions. Underpinning this model is **force field analysis**, which maps out forces driving change (e.g., market competition, new leadership vision) and forces resisting change (existing norms, fear of the unknown). By identifying and amplifying the drivers while reducing or removing barriers, organizations can move more smoothly into new states of equilibrium.

- ✓ **Unfreeze**: Question existing processes, create readiness for new ideas.

- ✓ **Change**: Implement interventions—like new structures or training—that guide employees toward new behaviors.

- ✓ **Refreeze**: Stabilize these new practices, reinforcing them through updated policies, metrics, or cultural celebrations.

Action Research Model

Prominent in OD practice, action research is a cyclical process blending **diagnosis**, **planning**, **action**, and **evaluation**. It emphasizes collaboration between OD practitioners (or HR professionals) and organizational members. Data is collected (via surveys, interviews, or observations) to pinpoint issues, collaborative solutions are developed, and progress is continually measured. This iterative approach ensures real-time adaptation, cultivating a sense of ownership among employees who co-create the interventions.

Socio-Technical Systems Theory

A core concept in OD is aligning both social aspects (people, teams, relationships) and technical aspects (tools, processes, infrastructure). Socio-technical systems theory asserts that changes in either dimension ripple through the other, necessitating a balanced design.

For instance, introducing advanced automation might require new team structures or skill-building to fully capitalize on the technology's potential. Neglecting the human side of such a shift often leads to suboptimal outcomes or resistance.

Weisbord's Six-Box Model

Marvin Weisbord formulated a diagnostic framework that partitions organizational functioning into six interrelated areas: **Purpose**, **Structure**, **Rewards**, **Helping Mechanisms**, **Relationships**, and **Leadership**. By systematically examining each "box," practitioners can identify misalignments—like a mismatch between formal structure and actual communication flows—and propose targeted interventions. The model also underscores that each element influences the others, reflecting OD's holistic ethos.

Likert's Systems Theory

Rensis Likert introduced the idea of four management systems, ranging from authoritative to participative. The more participative a system, the more likely employees are to be motivated, collaborative, and productive. OD interventions that champion participative methods—such as problem-solving groups or leadership that nurtures open communication—find theoretical support in Likert's observation that involvement and empowerment bolster performance and satisfaction.

Practical Implications in Modern Organizations

Real-world OD initiatives often weave together these foundational theories. For example, a multinational company embarking on digital transformation might blend Lewin's unfreeze-change-refreeze stages with an action research approach to continuously refine strategies across different regions. Meanwhile, socio-technical systems thinking ensures the new software rollout considers not just IT architecture, but also how employees collaborate or adapt their workflows. Tools like Weisbord's Six-Box or Likert's continuum can serve as diagnostic checklists, highlighting whether organizational culture and leadership style support or hinder the desired changes.

OD theories offer guiding principles for diagnosing organizational challenges and implementing effective, collaborative change. By understanding how workplaces evolve (Lewin), how data-driven cycles of improvement proceed (Action Research), or how social and technical elements intertwine (Socio-Technical Systems), HR and OD practitioners can better craft interventions that resonate with employees and drive sustained progress. Each theory underscores the importance of inclusive, evidence-based processes—ensuring that transformation efforts become more than just top-down mandates.

8.2.2 Change Management Models (e.g., Kotter's Steps)

Change management models provide structured methods for guiding an organization through shifts in strategy, structure, or culture. Among the most recognized is John Kotter's eight-step approach, which offers a comprehensive framework for creating urgency, fostering buy-in, and ensuring new processes or behaviors stick over time. By following these or similar models, HR and Organizational Development (OD) professionals can more effectively navigate transitions and maintain employee commitment throughout periods of uncertainty.

Kotter's Eight-Step Model: Core Principles

Although every change initiative varies in scope and complexity, Kotter's method underscores the importance of establishing momentum early and sustaining it until the transformation is fully embedded. The steps help clarify the sequence of leadership actions and empower employees to embrace new ways of working.

1. **Create a Sense of Urgency**

   Highlight why the change is critical—perhaps due to shifting market demands or technological advancements. Without a shared understanding of why action is needed, employees may remain complacent or indifferent.

2. **Build a Powerful Coalition**

   Gather influential champions who support and can advocate for the change. Their enthusiasm and credibility encourage broader acceptance, especially if they represent multiple levels or functions within the organization.

3. **Form a Vision and Strategy**

   Develop a concise vision that paints a compelling future and aligns with overarching organizational goals. Laying out clear objectives and strategies ensures that everyone understands both the destination and the route.

4. **Communicate the Vision**

   Messages about the change should be frequent, transparent, and accessible to all employees. Leaders who actively model the new behaviors and consistently reinforce key points can reduce confusion or skepticism.

5. **Remove Obstacles**

   Identify and address barriers—like outdated processes, resource constraints, or resistant mindsets—that could derail progress. HR's role often involves revising policies, clarifying new responsibilities, or offering additional training and support.

6. **Generate Short-Term Wins**

   Celebrating early achievements boosts morale and demonstrates tangible benefits of the transformation. Small successes also help counter "change fatigue" and maintain momentum by showing that efforts lead to real improvements.

7. **Sustain Acceleration**
   Avoid declaring victory too soon. Build on early results, deepen the scope of transformation, and continue refining processes or strategies. This phase often involves fine-tuning roles, embedding new technologies, or broadening initiatives across more teams.

8. **Anchor Changes in the Culture**
   Reinforce new norms by incorporating them into leadership development, performance criteria, or reward systems. Ensuring that updated behaviors and practices become part of the organizational DNA prevents regression to the old status quo.

Other Model Variations

While Kotter's approach remains influential, some organizations employ other frameworks like ADKAR (Awareness, Desire, Knowledge, Ability, Reinforcement) or Bridge's Transition Model. Each highlights unique angles—such as the emotional journey of individuals or the mechanics of skill-building and reinforcement. Regardless of the chosen model, principles of clear communication, inclusive collaboration, and continuous feedback apply across the board.

Practical Application Tips

✓ **Match Model Steps to Organizational Culture**: If a company values rapid experimentation, focusing on quick pilot initiatives early on may suit them better than a lengthy planning phase.

✓ **Stakeholder Engagement**: Securing endorsement from informal influencers can be as pivotal as winning over formal leaders. Their support or criticism often shapes peer opinions of the initiative.

✓ **Ongoing Measurement**: Tracking outcomes—like process efficiency gains or shifts in employee sentiment—helps identify which interventions work and where adjustments are needed. Post-change reviews can also inform future transformations.

Whether using Kotter's eight steps or another recognized model, the core objective is to guide employees through transitions in a structured, empathetic way. By sustaining momentum, celebrating milestones, and embedding new practices into the culture, organizations stand a better chance of achieving lasting change that advances strategic goals.

8.2.3 Interventions for Improving Effectiveness

Organizational Effectiveness and Development (OED) interventions are deliberate efforts aimed at realigning structures, processes, or behaviors to enhance overall performance. These targeted actions often stem from diagnostic data—such as employee surveys, productivity metrics, or customer feedback—and typically involve collaboration among HR, leadership, and key stakeholders. By carefully selecting and implementing interventions that address underlying root causes, organizations can see sustained improvements in morale, efficiency, and adaptability.

Diagnostic Foundations

Any intervention begins with a thorough assessment. Whether through interviews, focus groups, or observation, OD practitioners gather insights on where bottlenecks or cultural misalignments exist.

From there, a clear plan emerges, pinpointing the specific areas—like communication gaps, skill deficits, or structural imbalances—that a targeted intervention must address.

Common Types of OD Interventions

Team Building: Often used when a team struggles with trust, unclear roles, or conflicts over goals. Facilitated workshops, off-site retreats, or structured activities can help members understand each other's work styles, realign on objectives, and practice open dialogue. Effective team-building goes beyond ice-breakers; it delves into real work challenges so the newly strengthened relationships translate into tangible performance gains.

Process Consultation: Focuses on the way tasks and decisions flow rather than the content of the tasks themselves. An OD consultant might observe a team's workflow, then suggest adjustments to meeting structures, data-sharing methods, or decision-making protocols. This intervention is particularly useful when inefficiencies or repeated miscommunications hinder progress, and direct input on operational improvements is needed.

Role Clarification and Redesign: Addresses confusion or overlap in responsibilities that can lead to tension or dropped tasks. Through discussions and negotiation, each position's scope is refined to ensure a coherent division of labor and accountability. This intervention may be triggered by rapid growth, departmental mergers, or newly introduced technology that changes how jobs interact.

Conflict Resolution and Mediation: Prolonged interpersonal or interdepartmental conflicts can undermine trust and stall projects. Mediation sessions, facilitated by an impartial party, encourage respectful airing of grievances and collaborative problem-solving. Establishing ground rules, focusing on future-oriented solutions, and following up on agreements help prevent the same issues from resurfacing.

Culture and Values Alignment: In some cases, an organization's stated values fail to manifest in daily behaviors. Initiatives might include defining desired cultural norms, revamping onboarding content to emphasize these norms, and rewarding employees who exemplify them. Leadership modeling—where managers visibly demonstrate key behaviors—reinforces new cultural standards.

Ensuring Successful Implementation

Simply introducing interventions doesn't guarantee lasting change. Key enablers include:

- ✓ **Leadership Sponsorship**: Senior leaders who champion the intervention, allocate resources, and publicly advocate its purpose increase the likelihood of acceptance.

- ✓ **Clear Communication**: Participants need to understand why the intervention is happening, how it will proceed, and what is expected of them. Transparent objectives quell uncertainty.

- ✓ **Follow-Up and Reinforcement**: After the initial activities—such as a team workshop or new role assignments—ongoing check-ins can confirm that progress sticks. Small adjustments and additional coaching may be required to sustain momentum.

Linking to Broader Goals

Effective interventions aren't merely about fixing an isolated symptom; they should tie back to strategic outcomes. If an organization seeks greater agility, for example, OD efforts around decision-making processes or team empowerment should explicitly mention how these changes enable faster innovation or improved customer responsiveness. Framing interventions in the context of larger organizational aspirations helps secure buy-in and clarifies success metrics.

OD interventions aim to bring about lasting improvements in how people collaborate, communicate, and work toward shared objectives. By diagnosing root issues, carefully choosing from a toolkit of methods—team building, process consultation, role clarification, and more—and ensuring robust follow-up, organizations can cultivate a high-performing environment that remains adaptable to shifting demands.

8.2.4 Measuring ROI of OED Initiatives

Organizational Effectiveness and Development (OED) initiatives often aim to improve collaboration, streamline processes, or boost innovation. Despite these worthy goals, stakeholders increasingly demand clear evidence that OED efforts produce tangible results. By applying a structured approach to measuring return on investment (ROI), HR and OD professionals can demonstrate how interventions contribute to organizational success—translating often-intangible outcomes into quantifiable value.

Clarifying the "Return" in ROI

Before launching an OED initiative, it's essential to define the specific problem being addressed and the desired results. "Success" might entail reduced turnover in a high-impact department, accelerated project completion rates, or a measurable rise in employee engagement scores. By articulating these targets early, practitioners can gather the right baseline data and plan relevant KPIs. In some cases, "return" may also encompass qualitative benefits, such as improved morale or strengthened leadership pipelines, which might require additional narrative or case study evidence to supplement financial metrics.

Collecting Data and Establishing Baselines

A compelling ROI calculation starts with baseline information that reflects current performance. This can include metrics like absenteeism, error rates, customer satisfaction, or productivity. During and after the OED intervention, new data on the same indicators are gathered, providing a comparison point that highlights changes:

> **Control Groups**: Whenever feasible, comparing outcomes in a group that did not receive the intervention with one that did can help isolate the effect of the OED program from external factors.

> **Time-Phased Tracking**: Checking progress at intervals—e.g., at three, six, or twelve months—captures both immediate impacts and longer-term stabilizations.

Quantifying Financial Impact

Where possible, organizations convert improvements into monetary terms. For example, if a department-wide conflict resolution program decreases turnover by 5%, HR can estimate the associated savings in recruitment costs, onboarding expenses, and productivity disruptions. Similarly, if a process improvement initiative shortens production cycles, the cost savings or extra revenue from faster delivery can be tied to the OED activity. By assigning real dollar figures, HR leaders can illustrate how the initiative pays for itself over time.

Outcome	Measurement	Potential Financial Conversion
Decreased Turnover	% reduction in turnover	Recruiting, training, and lost-productivity savings
Faster Project Completion	Days/weeks saved per project	Opportunity cost reduction, speed-to-market benefits
Improved Team Communication	Feedback survey scores, error rates	Lower rework costs, stronger customer satisfaction

Addressing Intangible and Long-Term Benefits

Not all benefits lend themselves to immediate or precise ROI calculations. Gains in organizational culture, leadership readiness, or cross-departmental trust might take longer to manifest financially. In these cases, documenting shifts through engagement surveys, interviews, or anecdotal success stories offers complementary evidence. Such qualitative data, when paired with any quantitative milestones, provides a fuller picture of how the intervention fosters strategic health and adaptability.

Communicating Results to Stakeholders

Merely calculating ROI does not guarantee broader buy-in. Presenting findings in a format that resonates with top executives and other relevant audiences is equally crucial. Condensing outcomes into clear, succinct reports—perhaps with visuals that compare pre- and post-intervention metrics—can convey how the OED project aligns with major corporate goals. Where feasible, showcasing success stories or champion testimonials heightens credibility and keeps the momentum for future OD efforts.

By systematically defining goals, collecting baseline and post-intervention data, and translating improvements into financial or strategic gains, HR and OD professionals can deliver solid evidence of how OED initiatives create real value. This transparent, data-oriented approach not only secures support for ongoing development projects but also positions HR as a strategic partner in fueling the organization's continuous evolution.

8.3 Functional Area 8: Workforce Management

8.3.1 Forecasting Workforce Needs

An organization's ability to execute its strategy often hinges on having the right talent—both in terms of quantity and skill sets—at the right times. Forecasting workforce needs aligns anticipated demand for labor with projected supply, helping HR leaders proactively address gaps or surpluses. By combining data-driven analysis with insights into emerging trends, organizations can minimize disruptions, control labor costs, and stay agile in the face of industry shifts.

Identifying the Drivers of Future Demand
Workforce forecasting typically begins with understanding what fuels the organization's staffing requirements. Factors might include anticipated product launches, expansions into new markets, technological upgrades, or strategic shifts such as outsourcing. If a company plans to double its R&D capabilities over the next two years, for instance, HR must predict which roles—engineers, data

scientists, project managers—will be in high demand and in what volumes.

Data and Methods for Forecasting

> ➤ **Quantitative Approaches**: Some organizations use historical data on turnover, hiring patterns, or productivity to model staffing needs. Sophisticated tools like regression analysis or time-series forecasting can reveal trends or seasonality in workforce demands.

> ➤ **Qualitative Forecasting**: Discussions with department heads, scenario planning, and expert judgments also shape projections. If an emerging technology is likely to disrupt an industry, quantitative methods alone may not capture its impact on required roles.

Internal vs. External Supply Analysis
Once projected demand is clear, HR reviews where talent can originate:

Internal Supply: Succession pipelines, internal transfers, and upskilling programs contribute to meeting future needs. Detailed knowledge of employees' competencies—often tracked in skill inventories—pinpoints who might fill critical roles.

External Supply: Labor market conditions, local or global talent availability, and demographic factors (e.g., a retiring workforce) determine how feasible it is to recruit externally. If the needed skills are scarce in-house or time to fill is likely to be extensive, early planning is essential to avoid project delays.

Bridging Workforce Gaps
When forecasts reveal shortfalls, HR leaders can pursue multiple strategies:

✓ **Recruitment Initiatives**: Launching targeted hiring campaigns, possibly with signing bonuses or specialized marketing to attract niche experts.

✓ **Upskilling or Reskilling**: Implementing learning programs so current employees can adapt to new technologies or responsibilities.

✓ **Alternative Staffing Models**: Engaging contingent workers, consultants, or gig arrangements to handle peak workloads or specialized tasks without permanent headcount growth.

Monitoring and Adjusting the Forecast

Forecasting is not a one-and-done activity. Economic conditions, competitor moves, and internal changes can shift workforce realities quickly. Regular check-ins—quarterly or biannually—allow HR to compare actual staffing metrics against the plan. If the gap is larger than anticipated, HR can accelerate recruitment or intensify training. If a downturn reduces demand for certain roles, a redeployment strategy or hiring freeze might be warranted.

By systematically assessing future labor demands and balancing them against both internal talent readiness and external market availability, HR leaders can avert crises in resource allocation. Proactive workforce forecasting ensures that as strategies evolve— whether through growth, transformation, or contraction—the organization remains equipped with the people and capabilities it needs to thrive.

8.3.2 Succession Planning & Knowledge Management

Maintaining a steady pipeline of future leaders and critical talent is pivotal for organizational resilience. Succession planning ensures that when key individuals leave or move on, capable successors are ready to step in. Meanwhile, knowledge management captures and preserves essential expertise—ranging from technical processes to stakeholder relationships—so transitions happen smoothly without costly lapses. Together, these processes help the organization retain critical know-how and mitigate risks associated with turnover or rapid expansion.

Succession Planning: Identifying and Developing Future Talent
Succession planning is more than a list of potential replacements. At its best, it's an ongoing strategy that nurtures high-potential employees, matches them with development opportunities, and prepares them for eventual promotion into critical roles. Some essential elements include:

✓ **Defining Critical Roles**: Organizations look beyond the C-suite, noting positions that significantly influence operations or customer satisfaction. A specialized engineering role or a global sales lead, for example, can be just as critical as top executive jobs.

✓ **Assessing Potential**: High performers are not always suitable for more complex leadership challenges. Tools such as competency evaluations, 9-box grids, and multi-rater feedback can help gauge both current performance and future potential.

✓ **Targeted Development**: Once potential successors are identified, tailored learning pathways—such as cross-functional projects or formal leadership programs—build the skills they'll need. Periodic check-ins keep progress on track, clarifying whether they are truly ready for upcoming openings.

Knowledge Management: Preserving and Sharing Expertise
While succession planning prepares individuals, knowledge

management ensures they (and others) have access to the information they need. This involves capturing critical insights from subject matter experts and making them readily available:

1. **Documentation and Repositories**: Organizations create internal wikis, digital libraries, or collaboration tools where process guidelines, project histories, and best practices are systematically stored. Regular content reviews keep these repositories current, preventing them from becoming "digital graveyards" of outdated data.

2. **Communities of Practice**: Bringing together employees with shared professional interests fosters ongoing learning and the exchange of fresh ideas. Whether discussing solutions to common challenges or brainstorming product innovations, these groups nurture collective intelligence. Mentorship and peer coaching can emerge organically within these communities, strengthening ties between seasoned professionals and newer hires.

3. **Structured Handoffs and Transitions**: When a valued employee is set to depart or rotate to another role, formal handoff sessions capture critical contacts, client nuances, or project intricacies that might otherwise walk out the door. Pairing an outgoing expert with an incoming employee for a set period ensures real-time Q&A and preserves context-laden knowledge that's often missing from written documents.

Synergy Between Succession Planning and Knowledge Management

An integrated approach maximizes the impact of both. If potential successors are already identified, pairing them with mentors or rotating them into key projects naturally links them to the organization's deeper knowledge base. Conversely, robust knowledge repositories can accelerate the learning curve for future leaders, helping them gain situational awareness faster:

➢ **On-the-Job Learning**: High-potential employees can consult well-documented processes or tap into communities of practice, complementing their hands-on experiences.

➢ **Risk Mitigation**: Should a senior leader exit unexpectedly, not only is a trained successor ready to assume the role, but the essential knowledge about clients, processes, or products also remains accessible and up to date.

Measuring Impact and Adjusting Strategy

Assessing the effectiveness of succession and knowledge management efforts can involve indicators such as reduced time-to-fill for critical roles, improved project continuity, or direct feedback on the usability of knowledge repositories. Periodic "health checks" reveal whether employees find these tools valuable or if certain skill gaps still persist. Over time, iterative improvements help fine-tune the design and implementation of both programs, ensuring they stay aligned with evolving business demands.

Succession planning secures the future of key roles, while knowledge management ensures expertise is documented and shared across the workforce. When integrated, they create a robust talent infrastructure: high-potential employees are groomed for leadership, and the vital organizational knowledge that fuels day-to-day success is safeguarded and easily transferred. This dual approach fortifies an organization's ability to adapt, innovate, and thrive in changing markets.

8.3.3 Flexible Work Arrangements

Shifts in technology, evolving employee expectations, and a global talent pool have all accelerated the demand for flexible work arrangements. By giving employees more control over where, when, or how they perform their roles, organizations can boost engagement, tap into broader talent markets, and adapt to fast-paced business cycles. Whether offering remote options, compressed schedules, or job sharing, each approach has unique benefits and considerations that impact both employee well-being and organizational effectiveness.

Common Flexible Work Models

Remote or Hybrid Work

> ➢ **Overview**: Employees complete some or all tasks outside the central office, using digital tools to communicate and collaborate.
> ➢ **Key Advantages**: Offers access to a geographically diverse talent pool, can reduce overhead costs, and often improves work-life balance.
> ➢ **Challenges**: Requires robust IT security measures, consistent communication practices, and clear performance metrics to manage productivity effectively.

Compressed Workweeks

> ➢ **Overview**: Employees fulfill their required weekly hours in fewer but longer workdays—such as four 10-hour days instead of five 8-hour days.
> ➢ **Key Advantages**: Frees employees for extended weekends or personal obligations, potentially reducing commuting time.

> ➤ **Challenges**: Can lead to fatigue if days are excessively long, and might complicate scheduling for roles needing consistent weekday coverage.

Flextime

> ➤ **Overview**: Staff set their start and end times within agreed-upon "core hours" when presence or real-time collaboration is required.
> ➤ **Key Advantages**: Accommodates varying personal schedules, rush-hour avoidance, or peak productivity preferences.
> ➤ **Challenges**: May complicate team synchronization if core hours are minimal or if employees choose widely divergent schedules.

Job Sharing

> ➤ **Overview**: Two or more employees split a single full-time position, dividing responsibilities and overlapping as needed.
> ➤ **Key Advantages**: Access to specialized talents or complementary skill sets that might not be available in one individual, plus improved continuity if one partner is unavailable.
> ➤ **Challenges**: Requires thorough handoffs and transparent communication protocols to ensure consistent coverage and avoid confusion about accountability.

Aligning Flexibility with Organizational Goals

When implementing flexible options, the end goal should extend beyond employee satisfaction. Understanding how these arrangements support strategic needs—like extending operating hours, increasing agility, or reducing real estate costs—helps secure executive and managerial buy-in. For instance, an international operation might use flextime and remote work to bridge time zone gaps, ensuring round-the-clock customer support or project progress.

Ensuring Equitable Access and Accountability

Not every role is equally suited to all forms of flexibility; certain positions might require on-site presence or specialized equipment. Still, communicating transparent criteria for eligibility mitigates perceptions of unfairness. Once arrangements are in place, consistent performance metrics—like project milestones, client satisfaction, or quality indicators—help managers assess productivity rather than relying on physical presence as a proxy for effort.

Maintaining Engagement and Collaboration

Though flexible work can enhance autonomy, it also alters team dynamics. Proactive steps like scheduled check-ins, virtual coffee breaks, and collaborative platforms maintain a sense of unity. In a hybrid environment, ensuring that remote participants are included in brainstorming sessions or quick hallway discussions can prevent information silos and isolation.

Consideration	Implementation Tip
Communication Rhythms	Regular stand-ups or weekly team huddles reduce misalignment
Tech Infrastructure	Secure, user-friendly tools for video conferencing, file sharing
Performance Measurement	Output-focused KPIs (project completion, customer satisfaction)
Cultural Integration	Encourage informal social moments, mentorship, or ERGs that connect staff

Evaluating Impact

Assessment of flexible arrangements typically includes metrics around retention, absenteeism, and productivity. If turnover declines or employee satisfaction surveys improve notably after a flexible work rollout, that signals value. In roles where quantitative output is measured—like code commits or sales calls—organizations can check whether productivity rises or stays stable under new scheduling patterns.

Well-structured flexible work programs can foster a more engaged and diverse workforce, aligning employee autonomy with organizational demands. By balancing robust technology, clear performance measures, and inclusive practices, employers can reap the advantages of greater flexibility—positioning themselves as forward-thinking while efficiently meeting both market and employee needs.

8.3.4 Contingent Workforce Considerations

Relying on contingent workers—such as freelancers, consultants, temps, or gig-economy personnel—can introduce agility and cost savings into workforce management. Organizations often turn to contingent talent for specialized skills, short-term surge capacity, or support during project spikes without having to sustain long-term headcount expenses. Yet, managing this workforce pool effectively demands attention to legal, operational, and cultural factors.

Reasons for Engaging Contingent Talent

Many employers find value in contingent labor due to the flexibility it provides, particularly when forecasted workloads fluctuate or when niche expertise is temporarily needed. Contract-based hires can bridge skill gaps or cover parental leaves without permanently expanding the payroll. However, the line between strategic utilization and overreliance can be thin—overusing contingent labor risks diluting institutional knowledge and hindering cohesive team dynamics.

> **Specialized Expertise**: Certain roles, like digital marketing analytics or AI consulting, might only be needed for a specific project scope.

> **Cost Control**: Paying only for the duration of the project or assignment can lower overhead, especially if training and long-term benefits aren't required.

> **Talent Pipeline Exploration**: Sometimes contingent workers transition to full-time if their performance and cultural fit align with organizational needs.

Key Compliance and Classification Concerns

Contingent arrangements carry legal implications. Misclassification—treating someone who meets the definition of an employee as an independent contractor—can result in substantial penalties, including back taxes and benefit liabilities. HR professionals typically review job duties, managerial oversight, and work conditions to ensure roles align with their labeled status. Co-employment issues may arise if both the employer and a staffing agency share control over a temporary worker's duties or supervision, potentially complicating liability or benefits obligations.

Risk Area	Typical Cause	Mitigation Strategy
Misclassification	Treating contractors as employees	Use clear contracts, consult legal guidelines
Co-Employment	Overlapping supervision or	Clarify managerial roles, define separate HR

	benefits	processes
IP Ownership Confusion	Lack of clarity around work product	Include robust contract clauses, detail IP transfers

Practical Management Approaches

Effective contingent workforce strategies go beyond short-term hiring. Organizations may establish centralized vendor management or a dedicated contingent workforce coordinator to oversee consistent engagement terms and safeguard compliance. Equally important is integrating contingent staff into relevant communication channels so they remain informed about project objectives and timelines—while still respecting boundaries that differentiate their status from core employees.

Furthermore, performance oversight should remain outcomes-based. Since contingent workers may operate outside traditional structures, focusing on deliverables and milestones ensures accountability without imposing unneeded layers of corporate policy. At the contract's conclusion, a structured offboarding process helps capture lessons learned, potential intellectual property, or references for future collaboration.

Contingent work arrangements can offer flexibility and specialized expertise at critical moments, but successful utilization requires thoughtful planning around legal compliance, role clarity, and practical management. By handling classification rigorously, coordinating oversight, and fostering clear communication, HR can leverage the contingent workforce to enhance agility without undercutting team cohesion or raising compliance risks.

8.4 Functional Area 9: Employee & Labor Relations

8.4.1 The Employment Relationship and Contract Basics

An employment relationship extends beyond mere hiring; it establishes legal and practical parameters around duties, compensation, and mutual obligations. In many organizations, this connection is governed by contracts or agreements—whether implied, verbal, or written—that spell out expectations and protections on both sides. By clarifying terms at the outset, employers and employees reduce uncertainties and can address potential disputes more efficiently.

Foundations of the Employment Relationship

At its core, an employment relationship involves an exchange: the employee provides labor and expertise, while the employer delivers wages, benefits, and working conditions. In some jurisdictions, employment can be "at-will," allowing either party to end the relationship with limited notice. However, certain regions or industries impose stricter frameworks, requiring just-cause terminations or specific notice periods to protect employee rights.

Components of an Employment Contract

While not all roles require a formal written contract, many organizations draft at least a basic agreement for clarity. Common clauses might include:

1. **Job Title and Duties**: Outlining responsibilities, reporting lines, and any special requirements (like travel or certifications).

2. **Compensation and Benefits**: Specifying salary, bonuses, or allowances, plus an overview of benefits such as health coverage or paid leave.

3. **Work Hours and Location**: Establishing expected working schedules and any flexibility or remote work options.

4. **Confidentiality and IP**: Securing proprietary information and clarifying ownership of work-related intellectual property.

5. **Termination and Notice**: Explaining conditions under which the contract ends, notice periods needed, and any severance arrangements.

These components help shape the day-to-day employment experience and clarify obligations around confidentiality, loyalty, or non-compete terms.

Differences Between Written vs. Implied Contracts

Although written agreements provide the clearest record of terms, many employment relationships proceed based on policy manuals, offer letters, or even implied understandings established through consistent employer practices. A regularly enforced handbook policy, for instance, can carry contractual weight if it sets out disciplinary procedures employees reasonably expect to be followed. Such unwritten arrangements, however, can lead to ambiguities if the employee's perceptions differ from the employer's intentions.

Navigating Local Laws and Regulations

Each jurisdiction imposes varied rules affecting contracts. For instance, some regions demand written documentation of specific clauses—like mandatory overtime rates—while others allow broad flexibility. Ensuring compliance may involve verifying:

> ➢ **Minimum Terms**: Statutory benefits (e.g., vacation allotments, maternity/paternity leaves) or mandatory notice periods.

> ➢ **Works Councils or Labor Codes**: In certain countries, employee representatives must be consulted about major contract changes or workforce restructures.

> ➢ **Industry-Specific Guidelines**: Fields like healthcare, finance, or transportation may impose additional licensing or shift constraints.

Staying updated on changes to labor regulations is crucial; even small oversights could lead to legal disputes or penalties.

When Contracts Become Critical

Special contractual terms can carry heightened importance in roles involving sensitive data, valuable intellectual property, or high-level decision-making:

1. **Non-Disclosure Agreements (NDAs)**
   Protect confidential business details—client lists, product roadmaps, or trade secrets—by preventing unauthorized disclosure.

2. **Non-Compete or Non-Solicitation Clauses**
   Restrict employees from joining competitors or poaching clients for a set duration after leaving. While potentially safeguarding business interests, they must be reasonable in scope or risk invalidation by courts.

3. **Arbitration or Dispute Resolution**
   Detail how conflicts will be handled—mediation, arbitration, or litigation—and which jurisdiction or venue governs if problems arise.

Maintaining Clarity Throughout the Relationship

Employment contracts aren't static. Promotions, major strategy shifts, or departmental reorganizations can significantly alter duties or compensation, warranting updated documentation. Periodic check-ins—especially during performance reviews—help ensure the contract terms still match reality. For global employers, extending these updates or clarifications to foreign subsidiaries helps achieve consistent practices across borders.

A well-defined employment relationship, bolstered by transparent contract terms, anchors trust and reduces misunderstandings for both employers and employees. Through clear clauses, adherence to local laws, and ongoing updates, HR professionals can establish stable grounds on which to build positive working dynamics—even as roles and business conditions evolve.

8.4.2 Managing Grievances and Disciplinary Actions

Organizations strive to maintain a fair and productive environment, yet disputes or rule violations inevitably arise. Handling these issues transparently and consistently is critical, both for preserving employee trust and minimizing legal risks. By establishing structured grievance channels and a clear disciplinary framework, HR professionals help ensure that conflicts are addressed promptly, thoroughly, and in a way that respects all parties involved.

Recognizing and Processing Grievances

Employees may raise grievances for a variety of reasons—ranging from perceived unfair treatment or harassment to disagreements over work assignments. A well-defined grievance process typically includes straightforward steps for an employee to lodge a complaint, designated individuals responsible for receiving and investigating it, and established timelines to ensure that grievances don't linger unresolved:

✓ **Open Communication**: Encouraging employees to voice concerns early (e.g., through an internal hotline or direct supervisor) can prevent escalation. A prompt, empathetic response often reassures them that their issues matter.

✓ **Neutral Investigation**: Assigning a manager or HR representative not directly involved in the dispute helps preserve objectivity. Detailed documentation of all relevant interviews and evidence gathered creates a robust record if further review or external scrutiny occurs.

✓ **Resolution and Follow-Up**: Where possible, solutions are reached through consensus—like clarifying misunderstandings or mediating interpersonal conflicts. If an employee remains dissatisfied, escalation to a higher-level review or appeals process may be built in.

Disciplinary Framework: Balancing Fairness and Accountability
When an employee's conduct, performance, or rule violation calls for disciplinary action, consistency and clarity are paramount. Different infractions or performance issues may prompt different responses, ranging from verbal warnings to termination, but the guiding principle remains a proportional, well-documented approach:

1. **Progressive Discipline**
   Many employers adopt a tiered model: verbal counseling, then written warnings, possibly followed by suspension or eventual termination if issues persist. This approach gives employees opportunities to correct behavior or performance before reaching more severe consequences.

2. **Documentation**
   Detailed records of each step—from the initial conversation to final decisions—protect against claims of arbitrary or

discriminatory treatment. These records typically describe the misconduct, the policy violated, the date of discussion, and any improvement goals set.

3. **Consistency Across Cases**
   Applying similar disciplinary measures for similar types of infractions reduces perceptions of favoritism or bias. Any apparent inconsistencies—such as imposing harsher penalties on one individual than another for the same offense—can create distrust and expose the organization to legal challenges.

Special Considerations in Unionized Environments
In workplaces with labor union representation, disciplinary actions often must conform to a collective bargaining agreement (CBA). Such agreements might dictate specific investigation procedures, require a union representative's presence in disciplinary meetings, or allow for grievance arbitration. HR teams collaborate closely with both management and union officials to ensure compliance with these contractual obligations.

Maintaining Employee Relations During Conflict
Even a straightforward disciplinary case can affect morale if coworkers sense an unfair or overly punitive approach. Transparency around policies—letting employees know what behavior is expected and how infractions will be handled—helps mitigate this concern. In more complex grievances, such as allegations of harassment or discrimination, discreet yet thorough processes show the organization's commitment to a safe, inclusive environment.

Grievance handling and disciplinary procedures are the guardrails that keep workplace standards clear and reinforce fairness. By responding to complaints promptly, documenting each step carefully, and administering discipline consistently, HR nurtures a culture of accountability while upholding employees' rights. This balance fosters trust, reduces conflict, and ultimately supports a more harmonious, productive workforce.

8.4.3 Union Environments (Collective Bargaining)

When a portion of the workforce is unionized, the employer-employee relationship extends beyond individual discussions and involves formal negotiations with a collective voice. **Collective bargaining**—the process by which employers and unions negotiate wages, hours, and working conditions—shapes the workplace environment in significant ways. Effectively navigating these discussions requires strategic preparation, mutual respect, and a thorough understanding of relevant labor laws.

Foundations of Collective Bargaining

Union environments revolve around collective agreements that address a wide range of employment terms. Once a union is recognized as the bargaining representative, the employer typically must engage in good-faith negotiations regarding mandatory subjects—often including pay structures, benefits, grievance mechanisms, and work rules. While each negotiation session can be distinct, certain principles remain consistent:

> ➢ **Good-Faith Requirement**: Both sides are expected to present proposals, consider each other's positions, and make sincere attempts to reach a compromise. Unyielding stances or surface-level talks risk allegations of bad-faith bargaining.

> ➢ **Written Agreements (CBAs)**: The outcome of successful negotiations is often a collective bargaining agreement (CBA). This contract, binding for a specified term (e.g., three years), outlines obligations and restrictions for both parties.

Negotiation Dynamics

Negotiations can vary in tone and complexity, influenced by economic conditions, union priorities, or past labor-management relations. While some talks proceed amicably, others may be protracted or confrontational:

1. **Preparation and Research**
   Both sides typically analyze financial data, workforce metrics, and industry benchmarks to craft realistic proposals. Employers might examine production costs or competitor wage rates; unions might survey their members for pressing concerns.

2. **Tentative Agreements and Packages**
   Not every term is resolved instantly. Negotiations may involve multiple rounds of discussion, culminating in "package" proposals that link several issues together (e.g., wage increases with modifications to overtime rules).

3. **Ratification**
   After reaching a tentative agreement, union members often vote on whether to accept the new contract. A rejected proposal may send negotiators back to the table or escalate tensions if a strike is on the horizon.

Handling Strikes and Work Stoppages

In some instances, if a deadlock arises and no resolution is forthcoming, unions may strike as a pressure tactic. Strikes vary in scope—ranging from short symbolic walkouts to prolonged shutdowns. Employers facing a work stoppage might temporarily replace workers, adjust operations, or seek legal relief if picketing activities breach permissible behavior. Meanwhile, the union often relies on strike funds and community support, hoping the economic impact convinces management to reconsider its stance.

Day-to-Day Labor Relations

Even after signing a CBA, labor relations continue through daily enforcement of contract terms. Common areas include:

➢ **Grievances**: If an employee believes contract provisions are violated—say, regarding seniority rights or shift assignments—they may file a grievance. The union and management then collaborate to resolve the dispute, possibly escalating to arbitration if unresolved.

➢ **Contract Administration**: Union stewards and HR representatives frequently engage in consultations around scheduling changes, layoffs, or new policies to verify alignment with the CBA. Clear communication channels and respectful dialogue often reduce potential conflicts.

➢ **Mid-Term Negotiations**: Significant organizational shifts—like adopting new technology or reorganizing a department—may require additional discussions, even if the current contract is not up for renewal. This allows both parties to address unforeseen impacts without waiting for the next bargaining cycle.

Impact on Organizational Culture

Working under a collective bargaining agreement can instill predictable processes for conflict resolution and job security. Employees may feel more empowered to voice concerns through formal channels. However, tension can arise if union goals clash with rapid operational changes or if management perceives the CBA's conditions as rigid. Cultivating collaborative labor-management committees or joint problem-solving sessions can foster trust and innovation, benefiting both parties over time.

Union environments revolve around the principle of shared decision-making, with collective bargaining as the cornerstone. By preparing thoroughly, engaging in transparent negotiations, and respecting the contract's terms, employers can maintain constructive labor relationships that serve both business objectives and employee welfare. An atmosphere of mutual respect, even amidst challenging talks, typically results in more stable, cooperative workplaces.

8.4.4 Non-Union Employee Relations Strategies

Organizations without a union presence often have more autonomy in shaping their employee relations frameworks, but they still need methods to engage staff, resolve conflicts fairly, and align the workforce behind common objectives. Approaching these issues proactively—rather than waiting for disputes to arise—can create a supportive environment and lessen the likelihood that employees feel compelled to seek third-party representation. By establishing trust, offering meaningful involvement, and administering consistent policies, HR can maintain productive non-union relationships.

Fostering Open Communication and Trust
In non-union settings, employees may lack formal representation, so clear communication channels become even more vital. Two-way feedback mechanisms encourage staff to raise concerns or suggestions before problems fester:

➢ **Open-Door Policies**: Inviting employees to speak with managers or HR at any time signals a willingness to hear about workplace difficulties or improvement ideas. Although symbolic, a transparent process for escalations can clarify how quickly and thoroughly leadership will respond.

➢ **Employee Forums or Councils**: Even without a union, companies can create committees representing various departments or shifts. These councils meet regularly with management to discuss current challenges—like scheduling or safety—and propose solutions, fostering joint ownership of outcomes.

Respectful and Consistent Conflict Resolution

Without collective bargaining agreements to dictate disciplinary or grievance procedures, employers should still articulate fair, standardized policies. Employees who trust that investigations are impartial and that punishments fit the offense are less likely to perceive favoritism or hidden agendas. Posting such policies, training supervisors on their consistent application, and following up swiftly on complaints sustain transparency.

Proactive Engagement Initiatives

Much like unionized environments, non-union organizations benefit from intentionally boosting morale and connection:

> - **Recognition and Rewards**: Structured recognition programs—whether peer-nominated awards or manager-driven kudos—can bolster engagement, giving employees a shared sense of accomplishment. These initiatives encourage employees to feel invested in team success without requiring formal bargaining.

> - **Development Opportunities**: Offering avenues for career growth—like internal mobility or professional certifications—underscores management's commitment to individual advancement. Employees who see a clear trajectory in the organization often invest more loyalty and effort.

Maintaining Credibility and Deterring Union Interest

In many industries, a high level of employee satisfaction can diminish interest in union formation. While the strategic goal of union avoidance shouldn't overshadow genuine employee well-being, ensuring staff have a voice and feel respected can reduce the impetus for union campaigns:

> ➢ **Competitive Pay and Benefits**: Regular benchmarking of wages, benefits, and flexible work arrangements helps confirm that employees receive market-aligned packages. A sense of economic security typically correlates with lower turnover and less impetus for external representation.

> ➢ **Problem-Solving Culture**: When managers are trained to listen actively, address concerns promptly, and invite staff feedback, employees often view their concerns as solvable internally. This collaborative stance bolsters trust in management's willingness to correct issues.

Addressing Complex Situations or Resistance

Even in a non-union setting, friction can develop if employees feel unheard or policy changes appear arbitrary. Ensuring that any major transformation—like shifting to a new compensation model or reorganizing departments—includes sufficient consultation and explanation is critical. Engaging employees in pilot programs or seeking volunteer participation before rolling out major changes can also help offset resistance.

By focusing on open communication, fair processes, and shared development opportunities, non-union employers can nurture an atmosphere where employees feel valued and confident in resolving workplace concerns internally. This approach not only curbs potential labor unrest but also promotes a more cohesive, innovative, and responsive organizational culture.

8.5 Functional Area 10: Technology Management

8.5.1 HR Information Systems (HRIS) and Data Security

Modern HR relies heavily on digital platforms to manage the full employee lifecycle—from recruitment and onboarding to payroll and performance tracking. A well-chosen Human Resource Information System (HRIS) provides a central repository for storing and analyzing workforce data, streamlining day-to-day processes and enabling data-driven decisions. Yet, with the volume of sensitive personal and financial information these systems hold, safeguarding data has become a paramount concern. Robust security measures and careful access controls are crucial to prevent breaches and ensure compliance with privacy regulations.

Core Functions of an HRIS

A robust HRIS goes beyond basic recordkeeping, offering functionalities like applicant tracking, benefits enrollment, training administration, and real-time analytics. By integrating these activities, organizations gain:

Data Centralization: A single source of truth for employee records, eliminating inconsistencies that arise when data is scattered across multiple spreadsheets or platforms.

Workflow Automation: Self-service portals allow employees to update personal information or submit leave requests, reducing administrative burdens on HR personnel.

Reporting and Analytics: Dashboards track metrics—like turnover, skill gaps, or compliance data—supporting proactive workforce planning.

While this unified approach drives efficiency, it also magnifies potential risks if security practices are lax. One breach in a centralized system can compromise the entire organization's HR data.

Addressing Data Security and Privacy

Protection measures must align with the sensitivity of the information being handled, especially when personal identifiers, salary details, or health-related data are in play:

Encryption and Secure Transmission: Storing data "at rest" with encryption—often using strong ciphers like AES—helps ensure that even if hardware is lost or stolen, the contents remain unreadable. Enforcing encrypted channels (e.g., HTTPS, VPN) when data is in transit between remote users or third-party vendors safeguards it from interception or man-in-the-middle attacks.

Role-Based Access Controls (RBAC): Determining who can view, edit, or delete records rests on each user's defined role. For instance, line managers might see direct reports' performance info but not broader departmental compensation. Such controls minimize the internal risk of unauthorized disclosure, whether accidental or intentional. Auditing features that log user actions further reinforce accountability.

Compliance with Data Protection Laws: Regulations like the GDPR (General Data Protection Regulation) impose strict rules on obtaining consent, handling data transfers, and providing data-subject rights. Non-compliance can lead to steep fines. HR must also consider local privacy statutes, especially if operating globally. Laws vary in terms of data retention periods, allowable data collection, or required breach notifications.

Vulnerabilities and Mitigation

Even advanced HRIS solutions can be exploited if security fundamentals are neglected:

➢ **Phishing and Social Engineering**: Employees with privileged system access may become targets of phishing attempts seeking to steal credentials. Regular security awareness training and multi-factor authentication (MFA) reduce this risk.

➢ **Misconfigured Cloud Services**: Shifting an HRIS to the cloud introduces shared responsibility with the vendor. Companies should confirm that default settings, such as open access or lax firewall rules, are tightened to align with best practices.

➢ **Outdated Software and Plugins**: Regular patches and system updates close known vulnerabilities. Postponing upgrades increases the chance of an attacker leveraging known exploits.

Best Practices for Implementation and Ongoing Management

When introducing a new HRIS or revamping an existing one, a methodical approach to security fosters resilience from the start:

✓ **Vendor Due Diligence**: Investigate a provider's track record, encryption standards, and incident response capabilities. Contracts should specify data ownership rights and clarify how data is returned or deleted if the partnership ends.

✓ **Employee Training and Clear Policies**: Comprehensive user guides help employees understand correct system usage, highlight data confidentiality rules, and remind them of reporting procedures for suspected breaches.

✓ **Disaster Recovery and Backups**: Catastrophic events, whether cyberattacks or natural disasters, can disrupt systems.

Maintaining secure, regularly tested backups ensures quick restoration of HR data.

✓ **Periodic Audits**: Independent security assessments verify that access controls remain relevant, vulnerabilities are patched, and processes still align with evolving regulations.

An HRIS can transform HR operations through unified data, automated workflows, and actionable analytics. However, the same centralized architecture that makes life easier for HR teams can also magnify risk if data security and privacy are not meticulously managed. By incorporating strong encryption, role-based access, regulatory compliance measures, and a culture of continual vigilance, organizations can leverage the full potential of an HRIS while safeguarding their workforce's sensitive information.

8.5.2 Big Data and Analytics in HR

As Human Resources moves from an administrative function to a strategic partner, data-driven insights increasingly shape how talent is sourced, developed, and retained. **Big data** refers to vast volumes of information—ranging from applicant tracking records and performance reviews to social media activity—that, when analyzed effectively, can guide HR decisions with greater precision. These insights help forecast workforce needs, pinpoint skill gaps, and even predict turnover risks. By weaving analytics into everyday processes, HR leaders can spot patterns and trends, making more informed recommendations that impact productivity and employee satisfaction.

Transformative Uses of Data in HR

Predictive Hiring: Analyzing candidate profiles, past hiring outcomes, and performance results can highlight which attributes predict long-term success in specific roles. This approach moves beyond gut feel, allowing recruiters to home in on applicants whose backgrounds align strongly with proven indicators.

Retention and Turnover Prediction: Identifying the factors that drive resignation—like inadequate career growth or compensation misalignment—enables early interventions. Data models might flag employees at higher flight risk, prompting targeted engagement strategies or development opportunities to encourage them to stay.

Employee Engagement Analysis: By correlating survey results, absenteeism records, and project performance data, organizations can uncover hidden morale issues. If a spike in missed deadlines correlates with negative engagement feedback, leadership can intervene before it escalates into burnout or team conflict.

Key Analytical Techniques

- ➤ **Descriptive Analytics**: Summarizes historical HR data (e.g., turnover percentages, average days to fill roles). This sets a baseline for performance comparisons.

- ➤ **Diagnostic Analytics**: Explores why certain trends occur—such as investigating why turnover is consistently higher in one department than another.

- ➤ **Predictive Analytics**: Leverages statistical models or machine learning to forecast future developments. Examples include anticipating which employees might be ready for promotion or which recruiting sources yield the best hires.

- ➤ **Prescriptive Analytics**: Provides recommendations for action, such as suggesting an optimized workforce schedule or pinpointing training initiatives that likely yield the strongest ROI.

Balancing Opportunity with Privacy and Ethics

Although analytics can spark smarter decisions, HR professionals must address privacy, compliance, and fairness. Overly invasive data collection—especially in sensitive areas like biometric tracking or personal social media use—can spark mistrust or even legal repercussions:

➤ **Data Minimization**: Collect only the information needed for legitimate organizational purposes, reducing exposure to privacy breaches or misuse.

➤ **Algorithmic Bias Monitoring**: Models trained on historical data risk perpetuating biases if that data reflects systemic inequities. Regular audits of HR algorithms can catch unintended discrimination in screening or promotion processes.

➤ **Transparent Policies**: Employees should know what data is gathered, how it's used, and who can access it. Clear communication fosters acceptance and trust in data-driven HR strategies.

Implementing HR Analytics Platforms

Adopting robust tools that integrate applicant tracking, learning management, payroll, and performance metrics typically provides a more holistic view of the employee lifecycle. Modern systems may feature:

✓ **Real-Time Dashboards**: Offer instant snapshots of essential indicators—like headcount, absenteeism trends, or compensation benchmarks—allowing HR to spot anomalies quickly.

✓ **Data Visualization**: Graphical interfaces help non-technical stakeholders interpret complex metrics, bridging HR insights to executives or line managers more effectively.

✓ **Integration with External Sources**: For instance, blending labor market data (wage levels, skill availability) can refine workforce planning. If external data suggests a rising demand for a certain skill, internal analytics might show which employees could be reskilled more efficiently than recruiting new talent.

Measuring Success and Evolution

Data efforts in HR should lead to tangible results, whether that's reducing time-to-fill, enhancing diversity in leadership, or cutting turnover among high performers. Tracking these metrics verifies whether analytics initiatives are worth the investment. As business conditions shift, analytics approaches must also adapt— incorporating new datasets, refining predictive models, or tackling emerging ethical questions about data usage.

Big data and analytics offer HR a powerful lens on workforce behaviors and outcomes, enabling predictive and prescriptive insights that were previously out of reach. By pairing advanced tools with careful privacy safeguards and a focus on practical application, organizations can better align people strategies with business goals—and ultimately foster a more engaged, productive workforce.

8.5.3 Leveraging Technology for Recruitment and Onboarding

Digital tools have transformed how HR professionals attract and integrate new talent, streamlining everything from job postings to the first days of employment. By automating repetitive tasks, improving candidate experiences, and fostering consistent onboarding practices, technology not only shortens hiring timelines but also establishes a stronger initial connection with new hires. As remote and hybrid work expand, tech-driven processes become even more essential for engaging candidates regardless of their geographic location.

Elevating the Candidate Experience

Many organizations implement specialized software—like applicant tracking systems (ATS)—to manage résumés and monitor candidates through each hiring phase. Beyond ensuring no application gets lost, advanced features support automated communications to confirm application receipt or deliver feedback, sparing recruiters from manual follow-ups. Some systems integrate with social media or job boards, enabling a wider reach and real-time updates on application flow.

Chatbots and AI-driven assistants can also enhance how candidates interact with the company's career site. Prospects may ask basic questions about role requirements, benefits, or hiring timelines, receiving instant responses that free recruiters' time while keeping potential hires informed and engaged.

Efficient Selection and Screening

Virtual interviewing tools allow recruiters to screen large candidate pools more swiftly. Pre-recorded video interviews, for instance, enable applicants to respond to standardized questions on their own schedule, and recruiters can review these submissions at their convenience. Such asynchronous evaluations cut back on scheduling complexities and let hiring teams focus on high-potential finalists.

When in-person (or live video) interviews are appropriate, integrated scheduling platforms help avoid time conflicts by matching candidate availability with interviewer calendars. Some solutions even provide interview templates, ensuring consistent questions across applicants while centralizing feedback for easy team consensus.

Integrating Onboarding Platforms

Once a candidate accepts an offer, technology ensures the onboarding experience begins immediately rather than waiting until day one. Online portals or mobile apps can guide new hires through digital forms, policy acknowledgments, and benefits enrollment, eliminating tedious paperwork on their first morning. Interactive modules—such as short videos or welcome messages from company leadership—reinforce a sense of belonging before the individual even steps on-site or logs in remotely.

Key Automation and Engagement Features

- ✓ **Electronic Document Management**: Automates the flow of employment contracts, NDAs, and tax forms, reducing error risk and creating an accessible digital record.

- ✓ **Self-Guided Learning Paths**: Combines training modules tailored to specific roles with quizzes or knowledge checks to verify comprehension. This approach personalizes development from the outset and can accelerate time-to-productivity.

- ✓ **Mentor Pairing and Networking Tools**: Some onboarding platforms facilitate connecting new hires with buddies or mentors, expanding their internal support network. Automatic scheduling of "meet-and-greet" sessions fosters early integration.

Ensuring a Smooth Experience for Remote and Hybrid Hires

Virtual onboarding becomes particularly critical when employees begin their roles offsite. Tools like virtual meeting platforms, e-signature applications, and digital collaboration spaces keep them engaged. Companies might stage remote orientations that combine live video introductions, prerecorded culture overviews, and interactive Q&A sessions, maintaining connection and clarity for employees who have never visited the physical workplace.

Balancing Technology with Personal Touch
Despite the convenience and efficiency of automated processes, organizations should preserve meaningful human interaction. For instance, scheduling one-on-one feedback calls or small-group meetings can maintain the social fabric, helping new hires feel genuinely welcomed. The best experiences merge streamlined digital workflows with personal check-ins, giving candidates a sense that the organization values both efficiency and genuine relationships.

By embracing HR technologies—from advanced ATS integrations to sophisticated onboarding portals—organizations can create a seamless journey for candidates and new employees. These innovations free recruiters to concentrate on high-value tasks like relationship-building and nuanced evaluations, while new hires benefit from clarity, timely support, and a head start on connecting with the team.

8.5.4 Remote Work Technology Considerations

Remote and hybrid work models have quickly become a mainstay in many organizations. While they offer flexibility and global talent access, they also demand robust technological infrastructure and policies to keep distributed teams connected, productive, and secure. From selecting the right communication tools to maintaining data protection across varied network environments, HR professionals must collaborate with IT to ensure remote employees can perform effectively without compromising sensitive information.

Enabling Collaboration and Communication
Effective remote operations hinge on more than just email. Video conferencing platforms, project management apps, and real-time

messaging systems help replicate the immediacy of an office setting. However, these tools must align with an organization's workflow and culture to be truly beneficial. Quick chat channels allow for informal brainstorming, while structured virtual meetings keep larger teams aligned on progress. Investing in high-quality audio/video solutions and stable infrastructure can reduce technical glitches, preventing meeting fatigue and maintaining professional standards even at a distance.

Equipping Employees and Supporting Hardware

When staff work offsite, the line between personal and corporate devices can blur. Many companies adopt policies on bring-your-own-device (BYOD), requiring security standards such as up-to-date antivirus software or password protection. Others opt to supply laptops and peripherals configured with organizational security measures, offering consistent user experiences. Regardless of approach, clearly documented guidelines outlining support processes—like who to contact for hardware malfunctions or how to request repairs—minimize downtime and frustration.

Data Security and Confidentiality

Remote workers often rely on home Wi-Fi or public hotspots, increasing exposure to cyber threats. HR's role in defining safe practices, alongside IT, involves:

- ✓ **VPN and Encrypted Connections**: Mandating secure tunnels for accessing internal systems ensures sensitive data remains encrypted, even on unsecured networks.

- ✓ **Access Controls**: Role-based permissions dictate which folders, drives, or applications staff can open. This model mitigates the risk of accidental or malicious data access.

✓ **Regular Training**: Brief, targeted training on recognizing phishing attempts or handling confidential files fosters a security-aware culture. When employees regularly handle private HR records or client data, this vigilance is crucial.

Performance and Work Monitoring

In remote setups, managers may wonder how to gauge productivity without direct line of sight. Tools exist that track keystrokes or screenshots, but relying excessively on such monitoring can undermine trust and morale. Instead, a more balanced approach emphasizes goal-oriented metrics—like project milestones, deliverables, or client feedback—rather than time-based observations. HR can guide leaders toward outcomes-based performance management, building mutual confidence between employees and supervisors.

Troubleshooting and IT Support

Tech disruptions impact remote staff differently than in-office teams, where an IT specialist can drop by. Creating systematic support channels—via helpdesk ticketing systems or phone lines—ensures employees receive timely assistance. Some organizations also establish "IT ambassadors" who possess intermediate troubleshooting knowledge and can lend local help to teams in their region or department, further speeding resolution times.

Future-Proofing Remote Work Tech

With technology evolving rapidly, what works today may be outmoded tomorrow. HR practitioners stay attuned to new tools that enhance virtual onboarding, digital whiteboarding, or asynchronous collaboration. Regular review cycles—assessing employee feedback on the functionality of existing platforms—can spotlight upgrade needs early. Piloting emerging solutions with a small cohort also helps refine adoption strategies before a full rollout.

Remote work thrives on reliable communication platforms, well-managed hardware, and robust security protocols—yet these must be supported by effective HR strategies that focus on building trust, guiding performance, and continuously updating technology. By thoughtfully selecting and maintaining the right tools, organizations can keep distributed teams connected, efficient, and protected no matter where they operate.

Chapter 9: Workplace Domain

9.1 Functional Area 11: Managing a Global Workforce

9.1.1 Working Across Borders: Key Considerations

Organizations that operate across national boundaries encounter an array of complexities—ranging from legal compliance to cultural nuance. A global footprint can enhance market presence and diversify talent pools, yet it also requires HR to reconcile different labor laws, manage language or time zone barriers, and facilitate cohesive team dynamics. By addressing these challenges proactively, companies can capitalize on cross-border collaboration while mitigating risks related to miscommunication or regulatory noncompliance.

Navigating Legal and Regulatory Variations

No two countries share an identical set of employment laws or social norms. Even fundamental concepts—such as at-will employment in the United States versus stringent notice periods or just-cause requirements elsewhere—necessitate careful planning. Before assigning employees abroad or hiring local staff in new markets, HR must research:

➢ **Employment Contracts and Termination Rules**: Some regions mandate written agreements with explicit clauses, while others expect indefinite contracts after probation periods. Failing to meet local standards can trigger hefty penalties.

➢ **Wage and Hour Laws**: Overtime eligibility, minimum wage rates, or mandated rest breaks differ widely. Ensure that payroll systems and scheduling tools handle regional rules without error.

➢ **Immigration and Work Permits**: Seconding employees to foreign locations may require specific visa categories or sponsorship processes. Delays in securing permits can disrupt project timelines.

Cultural Competence and Communication

A globally distributed workforce often features diverse languages, time zones, and workplace norms. Understanding and respecting these differences not only facilitates seamless collaboration but also protects against inadvertent offense or exclusion.

1. **Language and Communication Styles**: Establish a shared corporate language for official documentation (often English), yet remain mindful of local-language adaptations for training or policy materials. Encourage clarity in virtual meetings: Summaries or meeting minutes help non-native speakers confirm their understanding and reduce chances of misinterpretation.

2. **Local Etiquette and Business Customs**: Simple gestures—like greeting styles, punctuality expectations, or gift-giving practices—can vary significantly. A quick briefing on these cultural nuances goes a long way in building rapport and avoiding awkward scenarios. Sensitivity training or cultural onboarding for expatriates and managers helps align team interactions with local norms, fostering inclusive relationships.

Coordination of HR Policies and Benefits

While global employees may share core organizational values, attempts to standardize benefits or performance management can overlook local nuances. Striking a balance between consistency and flexibility ensures fairness without imposing irrelevant policies:

Policy Area	Global Consistency	Local Adaptation
Compensation	Benchmark roles	Adjust for local market

	using global job families	rates, currency, and pay cycles
Performance Reviews	Common competency framework	Culturally relevant feedback styles and goal formats
Benefits Packages	Align major pillars (health, retirement)	Incorporate region-specific perks or statutory provisions

Regular communication among regional HR leads can help identify where uniformity serves strategic goals—and where customization enhances employee satisfaction or compliance.

Supporting Cross-Border Assignments
Global mobility programs that send employees abroad (as expatriates) or into other regions within a multinational company can deepen skill sets and cross-pollinate ideas. However, they demand careful oversight:

✓ **Compensation and Tax Considerations**: Cost-of-living adjustments, tax equalization policies, and housing stipends keep employees financially secure. Omitting these details risks dissatisfaction or tax penalties.

✓ **Cultural and Family Support**: Pre-departure training helps employees and dependents adapt. Language lessons, cultural briefings, or destination services ease relocation stress.

✓ **Reintegration Planning**: Employees returning from overseas bring fresh perspectives. Without proper re-onboarding, the organization risks losing that expertise if they feel underutilized or culturally disoriented in their home office.

Working across borders necessitates an interplay of legal knowledge, cultural finesse, and flexible policy-making. From verifying compliance with local labor laws to shaping inclusive communication practices and managing expatriate life cycles, organizations that invest in robust frameworks and cultural understanding can harness global talent and tap into new markets effectively—turning cross-border operations into a competitive asset rather than a logistical hurdle.

9.1.2 Cultural Competency and Inclusion in Global Teams

When workforces span multiple countries and cultural backgrounds, daily interactions can become a dynamic intersection of perspectives and social norms. While such diversity often fuels innovation and creativity, it also demands intentional strategies to build trust and prevent misunderstandings. **Cultural competency**—the ability to function effectively and respectfully in varied cultural contexts—enables team members to collaborate smoothly across borders. Coupled with deliberate inclusion efforts, it fosters an environment where diverse voices feel valued and integrated into decision-making.

Building Cultural Awareness and Sensitivity

Team members who operate in multinational settings benefit from recognizing how communication styles, hierarchy norms, and conflict resolution approaches differ by culture. Even small gestures—like using the correct form of address or understanding the significance of certain holidays—can influence how respectfully colleagues perceive each other. In global virtual meetings, for instance, showing awareness of time zone constraints or local holidays sends a message of respect. Some organizations encourage short "cultural snapshots," where employees from different regions briefly introduce customs or etiquette, helping colleagues grasp subtle cultural cues.

Techniques for Developing Cross-Cultural Skills

- ✓ **Cross-Cultural Training Sessions**: Structured workshops can go deeper than surface-level tips, guiding participants through scenarios where cultural assumptions might derail collaboration.

- ✓ **Mentoring and Buddy Systems**: Pairing employees from different locations often reveals day-to-day nuances around communication and decision-making, strengthening empathy on both sides.

- ✓ **Self-Reflection Tools**: Individual assessments or quizzes on cultural orientation highlight personal biases and growth areas, prompting employees to adapt how they approach global counterparts.

Promoting Inclusion in Global Teams

Diversity alone does not guarantee inclusive outcomes. Leaders and HR practitioners should create systems that empower every employee—regardless of location or background—to voice ideas and feel part of the collective success.

1. **Equitable Participation**: Synchronous meetings can disadvantage colleagues in distant time zones if scheduled at inconvenient hours. Rotating meeting times or employing asynchronous collaboration (like pre-recorded video updates) ensures no single group perpetually shoulders inconvenience. Collaborative software that captures contributions in real time (or offline)

fosters equal input. This might include shared whiteboards or discussion threads, preventing more vocal or centrally located members from dominating.

2. **Inclusive Decision-Making**: Transparent processes define how decisions are made and whose input is solicited. If remote teams consistently feel bypassed, engagement drops, and creative ideas remain untapped. Encouraging local or site-specific committees to weigh in on regionally relevant topics highlights that the company values local perspectives, not just headquarters-driven mandates.

3. **Adapted Leadership Approaches**: Effective global leaders recognize that employees from some cultures expect direct instructions, while others thrive on autonomy. Cultivating cultural intelligence entails adjusting feedback styles, balancing formality with warmth, and interpreting silence or indirect communication accurately. Demonstrating curiosity—asking open-ended questions about local practices—and responding constructively to new suggestions signals genuine respect for different cultural lenses.

Addressing Bias and Fostering Psychological Safety

Unconscious biases or stereotypes can hamper inclusivity, especially when employees come from varied cultural, ethnic, or linguistic backgrounds. Creating a psychologically safe atmosphere, where people can respectfully challenge or clarify points, involves managers modeling open-mindedness and swiftly addressing microaggressions or dismissive behavior.

Bias/Challenge	Mitigation Strategy
Language Fluency	Encourage multiple communication

Assumptions	modes, offer language support if needed
Stereotyping Based on Region	Provide cultural awareness training, promote first-hand experiences
Power Dynamics in Virtual Spaces	Rotate meeting facilitators, clarify turn-taking protocols

Measuring and Reinforcing Inclusivity

Organizations can evaluate cultural competency through employee surveys, engagement metrics, or 360-degree feedback focusing on cross-cultural collaboration. Feedback loops—such as open forums or focus groups—clarify if certain teams feel sidelined or if staff lack clarity about inclusive behaviors. Senior leaders who reward and recognize exemplary cross-border teamwork reinforce the importance of embracing cultural diversity as a strategic advantage.

Nurturing cultural competency goes beyond awareness sessions; it involves consistent organizational structures, leadership mindsets, and communication norms designed to celebrate and leverage cultural differences. By blending targeted training, inclusive leadership practices, and technology that equalizes collaboration, global teams can unlock creative synergy—turning cultural variety into a genuine competitive edge.

9.1.3 International Assignments (Expatriates, Repatriates)

Global expansion often hinges on moving talent across borders, allowing key employees to transfer expertise, cultivate local teams, or oversee critical projects. Assigning staff to overseas locations— whether on short-term stints or multi-year placements—presents both opportunities for career growth and challenges in cultural adaptation. Upon returning, repatriates also need support to reintegrate and leverage their international insights effectively. By planning thoroughly at each stage—pre-departure, on assignment, and re-entry—organizations maximize the impact of these global transitions.

Crafting Effective Expatriate Assignments
Many expatriates experience a cycle of excitement, culture shock, and eventual adjustment as they settle into a new environment. Providing structured resources helps them navigate these phases smoothly:

➢ **Pre-Assignment Preparation**: This might include language training, cultural briefings, and tax/legal orientation. Clear terms on housing, schooling (for accompanying dependents), and remuneration reassure the expatriate and set realistic expectations.

➢ **Ongoing Support**: Once abroad, expats often benefit from a designated local mentor or HR liaison who can answer questions about day-to-day issues—whether about healthcare, social customs, or workplace practices. Performance expectations should be explicit, helping them balance home-office goals with local operational demands.

➢ **Communication with Home Office**: Regular check-ins maintain alignment and reduce "out of sight, out of mind" risks. Sharing successes and challenges back home keeps the expatriate connected to the parent organization's evolving culture and strategy.

Managing Repatriation
Returning employees—repatriates—face a unique set of challenges, often overlooked. After adapting to a foreign culture, they may

experience reverse culture shock when re-entering their home country, especially if the organization has changed significantly during their absence.

Reintegration Planning: Employers can schedule debrief sessions where repatriates share newly gained knowledge or networks. This approach highlights the assignment's value and helps integrate fresh perspectives into domestic operations. Assigning them a suitable role that recognizes their expanded skill set and global insight reduces disappointment. If they return to a lateral or less influential position, they might question the worth of the entire assignment.

Retention and Career Pathing: Some studies indicate higher turnover rates among repatriates if they see little opportunity to leverage their international experience. Mapping a clear post-return path—including possible leadership or cross-functional roles—can keep them engaged. Leveraging mentorship or internal networking sessions allows them to mentor future expatriates, thus institutionalizing lessons learned and sustaining global knowledge transfer.

Addressing Compensation and Tax Complexities

International assignments often entail cost-of-living allowances, hardship premiums, or tax equalization policies:

➢ **Cost of Living Adjustments**: Companies may provide housing subsidies, educational allowances, or relocation support to maintain the employee's standard of living. Clear, transparent calculators for these allowances minimize confusion.

➢ **Tax Equalization**: Because expatriates may face dual taxation, organizations commonly adopt policies that keep an assignee's overall tax burden similar to what it would be at home. Additional complexities arise if the assignee frequently travels or if multiple jurisdictions lay claim to certain income.

Cultural Integration and Family Considerations
Spouses or children accompanying expatriates can significantly influence assignment success. Providing language resources, access to local communities, or schooling assistance fosters a smoother family transition, reducing stress that might otherwise impede work performance.

Global assignments are a powerful way to distribute expertise, strengthen international relationships, and develop leaders with cross-cultural fluency. Yet, without careful planning—covering pre-departure preparation, on-assignment support, and structured repatriation—expatriates and repatriates alike may struggle to realize the full value of their international experiences. By supporting them holistically, organizations ensure that both the overseas operation and the home office benefit from the knowledge, leadership development, and global perspective gained.

9.2 Functional Area 12: Risk Management

9.2.1 Identifying and Evaluating Workplace Risks

Organizations face a range of potential threats, from physical hazards on production floors to cyber vulnerabilities in corporate offices. Systematically recognizing and assessing these risks not only safeguards employee well-being but also supports productivity, reputation, and regulatory compliance. By using a structured approach to pinpoint where hazards lie, HR and risk management professionals can prioritize mitigation strategies and allocate resources more efficiently.

Building a Proactive Risk Assessment Framework

A well-rounded process for identifying and evaluating risks typically begins with mapping out how work is done—who performs which tasks, under what conditions, and using which tools. Gaining this clarity helps isolate areas where the chance of injury, data breaches, or other incidents is higher. HR teams often collaborate with operations, security, and line managers to gather input on day-to-day vulnerabilities.

Hazard Inventories

Physical Hazards: Might include slipping or tripping obstacles, faulty machinery, or exposure to harmful substances. Even office roles can encounter repetitive strain or ergonomic problems if workstations are poorly set up.

Environmental and Health Risks: Poor ventilation, extreme temperatures, or biological hazards (in healthcare or food processing) require specific controls and regular monitoring.

Security Threats: Risks such as unauthorized access to facilities, theft of sensitive documents, or potential workplace violence can disrupt operations and endanger staff.

Data Collection Methods

Observations and Walkthroughs: A direct look at worksites, watchful for housekeeping issues, equipment misuse, or employee workarounds that bypass safety features.

Surveys and Focus Groups: Employees often know best where hazards exist. Encouraging staff to share concerns or near-miss incidents can uncover hidden weaknesses.

Historical Records: Past incident reports, claims data, and absenteeism statistics reveal patterns—like recurring shoulder injuries in a certain department or repeated security breaches during off-hours.

Applying Risk Assessment Tools
Once potential hazards surface, organizations need a consistent framework for evaluating how severe each one might be. A common approach blends **likelihood** (probability that a hazard event will occur) with **impact** (scale of potential harm, such as injury severity or financial cost).

➤ **Risk Matrices**: Use color-coded grids to rank hazards from low to high priority. A risk that is moderately likely but could cause severe harm might prompt immediate remedial action.

➤ **Job Hazard Analysis (JHA)**: Breaks down each task step-by-step, pinpointing possible dangers at each phase. This detail helps in designing more specific controls or training content.

Risk Factor	Example	Possible Impact
Likelihood	Frequency of forklift collisions in a cramped warehouse	Probability of monthly or quarterly incidents
Severity	Extent of injury or downtime if collisions happen	Range from minor damage to major injury

Key Considerations in Evaluation

✓ **Regulatory Requirements**: Certain sectors must comply with Occupational Safety and Health Administration (OSHA) guidelines or equivalent authorities. Non-compliance can lead to fines or legal repercussions.

✓ **Varying Work Environments**: Remote or field-based employees might face unique risks—like data security gaps for telecommuters or weather hazards for traveling technicians.

✓ **Psychosocial Factors**: Stress, bullying, or fatigue can exacerbate accident risks. Evaluations should consider intangible elements that affect morale and attention.

Turning Insights into Action

After identifying risks and gauging severity, organizations generally devise control measures—ranging from engineering changes (e.g., installing machine guards) to administrative policies (rotating tasks to reduce strain). HR plays a vital role in:

1. **Developing Training Programs**: Focusing on safe work procedures, emergency responses, or cybersecurity best practices, depending on identified vulnerabilities.

2. **Integrating Controls into Policies**: Writing or updating SOPs (Standard Operating Procedures) that directly address each key risk, ensuring employees know the correct steps to avoid hazards.

3. **Enforcing Accountability**: When metrics reveal persistent shortfalls (like repeated near-miss incidents in a specific area), managers and supervisors must revisit daily routines, equipment, or staff competencies. Transparent accountability fosters consistent, proactive improvement.

Systematically detecting and evaluating workplace risks forms the cornerstone of an effective risk management strategy. Through thorough hazard inventories, structured analysis tools, and a data-driven approach to prioritizing interventions, organizations can guard against accidents and disruptions—fostering a safer, more resilient work environment for all employees.

9.2.2 Safety, Security, and Emergency Preparedness Plans

Organizations face an array of potential emergencies—ranging from natural disasters and security breaches to fires or pandemics. Proper planning minimizes harm to employees, protects physical and digital assets, and preserves the continuity of operations. HR plays a pivotal role here, often collaborating with facilities, security, and IT departments to implement comprehensive measures. By developing clear protocols and regularly training staff, companies can respond to crises swiftly and methodically, reducing confusion and panic when minutes truly matter.

Building a Risk-Aware Culture
Safety and security begin with an organizational mindset. When employees understand that management prioritizes their well-being—and consistently communicate potential risks—they are more likely to follow protocols. Detailed signage (e.g., evacuation routes, hazard warnings) and frequent reminders (through newsletters or digital bulletins) keep awareness levels high. Encouraging employees to report hazards or suspicious activity without fear of reprisal can further strengthen safety and security vigilance.

Key Components of a Preparedness Plan
Many companies structure their plans to address different scenarios

separately, but certain foundational elements appear across all types of emergencies:

> **Evacuation and Shelter-in-Place Procedures**: Clear instructions guide employees on where to assemble outside or how to find safe interior zones when leaving the building is unsafe (e.g., severe weather or a chemical spill).

> **Communication Protocols**: Rapid alert systems—such as mass text messages or public announcement tools—update everyone on the nature of the emergency and next steps. Backup communication channels prove essential if primary systems fail.

> **Roles and Responsibilities**: Assigned crisis team members, from floor wardens to first-aid leads, know exactly what to do, lessening the chaos. HR often maintains updated contact lists and ensures critical documents (employee rosters, emergency contact data) remain accessible.

Coordinating Safety and Security

While emergencies can be unpredictable, organizations can reduce vulnerability through physical security measures and ongoing vigilance:

1. **Access Controls:** Restricting building entry via ID badges or biometric authentication deters unauthorized individuals. Visitor logs and escorted visits add extra layers of oversight.

2. **Surveillance and Monitoring:** Cameras, motion detectors, or alarm systems offer real-time alerts if unusual activities occur. However, privacy considerations should guide where and how surveillance is employed.

3. **Cyber-Physical Integration:** As physical systems increasingly connect to digital platforms (smart locks, IoT sensors), organizations must protect these interfaces from hacking or tampering. HR ensures employees understand secure usage of any integrated devices, reducing accidental vulnerabilities.

Regular Drills and Training

Even the most thorough emergency plan can falter if employees are unsure how to act under pressure. Scheduled drills—whether fire evacuations or lockdown scenarios—familiarize staff with procedures and highlight operational gaps:

✓ **Varied Scenarios**: In some cases, focusing on less typical emergencies (like active assailant incidents or chemical leaks) underscores the need to treat each threat seriously.

✓ **Post-Drill Debriefs**: Gathering feedback reveals confusion points or logistical hiccups. Updating procedures soon after these reviews helps maintain readiness.

✓ **Leadership Modeling**: If managers demonstrate calm compliance during exercises, employees are likelier to do the same when real incidents occur.

Ensuring Business Continuity

Safety and security efforts link closely with broader continuity plans. Even a well-executed evacuation might lead to prolonged downtime if systems are damaged or crucial records are inaccessible:

✓ **Redundant Systems**: Off-site data backups, alternate worksites, or cloud-based platforms allow core functions to persist if a main facility is compromised.

✓ **Vendor and Supply Chain Planning**: Identifying secondary suppliers can soften the blow if primary partners face their own disaster.

✓ **Return-to-Work Protocols**: Once conditions stabilize, clear instructions guide staff on re-entering the site, checking equipment, and resuming normal operations. HR and facilities teams coordinate to ensure both safety and an orderly ramp-up.

Effective safety, security, and emergency preparedness plans go beyond written protocols. They rely on regular training, open communication, and continuous refinement based on drills and potential new threats. By uniting employees under clear guidelines, ensuring robust physical and technological safeguards, and mapping out recovery strategies, organizations protect both their people and their ongoing viability in the face of crisis.

9.2.3 Business Continuity and Disaster Recovery

Maintaining day-to-day operations during a crisis and returning to normal as quickly as possible after disruptive events are significant challenges for organizations. Business continuity and disaster recovery efforts combine strategic foresight with a deep commitment to safeguarding people, assets, and brand reputation. Together, these plans ensure that disruptions—whether natural disasters, cyber incidents, or other emergencies—do not bring organizational processes to a prolonged standstill.

A key first step involves assessing which functions are truly essential. By mapping out dependencies—such as key suppliers, major software systems, or critical departments—management can determine which areas require the fastest restoration. This prioritization helps focus resources on the most vital processes when time and capacities are limited. In many organizations, certain customer-facing tasks or production lines represent critical revenue streams, so ensuring their rapid recovery reduces losses and preserves stakeholder confidence.

While **business continuity** typically focuses on keeping critical operations active despite difficulties, **disaster recovery** zeroes in on the technical and infrastructural aspects of bringing systems back online. In practice, the two go hand in hand. For instance, a thorough continuity plan might specify how employees can access remote worksites or alternative IT networks if a primary facility is compromised. Disaster recovery, meanwhile, handles the detailed steps for restoring damaged servers, retrieving backups, or reconfiguring secure connections so employees can continue their tasks with minimal disruption.

Having robust backup solutions is essential. Storing data in offsite or cloud environments can expedite recovery if local servers are struck by flood, fire, or hardware failure. Equally important is verifying that these backups function correctly through periodic tests—many an organization has discovered too late that untested backups were corrupted or incomplete. Likewise, ensuring that software patches, firewall rules, and virus definitions remain current helps keep the entire network resilient against cyberthreats that might trigger a forced shutdown or lock employees out of core systems.

People management also plays a critical role. When an event occurs—such as a severe weather warning or active threat—rapid communication channels allow HR and leadership to broadcast instructions. Employees should know where to find status updates, how to handle their workloads, and whether to stay home or shift to an alternative location. Practical guidance on safeguarding personal safety or preserving crucial documents reduces confusion. After immediate dangers pass, protocols typically outline how staff transition back, including any mental health support or flexible arrangements that aid them in re-establishing routines.

Even the best plans can become outdated as an organization evolves. Mergers, expansions, and new product lines alter what is deemed "mission-critical," so a living document approach—where continuity and recovery plans undergo scheduled reviews and simulations— helps maintain accuracy. Simulated drills, such as surprise power outage exercises or cybersecurity breach run-throughs, let teams rehearse their roles. These exercises highlight overlooked vulnerabilities, spark fresh ideas for improvement, and bolster team confidence in navigating real crises.

Below is a brief illustration of how business continuity and disaster recovery can work together during a severe event:

Phase	Continuity Actions	Disaster Recovery Focus
Incident Occurs	Invoke work-from-home protocols if the site is unsafe	Protect servers from ongoing damage, isolate impacted systems
During Disruption	Keep core functions operational via backup processes	Assess data loss, begin restoration from verified backups
Post-Incident	Guide staff on returning to normal schedules	Validate restored systems and confirm data integrity

However, planning isn't enough without continuous improvement. Gathering feedback after each drill or actual incident fosters an adaptive mindset, enabling leaders to refine both processes and technology solutions. Over time, these refinements bolster organizational resilience, ensuring a temporary setback does not spiral into a full-blown catastrophe.

In the end, successful continuity and recovery hinge on realistic expectations, well-practiced procedures, and a clear sense of priority. By regularly updating plans, involving employees in drills, and leveraging robust data security measures, organizations create a safer environment in which unforeseen disruptions become manageable—rather than crippling—events.

9.3 Functional Area 13: Corporate Social Responsibility (CSR)

9.3.1 Environmental, Social, and Governance (ESG) Practices

Amid growing scrutiny from investors, customers, and employees, organizations increasingly adopt **ESG** frameworks to guide sustainable, ethical operations. Environmental, Social, and Governance considerations move beyond traditional philanthropy or basic compliance; they infuse decision-making with a focus on long-term impact and accountability. Companies committed to ESG principles often find it easier to win customer loyalty, attract talent, and maintain investor confidence—while also mitigating risks tied to resource depletion or reputational damage.

Defining ESG Pillars

Although each enterprise tailors its ESG strategy to its unique context, the pillars remain consistent:

1. **Environmental**
   Organizations evaluate how their activities affect ecological well-being. Whether by reducing carbon footprints, minimizing waste, or safeguarding biodiversity, these

initiatives aim to preserve natural resources for future generations. Manufacturing firms might invest in cleaner production methods or adopt renewable energy sources, while service-based enterprises might emphasize paperless policies or energy-efficient office layouts.

2. **Social**

   This component addresses how companies manage relationships with employees, suppliers, customers, and local communities. Efforts can range from promoting diversity and inclusion (D&I) in hiring and leadership pipelines, to ensuring fair labor standards in global supply chains. Some organizations deepen community ties by actively engaging in local education programs or supporting volunteer opportunities. Effective social practices help build trust and cultivate a positive brand identity—both locally and internationally.

3. **Governance**

   Under governance, the spotlight falls on an organization's leadership structure, ethical guidelines, and risk controls. Transparent boards of directors, anti-corruption policies, and ethical codes of conduct collectively reinforce accountability. Governance also shapes how companies manage crises, data privacy, and executive compensation, affirming their commitment to responsible oversight.

Integrating ESG into Business Strategy

Rather than treating ESG as an external add-on, many companies embed these values into core processes. For instance, procurement teams might establish supplier criteria that mandate environmental certifications or fair labor conditions. Meanwhile, HR can implement robust D&I policies, track their progress through metrics, and ensure leadership development programs embody inclusivity. By weaving ESG standards into budgeting and planning cycles, organizations create a consistent, values-driven approach that resonates across all departments.

Measuring and Reporting ESG Impact

Stakeholders often demand tangible proof of ESG performance. As a result, companies may adopt frameworks like the Global Reporting Initiative (GRI) or the Sustainability Accounting Standards Board (SASB) standards. Detailed ESG reports typically include:

- ✓ **Environmental Indicators**: Metrics around emissions, energy usage, water consumption, or waste management.

- ✓ **Social Benchmarks**: Data on workforce demographics, labor practices, community investments, or product safety records.

- ✓ **Governance Metrics**: Information on board composition, shareholder rights, or executive compensation structures.

These disclosures not only assure transparency but guide internal improvements. If carbon emissions fail to meet reduction targets, for instance, leadership can revisit operations and technologies to find more sustainable solutions.

Linking ESG to Employee Engagement

Aligning organizational values with ESG commitments often appeals to staff who prioritize purpose in their careers. Encouraging involvement in green initiatives, socially beneficial projects, or ethical oversight committees helps employees see how their roles contribute to broader societal goals. Some organizations connect performance evaluations or bonuses to ESG objectives, reinforcing the message that sustainability and responsible governance count as core responsibilities.

Such alignment can make a difference in attracting and retaining talent, particularly among younger professionals who weigh an employer's social and environmental track record alongside compensation. Moreover, employees who feel proud of their company's ethical stance tend to demonstrate higher engagement, collaboration, and loyalty.

Overcoming Implementation Hurdles

Embedding ESG values may involve overhauling supply chains, revamping corporate policies, or investing in more sustainable technologies. Resistance sometimes emerges if these changes affect short-term profitability, require capital expenditure, or alter long-standing processes. However, open communication about the long-term value—reduced risk of regulatory fines, enhanced brand reputation, and possible cost savings from efficient resource use—helps secure buy-in from stakeholders.

Additionally, maintaining momentum requires senior leadership commitment. When executive leaders champion ESG goals, from energy reduction to community programs, they set a tone of authenticity ·rather than lip service. Establishing cross-functional committees or designating an ESG officer can also keep these priorities front and center, ensuring efforts do not become siloed in a single department.

ESG practices serve as a roadmap for businesses striving to be responsible global citizens while sustaining financial health. By attentively managing environmental footprints, fostering social integrity, and upholding rigorous governance standards, companies not only avoid reputational pitfalls but also build stronger bonds with investors, consumers, and employees alike. As ESG becomes a benchmark of corporate maturity, organizations that actively integrate these principles are better positioned for long-term resilience and relevance.

9.3.2 Developing CSR Strategies

Crafting a Corporate Social Responsibility (CSR) strategy involves translating broad principles—like ethics, sustainability, and community stewardship—into actionable plans that align with organizational aims. Unlike standalone charitable activities, a well-structured CSR strategy links to the company's brand identity, employee engagement, and even long-term financial success. By matching community needs with internal capabilities, businesses create meaningful initiatives that resonate with stakeholders and maintain momentum over time.

Linking CSR to Core Business Objectives

The most impactful CSR initiatives complement organizational goals, rather than operate as side projects. If a technology firm prides itself on innovation, for instance, it might sponsor STEM education programs or donate refurbished devices to underserved schools. Likewise, companies with strong logistics expertise could help streamline relief supply chains in disaster-prone areas. By leveraging in-house strengths, a CSR effort not only provides external benefits but also reinforces the company's value proposition, motivating employees who see how their everyday work can extend to broader societal contributions.

Engaging Stakeholders Early

When planning CSR, companies should consult a range of stakeholders—customers, employees, community representatives, and possibly local government officials. Gaining diverse input can reveal pressing social or environmental issues that might not be obvious from a boardroom perspective. Where feasible, forming a cross-functional CSR advisory group fosters shared ownership of projects and encourages each department to identify potential synergy with philanthropic or environmental goals. Involving frontline employees ensures the programs match local realities and feel authentic, rather than top-down mandates.

Defining Clear Targets and Scope

A common pitfall is adopting lofty ambitions without specifying measurable outcomes. Effective CSR strategies break down overarching aims—like reducing carbon emissions or improving local education—into concrete, time-bound goals. For example, committing to cut energy usage by 20% over three years sets a clear benchmark. Similarly, establishing the scope (e.g., focusing on three key regions or one primary cause area) helps avoid fragmenting resources. Concentrated efforts can demonstrate deeper impact and create case studies that showcase the program's success.

Implementation and Resource Allocation

Once objectives are in place, the next challenge is to integrate CSR into daily operations. Some organizations form dedicated CSR teams or assign designated hours for employees to volunteer. Others weave volunteer or sustainability targets into performance metrics, ensuring accountability. Funding models vary—some rely on a percentage of annual profits for philanthropic budgets, while others generate micro-donations via product sales or matching employee contributions. Regardless of the approach, transparent communication about how funds and labor are allocated builds trust among participants and external observers.

Measurement and Communication

Demonstrating progress and impact underpins a CSR strategy's credibility. Qualitative stories—like student feedback on an after-school coding program—add emotional resonance, while quantitative metrics, such as pounds of recycled materials or scholarship recipients, present tangible results. Public-facing CSR reports or webpages highlight these data points, allowing stakeholders to see both the initiative's aspirations and its real-world outcomes. Internally, employees appreciate seeing how their involvement drives community or environmental benefit, boosting engagement and retention.

Sustaining and Evolving the Strategy

As community needs shift or the company's own capacities evolve, CSR strategies require periodic reviews. Regular check-ins—where project leads share updates and recommend course corrections—keep efforts relevant and adaptive. If an initiative fails to meet benchmarks or community interest wanes, organizations can learn from these experiences, pivot resources to more effective endeavors, or invite fresh ideas from staff. This cyclical improvement process ensures CSR remains a living, responsive part of organizational culture rather than a static box on an annual report.

An impactful CSR strategy is deeply woven into the organization's fabric, reflecting both its unique expertise and the pressing needs of the communities it serves. By setting clear goals, involving stakeholders from the start, allocating appropriate resources, and rigorously measuring outcomes, companies create CSR programs that not only foster goodwill but also reinforce strategic priorities. Over time, these purposeful efforts can help build resilient communities, strengthen employee morale, and uphold the organization's commitment to responsible, sustainable growth.

9.3.3 Philanthropy, Community Outreach, and Volunteering

Many organizations move beyond internal operations to make a positive impact on the communities they serve. By investing in local or global causes, inviting employees to volunteer, or forming partnerships with nonprofit groups, businesses not only do good but also inspire higher engagement and pride within their workforce. A well-planned philanthropic strategy typically arises from a genuine alignment with company values—helping the organization build lasting relationships and credibility in the public sphere.

Defining Philanthropic Focus Areas

Rather than scatter resources across myriad causes, many companies concentrate on one or two domains that resonate with their mission or industry expertise. For instance, a software firm might focus on STEM education or digital literacy, whereas a consumer goods manufacturer might back environmental cleanups or recycling programs. Selecting a focal theme helps ensure consistent messaging, fosters deeper impact, and sustains employee enthusiasm, as staff can see progress in a defined area over time.

Encouraging Employee Involvement

Philanthropy gains momentum when employees actively participate:

➢ **Volunteer Days or Paid Time Off (PTO)**: Allowing staff to take dedicated hours or days to support nonprofits fosters a spirit of service while acknowledging the demands of busy schedules. Employees often appreciate the endorsement of their personal passions, feeling that the organization values both community and work-life balance.

➢ **Company-Matching Programs**: When employees donate to qualified charities, some employers match those contributions dollar-for-dollar. This model amplifies philanthropic impact, giving employees a direct sense that their choices matter and doubling the overall donation to selected causes.

> **Group Activities**: Team-based volunteering—like building homes, organizing fundraising events, or mentoring youth—can double as a bonding experience. Such efforts break down departmental silos and create shared memories that enrich workplace culture.

Community Partnerships

Connecting with established community organizations can elevate a company's outreach:

> **Long-Term Collaborations**
> A sustained relationship with a local school district, for example, might see employees tutoring students each semester or assisting in after-school programs. This ongoing engagement allows deeper trust-building and measurable progress.

> **Co-Branding Opportunities**
> Joint public events—like charity runs or awareness campaigns—blend the brand's visibility with a community cause. In these instances, marketing departments can spotlight philanthropic commitments in a way that also aligns with corporate social responsibility (CSR) messaging.

Tracking and Communicating Impact

While philanthropic and volunteer initiatives aim at altruism, businesses still benefit from gauging their effectiveness. Some use formal metrics—like the number of volunteer hours, dollars raised, or program participants served. Others collect stories or personal testimonials showing how donated funds or volunteer efforts have changed lives. Sharing these outcomes internally helps maintain employee motivation, while external stakeholders (customers, investors) often appreciate transparent updates on community projects.

Avoiding Pitfalls and Ensuring Authenticity

Employees and the public can sometimes spot superficial or purely PR-driven efforts. Balancing visibility with substance is crucial. If a company sponsors a local event, ensuring actual staff presence or in-kind support (like providing expertise or resources) adds authenticity. Additionally, being mindful of cultural and regional differences, especially in multinational contexts, prevents well-intentioned initiatives from overlooking local realities.

Philanthropy, community outreach, and volunteering reveal an organization's commitment to more than profit margins. By choosing focus areas aligned with corporate capabilities, facilitating broad employee participation, and measuring impact, companies create sustained relationships that benefit society, shape a reputation for integrity, and galvanize employees who appreciate working for a values-driven employer.

9.4 Functional Area 14: U.S. Employment Laws & Regulations

9.4.1 Ongoing Compliance and Maintenance

Staying compliant with U.S. employment laws requires more than a one-time review of regulations. Even after policies and processes are developed, organizations must continually monitor changes in federal, state, and local rules, ensuring that day-to-day practices remain valid and up to date. This focus on continuous improvement helps avoid legal pitfalls, fosters trust among employees, and keeps internal policies aligned with evolving business realities.

A core strategy often involves periodic self-audits or internal reviews to confirm that documented procedures—such as hiring checklists or overtime calculations—are being followed correctly. These reviews might uncover minor deviations, like outdated forms or inconsistent application of overtime exemptions, that can be addressed before they escalate into compliance violations. In some cases, using a standardized audit framework or external consulting support can provide a fresh perspective, flagging issues an internal team might overlook.

Legal updates also demand vigilance. New rulings or changes in wage-and-hour, leave, or anti-discrimination legislation can appear with limited notice, especially at state or municipal levels. Tracking these developments typically involves assigning someone—often within HR or legal counsel—to monitor news alerts, subscription services, or government agency bulletins. Once relevant changes surface, a transparent communication plan ensures both leadership and affected employees understand upcoming adjustments, whether that's a revised sick leave policy or an updated salary threshold for overtime eligibility.

Employee training further reinforces compliant behavior. Front-line managers, in particular, need clarity on how to implement updated regulations—for instance, clarifying which roles qualify for specific accommodations or how to handle requests for paid family leave. Conducting brief refreshers as laws shift keeps everyone aware of rights and responsibilities. Even employees who don't handle managerial tasks benefit from knowing how changes affect them— such as added protections or new leave entitlements—reducing confusion or misapplication of rules.

Documentation and record retention practices also play a vital part in maintaining compliance. Employment records, ranging from I-9 forms to disciplinary notes, must be retained according to statutory timelines. Regularly purging expired files prevents data overload while cutting the risk of exposing sensitive information beyond what's legally required. At the same time, ensuring that active records remain accessible and well-organized provides a clear audit trail if agencies like the Department of Labor or the Equal Employment Opportunity Commission request evidence during routine checks or investigations.

By weaving compliance maintenance into routine operations— through audits, timely legal updates, ongoing training, and diligent recordkeeping—organizations can uphold both the letter and spirit of U.S. employment laws. This steady approach helps avert penalties, protects employee rights, and sustains the organization's reputation for fair, ethical practices over the long haul.

9.4.2 Recordkeeping Strategies

Maintaining accurate and secure employment records is an integral part of U.S. employment law compliance. From job applications to payroll documentation, HR must manage a wide array of files—each governed by specific retention periods and accessibility requirements. Beyond meeting statutory obligations, robust recordkeeping practices help preserve organizational memory, facilitate prompt responses to employee inquiries or legal requests, and reduce confusion when policies or leadership change.

Identifying Essential Documents

A first step in effective recordkeeping is determining which files are truly necessary. While some records—like I-9 forms or wage and hour logs—are explicitly mandated, others (such as documentation of training or performance notes) might be maintained for practical, rather than purely legal, reasons. Conducting a thorough inventory of all HR-related documents clarifies where duplicates exist and highlights which information is most critical. This mapping exercise also aligns with broader data privacy considerations, ensuring unnecessary details are not stored indefinitely.

Establishing Clear Retention Schedules
Different laws stipulate how long an employer must keep certain records. For example, the Fair Labor Standards Act (FLSA) may require three years for payroll data, while Equal Employment Opportunity Commission (EEOC) guidance might suggest a separate retention window for hiring-related documents. Creating a retention schedule—often in a spreadsheet or policy handbook—defines each record category (e.g., job applications, time sheets) alongside the exact duration to store them. Linking these schedules to relevant statutes avoids guesswork and ensures consistency across all HR staff.

Secure Storage and Organization
With the volume and sensitivity of HR data, choosing the right storage method is key. Organizations blend physical archives (for older paper-based records) with digital platforms. In a digital environment, a well-structured folder hierarchy or an HR information system (HRIS) that tags documents by type and date can greatly simplify retrieval. While advanced search tools aid efficiency, a consistent naming convention often prevents confusion. Regarding security, role-based access control ensures only authorized individuals can view or modify certain files, protecting personal employee information from internal and external misuse.

Periodic Audits and Disposal
Simply collecting documents is not enough. Scheduled reviews—perhaps annually—verify if some records have reached their retention limits. Timely destruction of outdated files reduces exposure to data breaches or legal discovery requests, because extraneous information can inadvertently complicate legal proceedings. When disposing of records, especially those containing personal identifiers or financial details, using secure shredding or data wiping methods is crucial to maintain confidentiality. A disposal

log can document that items were discarded properly, safeguarding the organization if questions later arise.

Handling Digital and Hybrid Environments

In hybrid workplaces, employees may upload documents from multiple locations, sometimes bypassing standard procedures. To avoid scattering critical records across personal drives or unapproved cloud services, HR needs formal guidelines on where documents are to be stored and how backups are managed. For any external storage providers or collaborative tools, contracts should clarify data ownership, security measures, and retrieval processes if the vendor relationship ends.

Solid recordkeeping strategies balance meticulous retention with thoughtful disposal, underscored by clear schedules and robust security. By defining essential documents, tracking retention deadlines, and instilling structured storage protocols, HR departments stay on top of regulatory demands while supporting a transparent, efficient approach to managing sensitive employee data. This diligence not only averts compliance pitfalls but also upholds trust with employees and other stakeholders who rely on the accuracy and confidentiality of their personal information.

9.4.3 Handling Audits and Investigations

Federal and state agencies periodically investigate whether organizations are adhering to labor laws, tax regulations, or safety standards. These reviews can arise from routine scheduling, employee complaints, or random selection. Being prepared for potential audits or inquiries—such as those from the Department of Labor (DOL), Equal Employment Opportunity Commission (EEOC), or Occupational Safety and Health Administration (OSHA)—minimizes disruption and demonstrates good-faith compliance. Beyond government authorities, internal investigations may also occur in response to allegations of discrimination or misconduct. Regardless of the catalyst, a careful, well-structured approach ensures fairness, reduces liability, and bolsters the organization's credibility.

Establishing Clear Response Protocols
When an audit notice arrives—whether by letter or an unannounced visit—HR should know exactly which steps to follow. Typically, designated point persons coordinate the collection of requested documents, arrange interview schedules, and liaise with internal or external legal counsel if needed. Defining this chain of command in advance prevents last-minute confusion, especially if the inquiry is urgent or unexpectedly broad in scope.

> ➢ **Document Gathering**: Agencies may request payroll records, hiring forms, benefits data, or internal communications. Having a centralized repository or well-maintained HR information system (HRIS) smooths the retrieval process.

> ➢ **Legal Consultation**: Even a friendly audit can quickly shift if compliance gaps emerge, so clarifying the scope of the inquiry with legal advisors helps HR remain transparent without disclosing superfluous information.

Ensuring Consistent and Accurate Information
During official interviews or document handovers, consistent narratives matter. Discrepancies between statements or incomplete files can raise red flags:

1. **Prepared Spokespersons**: Whether it's an HR manager or in-house counsel, those who speak on behalf of the organization should have a solid grasp of relevant policies. They can confirm the timeline for providing any missing records or clarifying ambiguous points.

2. **Policy Familiarity**: If an audit centers on wage and hour matters, for instance, managers who oversee time tracking or scheduling must be fully conversant with the system's operation and the rationale behind any anomalies.

3. **Integrity in Data Presentation**: Attempts to mask or alter documents can severely damage the organization's standing, compounding legal troubles. Submitting accurate records and clarifying any discovered mistakes often yields better outcomes than trying to conceal errors.

Internal Investigations for Complaints or Allegations

Not all investigations come from outside regulators; some involve handling employee complaints about discrimination, harassment, or policy violations. While these may not carry external deadlines, the organization still has a duty to examine facts impartially and conclude matters in a timely manner:

- ✓ **Confidentiality and Neutrality**: Assigning an investigator who isn't directly linked to the parties involved reduces bias. Communicating the importance of confidentiality to witnesses also preserves trust.

- ✓ **Thorough Documentation**: Capturing each interview's key points, relevant evidence, and final resolutions forms a clear record if the matter escalates to legal dispute. Equally important, it shows employees that leadership takes concerns seriously.

- ✓ **Follow-Up and Remediation**: Should wrongdoing be uncovered, swift corrective action—ranging from disciplinary measures to policy revisions—demonstrates accountability. Communicating broad lessons learned to the workforce can reinforce a culture that prioritizes respect and fairness.

Managing Aftermath and Continuous Improvement

Once an audit or investigation concludes, the organization may receive findings or directives for corrective action. Some steps might be straightforward—like updating certain forms to reflect new compliance rules—while others, such as recalculating back wages or modifying major policies, can be more involved. In the case of internal probes, ensuring that promised changes (perhaps around team dynamics or manager conduct) are implemented and tracked fosters confidence in the company's processes.

Over time, analyzing patterns from previous audits or internal investigations can guide HR in reinforcing training, refining policy language, or adopting better recordkeeping systems. Early detection and remediation of minor inconsistencies often preempt more severe challenges. Regular self-audits and open communication about compliance expectations build a workforce that collaborates toward sustaining lawful, ethical operations—reducing the likelihood of future disputes or external probes.

Audits and investigations—whether government-led or internally driven—need not disrupt the organization if HR has a clear plan, accessible records, and collaboration with legal counsel. By responding promptly, maintaining transparency, and learning from the results, companies not only address immediate compliance needs but also reinforce a culture of integrity and continuous improvement.

Chapter 10: Strategy Domain

10.1 Strategic Planning Fundamentals

10.1.1 Environmental Scanning (SWOT, PEST)

Strategic planning often begins with a thorough understanding of the context in which an organization operates. **Environmental scanning** provides the foundation for developing and refining these strategies, helping leaders discern internal capacities as well as external threats or opportunities. Two widely recognized tools—**SWOT** (Strengths, Weaknesses, Opportunities, Threats) and **PEST** (Political, Economic, Social, Technological)—guide this process by systematically structuring observations and prompting data-driven discussions. Through these analyses, HR and executive teams can shape more adaptable plans and anticipate shifts that may require rapid response.

The Role of Environmental Scanning in Strategic Planning
When organizations face volatile markets, changing labor forces, or emerging technologies, ad hoc reactions can fall short. Environmental scanning ensures a proactive stance, allowing leadership to incorporate both broad macro factors and specific organizational nuances. HR departments in particular rely on these insights to forecast talent requirements, design robust policies, and advise leadership on workforce implications of new business directions. By weaving environmental insights into everyday decision-making, companies reduce the risk of blind spots that could undermine their longer-term objectives.

SWOT Analysis: Balancing Internal and External Factors
A classic SWOT framework requires teams to look inward to identify strengths and weaknesses, then outward to outline potential opportunities and threats. In many cases, **SWOT** sessions become collaborative workshops, gathering perspectives from different

functions—such as HR, finance, operations, and marketing—to build a comprehensive picture of the organization's current posture.

Strengths: An organization's internal capabilities or resources that give it a competitive edge. This might include a strong employer brand, a track record of innovation, or a highly skilled workforce. Recognizing these strengths helps leaders leverage them strategically—like doubling down on effective recruitment channels or investing further in specialized training programs that yield strong results.

Weaknesses: Areas needing improvement or inherent limitations. Outdated technology, high turnover in specific units, or gaps in leadership development could fit here. Identifying these weaknesses leads to targeted improvement efforts that can significantly raise performance.

Opportunities: External trends or conditions that the company can capitalize on—perhaps a growing interest in remote solutions or an emerging market for one of its product lines. For HR, this might translate into recruiting specialized talent that competitors have yet to pursue, or building new partnerships in communities where strong brand affiliations exist.

Threats: External hazards that could impede progress, such as regulatory changes that might limit expansion or new competitors entering the market with fresh offerings. HR might examine how changing labor regulations or shifts in workforce demographics pose potential threats if not managed proactively.

A well-executed SWOT session culminates in actionable priorities. For example, if a company's recognized strength is "highly engaged employees" and an opportunity is "rapidly expanding e-commerce markets," it might launch a strategic initiative to upskill its workforce for digital transformation. Conversely, if turnover is a key weakness and an economic downturn looms as a threat, HR could expedite retention strategies before the broader slowdown magnifies the issue.

PEST Analysis: Scanning the Broader Environment
While SWOT delves into both internal and external elements, **PEST** focuses almost exclusively on external macro forces—**Political, Economic, Social, and Technological**. This vantage point helps organizations adapt to evolving landscapes that could reshape consumer behaviors, labor pools, or operational costs.

- ✓ **Political**: Governments may introduce new labor laws or shift tax policies. For instance, more stringent employment regulations could force employers to revise recruitment processes or restructure compensation frameworks.

- ✓ **Economic**: Fluctuations in inflation, unemployment rates, or consumer spending often prompt business expansions, contractions, or shifts in hiring strategies. By monitoring these indicators, HR can gauge talent availability and adjust salary benchmarks to remain competitive.

- ✓ **Social**: Cultural values, demographic changes, or trending social issues frequently sway workforce expectations. Rising interest in flexible work, for example, might require policy revisions or new remote collaboration tools.

- ✓ **Technological**: Disruptive innovations, automation, or new digital platforms may redefine skills needed in the workforce. HR strategists who stay current on emerging tech can advise leadership on reskilling or upskilling employees in time to maintain competitiveness.

By regularly reviewing the PEST factors, companies detect early warning signals—such as shifting consumer demands or looming legislative proposals. This foresight is especially vital for HR, as it shapes workforce planning and ensures training programs align with anticipated future skill needs. The more fluidly HR can integrate these external insights, the more readily an organization can fine-tune its strategic trajectory.

Leveraging SWOT and PEST for Organizational Benefit

In practical terms, **SWOT** and **PEST** analyses often feed a single strategic planning cycle. A company might begin with a broad PEST scan to understand the market environment, then refine and prioritize issues via a SWOT assessment that weighs internal readiness against potential external challenges. The outcome is a more nuanced strategic roadmap, complete with measurable objectives and an alignment across departments.

Sample Integration of SWOT and PEST Insights

Identified Factor	Action/Strategy
Growing legislative push for workplace diversity (Political, PEST)	Enhance D&I programs, incorporate targeted hiring initiatives
Strong brand reputation in sustainability (Strength, SWOT)	Expand eco-friendly product lines, marketing aimed at environmentally conscious consumers
Rising unemployment, leading to larger applicant pools (Economic, PEST)	Revamp recruiting channels, refine candidate screening for top talent

Inconsistent training outcomes in certain departments (Weakness, SWOT)	Implement standardized learning & development framework

Environmental scanning through frameworks like **SWOT** and **PEST** positions HR and senior leadership to navigate uncertainties more confidently. By merging insights on internal capabilities with signals from the broader environment, organizations remain agile, turning challenges into opportunities for growth. As strategic planning evolves, these tools provide a steady compass—one that guides both immediate adaptations and long-term aspirations.

10.1.2 Strategy Formulation and Alignment

Developing an effective strategy involves more than outlining grand objectives. Organizations must translate high-level aspirations into concrete, coordinated plans that engage every department. After gathering insights from environmental scanning and internal assessments, the next step is to convert these findings into a cohesive roadmap that fosters growth and resilience. By ensuring each layer of the company—from executive leadership to front-line teams—understands and supports core strategic goals, businesses can more reliably execute on their ambitions.

Defining Objectives and Priorities

Once decision-makers interpret market trends, competitive pressures, or organizational capabilities, they typically establish a small set of primary objectives. Some might focus on revenue growth or market share increases; others may target product innovation or operational efficiency. However, clarity is essential: a strategy with too many overlapping aims can scatter efforts and dilute impact. Instead, leadership often narrows objectives to a handful of major pillars—each reflecting a distinct purpose, such as expanding into a new region or reengineering a product line.

These overarching pillars help rally the organization around shared goals, providing a reference point when debates arise about resource allocation or project feasibility. If accelerating digital transformation is a top priority, for instance, departments know to align technology upgrades, training plans, or budget requests to that theme, ensuring synergy across functions.

Translating Strategy into Functional Plans

A common barrier to strategic success is the gap between corporate-level declarations and day-to-day departmental actions. Bridging this divide means each division—whether marketing, finance, or HR—needs to interpret the broader directives in terms of their own deliverables. For example, a corporate goal to "enhance customer satisfaction" might become a marketing objective to "reduce response times by 20%," or an HR initiative to "train all service staff in advanced communication skills within six months."

While the final form of these functional plans may differ, ensuring consistency among them is key. Regular cross-functional reviews or steering committees can detect misalignments early—such as an IT department's timeline for implementing new software not matching HR's schedule for training. By reconciling these disparities, the organization fosters a collective pace, preventing bottlenecks that might otherwise stall progress.

Empowering and Engaging Employees

Aligning strategies does not mean forcing a top-down model of compliance; on the contrary, it often benefits from input at multiple levels. When managers and employees grasp why certain strategic aims matter—how they respond to competitive pressures or leverage the company's internal strengths—they become more motivated to contribute solutions. Internal communications play a vital role here, whether through town halls, intranet forums, or manager-led briefings that clarify objectives and invite practical feedback.

Empowerment also appears in how performance management systems integrate strategic objectives. Employees who see their targets or key result areas (KRAs) explicitly linked to overall goals can measure their contributions in a larger context. For instance, if one strategic pillar centers on market expansion, a sales representative's targets might include leads generated in new territories, reinforcing that shift in focus.

Monitoring and Adjusting

An aligned strategy is not static. As market conditions, technology, or competitor moves evolve, leadership may revise or refine priorities. Adopting an iterative approach allows for mid-course corrections if data reveal that certain tactics are not yielding results. Routine check-ins—like quarterly reviews with department heads—verify whether the organization remains on track or needs to pivot. This approach discourages a "set it and forget it" mindset, replacing it with dynamic adaptation that keeps the business responsive in changing environments.

In practice, these reviews might highlight a higher-than-expected adoption rate for a new product line, prompting leadership to invest further in marketing or distribution. Conversely, if progress lags in an initiative meant to slash operating costs, the organization can re-examine budget allocations, vendor choices, or employee training. By using real-time feedback, the strategy stays fresh and relevant rather than becoming a document remembered only at annual planning sessions.

Strengthening the Strategic Culture

Beyond formal processes, an organization's culture also underpins successful strategy formulation and alignment. Leadership that champions transparency, open dialogue, and accountability encourages employees to voice their concerns if certain strategic directives conflict with on-the-ground realities. When teams feel safe challenging assumptions or raising potential risks, strategic planning becomes more robust, as multiple perspectives test and refine the original ideas.

Additionally, celebrating milestones—whether a key contract is secured or a cost-reduction target is met—reinforces the behaviors and collaboration that contributed to success. Over time, this recognition builds a climate where pursuing strategic objectives is normal rather than an occasional push. Employees begin to view strategy not as a one-off event but as a guiding framework that shapes everyday decisions, fueling sustainable performance.

Formulating strategy involves setting clear, measurable objectives drawn from thorough analyses, while alignment requires weaving these goals into every department's agenda. By ensuring functional plans match overarching directives, empowering employees to understand their role in the bigger picture, and staying open to adjustments as conditions shift, organizations can unify around a coherent strategy. This unity paves the way for deliberate, coordinated progress and a culture that consistently delivers on its strategic ambitions.

10.1.3 Implementing and Monitoring the Strategic Plan

Developing a strategic plan is only the beginning; bringing it to life requires careful coordination, continuous oversight, and the willingness to adapt as conditions evolve. Once goals and tactics are set, leaders typically turn to structured processes—like project teams, regular progress check-ins, and transparent reporting mechanisms—that unify efforts across departments. By weaving strategic initiatives into daily operations and measuring outcomes, organizations increase the likelihood of converting aspirational objectives into visible, sustained results.

Translating Strategy into Action

For many, the biggest hurdle is transitioning from conceptual plans to concrete projects. After the executive team approves the strategy, departmental leaders often identify specific responsibilities, timelines, and resource needs. Key performance indicators (KPIs) help measure progress. For instance, if a strategic priority involves entering a new market, the sales department might track the number of qualified leads, while marketing measures brand recognition through local surveys. Encouraging each department to propose implementation roadmaps empowers local ownership— ensuring not just compliance but genuine commitment.

Mid-level managers, in particular, serve as a bridge between high-level directives and front-line activities. They translate broad goals into tasks, assign them to teams, and clarify how daily work supports bigger-picture aims. Clear role definitions and aligned incentives— such as performance reviews or bonus structures tied to strategic milestones—reinforce accountability. Employees see how their contributions, whether in product development or client service, directly feed into the plan's overarching targets, motivating them to uphold or exceed the expected standards.

Governance and Accountability Structures

Once implementation begins, routine governance practices keep the organization on course. Steering committees or strategy councils composed of cross-functional leaders can meet monthly or quarterly to review progress, discuss challenges, and propose mid-cycle revisions if needed. These sessions should be grounded in tangible data—like budget usage, KPI updates, or risk assessments—ensuring decision-making remains fact-based. When issues emerge, such as a significant delay in technology rollouts or unexpected budget overruns, the committee can quickly mobilize corrective measures.

Meanwhile, a designated strategy champion—or small team—often oversees the whole plan, spotting dependencies among projects and ensuring synergy. If the marketing department's timeline for a product launch slips, for example, the champion can coordinate with operations to adjust promotional campaigns or shift resources in a timely manner. In large or geographically dispersed organizations, digital dashboards help leaders visualize progress, offering real-time snapshots of milestone completions, resource allocations, and any deviation from initial forecasts.

Monitoring and Adapting to Change

Even the best-conceived plan may need recalibration in dynamic markets. External shifts—like evolving regulations or a competitor's unexpected move—can render some elements of the strategy less relevant or reveal new opportunities to explore. This is where a culture of agility proves invaluable: by regularly assessing the plan's assumptions and outcomes, leadership can pivot resource distributions or recalibrate deadlines without losing overall momentum.

Frequent data reviews sharpen this adaptive process. Teams compare actual vs. planned results, analyzing the root causes of any gaps. If a certain product fails to generate expected interest, marketing and product management might adjust pricing or features. In some cases, the root cause could be internal—like inadequate staff training or supply chain disruptions. Transparent reporting ensures that when departments highlight stumbling blocks, problem-solving is collaborative rather than defensive. Over time, these iterative course corrections form a virtuous cycle of continuous improvement.

Sustaining Engagement and Celebrating Milestones

While performance metrics inform leaders of progress, employees also benefit from regular updates that detail how various initiatives unfold. Communication channels—like intranet announcements, town hall meetings, or departmental briefings—keep everyone aligned and energized about their collective journey. When key milestones are reached, acknowledging the teams involved underscores the company's appreciation, reinforcing desired behaviors and spurring further dedication.

Recognition can come in many forms, from simple thank-you notes to departmental awards. The important element is to ensure employees see the connection between their hard work and the organization's advancing strategy. By tying accomplishments back to the initial vision, leadership fosters a sense of forward momentum, reminding all stakeholders that strategic planning is not merely an annual event but an ongoing, dynamic process.

Effective strategy implementation blends well-defined responsibilities, robust oversight, and an openness to evolution when real-world conditions diverge from initial assumptions. By linking tactical tasks to established KPIs, maintaining transparent governance, and celebrating successes, organizations can transform a static strategic document into continuous, purposeful action. This systematic, inclusive approach not only delivers on immediate targets but also cultivates a workforce that remains agile and enthusiastic about contributing to the long-term vision.

10.2 HR as a Strategic Partner

10.2.1 Positioning HR at Executive-Level Decision Making

HR's strategic importance grows clearer when executives realize that workforce dynamics directly impact organizational outcomes. Yet securing a permanent seat at the leadership table demands more than simply offering well-run payroll and benefits systems. By presenting credible data, guiding talent-related policies, and demonstrating a nuanced understanding of business drivers, HR professionals can become indispensable advisors on issues ranging from expansion plans to emerging market trends.

Elevating HR's Role Through Data and Business Acumen

One key factor in earning executive trust is the ability to frame workforce initiatives in bottom-line terms. When HR leaders articulate how a proposed training program could reduce error rates or when they illustrate how proactive recruitment strategies cut time-to-fill and associated costs, they show they're not just stewards of soft skills but contributors to operational efficiency. In many organizations, the HR function evolves from a purely administrative or compliance-focused unit to a partner that harnesses analytics— like predictive turnover models—to shape strategic dialogue. By blending these insights with broader industry context, HR makes a persuasive case that it can detect risks (e.g., skill shortages) or validate opportunities (e.g., global expansions) before they derail timelines or budgets.

Influencing Major Organizational Choices

Once HR establishes credibility, it can influence executive decisions around mergers, reorganizations, and product launches. For instance, if the CEO plans to enter a new geographic market, HR can highlight the availability of specialized talent in the region or alert the team to local labor regulations that might necessitate adjustments. This input ensures top leaders think about human capital from the outset, rather than scrambling mid-initiative to address workforce shortfalls. In effect, HR leaders who understand both the strategic plan and the workforce implications become translators, articulating how each choice—like a new tech stack or a refined marketing approach—reverberates within the talent ecosystem.

Strengthening Cross-Functional Alliances
Positioning HR in executive decision-making also entails building alliances across finance, operations, and other key departments. If finance lacks clarity on the cost-saving potential of a robust training program, HR can quantify projected impacts, referencing known benchmarks or success stories. If operations wrestle with efficiency challenges, HR might propose realignment of team structures or skill sets that reduce bottlenecks. By consistently delivering solutions that enhance other units' performance and championing collaborative efforts (e.g., cross-departmental task forces on workforce planning), HR becomes a valued resource rather than an obligatory gatekeeper.

Demonstrating Forward-Thinking Leadership
Leaders often look to HR for a pulse on internal culture and external workforce trends. In high-level discussions, HR can highlight emergent employee attitudes—like the demand for flexible work arrangements or heightened focus on diversity and inclusion—that shape organizational reputation. Leveraging external data, such as competitor hiring rates or demographic analyses, HR can forecast shifts in talent availability, pressing the executive team to invest in upskilling or pipeline development. This proactive stance aligns talent strategies with visionary business goals, underscoring that HR stands ready to guide transformations, not merely react to them.

Positioning HR at the executive level calls for a blend of evidence-based advocacy, deep business understanding, and a willingness to take ownership of strategic outcomes. By consistently translating human capital proposals into business-relevant language, forging cross-departmental partnerships, and flagging emerging workforce trends, HR cements its role as a core contributor to organizational growth and resilience. This elevated status allows HR leaders to shape decisions at their inception, ensuring that talent considerations remain central to every major move the company undertakes.

10.2.2 Influencing Organizational Culture and Change

Successfully guiding organizational culture and change requires more than setting policies or declaring new values—it demands shaping a collective mindset and everyday practices that reflect a shared vision. **HR professionals** often stand at the forefront of these efforts, bridging leadership directives with the realities of day-to-day staff experiences. Through consistent communication, modeling desired behaviors, and developing relevant initiatives, HR can orchestrate an environment where culture aligns with strategic priorities and employees adapt more readily to evolving business needs.

Diagnosing the Current Culture

Before proposing any transformation, HR typically starts by understanding what the workforce currently values and how employees actually behave. Standard approaches like anonymous surveys, focus groups, and informal feedback sessions highlight whether the stated culture (often found in mission statements or handbooks) truly matches the lived experience. Through these diagnostics, HR uncovers disconnects—such as teams that prioritize risk-taking while corporate leaders espouse conservative approaches—and identifies pockets of strong engagement or persistent friction. Gaining this insight ensures that subsequent interventions target real issues rather than superficial fixes.

Shaping and Reinforcing Cultural Norms

Once the organization clarifies its preferred culture, HR finds ways to weave these values into everyday routines. Rather than rely on top-down announcements alone, HR can incorporate cultural expectations into performance assessments, leadership development sessions, and reward mechanisms. For instance, if collaboration is a key principle, performance reviews might explicitly measure how individuals share knowledge or support cross-functional projects. Likewise, internal communications—like regular newsletters—can spotlight success stories where employees embody the desired culture, promoting these examples as models for the entire workforce. Over time, these repeated reinforcements create a shared narrative about "how we do things here."

Facilitating Change Management Processes

As the company evolves—whether merging with another organization, restructuring, or pivoting to new markets—HR leads the human side of change. Alongside executives, HR clarifies the rationale behind each shift, helps employees see what the change means for them personally, and identifies skills that may need upgrading. Equally important is the pace of transition: abrupt overhauls often cause confusion or resistance, so HR frequently advises leaders on phasing in new policies or organizational designs gradually. By listening to employee feedback during these transitions, HR also stands ready to address morale concerns, adapt communication strategies, or refine training programs to maintain momentum without overwhelming staff.

Modeling Leadership Behaviors

Ultimately, culture and change efforts hinge on role-modeling. If managers contradict the new direction—say, by penalizing prudent risk-taking in a company that aims to be more innovative—employees will receive mixed signals. HR professionals work closely with top management to ensure leaders demonstrate consistent behaviors, such as openness to employee suggestions or readiness to praise cross-departmental initiatives. By coaching executives on how to communicate big-picture aims in relatable terms, HR ensures that messages about cultural change remain authentic and credible. Over time, these leadership behaviors trickle down, influencing how mid-level managers and frontline teams operate, thereby embedding new norms more deeply.

By integrating these elements—a clear understanding of the current culture, the reinforcement of desired norms through HR processes, a measured approach to change, and demonstrable leadership commitment—HR helps organizations adapt and thrive. When these cultural transformations succeed, employees experience greater alignment with strategic objectives, forging a workplace identity that supports ongoing innovation and resilience in the face of shifting challenges.

10.2.3 Communicating the Value of HR Initiatives

HR teams regularly introduce or refine programs—whether to enhance employee engagement, boost productivity, or address compliance needs. However, the full impact of these efforts often goes unseen unless HR clearly and compellingly articulates their benefits. By framing initiatives in terms that resonate with key stakeholders—like executive leadership, middle managers, and employees—HR professionals can build broader support, justify resource allocation, and highlight how their work underpins the organization's strategic goals.

Translating HR Outcomes into Business Metrics

One of the most effective ways to showcase HR's value is by drawing direct connections to measurable results that matter to decision-makers. For instance, if a new onboarding program shortens time-to-productivity for new hires by 20%, leadership can translate that improvement into tangible gains (like reduced training costs or faster project completions). Even traditionally qualitative areas—like leadership development—can be linked to lowered turnover in key positions or higher engagement survey scores, demonstrating positive returns on the company's investment in people processes.

Tailoring Messages to Different Audiences

HR initiatives typically affect various groups in distinct ways. Tailoring communications ensures each stakeholder sees how a program answers their specific pain points or objectives:

> - **Executives**: Focus on strategic and financial outcomes—such as improved market competitiveness, risk mitigation, or cost savings—when proposing or reporting on initiatives.

> - **Managers**: Emphasize how changes streamline daily tasks, address skill gaps, or provide new tools for motivating and retaining team members. Real-life examples—like how a revised performance management system reduces paperwork—can strengthen buy-in.

> - **Employees**: Speak directly to individual benefits—career growth paths, flexible scheduling, or personal development opportunities. Clarity on "what's in it for me" helps staff embrace new programs more enthusiastically.

Showcasing Success Stories and Data

Hard statistics and personal narratives both help clarify HR's contributions. Simple, visually appealing dashboards or scorecards may highlight progress against key metrics—like fill rates in critical roles or improvements in diversity representation. Meanwhile, brief success stories from employees or managers highlight the human impact. For example, an employee's testimonial about how a mentoring initiative boosted their confidence and performance can powerfully reinforce the broader data about participant satisfaction.

Establishing Consistent Communication Channels

Sporadic updates can leave stakeholders unsure of HR's day-to-day contributions. By integrating regular touchpoints—like quarterly reports to leadership or short monthly bulletins to managers—HR maintains visibility for ongoing initiatives. In more dynamic situations, such as rolling out new digital platforms for remote teams, HR might hold short, open Q&A sessions to gather immediate feedback and clarify any confusion. The key is to keep messages timely and relevant, ensuring HR's voice remains part of critical operational discussions rather than an afterthought.

Embedding HR as a Strategic Partner

Beyond campaign-based communications, an overarching strategy places HR leaders in forums where key decisions emerge. Frequent involvement in cross-functional planning or executive committees lets HR highlight workforce implications before finalizing major projects. By consistently tying HR recommendations to big-picture results—such as competitive advantage or risk mitigation—HR solidifies its reputation as a trusted advisor. Over time, this presence means top management looks to HR for guidance not only on tactical matters like hiring or training but also on shaping culture and long-term workforce strategy.

Communicating HR's value involves more than publishing data or distributing memos. It requires crafting messages that resonate with diverse stakeholders, tying proposals and updates to measurable business and employee impacts, and maintaining a steady dialogue about progress. By deliberately aligning their communications with organizational priorities, HR can reveal the transformative role it plays—from setting strategic plans into action to elevating the employee experience—and secure the recognition and backing essential for sustained success.

10.3 Case Studies in Strategic HR

10.3.1 Real-World Examples of Strategic Interventions

Translating HR's strategic role into practical results often involves creative, data-driven solutions that address pressing organizational challenges. These interventions, designed with long-term business goals in mind, demonstrate how HR can spark notable improvements in workforce performance, engagement, and adaptability. While the specific tactics may vary by industry or region, the underlying principle remains consistent: aligning people strategies with broader corporate objectives to realize tangible outcomes.

Revamping Performance Management to Drive Innovation
A mid-sized technology firm, seeking to sustain a competitive edge, realized its traditional annual review cycle barely captured the rapid skill shifts required for new projects. Recognizing that delayed feedback and vague goal-setting undermined progress, HR led the charge to introduce a more frequent, agile performance management model. Instead of once-a-year appraisals, employees now participated in quarterly check-ins with team leaders. Each conversation centered on near-term goals and real-time coaching, enabling swift course corrections.

Six months into this approach, the company noted reduced project delays and higher rates of cross-departmental collaboration. Managers reported feeling better equipped to detect early signs of skill mismatches or burnout. Most importantly, innovation metrics—like the number of new product features released each quarter—increased, reflecting how timely feedback and updated objectives kept teams aligned. This intervention underscored HR's capacity to foster a culture of continuous improvement and responsiveness to market demands.

Building a Robust Internal Talent Marketplace

In a global manufacturing conglomerate known for frequent product-line pivots, HR observed that some highly specialized roles faced chronic underutilization, while other departments struggled with skill shortages. Departing from standard functional silos, the HR team launched an internal talent marketplace where employees could "bid" on short-term assignments or cross-functional projects that matched their expertise and interests.

Participation exceeded expectations: engineers from the R&D unit tested their skills in the logistics department to streamline inventory systems, while sales associates joined marketing sprints to bolster customer insights. Over time, turnover in specialized roles dipped because staff discovered fresh challenges without leaving the company. Meanwhile, managers praised the marketplace for accelerating product launches and problem-solving initiatives. By systematically matching latent skills with strategic needs, HR demonstrated how people-centric innovations can power organizational agility.

Promoting Leadership Diversity for Strategic Growth

A fast-growing retail chain aimed to diversify its leadership pipeline, recognizing that varied perspectives could help it navigate evolving consumer tastes across multiple regions. Initially, HR encountered skepticism about altering long-standing promotion paths. Yet data confirmed a correlation between more diverse leadership teams and better local market performance.

Acting on these insights, the HR function spearheaded a targeted leadership development program. Mid-level managers from underrepresented groups received mentoring, structured rotations, and networking opportunities. Branch-level data soon revealed that newly promoted managers brought fresh merchandising ideas and localized community engagement, boosting sales. Internal engagement surveys also showed stronger morale and sense of fairness. By broadening pathways to leadership, the retailer tapped into a broader range of ideas—serving both its social responsibility aims and its strategic push to stand out in saturated markets.

Investing in Employee Experience Post-Acquisition
Following a high-profile acquisition in the financial services sector, employees from both legacy companies found themselves grappling with cultural differences and overlapping roles. Recognizing the risk of talent flight and productivity dips, HR designed a robust integration plan that emphasized open dialogue. Dedicated "listening tours" brought managers, newly merged teams, and executive leadership together to outline perceived barriers and clarify newly formed structures.

Simultaneously, the HR team launched skill-based workshops that cross-trained employees from each firm in the other's products and systems. This not only curbed redundancies but also created a sense of unity among staff anxious about changes. Over the subsequent quarter, retention remained stable, avoiding the spike in voluntary departures typical in large-scale mergers. The new cross-functional expertise led to smoother client handovers and an uptick in cross-selling financial products, confirming that proactive, people-focused strategies can secure business continuity and enhance growth opportunities during major organizational shifts.

Strategic HR interventions thrive when they align closely with business imperatives—whether driving innovation, enhancing role flexibility, strengthening leadership diversity, or easing post-merger integration. These real-world examples demonstrate that, by pinpointing workforce challenges and crafting tailored solutions, HR can move beyond transactional duties to become a genuine catalyst for sustained competitive advantage.

10.3.2 Mergers & Acquisitions: HR's Role

When organizations combine through mergers or acquisitions, the deal's success hinges on more than just financial calculations. Seamlessly blending workforces, harmonizing policies, and addressing cultural differences are critical tasks that often fall under HR's purview. From the earliest stages of due diligence through post-merger integration, HR professionals serve as strategic advisors, anticipating talent concerns and implementing solutions that preserve morale, maintain productivity, and unlock the full value of the transaction.

Early Due Diligence and Risk Assessment
Long before an acquisition is final, HR can help validate whether the target company is a good cultural and operational fit. This might involve reviewing compensation structures, benefits liabilities, or existing union contracts that could introduce new complexities. In parallel, understanding the target's leadership pipeline or critical roles informs leadership succession planning post-deal. HR's early involvement ensures that potential obstacles—like overlapping roles or drastically differing workplace cultures—are identified up front, allowing negotiators to shape deal terms with people-focused insights.

Cultural Integration and Change Management

Once a merger is announced, employees typically have questions about job security, benefits, and reporting lines. HR can help address these concerns promptly and openly, limiting speculation and rumors. In many cases, the acquiring firm's culture does not simply overwrite the acquired entity's norms; instead, the newly combined workforce often merges elements of both cultures. HR teams can facilitate "cultural audits," collecting feedback on values, communication styles, and decision-making processes to clarify shared ground and design bridging activities. Workshops or joint committees may help employees from both organizations gradually acclimate to any new mission statements or operating principles.

Aligning Compensation, Benefits, and Roles

M&A often leads to reorganization, with certain positions redefined or consolidated. Harmonizing job titles, pay ranges, and employee benefits demands careful planning:

> ➢ If the acquiring company's retirement program differs drastically from what employees in the acquired firm are accustomed to, HR must craft a clear transition plan and communicate why it benefits the entire entity.

> ➢ When roles overlap, a transparent selection process helps identify who will occupy leadership positions in the new structure. HR can champion objective criteria—like performance history or required skill sets—so these decisions appear fair and performance-based rather than arbitrary.

Throughout these alignments, consistent internal messaging reassures employees that even where redundancies are unavoidable, the process is handled with respect and fairness.

Maintaining Engagement and Productivity

In the immediate aftermath of a merger, distractions run high as personnel worry about structural changes or cultural mismatches. HR teams often partner with managers to ensure workstream continuity. Regular Q&A sessions, simple one-page guides on updated policies, and group orientations reduce confusion. If the organization intends to introduce new collaboration tools or adopt the acquiring company's performance review systems, short trainings or job aids prevent day-to-day tasks from stalling. Meanwhile, recognized "change champions" in each department can monitor sentiment and escalate staff concerns as needed.

A well-thought-out communication strategy during the integration phase—featuring town halls or routine email bulletins—keeps employees informed of milestones, new leadership appointments, and any synergy gains (like expanded career paths or cross-functional project opportunities). By fostering openness, HR can transform apprehension into cautious optimism.

Leveraging Synergies and Skill Development

While cost savings and market expansion are often top-of-mind for leadership, mergers can also reveal beneficial synergies that involve people. HR specialists analyze skill inventories across both entities to pinpoint where combining teams can amplify innovation. For example, an R&D unit from the acquired firm might complement the acquiring company's sales reach. HR can design cross-training programs or strategic project assignments that bring these skill sets together, accelerating knowledge exchange and new product development.

In addition, identifying employees with high potential in the acquired entity ensures their retention. Targeted retention bonuses or leadership development programs can prevent the outflow of crucial talent that might have concerns about the new ownership's direction.

Post-Merger Review and Continuous Improvement
As the dust settles, HR continues to refine processes and address lingering cultural gaps. Feedback loops, such as employee surveys or focus groups, gauge how effectively staff have adapted and whether new policies are functioning as intended. If unexpected friction persists, HR might revisit certain integration decisions—perhaps adjusting leadership structures or reintroducing specialized training. Periodic check-ins enable the organization to remain nimble, further unifying the workforce over time.

In a successful merger or acquisition, HR's strategic role spans from initial due diligence—anticipating cultural and staffing pitfalls—to long after the formal deal closes, uniting people under a cohesive vision. By integrating cultures, aligning compensation and roles, and fostering transparent communication at every stage, HR not only mitigates risks but also unlocks the full potential of the newly combined workforce.

10.3.3 Global Expansion Strategies

When organizations decide to scale beyond their home country's borders, they must balance market ambitions with the operational realities of managing diverse cultures, regulatory landscapes, and talent pools. Effective global expansion strategies can propel brand recognition, drive revenue from new segments, and distribute risk across multiple geographies. However, launching a product or establishing offices abroad involves more than business plans and market analyses: it also requires HR to play a pivotal role, ensuring that workforce dynamics align seamlessly with overall strategic objectives.

Assessing Market and Workforce Potential

A foundational step in global expansion is determining which regions offer the most favorable blend of customer demand, logistical feasibility, and skilled labor. While sales projections often dominate these discussions, HR contributes crucial insights about local talent availability or wage structures. For instance, if the company's product relies heavily on specialized R&D roles, the HR team can examine whether a potential market has a thriving ecosystem of universities or tech clusters. Conversely, if labor costs in a particular region appear attractive, HR helps confirm whether those roles can be effectively recruited and retained within local cultural norms.

Adapting Organizational Structures

Expanding abroad frequently compels organizations to revise decision-making frameworks. In some cases, it may be beneficial to create a regional headquarters with autonomy over day-to-day operations. Alternatively, certain expansions might remain closely coordinated from the company's main office. Either approach influences how local teams interact with central leadership. HR ensures that any resulting hierarchy or reporting lines remain clear to avoid confusion, and that accountability is properly allocated. This structural decision can set the tone for local empowerment, strategic agility, and how quickly the new location can respond to market shifts.

Navigating Cultural and Regulatory Nuances

New markets inevitably introduce fresh business norms, from how contracts are negotiated to how employees expect to be managed. HR professionals must translate broader organizational standards into policies that resonate locally—balancing central values with region-specific legal and cultural obligations. For instance, some locations may demand robust union relations, while others might have unique statutory requirements for vacation or maternity leave.

A mismatch between corporate policies and local expectations can hinder early traction, leading to resentment or high turnover.

Beyond compliance, adjusting leadership and communication styles can improve local engagement. In a highly relationship-driven culture, managers might need to invest extra time in personal rapport-building, or adopt different feedback mechanisms than those used at headquarters. HR's role extends to briefing expatriates and local hires on these dynamics, creating a shared perspective that smooths day-to-day interactions.

Building Effective Talent Pipelines
Securing qualified professionals in a new market can be a critical gating factor for expansion. In some regions, hiring is complicated by fierce competition for top talent or strict work permit regulations. HR's strategic input can guide whether to staff up gradually, perhaps using contractors initially, or to invest in robust local recruitment from the outset. Partnerships with local universities, government job agencies, or specialized recruiters often streamline this ramp-up. If an internal rotational program is in place, certain high-potential employees might transfer overseas, seeding the new location with individuals who fully grasp the organization's culture and processes.

For roles that require specialized expertise, HR can create cross-border training or mentorship programs to ensure skill transfer. Conversely, local experts can be tapped to train or advise headquarters staff on regional peculiarities—whether that's consumer preferences or unique regulatory hurdles—fostering two-way learning.

Monitoring Progress and Adapting
As the global venture takes root, consistent evaluation prevents minor friction from escalating. HR's metrics might include turnover rates in the new market, speed of team formation, or local employee

engagement levels. If, for example, turnover spikes among specialized engineers, HR might reevaluate compensation packages, training support, or cultural integration tactics. Real-time responsiveness signals to local teams that the organization actively invests in their success, not just in revenue generation.

Frequent coordination calls between regional HR managers and global leadership helps keep policy alignment intact, especially if new legislation arises or if shifting economic conditions demand workforce recalibration. In more dynamic industries, staying agile allows local units to pivot quickly, whether acquiring a promising local startup or adjusting product lines in response to emerging trends.

Successful global expansion involves interlocking considerations: marketplace fit, regulatory awareness, local talent strategies, and an inclusive culture that balances corporate identity with regional uniqueness. By collaborating closely with executives to address these dimensions, HR stands as a strategic linchpin—guiding everything from organizational structure to workforce engagement—thereby maximizing the potential of each new venture abroad.

Chapter 11: Leadership Cluster

11.1 Behavioral Competency 1: Leadership & Navigation

11.1.1 Key Concepts and Definitions

Leadership and navigation within an HR context entail more than simply managing employees or administering policies. They involve guiding individuals and teams toward shared objectives, fostering unity, and steering the organization through change. At its core, leadership shapes how professionals inspire and motivate those around them, while navigation focuses on steering initiatives and resources efficiently, even amidst complexity or uncertainty. When these two elements intersect, HR practitioners become not just managers of human capital but also architects of direction and momentum within the organization.

Leadership as Influence and Vision

Within the behavioral competency model, leadership is often tied to an individual's ability to articulate a compelling vision, build trust, and energize colleagues around a set of common goals. Far from a one-size-fits-all approach, effective leadership adapts to situational nuances—sometimes emphasizing coaching and empathy, other times making decisive calls under pressure. The unifying thread is the capacity to model desired behaviors and align daily actions with overarching values. Whether one leads a small project team or shapes corporate policy at the executive level, leadership in HR underpins how employees perceive the function's credibility and fairness.

These attributes manifest in how an HR leader might champion equitable hiring practices or spearhead a new engagement initiative. By clearly explaining the rationale behind such efforts, anticipating challenges, and gathering stakeholders' input, leadership moves from abstract ideals to practical results. Meanwhile, transparent communication, consistent ethical conduct, and openness to feedback create the trust that leadership requires.

Navigation in Complex Environments

While leadership casts the vision, navigation deals with the practical act of guiding initiatives through organizational structures, resource constraints, and stakeholder alliances. HR professionals adept at navigation read the terrain—cultural norms, political dynamics, even external legal changes—and adjust strategies to maintain progress. This skill extends to anticipating roadblocks, whether that's securing buy-in from skeptical managers or handling budgetary limits that threaten a new training program.

In a simple example, an HR manager tasked with rolling out a performance management overhaul navigates by coordinating with IT for the right platform, consulting with legal to confirm compliance, and gathering department heads' perspectives on key metrics. Each step demands balancing competing priorities—like speed of implementation versus thorough user testing—so that the end result is integrated rather than siloed. Over time, an aptitude for navigation builds an HR team's reputation as a reliable partner that can steer even complex, cross-functional projects to a productive conclusion.

Interplay of Leadership & Navigation

The most effective HR leaders don't treat leadership and navigation as separate silos. Instead, they recognize that articulating an inspiring vision (leadership) and marshaling resources or relationships to fulfill that vision (navigation) go hand in hand. For instance, in championing a diversity and inclusion initiative, a leader might evoke the importance of diverse perspectives, but without the skill to navigate departmental politics or to adapt global frameworks to local cultural contexts, the project may stall. Conversely, skillful navigation absent a compelling sense of purpose can feel transactional or mechanical, failing to ignite genuine staff commitment.

Why It Matters for HR

When HR displays strong leadership and navigation competencies, it assumes a role well beyond traditional hiring or compliance responsibilities. HR professionals guide not only the workforce but also influence executive thinking on how people strategies fuel organizational success. Employees who see HR in this light tend to trust and consult the function more frequently, fostering a collaborative climate that can accelerate change. Moreover, in times of crisis or rapid transformation, HR's dual focus on people-centric leadership and strategic navigation can be the difference between organizational resilience and disarray.

By grasping these foundational concepts—leadership as a motivating force and navigation as the operational drive—HR practitioners can champion initiatives with depth and credibility. Through clarity of direction and adept handling of organizational complexities, they model the very competencies they seek to nurture across the enterprise, cultivating a workplace culture that unifies strategic ambition with the day-to-day realities of human collaboration.

11.1.2 Core Proficiency Indicators

Leadership and Navigation at the core proficiency level focuses on the everyday behaviors that allow HR professionals to guide colleagues, facilitate collaboration, and uphold trust. Although these indicators may not involve large-scale strategic influence, they lay crucial groundwork for more advanced leadership roles. By consistently demonstrating dependability, clear communication, and inclusion, HR practitioners establish a positive atmosphere where teams remain engaged and initiatives move forward smoothly.

Establishing Reliability and Trust

A central aspect of leadership is modeling steady follow-through. When employees or department heads approach HR with questions—perhaps about a new benefit or an upcoming policy change—core-level leaders respond promptly, offering accurate and transparent information. They also:

> **Honor Commitments**: If HR pledges to provide a clarified policy or training schedule by a certain date, they deliver on time, showing employees their requests matter.

> **Maintain Confidentiality**: Sensitivity around employee data or disciplinary issues requires careful discretion. Adhering strictly to privacy boundaries assures staff that HR safeguards personal information.

Such reliable conduct cements HR's credibility. Over time, teams learn to trust that HR acts in the best interest of employees and the organization alike, fostering open, supportive relationships.

Guiding and Motivating Teams

Beyond routine administrative tasks, HR professionals with core-level leadership skills facilitate the success of small projects and departmental undertakings. They focus on inclusivity and clarity:

✓ **Set Clear Project Goals**
   Whether coordinating an engagement survey or revamping a performance review process, leaders outline why the project matters, how success is measured, and who is responsible for specific milestones.

✓ **Encourage Collective Input**
   Early in the planning phase, they organize short meetings or roundtable discussions to gather perspectives from various

stakeholders. This step not only surfaces possible obstacles but also cultivates ownership among the contributors.

✓ **Foster a Positive Tone**
Leaders maintain an encouraging environment where team members feel comfortable sharing ideas or concerns. Even when addressing setbacks, they remain solution-oriented, directing focus toward collaborative problem-solving.

Communicating with Consistency and Purpose

Even small details in messaging can influence whether teams understand and support HR initiatives. Practical communication strategies at this level include:

➤ **Contextual Briefings**: Whenever a new program (e.g., a modified time-off policy) is introduced, HR explains how it aligns with broader objectives—like improving work-life balance or reducing burnout.

➤ **Regular Check-Ins**: Brief, periodic updates keep employees informed about progress or changes, easing uncertainty and reinforcing that HR remains accessible for questions.

Such consistent, purposeful communication prevents misunderstandings and builds organizational confidence in HR's direction.

Handling Resistance and Fostering Adaptability

When adjustments—like a revised overtime policy or a shift to online training—encounter initial pushback, HR's leadership capabilities help maintain momentum. Proficiency at this level means:

✓ Listening to Concerns: Leaders hold small-group sessions to hear fears or doubts, ensuring stakeholders feel respected.

✓ Highlighting Benefits: Emphasizing the advantages (e.g., simpler recordkeeping, flexible scheduling) can alleviate worries and show employees the rationale behind changes.

✓ Offering Incremental Steps: If major overhauls seem daunting, introducing pilot phases or partial rollouts allows staff to adapt gradually, reducing friction.

This measured approach to change underscores the collaborative spirit and reassures employees that HR balances organizational goals with individual comfort.

Upholding Ethical and Inclusive Standards
Though advanced ethics may be detailed elsewhere, core leadership proficiency requires consistently applying fair treatment in day-to-day interactions. This might entail forming diverse interview panels, ensuring that early career staff have equitable access to professional development, or transparently explaining compensation structures. As they interact with managers and employees, HR professionals build an environment where ethical norms and inclusion are woven into the organizational fabric—not merely stated ideals.

Sample Core Indicators in Practice

Indicator	Real-World Example
Maintains Reliable Communication	Delivers timely progress updates on a new HRIS rollout
Gathers Stakeholder Input	Hosts small-group meetings before rolling out a departmental policy
Clarifies Scope and Objectives	Uses short project briefs to outline responsibilities and success metrics

Respects Confidentiality	Properly stores disciplinary documents and limits data access
Offers Constructive Feedback	Conducts regular one-on-one sessions, addressing issues with empathy and directness

By consistently exhibiting these behaviors, HR leaders at the core competency stage create a trustworthy, motivating backdrop for initiatives. This foundation paves the way for more advanced leadership tasks in the future, ensuring employees feel guided, respected, and clear on how each policy or project meshes with the organization's broader ambitions.

11.1.3 Senior-Level Indicators

At a more advanced stage of **Leadership & Navigation**, HR professionals wield influence that goes beyond departmental management, driving strategic direction and embedding a leadership mindset across the organization. While core-level competencies emphasize dependable communication and team coordination, senior-level behaviors focus on shaping culture, steering top-level decisions, and ensuring that large-scale initiatives stay on track— even amidst complex, rapidly shifting conditions. These indicators typically surface when HR executives or seasoned managers take on enterprise-wide challenges that demand both strategic vision and the agility to navigate competing agendas.

Championing Enterprise-Wide Change and Vision
A hallmark of senior-level leadership is the ability to frame broad organizational objectives in a way that resonates with diverse departments. Rather than merely participating in high-level discussions, these HR leaders help craft the narrative around major

transformations—such as rebranding efforts, global expansions, or reorganizations—and ensure that people impacts remain front and center.

- ✓ They **collaborate closely with the C-suite** or board, providing data-driven insights on workforce capabilities, potential skill gaps, and cultural barriers that might impede success.

- ✓ Through town halls or executive briefings, they **articulate a unifying vision**, explaining how an organizational pivot, for example, aligns with employee growth opportunities and longer-term market advantages.

- ✓ In times of uncertainty—like acquisitions or budget cuts— senior-level HR professionals offer **calm, strategic counsel**, highlighting both immediate operational requirements and sustained cultural harmony.

Influencing Stakeholders at All Levels
While core-level leaders excel at guiding small teams, senior-level figures cultivate alliances that extend beyond their immediate sphere. Often, they:

Secure Cross-Functional Support: Engaging with finance, IT, operations, and other key business units to shape HR initiatives that address shared goals, such as digital transformation or new market penetration.

Negotiate Complex Conflicts: When departmental interests clash—like competing resource demands or divergent timeframes—senior HR leaders balance these perspectives, proposing solutions that optimize overall organizational benefit rather than favoring one side.

Leverage External Networks: Partnerships with industry peers or external advisors help them stay abreast of emerging trends, which they then relay to top executives. This external viewpoint adds depth to strategic choices, reducing the likelihood of blind spots.

Driving Cultural Integration and Maturity

At the senior level, leadership efforts shift from shaping small workgroup cultures to influencing the entire organizational ethos. This heightened role involves:

- ✓ **Embedding Core Values**: Beyond championing ethics or inclusion in isolated initiatives, senior HR leaders ensure these principles become integral to performance reviews, leadership pipelines, and recognition systems.

- ✓ **Sustaining Change Over Time**: In large-scale transformations (like a post-merger integration or a multi-year innovation strategy), they monitor cultural alignment months or even years after the initial rollout, adjusting approaches if employee sentiment or engagement metrics suggest drift from the desired norms.

In fulfilling this role, they sometimes convene cross-regional committees or sponsor leadership development programs that interweave skill-building with cultural reinforcement, ensuring employees at all levels share a consistent understanding of the organization's guiding principles.

Aligning HR Strategy with Business Priorities

Senior-level leaders do not merely execute strategic plans—**they shape them**. By aligning human capital decisions with the overarching corporate agenda, they validate that workforce investments yield measurable returns. For instance, if the company invests heavily in R&D, senior HR leaders might:

✓ Recommend specialized compensation structures to attract top-tier technical talent;

✓ Introduce advanced learning platforms that expedite skill development for product engineering teams;

✓ Outline predictive workforce analyses, anticipating attrition or the surge in hiring needed during product ramp-ups.

This synergy ensures that executive conversations about product expansions or cost-saving measures always factor in potential human resource implications. Consequently, HR becomes an indispensable driver of strategic progress, rather than a late-stage operational add-on.

Exercising Strategic Foresight Under Pressure

Under uncertain market conditions—like economic downturns or emergent industry disruptions—senior-level HR leaders deploy a range of contingency plans:

Scenario Planning: Collaborating with finance and other departments to model best-case, worst-case, and moderate outlooks, clarifying how workforce configurations might shift under each.

Transparent Crisis Communication: In a crisis, they ensure employees trust leadership by offering timely updates, explaining rationales behind tough decisions, and addressing morale concerns.

Selective Resource Allocation: Balancing short-term imperatives (e.g., preserving cash flow) with long-term workforce resilience (e.g., sustaining critical skill groups).

Such adept navigation cements HR's role as a stabilizing presence that mitigates risk while safeguarding the company's strategic vision, even under intense scrutiny from stakeholders or investors.

Sample Indicators of Senior-Level Leadership & Navigation

Indicator	Practical Illustration
Articulates Organizational Vision	Shapes communication plans for a major reorganization, explaining benefits to employees and linking changes to long-range goals
Negotiates High-Stakes, Cross-Functional Needs	Balances budget constraints with operational demands, guiding leaders to consensus in contested resource allocation
Aligns HR Strategy to Enterprise Goals	Develops workforce analytics that forecast skill requirements, driving targeted recruitment and upskilling solutions
Fosters Long-Term Cultural Maturity	Ensures that new leadership pipelines explicitly incorporate DEI standards and that executive reviews include cultural alignment metrics
Champions Stability During Shifts	Offers transparent updates during crisis events, providing scenario-based workforce strategies to minimize disruptions

By consistently displaying these capacities—encompassing vision-setting, adept negotiation, and cultural stewardship—HR leaders operating at the senior level become trusted advisors to top executives. Their perspective transcends departmental boundaries, tying human capital initiatives to bottom-line success and future readiness. This elevated influence cements their role in guiding the enterprise through evolving challenges, ensuring that strategic ambitions translate into tangible organizational outcomes.

11.1.4 Practical Scenarios (Leading Teams, Influencing Stakeholders)

Translating the concepts of Leadership & Navigation into day-to-day HR work can involve guiding diverse groups toward shared goals, reconciling competing priorities, and advocating for new initiatives that may face skepticism. In each scenario below, HR practitioners apply various aspects of leadership—from empathy and communication to proactive problem-solving—while maintaining a clear focus on organizational objectives. These examples illustrate how real situations test the ability to unite teams and influence critical stakeholders.

Scenario 1: Aligning Multiple Departments on a New HRIS

An HR manager proposes migrating to a modern Human Resources Information System (HRIS) that promises to reduce repetitive manual tasks and improve data integrity. However, department heads raise concerns about deployment timelines and potential workflow interruptions. Instead of issuing a top-down mandate, the HR manager opens initial discussions with each department, listening to concerns about training requirements and possible downtimes. Over a series of short, structured conversations, it becomes clear that one department needs specialized system configurations for shift scheduling,

404

while another department is primarily worried about data security.

By synthesizing these viewpoints, the HR manager develops a phased rollout plan. Certain modules launch sooner for areas with lower complexity, giving the more complex departments time to test custom features. Communication remains frequent: concise weekly updates reassure all parties that deadlines are being met, and minor adjustments emerge from user feedback without derailing progress. In the end, departments appreciate that the HR manager balanced their operational needs with the larger goal of modernizing HR processes.

Scenario 2: Convincing a Skeptical Executive to Support a Leadership Development Program

Context: The firm's CEO aims to accelerate internal promotions, yet the CFO questions the ROI of formal leadership training. Past workshops did not produce immediately visible performance gains.

HR's Strategic Response:

Compiles evidence from competitor case studies, demonstrating lower turnover and faster project completions when employees undergo structured leadership paths.

Pilots a small, six-month development track for mid-level managers, focusing on high-impact managerial skills (budgeting, cross-functional communication).

Shares interim results—reduced manager attrition, improved engagement scores among participants—at a subsequent executive review, highlighting tangible outcomes.

Seeing proof of incremental value convinces the CFO to fund a full-scale expansion. By relying on data and controlled experimentation, HR shows it can link skill-building programs to the organization's financial and operational metrics.

Scenario 3: Reducing Tension in a Project Team

A cross-functional squad, formed to revise the company's benefits offerings, encounters friction: the benefits specialist prioritizes thorough market research before changes, while the employee relations lead pushes for a quick launch to address staff complaints. As the HR leader overseeing this project, you realize that waiting too long may undermine morale, but rushing a launch could lead to flawed implementations.

Your first step is a brief mediation session where each party clarifies constraints and desired outcomes. Rather than imposing a compromise, you highlight the shared purpose: designing benefits that boost retention and satisfaction without spiking costs. Through guided questioning, the two parties recognize that phased improvements—like adding mental health support immediately and rolling out advanced benefits after sufficient market analysis—can satisfy both concerns. This approach alleviates tension and preserves the team's collaborative spirit, illustrating how patient facilitation can transform conflict into a joint solution.

Scenario 4: Instilling a New Cultural Value in Everyday Operations

Background: The leadership team introduces a focus on "innovation" as a core value, but employees express uncertainty about what that means for routine tasks.

HR's Leadership Approach:

Initiates monthly "Spotlight Sessions," where teams briefly present small process improvements or fresh ideas to solve workplace challenges.

Encourages department heads to integrate a "What did we learn?" moment into weekly staff meetings, reinforcing the normalcy of experimentation and reflection.

Recognizes staff who pilot creative approaches (e.g., an online scheduling tweak that cut wait times), publicizing their stories on the company intranet to highlight concrete benefits.

This steady reinforcement fosters a mindset where employees see innovation not as a buzzword but as a daily possibility. Over time, incremental changes yield fewer manual errors, quicker approvals, and greater willingness to test suggestions that might once have been dismissed.

Why These Scenarios Matter
In each of these examples, HR professionals embody leadership and navigation by listening actively, finding pathways through conflicting priorities, and anchoring decisions in business impact. The outcome is a more cohesive workforce that buys into new systems, skill development, or cultural shifts with less resistance. Whether mediating departmental tensions, persuading executives to fund a strategic project, or embedding fresh values, these real-life situations underscore that genuine leadership emerges through practical problem-solving and inclusive, goal-oriented communication.

11.2 Behavioral Competency 2: Ethical Practice

11.2.1 Ethical Frameworks in HR (Integrity, Fairness)

HR professionals often serve as the conscience of their organizations, guiding actions in ways that build trust and ensure that decisions reflect shared values. Underpinning this role are **ethical frameworks**—conceptual tools that define how HR practitioners uphold **integrity** and **fairness** in processes such as hiring, performance evaluations, and conflict resolution. When these frameworks are clearly understood, HR can more confidently address moral complexities, balancing the organization's needs with respect for individual employees.

Building on Integrity

Integrity involves acting according to consistent principles, even when expedient shortcuts appear tempting. For HR practitioners, integrity manifests in transparent and truthful communication, responsible stewardship of confidential information, and an unwavering commitment to the greater good of the workforce. Because HR holds sensitive data—ranging from compensation figures to disciplinary records—small lapses in integrity can undermine employee trust quickly.

When leaders demonstrate this virtue, they transcend mere rule enforcement and become guardians of a culture that prizes openness. For example, if a high-performing manager overlooks harassment complaints within their team, an HR professional guided by integrity would address the issue candidly, even if senior leadership is protective of that manager. The integrity-driven HR partner treats internal policies and values as genuine guardrails, not optional suggestions. Over time, repeated demonstrations of forthrightness shape an environment where employees feel safe voicing concerns without fear of hidden agendas or retaliation.

Promoting Fairness

Fairness in HR context means ensuring impartial treatment of employees and applicants, free from undue bias or preferential treatment. This principle applies to everyday decisions such as distributing assignments, designing pay structures, or considering promotions. Bias—whether conscious or unconscious—can creep into these processes, eroding the belief that the organization rewards merit and discouraging talented individuals from staying or applying.

An HR department operating under a fairness framework dedicates resources to evaluating potential disparities in pay or performance ratings, using data to pinpoint where systematic unevenness occurs. If certain groups are underrepresented in leadership or if performance reviews repeatedly skew against specific demographics, a fairness-based approach prompts deeper investigation. Corrective measures might include refining evaluation criteria or offering training on implicit bias. By embedding fairness checks into core HR activities, from candidate screening to grievance handling, HR practitioners help maintain a level playing field that fosters genuine employee engagement and motivation.

Integrating Integrity and Fairness into HR Practice

1. **Transparent Procedures**: Publicly documenting how hiring, promotions, and discipline decisions occur discourages favoritism. Employees who understand the reasoning behind personnel actions see HR's commitment to fairness in action.

2. **Consistent Accountability**: HR leaders uphold the same ethical standards for all staff, including executives or star

performers. Integrity loses credibility if higher-ups appear exempt from consequences faced by others.

3. **Regular Ethical Reflection**: Short, periodic discussions among HR teams or with departmental leaders encourage ongoing scrutiny of biases and decision patterns, reinforcing a culture that values moral reflection.

Why These Frameworks Matter

A workforce that trusts HR's ethical commitment tends to be more cohesive. Integrity ensures employees believe official pronouncements hold genuine weight, not empty rhetoric, while fairness helps cultivate a sense that advancement opportunities and disciplinary actions alike are conducted without hidden bias. In practice, the two concepts intertwine—consistently honest, transparent actions feed into an environment where fairness can thrive. For HR, embracing these frameworks ensures that even in challenging times, the function remains a force for consistency and equity.

11.2.2 Code of Conduct Development

A code of conduct provides a structured reference for expected behaviors and organizational values, guiding employees in everyday decisions. Rather than existing as a static document, it sets cultural benchmarks that shape an environment of trust, accountability, and ethical consistency. Developed thoughtfully, it balances broad guiding principles with specific examples that reflect the realities employees face—such as data confidentiality, fair conflict resolution, or respectful communication. When the HR function leads or co-leads this effort, the final product typically resonates with both leadership goals and grassroots concerns, thereby embedding ethics into the organization's operational fabric.

Establishing Purpose and Scope

Any code of conduct starts by clarifying its objective: ensuring staff understand not merely "what" actions are off-limits but also "why" those restrictions matter. Early on, HR professionals identify and consult key stakeholders (e.g., legal, compliance, departmental heads) to capture diverse viewpoints. This collaboration helps refine the code's scope—covering topics like conflicts of interest, anti-discrimination, data privacy, or insider trading—according to the organization's industry and regulatory obligations. A well-scoped code also addresses everyday workplace interactions, steering employees toward respectful collaboration.

Though legal requirements guide many provisions, going beyond minimal compliance can safeguard the company's reputation. For instance, a tech firm handling personal data might outline robust privacy commitments that exceed baseline regulations, reflecting deeper organizational values. In shaping these standards, HR ensures the language remains accessible, avoiding impenetrable legalese that might deter genuine engagement or comprehension.

Clarifying Ethical Expectations in Practical Terms

A code often gains traction when it offers real-world examples or short scenarios, rather than generic prohibitions. Employees respond better to a statement such as: "If you have a potential conflict of interest—like conducting personal business with a vendor—consult your manager or HR before proceeding," compared to simply, "Avoid conflicts of interest." By giving concrete guidance, the code preempts confusion and suggests appropriate escalation paths when gray areas emerge.

In addition, HR can demonstrate how certain behaviors align with the organization's core values. If "innovation" is prized, the code might articulate how employees are encouraged to propose ideas freely, so long as they respect intellectual property boundaries. Similarly, references to an "open-door policy" for reporting concerns illustrate the practical side of fairness, ensuring no one fears retaliation for raising ethical or compliance questions.

Building Awareness and Ownership

➤ **Inclusive Drafting**:
Rather than a small team finalizing the entire document in isolation, HR often invites representative employees to review early drafts. This "peer validation" ensures the tone and content reflect everyday work realities, rather than lofty but irrelevant ideals.

➤ **Integration into Onboarding and Ongoing Training**:
Introducing the code during new-hire orientation establishes clear expectations from day one. Periodic refreshers— through short e-learning modules or lunchtime talks— reinforce essential principles and keep the code's contents fresh in employees' minds.

Ensuring Accessibility and Relevance

A code of conduct can fail if it remains hidden or seen as purely symbolic. Posting it conspicuously on the intranet, referencing it during performance reviews, or incorporating it into team discussions signals management's seriousness about ethical standards. HR leaders can also collaborate with communications specialists to produce concise summaries or visual aids, highlighting key sections for quick reference. When employees know exactly where to find guidance—such as how to escalate a suspected fraud—they feel empowered to act consistently with the code's directives.

Finally, updating the code periodically maintains its relevance. If remote work expands or new social media policies become critical, the code can reflect these evolving contexts, reinforcing that ethical considerations must keep pace with organizational growth and societal changes. In each revision cycle, HR might solicit feedback on problematic sections or gather success stories about how the code helped resolve dilemmas. Over time, this process ensures the document remains a living framework—one employees turn to, rather than a static artifact rarely consulted.

Developing a code of conduct is a dynamic process—one that balances clarity about behavioral standards with a deeper articulation of organizational values. By involving stakeholders, using accessible language and scenarios, and regularly refreshing the content, HR keeps the code aligned with both current operations and the company's future trajectory. This focus on practical guidance and consistent reinforcement helps employees internalize the code, fostering a workplace culture defined by integrity, fairness, and responsible innovation.

11.2.3 Handling Ethical Dilemmas (Conflicts of Interest, Privacy Breaches)

Even within well-structured organizations, ethical dilemmas can arise unexpectedly, testing HR's role as a guardian of standards and employee trust. Two recurring issues—**conflicts of interest** and **privacy breaches**—require HR to balance empathy, compliance, and organizational best interests. Addressing these dilemmas effectively ensures that potential harm is minimized and that employees remain confident in the company's commitment to fairness and integrity.

Confronting Conflicts of Interest

A conflict of interest occurs when an employee's personal or financial interests collide with their professional responsibilities. At times, the matter is overt: someone awarding contracts to a friend's company, for instance. More subtle conflicts, however, may involve close relationships that could compromise objectivity—like a manager evaluating a direct report who also happens to be a family member.

Resolving these tensions typically begins with transparency. Once HR becomes aware of a potential conflict, it guides the individuals to disclose all pertinent details—whether it's a familial relationship or a stake in a vendor. By collecting facts, HR can assess the severity. Some conflicts might be neutralized by recusing an employee from certain decisions; others require reassigning duties entirely to avert suspicion or bias. Through calm, systematic questioning, HR ensures employees realize that acknowledging a conflict doesn't always imply wrongdoing—rather, it's about maintaining objectivity and trust in daily processes.

When managers balk at the notion of stepping away from a decision, HR underscores that preserving the credibility of the decision outweighs any inconvenience. Sharing brief examples of how unaddressed conflicts in other organizations eroded morale or led to legal scrutiny can illustrate the stakes. Ultimately, HR's role is to protect both the individual from allegations of favoritism and the organization from claims of compromised ethics.

Managing Privacy Breaches

Recognizing the Risks
From payroll data to health records, HR departments handle vast amounts of sensitive information. Even a minor slip—like forwarding an employee's personal file to the wrong department—can breach trust and potentially violate regulations. Large-scale data exposures, such as hacking incidents, amplify these risks, spurring legal consequences and reputational damage.

Swift Response and Communication

Once a breach is detected, quick action is crucial:

➢ Containing the exposure is the immediate priority, whether by revoking compromised accounts or isolating affected systems.

➢ Notifying those impacted—while adhering to relevant legal and regulatory requirements—demonstrates transparency.

➢ Coordinating closely with IT and, if necessary, legal counsel allows HR to provide accurate updates to stakeholders, avoiding rumor-driven panic.

Balancing Empathy and Accountability

Privacy breaches can feel personal, so employees expect sincerity and thoroughness from HR. Where errors involve an HR staff member, a clear, impartial investigation reinforces that no one is above organizational standards. Follow-up might involve additional data protection training or revised protocols for accessing sensitive files. The message is twofold: the company respects employees' confidentiality, and it's willing to tighten procedures to prevent recurrences.

Why Handling Dilemmas Matters

Whether they stem from conflicts of interest or privacy breaches, ethical lapses can damage credibility, both internally and in the broader marketplace. Employees who sense that transgressions are brushed aside—or that personal information might be misused—will hesitate to engage candidly with HR and may explore external solutions (such as legal filings or whistleblower hotlines). Conversely, consistent transparency and decisive action, however difficult, build a culture where ethical considerations guide daily decisions.

In the end, HR's approach to these dilemmas encapsulates the organization's broader moral stance. By promoting honest disclosure, safeguarding private data, and maintaining balanced procedures, HR upholds an environment in which employees trust that issues are addressed fairly, fostering ongoing loyalty and reducing distractions that arise from unchecked ethical vulnerabilities.

Chapter 12: Interpersonal Cluster

12.1 Behavioral Competency 3: Relationship Management

12.1.1 Establishing Trust and Credibility

In the relationship management domain, trust and credibility serve as a foundation that allows employees, teams, and organizational leaders to collaborate openly. Without these qualities, even skilled communicators or strategic thinkers struggle to unite people around shared goals. When HR professionals and managers earn trust, they can influence decisions more effectively and encourage genuine participation. Likewise, showing credibility—in terms of both competence and consistency—cements an environment where stakeholders believe in the rationale behind policies, initiatives, and feedback processes.

Demonstrating Consistency in Actions and Communications
One of the simplest yet most powerful ways to build trust is through predictable honesty and reliability over time. For instance, when employees raise concerns about compensation fairness or job safety, responding with clarity—even if the immediate answer is that further investigation is needed—reinforces the idea that leadership takes them seriously. Consistency can also appear in how managers handle performance appraisals or conflict resolution: if staff see that guidelines remain the same regardless of personal relationships or individual status, they infer the organization values fairness. This steadiness in day-to-day dealings fosters a sense that HR or management will handle more complex matters fairly as well.

Beyond policy enforcement, credible leaders treat small commitments as seriously as large ones. Returning calls or emails promptly and sharing updates according to previously announced timelines might seem minor, yet these everyday signals accumulate into a broader picture of trustworthiness. Over time, employees infer that the same dependable approach applies to more sensitive areas—like delivering difficult feedback or preserving confidentiality in investigations.

Ensuring Transparency to Strengthen Relationships

Transparency moves beyond fulfilling minimum disclosure requirements. It involves proactively sharing relevant information so that individuals can understand decisions and potential implications:

> ➤ **Clarifying Processes**: During reorganizations or job reclassifications, employees often worry about hidden agendas. Offering a step-by-step overview—outlining how roles will be evaluated, what criteria define pay ranges, or how reassignments are decided—alleviates suspicion.

> ➤ **Explaining Rationales for Changes**: When new policies emerge—say, switching to a different benefits provider— leaders who outline the considerations behind the change (like cost savings or improved coverage) help staff see the bigger picture. This level of openness reduces rumors and fosters acceptance.

A transparent approach does carry limits, particularly around legal constraints or strategic confidentiality. Yet even in those cases, stating openly that certain details remain under review or bound by nondisclosure underscores a respect for employees. By defaulting to as much clarity as possible, HR practitioners reinforce the sense that they operate in good faith, sparing employees the suspicion that emerges when managers appear guarded or evasive.

Key Aspects of Trust and Credibility in Practice

✓ **Admitting Uncertainties**

Leaders who acknowledge unknowns—like an evolving external regulation—earn authenticity points. Employees see they are not being misled and appreciate straightforward updates, even if the situation remains fluid.

✓ **Aligning Words with Behavior**

If a department commits to supporting remote work but then introduces policies discouraging flexible schedules, trust erodes. Credibility demands that policies reflect stated values, reinforcing that promises are genuine rather than superficial.

✓ **Enforcing Standards Equitably**

Applying the same disciplinary guidelines to a high-performing director as one would to a junior staffer signals integrity. Staff who witness impartial consistency become less cynical about managerial decisions.

Why Trust and Credibility Matter

When trust and credibility flourish, individuals feel safe voicing concerns, bringing forward innovative proposals, or investing extra effort in collaborative tasks. Absent these elements, relationships deteriorate into guarded compliance, with employees questioning motives behind each directive. In high-trust cultures, on the other hand, team members more readily adapt to changes, approach HR for guidance rather than as a last resort, and express loyalty to the company's goals.

Equally important, a credible HR team can shape more effective policies because employees contribute honest feedback. If staff doubt HR's commitment to confidentiality or fairness, they might mask the extent of job dissatisfaction, skill gaps, or interpersonal tensions. By contrast, an environment that values trust fosters candid discussions, unveiling potential problems early enough for constructive resolution. Ultimately, establishing trust and credibility is not an abstract ideal—rather, it's the backbone that underpins successful initiatives, fosters mutual respect, and propels healthy organizational relationships forward.

12.1.2 Conflict Resolution Techniques

Disagreements in the workplace can arise from clashing goals, communication breakdowns, or underlying personality tensions. While some friction stimulates creative problem-solving, unresolved conflict typically disrupts team morale and impedes productivity. HR professionals and leaders who skillfully navigate conflict help maintain a cooperative culture, ensuring that differences become growth opportunities rather than roadblocks. Rather than sidelining issues, they employ structured methods to clarify misunderstandings, explore win-win solutions, and uphold constructive dialogue.

Fostering a Non-Adversarial Atmosphere

An essential first step in resolving conflict is de-escalation. People locked in disagreement often feel threatened or misunderstood, causing them to dig in their heels. A leader or HR facilitator can help shift the tone by emphasizing shared objectives—perhaps both parties ultimately care about delivering projects on time or maintaining a healthy team dynamic. Actively acknowledging each side's concerns, without immediate judgment, diffuses tension and opens the door to finding common ground. Neutral phrasing like, "I see you're concerned about resource constraints, while your colleague feels timelines are tight," signals an understanding of both perspectives. This approach breaks down defensiveness and encourages collaboration.

Maintaining respectful communication also protects relationships. Sometimes, even small language shifts—saying "Let's explore options" rather than "You must change"—ease defensiveness. If emotions run high, a brief pause or cooling-off period can allow participants to gather their thoughts. When meetings resume, reiterating a sense of joint purpose reminds everyone that the ultimate goal is not to "win" but to find workable solutions that serve collective interests.

Structured Techniques for Conflict Resolution

Interest-Based Problem-Solving

In this approach, each party identifies the underlying interests behind their stated positions. For instance, if a project manager demands more budget while finance insists on austerity, the project manager might be worried about achieving quality standards, while finance tries to minimize cost overruns. By surfacing these deeper interests—quality vs. fiscal responsibility—the facilitator can suggest alternatives that balance both aims. This technique moves the dialogue away from entrenched stances (e.g., "I need X dollars" vs. "We won't approve that") toward shared or overlapping priorities.

Mediation and Facilitation

Sometimes a neutral third party—often someone from HR or an external mediator—guides a structured conversation. The mediator's role is not to dictate outcomes but to ensure each participant is heard fully and to brainstorm potential compromises. This format might involve each party sharing their viewpoint uninterrupted, followed by a joint problem-solving stage where the mediator prevents verbal sparring or personal attacks. Mediation can be especially valuable when disputes become emotional or when direct attempts at resolution stall.

Collaborative Brainstorming

For less polarized conflicts, a short brainstorming session can break the deadlock. This tactic suits situations where both parties have partial truths or constructive ideas but lack a platform for merging them. The group sets aside blame and focuses on solutions—perhaps listing multiple proposals and assessing each for feasibility. Even if the final plan merges elements from multiple suggestions, participants often appreciate that their voices shaped the outcome.

Sustaining Positive Dynamics After Agreement

Settling on a workable solution doesn't guarantee lasting harmony—follow-up matters. If teams agree to reallocate workloads, for instance, managers should track how well the new assignments function and revisit them after a brief trial period to confirm satisfaction. Ongoing check-ins reinforce transparency, reinforcing that leadership or HR isn't imposing a quick fix and abandoning the situation. By monitoring newly implemented measures, leaders catch minor snags early, preventing a relapse into old disputes.

It's also crucial to address any deeper interpersonal rifts that surface during conflict resolution. If the process reveals trust deficits or communication issues in a particular department, HR can step in with targeted workshops, mentoring, or facilitated discussions to strengthen relational skills. Investing in these after-care steps ensures that the benefits of resolving a single conflict extend more widely, setting a precedent for healthier discussions across the organization.

Conflict resolution in the workplace hinges on respect, clear communication, and a focus on shared aims. Rather than sidestepping disagreements or allowing them to fester, effective leaders acknowledge the legitimacy of each viewpoint and guide participants toward constructive outcomes. Through approaches such as interest-based problem-solving, facilitated mediation, or collaborative brainstorming—and by diligently following up on agreements—HR nurtures an environment where differences spark innovation and balanced compromise rather than protracted struggles.

12.1.3 Networking and Mentoring

Expanding professional connections and offering structured guidance are two powerful ways HR can foster a collaborative, growth-oriented culture. Networking opens avenues for sharing expertise, uncovering new resources, and forging cross-departmental alliances. Meanwhile, mentoring pairs individuals at different career stages, channeling institutional knowledge in a way that boosts retention, engagement, and succession planning. Both strategies deepen interpersonal bonds across the workforce, enabling employees to access support and wisdom they might otherwise miss in day-to-day operations.

Building Effective Networks

Strategic networking involves more than merely exchanging contact information at events. HR leaders often encourage authentic relationship-building by orchestrating group sessions or collaborative platforms where employees can learn from one another's specialties or experiences. For example, a newly hired recruiter might benefit from meeting seasoned managers in finance or IT, understanding department-specific workforce challenges. Through these interactions, the recruiter can spot broader organizational needs that inform more precise talent sourcing efforts, while also broadening internal alliances that expedite candidate evaluations.

Moreover, digital communities—from Slack channels to HRIS-based forums—provide a venue for employees in different offices or time zones to share insights. By seeding these groups with discussion prompts (e.g., best practices for remote training), HR kindles exchanges that encourage employees to see each other as go-to resources for problem-solving. Over time, these bonds can speed project execution, reduce duplicated efforts, and nurture a sense that staff are part of a supportive, interlinked network rather than isolated in functional silos.

Making Mentoring Programs Thrive
While informal mentoring relationships may flourish spontaneously, structured programs help spread these benefits organization-wide. In many programs, employees volunteer as mentors or mentees, with HR acting as the matchmaker based on aligned career goals or technical competencies. A strong mentoring initiative typically addresses:

- ✓ **Purposeful Matching**: Pairing participants who have complementary skills or aspirations (e.g., an up-and-coming project lead with a manager experienced in high-stakes negotiations).

- ✓ **Clear Expectations**: Setting a cadence of monthly or bi-monthly meetings, along with objectives that might include leadership development, project management tips, or navigating company-specific procedures.

- ✓ **Tracked Outcomes**: Soliciting feedback from both mentors and mentees to verify progress, identify stumbling blocks, and celebrate achievements. Tracking might reveal, for instance, that participants who regularly exchange feedback are more likely to stay with the organization, thanks to improved confidence or cross-functional collaboration.

Mentors themselves often find renewed motivation in guiding others, refining their coaching skills and staying alert to emerging challenges on junior employees' horizons. Mentees, meanwhile, gain tailored guidance that accelerates their ability to assume higher responsibilities—whether in specialized niches or broader leadership roles. Together, these relationships form a cycle of knowledge sharing that preserves institutional expertise and fosters a sense of community.

Ensuring Tangible Results

Networking and mentoring both lose impact if they remain superficial. HR can enhance effectiveness by:

✓ **Linking Goals to Business Outcomes**
Employees may respond more enthusiastically to a mentoring opportunity if it clearly supports career progression or project success. Similarly, encouraging cross-team networks might emphasize that improved collaboration yields real gains, such as faster product rollouts or increased customer satisfaction.

✓ **Rewarding Active Participation**
Recognizing mentor-mentee pairs that achieve specific milestones—like delivering a key presentation or launching a new process—validates the time they invest. Such recognition can appear in newsletters or at team gatherings.

✓ **Periodically Refining Structures**
Over time, large organizations may find that certain mentoring matches need adjusting (as individuals switch roles or priorities change). A mid-year checkpoint allows HR to reshuffle pairs or refresh networking formats, ensuring these programs remain flexible and relevant.

In the broader view, networking and mentoring flourish when they weave seamlessly into organizational culture. Leaders who showcase examples of successful knowledge-sharing or co-mentoring arrangements signal that these practices are not mere add-ons but integral to a thriving environment. Under this backdrop, employees confidently develop ties across departments, glean perspectives from mentors, and step forward to help others along the way—strengthening both individual development and collective resilience.

12.2 Behavioral Competency 4: Communication

12.2.1 Verbal, Written, and Nonverbal Communication Skills

Strong communication forms the backbone of effective HR leadership, shaping how employees perceive guidance, feedback, and organizational goals. Whether exchanging quick instructions in a meeting, composing policy updates, or conveying support through body language, HR professionals must ensure messages resonate across varied contexts. By refining verbal, written, and nonverbal cues, leaders create an atmosphere of clarity and respect that underpins collaboration and reduces misunderstandings.

Cultivating Verbal Clarity and Presence
A concise yet empathetic verbal style can resolve confusion before it takes root. This approach hinges on adjusting speech patterns—tone, pace, and phrasing—to suit each setting. In staff forums or one-on-one conversations, HR specialists often adopt a tone that combines authority with approachability, ensuring employees feel both reassured and guided. Meanwhile, summarizing key points at the close of a meeting solidifies shared takeaways, preventing differing interpretations after participants disperse.

When dealing with sensitive information—like performance concerns or discussions of personal hardship—selecting the right words matters greatly. Emphasizing neutral language (e.g., focusing on behaviors rather than personal traits) reduces defensiveness. Using measured pauses can also give the listener time to process emotionally charged topics. Over time, consistent verbal empathy fosters trust, helping staff feel comfortable raising questions or issues earlier.

Sharpening Written Communication

> ➤ **Matching Format to Purpose**: A formal memo might suit policy updates, but more urgent or motivational messages can find better expression in shorter, direct emails or chats. Clarity in the subject line and a succinct opening paragraph often set the right tone, allowing recipients to grasp essential content quickly.

> ➤ **Balancing Detail with Readability**: While robust documentation is essential for compliance or policy references, excessive jargon or repetitive clauses bury the key message. Strategic use of headings, bullet points (in moderation), and white space helps employees navigate lengthy procedures or detailed FAQ documents without confusion.

Written communication also leaves a more permanent record than a spoken exchange. Drafting with an eye for consistent terminology ensures employees don't receive contradictory guidance from different HR sub-teams. Revisiting documents with a fresh perspective—ideally after a short break—helps authors spot ambiguities or awkward phrasing that could lead to misinterpretations.

Interpreting and Projecting Nonverbal Signals

Even well-chosen words can fall flat if nonverbal cues undermine them. For HR professionals, mindful attention to posture, facial expressions, and physical gestures can either reinforce or contradict spoken intent. In group settings, making steady eye contact when explaining a new benefits plan underscores confidence and respect for the audience. Conversely, a slouched posture or arms crossed tightly may inadvertently suggest disinterest or defensiveness, regardless of the message.

In cross-cultural contexts, nonverbal norms vary widely. A direct gaze that signals sincerity in one culture might be deemed intrusive in another. By staying alert to local customs and gauging people's reactions, HR can adjust nonverbal communication on the fly, ensuring staff feel acknowledged and respected. During virtual calls, gestures become more subtle, and the focus may shift to facial cues and vocal intonations. Even the background environment—like bright lighting or a neutral, uncluttered space—affects how participants perceive an HR professional's attentiveness.

Aligning All Communication Channels

The power of communication arises when verbal, written, and nonverbal elements support one another. Confusion often occurs if an employee receives encouraging verbal feedback in a performance review but then reads an email that sounds overly critical, or if HR announces an "open-door policy" while nonverbal signals (e.g., staff seeing a manager often closed off in private discussions) suggest otherwise. Maintaining consistency across all channels prevents such disconnects.

At a broader level, cohesive communication means that employees understand updates—whether delivered in person, via email, or through an internal platform—convey the same priorities. Doing so fosters a sense of reliability that encourages employees to engage proactively, ask questions, and trust that HR's messages reflect genuine organizational intentions.

Verbal, written, and nonverbal communication skills reinforce each other to shape workplace dynamics. HR practitioners who adapt their language to the audience, structure messages for clarity, and match gestures to the tone of their words can significantly uplift collaboration and morale. By consistently attending to each dimension of communication, HR fosters respect, reduces the likelihood of misinterpretation, and ensures that important policies or cultural messages truly resonate with the workforce.

12.2.2 Listening and Feedback Mechanisms

An environment in which employees feel genuinely heard not only improves morale but also produces more effective decision-making. When leaders and HR professionals excel at listening, they uncover root causes of conflicts and spot opportunities for innovation. Meanwhile, structured feedback processes guide teams to refine performance, address misunderstandings, and adapt to shifting objectives. Both listening and feedback, when interwoven consistently into an organization's culture, can elevate trust and spark proactive engagement.

Cultivating Active Listening Skills

Truly absorbing another person's perspective goes beyond hearing their words. Active listeners remain alert to tone, pauses, and underlying emotions, reflecting these observations back to the speaker. This method—sometimes called reflective listening—discourages assumptions, providing a safer space for individuals to reveal concerns or share ideas they might otherwise hold back.

✓ In one-on-one meetings, paraphrasing the employee's statements ("It sounds like you feel overextended on tasks...") can confirm mutual understanding.

✓ During group settings, posing open-ended questions encourages each participant to clarify viewpoints, rather than default to superficial agreement.

✓ Consistent eye contact and minimal distractions—like avoiding phone checks or rushing to fill silent moments—demonstrate respect, reinforcing that the conversation matters.

When employees witness HR leaders practicing such attentiveness, they become more inclined to volunteer honest feedback early, rather than wait until an issue escalates.

Designing Effective Feedback Loops

➢ **Formal Reviews and Check-Ins**
Many organizations rely on periodic performance reviews. Yet short, scheduled check-ins—monthly or quarterly—can catch emerging issues long before annual cycles. Ensuring that feedback flows both ways (manager to employee, employee to manager) reduces the power imbalances that sometimes deter honest dialogue.

➢ **Anonymous Feedback Channels**
While open communication is ideal, certain cultural norms or personal reservations may hinder direct confrontation. Anonymous tools—digital surveys, suggestion boxes—offer a pathway for employees to highlight sensitive topics without fear of reprisal. HR can then examine trends or repeated concerns to decide on potential policy changes or training interventions.

> ### Real-Time Micro-Feedback
>
> In fast-paced environments, immediate observations prove invaluable. A quick note after a product demo or a short Slack message acknowledging successful conflict resolution can reinforce desired behaviors or clarify small oversights before they crystallize into larger issues. This immediate approach complements more formal processes by keeping day-to-day performance aligned with goals.

Maintaining Transparency and Follow-Through

Gathering candid input means little if employees see no subsequent action or explanation. After collecting feedback—whether from large-scale employee surveys or targeted team sessions—HR professionals and leaders should provide concise updates on what was gleaned, how concerns will be addressed, or why certain suggestions cannot be implemented. This transparency solidifies the perception that management listens seriously and responds thoughtfully. In turn, staff become more willing to share in the future, knowing their voices influence tangible outcomes.

When employees raise complex or sensitive matters—such as perceived favoritism or discomfort with a new policy—an empathetic yet structured approach is crucial. Clear timelines for responding, open invitations for follow-up questions, and thorough documentation shape an organizational culture where feedback is not just encouraged in principle but recognized as a valuable driver of improvement. As these habits take root, leaders and teams alike learn to adapt swiftly, refining both operational and interpersonal strategies based on continuous, constructive insights.

12.2.3 Communicating with a Global Workforce

As organizations expand across borders, the complexity of communication increases. Colleagues and teams may differ in language, cultural norms, time zones, and technological access. Under these circumstances, a well-crafted strategy ensures that information flows smoothly and consistently—enabling alignment on goals and reinforcing a sense of shared belonging. When HR and leadership tailor their messages, respect local nuances, and utilize diverse media channels, employees from every region feel equally informed and valued.

Addressing Language and Cultural Differences
When employees speak multiple languages, translation or interpretation can help—but authenticity and clarity matter more than merely converting words. Simple techniques like minimizing jargon, avoiding idiomatic phrases, and confirming understanding ("Does this make sense in your local context?") prevent misunderstandings. At times, adding brief explanations of cultural references may help employees in another region fully grasp the message's intent.

Cultural awareness extends to communication style. Some cultures prefer direct, concise updates, while others value relationship-building conversations before delving into task specifics. If a team in one country expects detailed written briefs, while another typically starts each project meeting with small talk, leaders who acknowledge these differences signal respect for local traditions. This respectful approach can make staff more receptive to company-wide priorities, ultimately smoothing collaboration across the enterprise.

Fostering Engagement Despite Time Zone Constraints

➢ **Rotational Meeting Schedules**
  Many global teams rotate meeting times so no single region regularly endures late-night or early-morning calls. This practice spreads inconvenience fairly and boosts morale: employees

recognize that leadership prioritizes inclusive planning rather than favoring one headquarters' schedule.

➤ **Asynchronous Collaboration**
In an international setting, expecting everyone to be available simultaneously is often impractical. Tools like shared drives, team chat platforms, or project boards let participants contribute updates at their convenience. This approach reduces waiting and allows individuals to craft thoughtful responses free from live "spotlight" pressure.

Maintaining Unified Messaging

Frequent organizational updates—sent through a combination of email, intranet, and brief video announcements—help unify scattered teams. Yet consistency is paramount: if one region hears a revised strategy or policy days before others, rumors and confusion may arise. Establishing a single "official" channel or time for major announcements can minimize these disparities. Where technology permits, short recorded messages from leadership, possibly with subtitles in multiple languages, reinforce the notion that each location receives the same core message at roughly the same moment.

In some cases, local HR representatives or team leads add brief explanatory notes, making large-scale communications more relevant to local audiences. For example, a new global benefits policy might require country-specific clarifications regarding eligibility or process steps.

Encouraging Interactive Feedback

Global communication thrives when it is two-way. If employees lack a straightforward method of voicing questions or concerns, they may disengage or rely on local guesswork. By designating accessible channels—like monthly "virtual office hours" or moderated discussion boards—leaders create opportunities for direct interaction. These forums accommodate various time zones and create a global dialogue, ensuring that leadership remains attuned to localized challenges or suggestions.

A supportive climate for feedback also benefits local managers, who often function as translators of corporate messages. When headquarters announces a reorg, for instance, local managers can relay front-line insights to leadership about how staff interpret or react to the news. Honest exchanges build on previously established trust, preventing potential misalignments from escalating.

Communicating with a global workforce demands cultural sensitivity, language awareness, and careful scheduling. By simplifying language where needed, accommodating diverse time zones, and offering consistent, interactive platforms for updates and feedback, organizations unify distant teams around shared purposes. This inclusive approach empowers employees across regions to remain fully engaged in the bigger organizational story, forging a sense of unity that transcends geography.

12.3 Behavioral Competency 5: Global & Cultural Effectiveness

12.3.1 Cultural Intelligence (CQ)

For organizations whose reach extends into multiple regions or involves a culturally diverse workforce, **cultural intelligence (CQ)** functions as a critical capability. At its core, CQ represents more than simple awareness of cultural differences. Instead, it captures an individual's capacity to adapt thinking, communication, and behavior across diverse cultural settings. By fostering this skill, HR leaders and managers can navigate international negotiations, cross-border project collaborations, or inclusive domestic teams with agility—aligning daily actions to local norms while preserving overall organizational cohesion.

Foundation of the CQ Concept

Cultural intelligence suggests that developing proficiency in multicultural interactions is not a fixed talent, but rather a skill set that can be honed through continuous exposure, reflection, and learning. Practitioners often break it down into four interrelated dimensions:

1. **Drive (Motivational CQ)**: The desire to engage with other cultures. Some individuals feel energized by cultural diversity, whereas others may experience reluctance or skepticism. Fostering a climate that rewards curiosity helps employees view cross-cultural scenarios as opportunities rather than obstacles.

2. **Knowledge (Cognitive CQ)**: Understanding rules of social interaction, gestures, and communication preferences in different cultures. For instance, a sales manager traveling to Southeast Asia might learn about hierarchical norms, ensuring that greetings or meeting protocols reflect local expectations.

3. **Strategy (Metacognitive CQ)**: The reflection process that occurs before, during, and after cross-cultural encounters. Leaders with strong metacognitive awareness pause to consider how their assumptions might differ from local perspectives, shaping how they plan meeting agendas or interpret ambiguous feedback.

4. **Action (Behavioral CQ)**: The practical adjustments made in real time—such as altering speech pace, adopting culturally appropriate body language, or following local etiquette in negotiations. This dimension makes the other elements of CQ manifest in actual workplace interactions.

Integrating CQ into Organizational Practices

When leaders and HR professionals embody cultural intelligence, they not only manage global teams more smoothly but also inspire employees to adopt more open, responsive mindsets. Several organizational approaches underscore this shift:

- ➢ **Inclusive Hiring and Onboarding**: HR can design job postings, interviews, and orientation programs that underscore cultural adaptability as a valued skill. New hires gain early signals that the organization respects varied backgrounds and viewpoints.

- ➢ **Targeted Training and Simulations**: In-house workshops or digital modules introduce practical cultural scenarios. For example, participants might role-play cross-cultural negotiations, receiving immediate guidance on how tone and phrasing shift in different cultural contexts.

- ➢ **Mentorship Pairings**: Employees from distinct cultural backgrounds can learn from each other's experiences. Mentors share region-specific knowledge, while mentees help refine the mentor's communication styles, generating two-way enrichment.

A robust CQ emphasis also aids in localizing policies effectively. From implementing regionally adapted performance metrics to adjusting holiday schedules that honor local customs, informed leaders minimize misunderstandings and demonstrate sincerity in accommodating different norms. This authenticity reduces friction, supports talent retention, and strengthens employer reputation.

Sustaining Cultural Intelligence Gains

HR and senior management can maintain momentum by continually highlighting success stories—like a marketing project that soared in a new country due to culturally tailored messaging—and by recognizing employees who excel in bridging cultural divides. Regular feedback loops encourage staff to reflect on their experiences abroad or in multinational teams, updating personal strategies to maintain or improve CQ. In growing enterprises, this collective growth helps flatten learning curves as the workforce tackles fresh geographic markets, fosters truly inclusive teams, and faces novel consumer behaviors.

Why CQ Matters

In an era of accelerated globalization, possessing cultural intelligence remains pivotal for seizing international opportunities and building cohesive, diverse workplaces. Leaders who model CQ instill confidence that the organization cares about cultural nuances, ensuring overseas partners or local minority communities feel respected. As CQ permeates the workforce, employees become more adept at spotting and resolving cross-cultural tensions early, turning potential stumbling blocks into distinct competitive advantages. Ultimately, robust CQ fosters trust, innovation, and resilience, all hallmarks of a future-ready enterprise.

12.3.2 Managing Global Teams Across Time Zones

Coordinating employees spread across different time zones goes beyond scheduling challenges—it tests how effectively leaders can sustain unity and maintain productivity when personal clocks and cultural habits vary widely. For HR professionals, ensuring equitable treatment and seamless collaboration hinges on strategic planning, thoughtful communication, and flexible structures that accommodate each region's constraints. By forging a framework where team members feel equally engaged, even if they rarely share real-time meetings, global organizations can tap into broader talent pools and ensure around-the-clock operations.

Balancing Schedules and Avoiding Meeting Fatigue

A key concern involves preventing any single group from repeatedly sacrificing off-hours for calls. Rotating "core meeting slots" helps distribute inconvenient times more fairly, so that different regions occasionally hold early-morning or late-evening sessions. Equally important, HR can encourage or mandate the use of asynchronous collaboration: employees share updates via project management tools or recorded video messages, enabling counterparts in distant locations to respond the following day without stalling progress. This approach not only respects personal boundaries but also harnesses employees' most productive windows. For instance, an engineer in one time zone can finalize code handovers at the end of their day, and a colleague across the globe picks up those tasks the next morning—creating a nearly continuous workflow.

Fostering Cohesion in Distributed Environments

➤ **Structured Communication Rhythms**
   Beyond formal tasks, casual interactions encourage deeper rapport. Some organizations schedule short, optional "virtual coffee breaks" where employees gather in small groups, bridging the distance with personal conversation. This nurturing of relationships often pays off in smoother professional collaboration, as team members become more than names on a digital interface.

➤ **Local Empowerment**
   If certain roles or decisions are always centralized at headquarters, employees in satellite offices can feel sidelined. Providing local managers or leads with decision-making authority demonstrates trust and speeds up processes. Regular check-ins ensure alignment but recognize that local teams often grasp cultural nuances better. This balance of autonomy and

oversight builds confidence: remote staff know they aren't simply executing instructions from afar.

Ensuring Continuous Knowledge Sharing

While teams in disparate time zones may see less real-time interaction, knowledge transfer remains crucial. Tools like shared knowledge bases or wikis let employees document experiences, tips, and project insights accessible to anyone at any hour. HR might also encourage short training videos recorded by subject matter experts, so a marketing specialist in Europe can learn from an Asia-based colleague's approach to product positioning without waiting for a synchronous session. Over time, this asynchronous learning fosters a sense of connectedness, as employees realize they have direct access to best practices from colleagues worldwide.

Promoting Inclusivity and Recognition

When employees rarely meet face-to-face, there's a risk of marginalizing those who operate on the fringes of a main hub's schedule. HR can proactively address this by encouraging managers to rotate who presents in global calls or who leads updates. Highlighting achievements from different regions in internal communications, such as newsletters or digital forums, also ensures visibility. If a Latin American team solves a complex product issue, sharing their success story fosters a culture of recognition and motivates other locations to contribute as well.

Leading global teams across time zones calls for more than logistical solutions—it requires a mindset that values asynchronous work, respects personal schedules, and actively promotes engagement. By adopting equitable scheduling, empowering local decisions, documenting knowledge effectively, and celebrating accomplishments from every corner, HR and leadership craft a cohesive atmosphere. As a result, employees remain connected to shared goals despite physical distance, translating geographic diversity into a genuine strategic advantage.

12.3.3 Diversity, Equity, and Inclusion (DE&I) Initiatives

Organizations embracing DE&I strive to appreciate the varied experiences and perspectives of their people. By broadening the talent pipeline, ensuring fairness in processes like promotion or compensation, and fostering an inclusive environment, HR not only supports ethical practice but also helps boost innovation and decision quality. A workforce rich in backgrounds and viewpoints is more apt to challenge assumptions and adapt to evolving marketplaces. However, achieving DE&I goes beyond policy statements—it requires systematic programs that embed equity considerations into daily operations, coupled with metrics that track genuine progress.

Driving Comprehensive DE&I Strategies

Leaders who view DE&I as integral to business outcomes, rather than a standalone initiative, tend to see deeper and more lasting improvements. HR takes an active role by integrating equitable recruitment, retention, and development practices into every stage of the employee journey. This involves:

- ➢ **Assessing Current Baselines**: A data-driven approach can reveal potential imbalances in hiring, turnover, or career progression. If certain demographics are underrepresented in leadership, HR might re-examine whether unconscious bias affects talent selection or if networking opportunities are unevenly distributed.

- ➢ **Embedding Inclusive Processes**: Overhauling job descriptions to use bias-free language, offering flexible work options, or structuring interviews around standardized criteria all help ensure that each candidate or employee receives equitable consideration. Where relevant, local legal requirements regarding equal opportunity also inform these reforms.

Once fundamental practices are aligned, organizations can go further by cultivating collaborative resource groups or community outreach efforts that build on employees' unique perspectives.

Measuring Progress and Accountability

✓ **Defining Concrete Metrics**: Tracking demographic shifts, pay equity data, and promotion statistics provides a baseline for evaluating whether interventions move the needle. Transparent reporting—shared internally and sometimes externally—strengthens accountability, signaling that leadership values honest self-evaluation.

✓ **Creating Shared Ownership**: Rather than limiting DE&I goals to HR, involving department heads or cross-functional committees ensures that teams integrate inclusivity into everyday decisions. Performance evaluations might include criteria for inclusive leadership, encouraging managers to actively mentor diverse staff or promote an environment where differing opinions are welcomed.

Sustaining an Inclusive Culture

Even with strong policies and numbers-based progress, employees sense the climate of inclusion in smaller interactions. Micro-affirmations—like acknowledging team members' contributions publicly—reinforce a sense of belonging, especially for individuals who may feel less represented. When HR fosters dialogues on subjects like implicit bias or cultural respect, it normalizes continuous learning. Over time, these collective efforts bolster trust, reduce turnover among underrepresented employees, and attract broader applicant pools eager to join a demonstrably inclusive organization.

Ultimately, DE&I initiatives transcend compliance—by weaving equitable and inclusive actions into the organization's fabric, HR supports stronger collaboration, creative thinking, and a workforce that authentically mirrors the diverse communities the business aims to serve.

Chapter 13: Business Cluster

13.1 Behavioral Competency 6: Business Acumen

13.1.1 Interpreting Financial Statements and Metrics

A sound grasp of financial data enables HR professionals to navigate conversations about resource allocation, workforce planning, and organizational priorities with greater credibility. When HR leaders understand income statements, balance sheets, and cash flow statements, they see beyond basic budget constraints and spot how factors like labor costs or benefits investments influence the broader financial picture. This knowledge positions HR to collaborate more effectively with finance and operations, ensuring that people strategies align with the company's overall fiscal health.

Core Financial Statements and Their Significance

Each of the primary statements offers unique insights into a firm's performance and stability:

1. **Income Statement**

   Also known as the profit and loss (P&L) statement, the income statement reports revenues, expenses, and net income over a specific period. For HR, fluctuations in labor expenses—such as overtime pay or benefits costs—often appear here. Detecting significant increases might prompt a review of staffing models, potentially indicating the need for more hires (to reduce overtime) or more cost-efficient benefits packages. By understanding gross margins and net profit, HR can evaluate how people-related initiatives (e.g., new training programs) affect profitability.

2. **Balance Sheet**

   The balance sheet lists assets, liabilities, and equity at a given snapshot in time. While often seen as finance's domain, the balance sheet helps HR professionals assess long-term obligations, such as pension liabilities or severance packages if employee turnover is high. In addition, intangible assets—like brand reputation—can be influenced by employee engagement or skill levels. Recognizing the balance sheet's composition encourages HR to weigh the impacts of workforce changes on the company's overall leverage or liquidity status.

3. **Cash Flow Statement**

Cash flow statements clarify how money moves in and out of the business—covering operating activities, investing, and financing. Even profitable companies can struggle if cash inflows lag behind outflows. For HR, this may mean certain short-term people initiatives (such as accelerated hiring sprees) could be delayed if the company's operating cash flow is tight. Conversely, strong cash flow might support more generous performance bonuses or expansion of learning programs.

Key Financial Metrics for HR Context

While the raw statements hold vital information, metrics such as gross margin, return on investment (ROI), or turnover ratio often prove more directly relevant for HR's decision-making. A few notable examples include:

- ➢ **Labor Cost as Percentage of Sales**: Indicates whether workforce expenses remain proportionate to revenue generation. If labor costs climb disproportionately, HR and line managers might evaluate process efficiencies, training to improve productivity, or even adjusting workforce structures.

- ➢ **Operating Margin**: Demonstrates how much profit remains after paying variable costs, including labor. When margins are thin, HR must be judicious with wage increases or staff expansions, balancing morale and retention against cost constraints.

➢ **EBITDA (Earnings Before Interest, Taxes, Depreciation, and Amortization)**: Provides a lens into operational profitability free from certain accounting nuances. HR can reference EBITDA to justify strategic initiatives that might require up-front investment but yield higher operational gains.

Why These Insights Matter

Decisions about headcount, compensation, or training frequently hinge on the company's financial capacity to absorb these costs. If an HR director can interpret shifts in revenues, margins, and cash reserves, they develop recommendations grounded in the company's present conditions. For instance, proposing a major recruitment drive is more persuasive if paired with data showing sufficient cash flow to handle the new payroll. Alternatively, if the organization's balance sheet indicates a heavy debt load, an HR plan might focus on internal talent development rather than expensive external hires.

Moreover, a broader understanding of financial statements boosts HR's credibility when partnering with executive leadership. By speaking confidently about how labor strategies affect the bottom line, HR practitioners ensure they're perceived not just as people specialists but as key strategic advisors. This comprehensive approach to financial data fosters a more integrated mindset, where cost controls, long-term profitability, and employee well-being are seen as mutually reinforcing facets of sustainable growth.

13.1.2 Budgeting and Cost-Benefit Analysis

A robust budgeting process, coupled with thorough cost-benefit analysis, underpins many HR-led initiatives—whether those involve new recruitment software, expanded training programs, or revised compensation structures. By approaching these activities with a strategic lens, HR not only justifies expenditures but also showcases how thoughtful investments in people yield concrete organizational returns. This level of financial acumen reassures executives that HR decisions contribute to overall stability and growth, rather than being seen as purely administrative costs.

Creating a Realistic HR Budget

Because HR departments juggle salary budgets, benefits, and various developmental programs, clarity is crucial. At the start of a budget cycle, HR practitioners typically gather data on current headcount, projected attrition, anticipated hires, and any significant changes in legislation (like benefits mandates) that may drive costs upward. They also consider intangible factors: if the organization intends to expand geographically, recruitment expenses might spike temporarily. By collating these details, HR can forecast essential spending accurately.

In practice, coordinating with department heads allows HR to identify potential skill gaps or major training needs. For example, if a technology team plans to adopt a cutting-edge platform, HR might account for specialized training sessions or an updated onboarding structure. These early consultations help avoid last-minute surprises: rather than discovering an urgent need for 50 new hires mid-year, HR plans accordingly, adjusting the budget to accommodate extra recruitment and orientation. Presenting these forecasts in a concise, data-backed format—often comparing prior periods—makes it easier for executives to grasp the rationale behind each line item.

Allocating Funds Within HR

Balancing the HR budget itself can be a delicate exercise. Beyond regular payroll and benefits, smaller categories—like employee engagement events, wellness initiatives, or online learning subscriptions—add up. When deciding which programs merit funding, HR must weigh both immediate returns (reduced overtime via improved scheduling) and strategic payoffs (succession planning or leadership development that might not show results for a year or two). Maintaining a degree of flexibility in allocations—enabling some reallocation mid-year—helps absorb unexpected costs, such as a surge in healthcare claims or accelerated software updates, without derailing high-priority projects.

Applying Cost-Benefit Analysis to HR Decisions

Quantifying Tangible and Intangible Returns

In many HR proposals—like launching a retention initiative—tangible outcomes include lower turnover expenses and shortened recruitment cycles. Intangible benefits might appear in boosted morale or stronger employer branding, which can indirectly reduce hiring costs. While intangible factors are trickier to put into exact figures, referencing industry benchmarks or internal analytics (like engagement survey trends) can supply supportive evidence.

Weighing Options and Trade-Offs

A cost-benefit lens encourages HR to compare multiple solutions. For instance, if a company faces a surge in repetitive injuries, leadership might consider purchasing ergonomic equipment or running a more robust safety training program. Assessing each proposal's cost, implementation timeline, and projected decrease in injury claims or missed workdays clarifies the best route. Cost-benefit analysis might even combine short-term metrics (reduced immediate healthcare costs) with long-term ones (fewer workers' compensation claims, better employee satisfaction).

Demonstrating ROI to Stakeholders
One recurring challenge in HR is persuading executives that certain projects—like upgrading an applicant tracking system or expanding a leadership development program—yield meaningful financial returns. Cost-benefit analysis allows HR to outline:

- ✓ **Initial and Recurring Costs**: Detailing software subscription fees, consulting support, or staff hours needed for rollout.

- ✓ **Likely Gains**: Reductions in manual data entry, faster time-to-fill for critical roles, or heightened promotion rates for internal candidates that translate to lower external hiring fees.

- ✓ **Time Horizon**: Some results manifest quickly, while others (such as leadership pipeline improvements) emerge over a longer period. Specifying these timelines helps manage expectations about when the organization will see payback.

By interspersing real-world examples—like how a prior training initiative or technology purchase enhanced productivity—HR professionals reinforce that their requests aren't speculative. They also solidify relationships with finance leaders, who appreciate consistent, systematic justification for outlays.

Sustaining Accountability
Putting a budget or cost-benefit projection into practice is only part of the cycle. Regular monitoring verifies whether spending tracks the allocated funds and whether the project's outcomes align with projections. Should actual results deviate—like a recruiting software failing to significantly cut hiring costs—HR can investigate

contributing factors and consider mid-course corrections. This iterative approach fosters an environment where data, rather than assumptions, guide ongoing resource distribution. If an initiative meets or exceeds objectives, that success story can inform future budgeting cycles and embolden leadership to support further HR investments.

By mastering budgeting and cost-benefit analysis, HR shifts from a purely cost-center mindset to that of a strategic partner shaping organizational resources. Aligning proposed expenditures with demonstrable returns—whether immediate or long term—heightens HR's influence in executive planning sessions. Ultimately, this financial acumen enables the department to secure the funds and support needed to drive employee-focused programs that keep the company competitive and prepared for evolving market demands.

13.1.3 Understanding Key Business Functions (Marketing, Operations)

Effective HR strategy often requires seeing the organization through the lens of other core functions, particularly **marketing** and **operations**. While HR supports talent acquisition, engagement, and development, its impact resonates most strongly when it aligns these initiatives with the main drivers of revenue, customer satisfaction, production efficiency, and service quality. By appreciating how marketing and operations shape business goals, HR professionals can design more targeted programs—such as skill development, performance metrics, or organizational structures—that support and accelerate those functions' objectives.

How Marketing Affects HR Needs

Marketing shapes brand perception in the marketplace, influences product positioning, and, ultimately, drives demand for the company's offerings. As campaigns scale up, HR frequently sees heightened recruitment needs for specialized marketing roles—like digital analytics or brand management. Additionally, a surge in lead generation might pressure sales teams to expand, requiring fresh hires or new training curricula.

When HR understands the nuances of marketing strategy, it can:

- ✓ Develop robust employer branding that echoes the same messaging marketing uses externally. This consistency reinforces a coherent brand identity and can boost the quality of job applicants.

- ✓ Prepare the workforce for seasonal fluctuations or major product launches, ensuring the right talent is in place before marketing ramps up.

- ✓ Align marketing skill development with evolving trends, such as new social media platforms or data analytics methods, providing structured learning paths to keep teams competitive.

Navigating Operations for HR Alignment

Operations involve the systems and processes that create goods or services, spanning areas like production, supply chain, and quality control. For HR, identifying where operational bottlenecks or expansions occur becomes crucial:

1. **Optimizing Workforce Deployment**: If operations forecast a spike in manufacturing due to higher customer demand, HR can preemptively recruit or cross-train existing employees to handle increased workloads. Conversely, if new automation technology reduces the need for certain manual tasks, HR can explore reskilling pathways for affected staff.

2. **Promoting Efficiency and Safety**: Operations teams often target lean techniques or improved logistical flows. With HR's backing, these efforts might extend to training employees on continuous improvement frameworks (e.g., Six Sigma) or ensuring safety protocols fit seamlessly into production routines. By weaving in recognized standards or certifications, employees develop valuable capabilities that maintain high performance and meet strict compliance requirements.

Integrating operational awareness into HR decision-making also drives consistent job design. For example, if the company invests in advanced robotics, job roles may shift from repetitive tasks to oversight or troubleshooting. HR can handle the redesign of roles, compensation adjustments for more specialized skill sets, and training interventions that maintain morale during transitions.

Why This Cross-Functional Understanding Matters
Marketing and operations can appear at opposite ends of a business pipeline: one stimulating demand, the other fulfilling it. But any imbalance—such as a marketing campaign promising short delivery times when operations lack capacity—harms customer satisfaction and brand credibility. By tapping into marketing's timeline for promotions, HR ensures staff readiness, preventing supply chain crunches or customer service overload. Similarly, if operations identifies a materials shortage that might delay production, marketing teams can adjust promotional schedules to maintain credibility. HR's role is to help unify these perspectives, ensuring the workforce remains agile in meeting shifting demands.

Long term, a deeper appreciation of these functions helps HR champion strategic initiatives that truly benefit the entire enterprise. For instance, an HR-led leadership development program might include rotations through both marketing and operations units, broadening managerial insight and improving cross-departmental collaboration. By facilitating this exchange of knowledge, HR underpins a culture that sees business success as a collective effort—one in which brand-building and efficient execution merge harmoniously to delight customers and sustain growth.

13.2 Behavioral Competency 7: Consultation

13.2.1 Internal Consulting Models

When HR professionals step into the role of internal consultants, they apply structured problem-solving and advisory techniques to help departments or executives navigate workforce challenges. Rather than passively executing commands, they collaborate with stakeholders to clarify issues, diagnose root causes, and recommend targeted interventions. A deliberate internal consulting model provides a roadmap for guiding these engagements from initial scoping to final evaluation, ensuring that HR's expertise resonates with real organizational needs and produces tangible outcomes.

Foundational Elements of Internal Consulting
At its core, internal consulting involves forging a trusted partnership with the client—often a department head, project team, or senior leader seeking to address a specific concern. Rather than presuming solutions, the consultant adopts an investigative stance, collecting insights before proposing a plan. This dynamic underscores mutual accountability: the HR consultant brings domain knowledge on talent and organizational practices, while the client provides context, data, and potential constraints (budget, timelines, or cultural norms). By aligning on objectives from the outset, both parties remain clear about scope and intended deliverables.

Model 1: The Collaborative Diagnostic Approach
In this model, the HR consultant works alongside the client team to

unravel performance gaps or efficiency bottlenecks. After defining the problem, they jointly assess underlying factors—perhaps collecting employee feedback, examining turnover stats, or mapping workflow processes. The consultant's role is to synthesize findings, highlight patterns, and facilitate brainstorming on potential remedies. Because clients actively contribute to the analysis, they gain a sense of ownership, making them more likely to back the final recommendations wholeheartedly. A brief, structured workshop can serve as the culminating event, where data-driven insights guide an action plan with milestones and metrics for follow-up.

Model 2: The Expert Advisory Approach

Sometimes, HR's specialized expertise around compensation, compliance, or organizational design leads the internal client to seek a more directive approach. Here, the consultant invests time upfront understanding context—like departmental structures or past policy issues—then prepares a solution proposal with documented rationales. The client reviews these recommendations and offers feedback, ensuring that the final plan suits operational realities. This model suits situations where time is tight or the problem demands deep HR knowledge (e.g., reconfiguring pay bands). Effective implementation, however, still benefits from iterative client check-ins; rigid mandates can falter if clients feel their insights were overlooked.

Embedding Value and Continuity

➢ **Trust-Building Over Transactions**
   Internal consulting models often differ from external ones in that the consultant–client relationship is ongoing, bound by shared organizational goals. While delivering a solution remains important, sustaining positive rapport is equally critical—clients likely have continuing HR needs. A track record of reliable advice

fosters repeat collaboration: managers know that returning to HR for future challenges yields constructive dialogue.

➢ **Documenting and Scaling Success**
If a particular model—like the collaborative diagnostic—resolves a major training gap or streamlines a hiring bottleneck, documenting the approach and outcomes can pave the way for replicating this success elsewhere. For instance, a short "case file" summarizing the problem, analysis, solution steps, and resulting metrics (e.g., a 15% drop in turnover) provides a reference for other units facing similar challenges. Over time, HR's portfolio of success stories raises the function's credibility as an internal consultancy hub, not just a policy administrator.

Significance of Choosing the Right Model

Adaptability is key. Some leaders prefer an expert advisory style if they lack the bandwidth for deep collaboration; others thrive on iterative workshops and hands-on diagnostic sessions. Matching the consulting model to the client's situation—time pressures, complexity level, or appetite for co-creation—maximizes acceptance of the final recommendations. Additionally, a well-chosen model reduces friction during the problem-solving phase, minimizing rework and accelerating the path to tangible improvements.

Ultimately, effective internal consulting elevates HR from a purely operational role to that of a strategic partner, shaping decisions and fostering solutions tailored to unique departmental contexts. By using structured models that balance expertise, collaboration, and accountability, HR professionals cultivate enduring relationships across the organization and help orchestrate meaningful change.

13.2.2 Diagnosing Organizational Issues

Identifying and tackling the root causes of performance gaps or structural dysfunctions requires a methodical approach. Instead of relying on surface-level impressions, effective diagnosis involves gathering data from multiple sources—quantitative metrics, employee feedback, process observations—and then interpreting the patterns that emerge. By combining systematic analysis with a nuanced grasp of company culture, HR practitioners can pinpoint genuine obstacles to productivity, engagement, or process efficiency, rather than addressing merely the symptoms.

Framing the Problem Accurately

Many organizational issues appear as vague dissatisfaction, high turnover, or missed project deadlines. If leadership jumps straight to solutions (e.g., offering pay raises, scheduling more training) without investigating underlying factors, they risk applying an incomplete or costly fix. During the diagnostic phase, HR may begin by clarifying the problem statement with relevant stakeholders:

- Are employees leaving because of compensation mismatches, or do they lack advancement paths?

- Are deadlines missed due to poor resource planning, communication breakdowns, or skill deficits?

Pose these clarifying questions early to move beyond general complaints into more precise territory. Once key lines of inquiry are established, designing data-collection methods—from structured surveys to in-person interviews—becomes more focused, yielding insights tied to genuine root causes.

Gathering Data for In-Depth Diagnosis

Workplace Metrics and Historical Trends

Analyzing patterns in turnover, absenteeism, or internal promotion rates can signal where tensions arise. For instance, an uptick in overtime hours might correlate with under-resourced departments, spurring stress or burnout. Tracking these trends over months or years illuminates whether certain problems are new or represent chronic, unaddressed concerns.

Qualitative Input via Interviews

One-on-one conversations with employees—especially those in pivotal roles—often reveal friction points that broad surveys fail to capture. A line manager might note that communication from senior executives feels sporadic, fostering confusion and project delays. Meanwhile, a junior staff member could highlight morale issues tied to a perceived lack of recognition. Integrating such anecdotes with quantitative findings shows how processes, culture, and leadership behaviors intersect.

Interpreting Patterns and Themes

Once data is collected, the next step involves synthesizing it into coherent narratives. Imagine a scenario where feedback suggests "lack of career growth," while turnover metrics confirm spikes in mid-level professionals leaving for external leadership roles. Coupled with interview comments about unclear succession planning, the data converges on a root cause: a deficiency in defined career pathways and targeted development. Rather than merely raising wages or offering one-off training sessions, HR might then propose a structured succession framework that explicitly outlines skill requirements for each managerial tier, providing clarity and genuine internal opportunities for advancement.

Throughout the interpretation process, an impartial mindset remains crucial. If data conflicts with an initial hypothesis—say, leadership believed poor communication was the main culprit, but the analysis indicates mismatch in skill sets—adjusting the narrative and solution path demonstrates good faith. Sharing early findings with key stakeholders and inviting their perspectives can fine-tune the diagnosis further, fostering collective acceptance of the final conclusion.

Validating and Refining the Conclusions

Before presenting the results to decision-makers, HR professionals typically confirm that interpretations align with operational realities. For instance, verifying that insufficient training truly slows production might involve comparing productivity rates for employees who completed advanced upskilling versus those who haven't. Or, if a climate survey suggests inadequate recognition policies, double-check whether teams with robust peer-nomination systems demonstrate stronger engagement than those lacking such processes. These validation steps reduce the likelihood that recommended fixes miss the mark or spark skepticism among leaders who demand evidence.

Why Accurate Diagnosis Matters

Misdiagnosed issues can lead to misguided efforts, wasted budgets, or even further decline in employee morale if solutions appear irrelevant. Conversely, well-founded diagnoses empower organizations to allocate resources where they're needed most, endorsing changes that employees recognize as addressing genuine pain points. By investing time in thorough, data-based exploration, HR cultivates deeper trust among staff and executives, reinforcing a reputation for approaching organizational challenges with rigor and empathy.

Ultimately, diagnosing organizational issues sets the stage for sustainable improvements—enabling HR, in partnership with other stakeholders, to craft interventions that truly align with the organization's strategic vision and operational demands. Through systematic inquiry, data triangulation, and a readiness to adapt, practitioners turn vague discontent into clear, constructive avenues for growth.

13.2.3 Presenting Recommendations to Leadership

Sharing well-researched proposals with top executives requires more than simply providing an attractive slide deck or issuing a confident statement. In many organizations, leaders look for concise evidence that ties each recommendation to the company's long-term vision and financial realities. For HR professionals—often functioning as internal consultants—success hinges on balancing credibility and brevity, illustrating how people-centric improvements address pressing business needs. A compelling presentation of findings and suggested actions can prompt executive endorsement and sustain momentum for organizational improvements.

Structuring Clear, Impactful Proposals

A coherent format helps leadership grasp the relevance and feasibility of any recommendation. Typically, an effective presentation unfolds in stages:

Context and Purpose: A brief recap of the organizational concern—whether it's high turnover, suboptimal training outcomes, or cultural misalignment—sets the stage. Stating the root issues gleaned from data or interviews ensures everyone remains on the same page.

Proposed Solution: Present the solution plainly, avoiding excessive jargon or technicalities. For instance, if the recommendation involves launching a new onboarding platform, highlight key features that directly respond to identified challenges (such as prolonged time to productivity).

Supporting Evidence: Concise data snapshots, anecdotal remarks from employee feedback, or external benchmarks supply credibility. By spotlighting relevant metrics—like how a similar approach cut costs or elevated engagement at another firm—you anchor the recommendation in verifiable outcomes. Steering clear of overloaded graphs or lengthy tables ensures leadership can absorb the key points rapidly.

Emphasizing Strategic Alignment

Leaders typically want to know how the proposed action contributes to broader objectives, such as market expansion, product quality, or revenue growth. Drawing an explicit link—e.g., how improved performance management feeds directly into the innovation pipeline—reveals the initiative's strategic relevance. Conversely, if the data suggests ongoing compliance risks, positioning the recommendation as a step to avert regulatory fines or reputational damage underscores the potential cost of inaction. This clarity about organizational impact often differentiates compelling proposals from routine suggestions that might be deprioritized.

Tips for Engaging Leadership

✓ **Tailor to the Audience's Focus**: Senior finance executives might appreciate cost analyses and ROI calculations, while an operations-focused CEO may respond more to efficiency and process flows. Refining the message based on known leadership preferences fosters receptivity.

✓ **Highlight Quick Wins and Phased Roadmaps**: Indicating a timeline for visible improvements—such as a pilot group demonstrating results within six weeks—helps executives visualize near-term payoffs before committing to large-scale adoption.

Handling Objections and Questions

Even thorough proposals can face scrutiny from executives worried about budget strain, implementation complexities, or cultural shifts. Anticipating likely concerns—like the cost of additional staff training or potential downtime during software rollouts—allows HR to preempt common pushbacks with reasoned solutions. If the question revolves around ROI, for example, show how employee retention statistics or a drop in error rates can offset initial investments. By validating executives' concerns, then demonstrating how the plan accounts for them, presenters showcase a balanced viewpoint that fosters trust.

Closing with a Defined Action Plan

A strong conclusion solidifies buy-in. Rather than relying on open-ended final slides, specify next steps—whether that's forming a cross-functional working group, scheduling a pilot program's launch date, or identifying key metrics to track progress. This clarity in "what happens next" reassures leadership that implementation is well thought-out, reducing inertia after the meeting. Ensuring accountability—e.g., stating who leads the project, who reviews milestones, and when the next update will occur—keeps momentum alive. If possible, highlight how success will be measured, so leaders have a straightforward gauge of ongoing results.

Compelling recommendations rest on thorough research and a persuasive narrative that aligns proposed interventions with broader organizational aims. By organizing findings into a clear structure, validating ideas with reliable data, and showing how progress will be monitored, HR professionals convey not just a recommendation but a roadmap for tangible outcomes. This approach elevates HR's role as a strategic partner, shaping informed decisions that resonate at the highest levels of leadership.

13.3 Behavioral Competency 8: Analytical Aptitude (Critical Evaluation)

13.3.1 Data Collection and Analysis Methods

Robust HR insights hinge on gathering the right information and interpreting it with care. Whether examining turnover patterns or gauging employee satisfaction, the choice of data sources and analysis techniques shapes the accuracy and relevance of conclusions. By tailoring methods to specific questions—such as understanding skill gaps or pinpointing the causes of productivity shortfalls—HR practitioners transform raw figures into meaningful intelligence. This ultimately supports evidence-based decisions that enhance workforce planning, development, and overall organizational success.

Key Approaches to Collecting Data

Obtaining reliable information often involves a mix of quantitative and qualitative channels. Surveys can measure broad sentiment on issues like engagement or manager effectiveness, providing numeric results that can be tracked over time. One-on-one interviews or structured focus groups, however, delve into the subtleties of employee experiences, unearthing concerns or motivations not easily captured by multiple-choice queries. Beyond direct feedback, operational metrics—like average time to fill roles or absentee rates—offer a fact-based lens on processes and workforce behavior. Cross-referencing these operational metrics with interview or survey findings can add depth, revealing why certain patterns persist. Meanwhile, more immersive methods, such as on-the-floor observations, can uncover routine inefficiencies, real-time group dynamics, or hidden cultural norms.

Combining Sources: Often, the most powerful insights emerge when organizations overlay data from multiple streams. For instance, if an uptick in project errors coincides with low engagement scores in a particular department, HR might investigate workload or resource allocation as a possible culprit.

Analyzing and Interpreting the Information

Once data is assembled, analysis turns raw inputs into insights. Standard statistical methods—like correlation or regression—can highlight relationships between variables, such as how salary levels correlate with turnover for certain job families. In the realm of predictive analytics, organizations use historical data to anticipate future scenarios: for example, modeling the effect of a new training program on employee retention. Even more straightforward methods, such as segmenting survey results by location or role, clarify whether problems are widespread or restricted to certain groups.

Yet analysis alone is not enough. Contextual factors—like economic conditions, pending organizational changes, or unique departmental cultures—must shape conclusions. A high absentee rate might reflect dissatisfaction, or it might simply indicate seasonal illness patterns. HR professionals who account for these nuances reduce the risk of implementing misguided solutions. They also refine future data collection methods, adjusting questions or metrics to target the most pertinent details.

Maintaining Data Integrity

Throughout collection and analysis, data integrity safeguards trust in the findings. Ensuring surveys remain anonymous preserves honesty, especially when staff critique leadership or sensitive policies. Similarly, verifying that each data point—like a line manager's budget or overtime figures—comes from a reliable system keeps subsequent analyses anchored in fact. Establishing clear protocols for data handling, including who has access and how results get documented, protects not just confidentiality but the credibility of the entire HR analytics function. When colleagues see that data is compiled and reviewed systematically, they become more open to data-driven insights and recommendations, knowing the processes behind them are transparent and robust.

Ultimately, well-chosen data collection and analysis techniques empower HR professionals to move beyond gut instincts. By carefully designing instruments, blending different sources, and interpreting patterns in context, they generate actionable knowledge that aligns workforce strategies with real organizational needs. From diagnosing morale challenges to forecasting staffing levels, effective data methodology remains a cornerstone of critical evaluation in HR.

13.3.2 Evidence-Based Decision Making

Implementing people-related initiatives based on reliable data and sound analysis—rather than intuition or tradition—lies at the heart of evidence-based decision making. For HR professionals and leaders, this approach entails gathering robust information, critically assessing its validity, and using the resulting insights to guide policies, processes, or strategic moves. By grounding recommendations in empirical evidence rather than anecdotes, organizations strengthen accountability and reduce the likelihood of costly missteps, ultimately building stronger credibility for HR's role in shaping workforce and operational decisions.

Sourcing and Evaluating Relevant Evidence

Evidence-based decisions typically integrate multiple layers of data. A well-designed employee survey might reveal morale challenges, while departmental performance metrics confirm precisely where productivity lags. External research—such as market wage analyses or case studies of how peer companies manage remote work—provides a broader context, enabling HR to benchmark internal findings against industry trends. Where possible, combining these sources yields a richer picture of root causes.

When gathering information, the quality of the data is paramount. A large-scale engagement survey might seem impressive, but if its questions are ambiguous or biased, the conclusions may prove unreliable. Similarly, correlational data—like noticing that high performers often receive certain benefits—doesn't guarantee causation. Evidence-based practitioners scrutinize each data source's methodology and relevance, weeding out weak or outdated references to ensure robust support for organizational initiatives.

Applying Evidence Across HR Functions

Recruitment and Selection

Instead of relying on "gut feelings," an evidence-based hiring manager might use validated assessment tools that predict job performance. Reviewing academic studies on structured interviews and analyzing internal data on past hires helps refine the selection criteria, reducing trial-and-error approaches.

Performance Management

If the goal is to enhance feedback processes, HR professionals gather evidence on effective review cycles—perhaps short, frequent check-ins versus annual evaluations. By reviewing internal data on turnover or engagement trends linked to feedback frequency and referencing external reports on high-performing cultures, leaders can restructure performance discussions more confidently.

Overcoming Organizational Resistance

Some stakeholders may prefer established practices or personal intuition. To bring them aboard, evidence-based HR professionals present transparent, concise findings that resonate with pressing concerns. For instance, if managers worry a new training approach will disrupt workflow, well-chosen data can show how similar interventions, in comparable businesses, led to a clear ROI or reduced errors. By translating the statistics into meaningful cost or productivity terms, HR ensures that evidence-based proposals speak to both minds and budgets.

In addition, evidence-based decision making gains traction when leaders demonstrate its utility. If top management references data-driven findings in meetings—citing a recent analysis on the positive impact of cross-training, for example—teams see that the organization values systematic inquiry. Over time, routines like "evidence check" segments in project reviews or staff briefings can normalize the habit of seeking data or documented reasoning before adopting a course of action.

Ensuring Rigorous Interpretation

Collecting data is only the first phase; how that data is interpreted can define success or sow confusion. Skilled HR professionals examine whether certain demographics, departments, or geographies skew results, or if external factors (e.g., seasonal workload surges) might influence the numbers. They also remain cautious about rushing to attribute cause-and-effect relationships when dealing with correlations. In practice, they might run a pilot or do small-scale testing before implementing major policy shifts, confirming that the insights truly hold under real conditions.

Evidence-based decision making distinguishes itself by integrating reliable data, critical scrutiny, and real-world testing into HR's strategic and operational activities. By systematically evaluating sources, blending internal and external evidence, and thoughtfully interpreting outcomes, HR practitioners deliver recommendations that resonate with leadership priorities. This discipline not only yields more effective initiatives—like streamlined hiring or better-tailored training—but also cements HR's standing as a grounded, analytics-savvy partner in organizational success.

13.3.3 Identifying Trends and Forecasting

Anticipating shifts in organizational needs—whether in talent supply, market demands, or operational costs—can deliver a competitive edge. When HR leverages historical patterns and emerging signals, it moves beyond reactive measures and helps steer strategic planning. The art of **identifying trends** involves spotting meaningful fluctuations in data, while **forecasting** uses those insights to project possible future scenarios. By systematically applying these techniques, HR aligns workforce strategies with evolving realities, preventing disruptions and seizing timely opportunities.

Uncovering Patterns in Workforce Data
A primary step in trend analysis is examining historical records across multiple dimensions—such as turnover rates, overtime frequency, or internal mobility paths. While minor fluctuations may be noise, consistent increases or decreases over months or years might reflect deeper structural issues:

> ➢ An elevated turnover trend in a key department could indicate leadership gaps, compensation mismatches, or cultural mismatches. Investigating the underlying causes allows HR to propose precisely targeted interventions (e.g., refined onboarding or managerial coaching).

> Seasonal peaks in absenteeism, correlated with major events or weather patterns, might prompt flexible scheduling or a reevaluation of staffing models.

Combining multiple data points—like cross-referencing performance ratings with exit interviews—can reveal hidden linkages that single metrics would conceal. If high-rated employees repeatedly leave soon after promotions, for instance, HR might explore whether new responsibilities lack corresponding support or compensation adjustments.

Approaches to Forecasting and Planning

Trend Extrapolation

This straightforward approach projects past patterns into the future. If hires for specialized engineering roles historically rose by 10% each quarter, one might anticipate a similar trajectory. However, HR professionals remain alert to contextual shifts—such as newly available automation tools or changes in the labor market—that may render straightforward extrapolation incomplete.

Scenario Planning

Instead of relying on a single linear projection, scenario planning imagines multiple plausible outcomes—ranging from best to worst case—and frames distinct HR responses. For example, if production lines might double output within two years, HR prepares a plan for aggressive hiring and skill development; if demand falls short, the plan adjusts to safeguard morale without overhiring.

In each scenario, identifying key indicators—like sales performance or legislative changes—allows the organization to pivot as certain "triggers" arise, minimizing guesswork. By encouraging leaders to debate different futures, HR anchors workforce decisions more firmly in real business drivers.

Integrating External Signals

Focusing purely on internal data risks missing critical shifts in the broader environment. An organization that tracks only its own turnover might be unprepared if a rival employer, newly arrived in the region, offers notably higher wages for similar skill sets. Likewise, looming regulatory changes—such as revised overtime laws—could upend payroll projections if not anticipated. Regular scanning of economic indicators, competitor actions, and technology advancements ensures forecasts remain grounded in the real-world context.

These external insights can also refine time horizons. A quick or unexpected jump in market demand might demand "just-in-time" hiring, while slower, predictable expansions allow for phased recruitment and training. By blending external intelligence into internal patterns, HR can pinpoint the sweet spot between agility and cost-efficiency.

Enhancing Credibility with Visual Tools and Transparent Methods

Communicating trend analysis to executives or departmental leaders often goes more smoothly when accompanied by visuals—like concise line graphs, heat maps, or scenario matrices. These tools let stakeholders grasp patterns at a glance, making it easier to discuss potential courses of action. Explaining assumptions behind forecasts (e.g., stable economic conditions, steady growth in the target demographic) clarifies the logic, bolstering trust in the methodology.

If certain unknowns remain, acknowledging them openly can spark collaborative thinking about risk mitigation.

By systematically identifying trends in both workforce and market data—and forecasting how these patterns may evolve—HR professionals transition from problem-solvers to proactive strategists. Whether the goal is ensuring adequate staffing, aligning budgets with future demands, or mitigating talent shortages, a disciplined approach to trend analysis and forecasting underpins better, more forward-looking decisions. This predictive lens strengthens HR's strategic contributions, positioning the function as a linchpin for organizational resilience and informed growth.

ACCESS CODE – ONLINE TOOLS

Unlimited Exam Simulator

Practice with our interactive exam simulator featuring a built-in timer and customizable options. Choose your exam duration, select the number of questions, and challenge yourself with randomized questions to sharpen your skills and track your progress. Scan the QR Code or type visit:

www.Apex-Academic.com/shrm_exam_sim

Exam Flashcards

Reinforce your understanding with digital flashcards designed for quick review. Cover key topics to boost your memory retention and exam confidence.
Scan the QR Code or type visit:

www.Apex-Academic.com/shrm_flashcards

Printable Exams & Answers

Access full-length practice exams that match the real SHRM-CP/SCP exam format and detailed answer keys in PDF format. Download, print, and simulate the real test-taking experience to prepare for success. Scan the QR Code or type visit:

www.Apex-Academic.com/shrm_exam_print

ACCESS CODE:

A A R S H R M 2 5

Chapter 14: Study Strategies and Test-Taking Techniques

14.1 Creating a Study Plan

14.1.1 Recommended Time Allotments per Domain

Effective preparation typically involves creating a balanced schedule that covers each domain proportionately to its representation on the exam. Although every candidate's strengths differ, a general rule is to align study hours with how prominently each domain appears in the test's question distribution. By doing so, you not only ensure a broad understanding of all areas but also mitigate the risk of overlooking key competencies.

Below is an example of approximate percentages to guide your daily or weekly study focus. These figures are not prescriptive for everyone—some individuals may need extra review in certain areas based on prior knowledge or comfort level:

✓ **Domain A (e.g., HR Foundations)**: ~20%
   This domain might cover core practices or essential terminology. If it includes topics you've previously encountered, you may allocate slightly less time, focusing on refreshing concepts rather than learning from scratch.

✓ **Domain B (e.g., Regulatory Compliance)**: ~25%
   Given that compliance can be detail-intensive, scheduling more frequent short study sessions often helps sustain familiarity with laws and guidelines. Incorporating mini-quizzes on essential regulations breaks up heavier reading.

✓ **Domain C (e.g., Strategy and Metrics)**: ~30%
   Because strategic knowledge might encompass broader frameworks and data interpretation, it often demands deeper comprehension. Setting aside uninterrupted blocks

for reading case studies or performing practice analyses can reinforce your grasp on these topics.

✓ **Domain D (e.g., Specialized Functions)**: ~25%
If your exam includes specialized content—like global HR or advanced analytics—distribute reading and practice questions evenly across these subsets. Touching on them regularly keeps technical details fresh.

Refining Time Allocations to Your Strengths
While these percentages serve as a baseline, tailor them by auditing your strengths and weaknesses. If initial diagnostic quizzes or practice tests show mastery in one domain, reduce its time share slightly and redistribute hours to areas that present consistent challenges. Conversely, if you're unfamiliar with certain regulations or have rarely managed strategic projects, more intense review sessions may be warranted.

Building flexibility into your plan—adjusting hours as you gain confidence—is often the difference between a rigid schedule that feels unmanageable and one that encourages steady progress. This dynamic approach ensures you remain focused on improving the domains that matter most, maintaining balance without ignoring areas where you already excel.

14.1.2 Setting Milestones and Checkpoints

A well-structured study plan keeps motivation high and prevents last-minute cramming. By setting clear milestones, you can measure progress in manageable increments rather than hoping everything comes together at the end. While the specific targets vary—some focus on finishing certain chapters, others revolve around hitting score thresholds on practice tests—the core idea is to create short-term goals that lead seamlessly toward exam readiness.

Aligning Milestones with Study Goals

In planning out a study timeline, each milestone should correspond to a pivotal benchmark. For instance, completing all reading on a specific domain or achieving a certain practice-test score might serve as signals that you're ready to move on. These smaller markers create momentum and let you course-correct if you discover an area of unexpected difficulty. Sometimes it helps to build in contingency time, ensuring that if you miss a milestone, you have space to catch up without derailing everything else.

Below is one way to structure these checkpoints:

✓ **Major Milestone**: Finishing your initial pass of key materials (including essential chapters or recorded lectures), usually set a few weeks into your study timeline. At this point, you should have a broad overview, allowing you to see which topics demand deeper review.

✓ **Intermediate Milestones**: Reviewing a subset of practice questions after each major topic, followed by short quizzes or flashcard sessions. These offer real-time evidence of which concepts stick and which need reinforcement.

✓ **Final Milestone**: A comprehensive rehearsal, such as completing a full-length mock exam under timed conditions, a week or two before the real exam date. The results guide any final reviews or clarifications.

Creating Feedback Loops

Regular checkpoints work best when they're tied to an immediate reflection process. If your practice exam score for a crucial section doesn't meet your target, it's a sign to revisit that domain thoroughly. Conversely, strong results might let you reduce the time allocated for that section in favor of another domain that remains challenging. This self-evaluation approach encourages adaptable planning, so that your schedule never feels locked in or detached from actual performance.

Sustaining Momentum and Adjusting

To maintain morale, build small rewards into your milestones—like allowing a weekend break or tackling a less intense domain after a demanding study sprint. If life events disrupt your schedule, reassess your checkpoints promptly. Sometimes compressing a couple of lesser domains or swapping practice-test days may suffice, preventing any sense of defeat. Ultimately, the flexible but deliberate nature of milestones fosters a habit of continuous improvement: each checkpoint is both a result of prior effort and a launch pad for whatever comes next.

By thoughtfully setting and reviewing these markers, you transform a broad study plan into a tangible, step-by-step journey. Each milestone or checkpoint yields valuable insight into your mastery, ensuring that you refine both time usage and study techniques as the exam date nears.

14.2 Reading and Note-Taking Techniques

14.2.1 Condensing Key Concepts

Examination content often spans multiple chapters, detailed policy guidelines, or intricate frameworks. Rather than attempting to memorize entire texts verbatim, it's far more efficient to **distill main ideas** into concise, accessible formats. By reducing complex topics into compact outlines, you can preserve core principles and logic flows, making it easier to revisit and strengthen recall. Additionally, an organized summary illuminates how various subtopics connect, reinforcing a big-picture understanding rather than scattered facts.

Identifying What Merits Summarization

Early on, decide which areas warrant a condensed overview. Not every paragraph or bullet in the source material carries equal weight. Focus on concepts that frequently appear in practice exams, domain outlines, or major headings—indicating their likelihood of exam prominence. If you're uncertain, cross-reference official exam objectives or past practice quiz results to find knowledge gaps. This approach helps you concentrate summarization efforts where it yields the biggest payoff.

Building Structured Outlines and Maps

Reducing content works best when you capture essential points in a hierarchical or visual format. Some learners prefer classic outlines— leading with a primary concept, then listing critical sub-points underneath. Others use concept maps, grouping related ideas and showing how they interlink with lines or arrows. Both approaches clarify relationships: for example, if you're summarizing compliance requirements, you might cluster them by function (like wage and hour, anti-discrimination, health and safety), then note the key regulatory bodies and deadlines.

When you periodically review these outlines or maps, each revisitation cements not only the fact but also how and why the topic fits into the broader HR landscape. By scanning a well-structured summary before diving into a practice exam, you reawaken major themes and data points quickly, leveraging the clarity you created during earlier reading sessions.

A Quick Example of Condensed Notes

Example Domain: Performance Management

➢ **Objective**: Ensure consistent evaluation of employees, fostering growth.

➤ **Core Elements**:

✓ Goal Setting (SMART goals)
✓ Ongoing Feedback (quarterly check-ins vs. annual reviews)
✓ Documentation (forms, timelines, improvement plans)
✓ Legal Considerations (fairness, anti-discrimination)

Such a concise block covers the essence of performance management, reminding you of the flow (setting goals → regular feedback → formal reviews) and the precautions (ethical and legal frameworks).

Maintaining a Recurring Review Cycle

Condensed notes prove most beneficial when you revisit them periodically throughout your study journey. One method is to **allocate brief daily or weekly refresh sessions**, quickly scanning your top-level outlines. This consistent repetition ensures that detailed material—like key regulations, methodological steps, or theoretical models—remains accessible in long-term memory. If you find certain areas still feel fuzzy, refine that segment in your notes to include a short, clarifying explanation or a practical example that crystallizes the concept.

Why Condensing Key Concepts Aids Mastery

By stripping down reading material to its core, you spend less time reprocessing extensive text each time you review. This efficiency keeps study sessions lively and helps avoid mental fatigue from sifting through repetitive paragraphs or irrelevant anecdotes. Moreover, seeing your material streamlined in your own words deepens comprehension: the act of deciding which details matter forces you to parse the subject's logic. Ultimately, well-crafted summaries serve as compact references you can rely on in the final lead-up to the exam, ensuring quick, targeted reinforcement of high-priority content.

14.2.2 Using Flashcards and Mnemonics

For many learners, **flashcards** and **mnemonics** provide an efficient method of locking key facts, formulas, or steps into memory without being bogged down by lengthy notes. By converting complex concepts into brief triggers or acronyms, you reduce cognitive load during review sessions. This technique works especially well for recall-based exam questions—like definitions, lists of compliance steps, or framework components—where you need quick retrieval rather than deep critical thinking.

Crafting Effective Flashcards

High-quality flashcards emphasize clarity, brevity, and relevance:

1. **Pinpoint the Core Idea**: Each card should revolve around a single concept or question, such as "Definition of Adverse Impact" or "Steps in a Performance Improvement Plan." Avoid packing multiple ideas on one card, which can clutter your recall process.

2. **Create Logical Clusters**: If a certain domain (e.g., labor laws) has many finer points, cluster related flashcards to help you see which subtopics interconnect. This way, studying them together fosters a contextual understanding instead of a random fact dump.

3. **Incorporate Examples**: While the front of the card might pose a question (like "What is constructive discharge?"), the back can include a quick scenario that cements the term in a real-world context. Examples can prevent memorized definitions from becoming too abstract or easily confused with similar concepts.

Though flashcards often bring to mind a physical deck you shuffle through, many learners choose digital platforms for added perks—

like randomization or spaced repetition algorithms. Whichever format you use, revisiting these cards routinely, and retiring those you consistently answer correctly, keeps your overall review targeted and time-efficient.

Enhancing Recall with Mnemonics

While flashcards handle discreet facts, **mnemonics** condense multi-step processes or multi-element lists into easily recalled phrases or acronyms. For instance, to remember "Factors Affecting Employee Engagement," you might build an acronym out of key words (Leadership, Autonomy, Recognition, etc.). The sillier or more vivid the mnemonic, the higher the chance it sticks:

- ➢ **Acronyms**: Combine first letters of items into a pronounceable word (e.g., "SCORE" for key metrics: Satisfaction, Costs, Outcomes, Retention, Engagement).

- ➢ **Visual Imagery**: Conjure a memorable mental picture linking each item in a sequence. For example, picturing a chain of tasks for onboarding new hires as a "conveyor belt of success" can lend a comedic but powerful association.

Because mnemonics often rest on personal associations, they are unique to each learner's imagination. Developing your own creative hooks can be more effective than adopting someone else's prefab memory trick. In fact, the very act of constructing a mnemonic helps reinforce the content in your mind, prompting you to isolate each essential component in a logical order.

Integrating Flashcards and Mnemonics Into Routine Study

Although flashcards and mnemonics typically serve quick-recall needs, weaving them into your broader review cycle amplifies their impact. For instance, after reading a chapter on compensation structures, select the top eight points that frequently appear in practice tests—like basic definitions or compliance thresholds—and transform them into succinct flashcards or an acronym. Over the ensuing days, revisit them during short daily study bursts, linking each to relevant real-world examples or HR scenarios. This layered approach ensures memorized items do not float freely but rather tie back to the deeper knowledge you've cultivated.

In group study contexts, you can gamify flashcard usage by challenging each other with random draws or by swapping custom mnemonics. This not only keeps the energy up but also exposes you to different memory strategies your peers create. Ultimately, these techniques help chunk information into approachable pieces, boosting your confidence in retrieval and sharpening your overall exam readiness.

14.3 Approaching Multiple-Choice Questions

14.3.1 Eliminating Wrong Answers

Multiple-choice questions often feature distractors—options that seem plausible but do not fully align with the scenario or underlying principle. Learning to rule out these incorrect choices systematically can raise your odds of selecting the right response, especially under timed conditions. By approaching each question with a logical, step-by-step strategy, you can focus on the crux of the query rather than being thrown off by cleverly worded (but ultimately flawed) alternatives.

Breaking Down the Question Stem
Before considering any answers, thoroughly parse the question stem. Identify exactly what it is asking—whether it's seeking a specific regulation, the "best" approach to a scenario, or an outcome based on a stated premise. If details mention certain constraints (like

budget limits or legal obligations), keep those in mind as you sift through potential responses.

Try to isolate keywords that clarify the question's scope (e.g., "immediate action," "long-term solution," "according to policy"). These cues help you recognize when an answer might be technically correct but mismatched in timing or focus.

Watch out for absolute language ("always," "never," "all employees") that might signal overly rigid answers unless the question's facts unequivocally support that level of certainty.

Spotting and Dismantling Distractors

In many exams, distractors lean on common misconceptions or misapplications of policy. Some ways to identify and eliminate them include:

> **Partial Truth**: Answers that address part of the question but fail to resolve the main issue. If an option fixes a secondary symptom but leaves the core challenge untouched, it's likely incorrect.

> **Overreach**: Responses that go beyond what the scenario permits—for instance, recommending a major structural overhaul when the question only concerns a short-term conflict. These answers may have an element of correctness but ultimately deviate from the scenario's scope.

> **Misaligned Terminology**: If an option uses key terms incorrectly (e.g., mixing up "exempt" vs. "non-exempt" roles), it may be trying to sound relevant without applying the right concept.

When a distractor appears close to the right logic but includes a small yet critical inaccuracy, scrutinize the wording carefully. Exams often design such items to trap hurried test-takers who latch onto familiar phrases.

Sample Process for Narrowing Down Choices

1. **Check Each Option Against the Question**
   Does it solve the primary concern or fully answer the prompt's "what" or "why"? If an option only addresses half the problem, set it aside.

2. **Evaluate Plausibility**
   Ask, "Could this realistically be the next step or solution given the scenario?" If legal, ethical, or policy constraints make it unlikely, dismiss it.

3. **Compare Remaining Options**
   If two or more answers remain viable, look for subtle differences in scope, timing, or alignment with organizational best practices. Identify which best fulfills the question's demand.

Leveraging Context Clues

Sometimes, exam questions embed small contextual hints—like referencing a newly passed regulation or an employee's distinct background. If a potential answer ignores these details or contradicts them outright, it becomes easier to rule out. Conversely, answers that seamlessly incorporate scenario nuances (like acknowledging an employee's stated preference for a flexible schedule) often reflect the exam's intention for "best fit."

When in Doubt

If you still find yourself torn between two plausible answers, revisit the question's core requirement. The difference might lie in the method (collaborative vs. top-down), scope (short-term vs. long-term), or alignment with known frameworks. Even if you cannot confirm with 100% certainty, eliminating less fitting options systematically increases your chance of choosing correctly.

Eliminating wrong answers requires a balance of reading comprehension, critical thinking, and familiarity with test content. By dissecting the question stem, systematically discarding partial or overreaching responses, and focusing on the scenario's finer points, you can handle distractors more confidently. This disciplined approach ensures that, rather than guessing blindly, you leverage each question's details to guide you toward the correct solution.

14.3.2 Tackling "Best/Most Likely" Scenario Items

Certain exams challenge you with scenario-based questions where multiple choices all sound plausible. The trick lies in identifying not just a valid response, but the one that represents the "best" or "most likely" solution given the specific conditions. These items test your understanding of context and priorities rather than just factual recall. Successfully navigating them requires careful reading, prioritizing relevant details in the scenario, and balancing multiple potential courses of action.

Analyzing the Context

When you read a scenario, zero in on **who** is involved, **what** the real issue is, and **why** the question is being posed. For example, a prompt might describe a department where morale is low and production errors are rising. If each possible answer addresses performance improvement in some way, your task is to decide which approach both recognizes the root cause (perhaps unclear leadership) and practically fits the environment (maybe a short pilot project or manager retraining). By methodically dissecting the scenario, you can more confidently select an answer that aligns with the subtle cues embedded in the text.

Look for phrases such as "suddenly," "recently hired," "long-time employees complaining," or "consistent patterns" to identify the scenario's urgency or historical precedents. A "sudden" problem might need immediate triage, whereas "consistent patterns" hint at deeper structural issues needing a more systematic fix.

Weighing the Underlying Principles

Many "best/most likely" questions revolve around applying policy, ethical norms, or strategic frameworks to real-world situations. If multiple options are technically permissible, the exam likely wants the one that best adheres to recognized principles—like ensuring fairness, mitigating risk, or fostering collaboration. Ask yourself:

- ✓ Does this option respect established laws or guidelines relevant to the scenario (e.g., anti-discrimination, safety regulations)?

- ✓ Does it address the immediate need or simply set up a distant solution with no short-term relief?

- ✓ Could it inadvertently create new problems, like undermining leadership credibility or ignoring key stakeholders?

Answers that meet the scenario's demands *and* uphold broader organizational or legal standards typically top the list.

Techniques for Deciding Among Similar Options

1. **Revisit Key Words in the Prompt**
   If the question highlights "financial constraints," an answer proposing a budget-heavy overhaul may not be the "best" choice. Alternatively, if it mentions "long-standing interpersonal conflicts," suggesting a quick one-hour training

might lack depth. Pinpointing these context clues helps differentiate two seemingly decent answers.

2. **Rank Potential Consequences**

   If each choice appears valid, sketch how each would play out. Which solution yields the greatest benefit with the least disruption or risk? If one choice resolves the scenario's immediate tension but violates a company policy or overlooks critical input, it may be less suitable than an option that's slightly slower but more compliant or inclusive.

Common Pitfalls

A frequent mistake is rushing to pick the first answer that "makes sense" without fully comparing it to the others. Another is failing to note subtle differences, such as one solution providing partial relief but ignoring the scenario's core driver. Pause to cross-check each possible response against the scenario's underlying facts. If you find an answer only partially addresses the scenario or introduces conflict with standard practices, keep looking.

Confidence Through Practice

Scenario-based questions can feel ambiguous, but consistent practice—whether through small case studies or formal practice exams—develops an instinct for reading between the lines. Over time, you'll better recognize which organizational values or regulations the question expects you to apply. If an item references progressive discipline or constructive feedback, recall how typical HR protocols approach these processes. That mental schema steers you to the solution that best fits real-world HR norms and exam expectations simultaneously.

When contending with "best/most likely" items, aim to identify a solution that aligns thoroughly with the scenario's context, addresses immediate and core issues, and respects guiding principles or policies. By systematically evaluating each option's relevance and potential consequences, you minimize the guesswork and maximize the chance of finding the single, most fitting approach.

14.4 Stress Management and Exam Day Tips

14.4.1 Sleep, Nutrition, and Mindset

Balancing study efforts with personal well-being can profoundly influence exam performance. While detailed review sessions and practice tests are crucial, how you care for your body and mind often determines whether you can absorb complex material and remain calm under pressure. By giving deliberate thought to sleep quality, dietary choices, and mental resilience, you set the stage for more productive study blocks and a confident exam-day showing.

Quality Sleep: Fueling Cognitive Function
Deep, restful sleep does more than just recharge your body—it consolidates new information into long-term memory. In the final weeks of exam prep, it's common to feel tempted to shave off an hour or two of rest for extra cramming. However, chronic sleep deficits impair focus and retention, potentially negating the benefits of that last-minute study. Making a habit of consistent bedtimes and wake-ups helps stabilize your internal clock, reducing drowsiness during daytime review.

If racing thoughts keep you awake, consider brief relaxation exercises before bed. This might involve a couple of minutes of slow breathing or noting down tomorrow's top tasks so your mind doesn't circle around them overnight. Setting digital devices aside 30 minutes prior to sleep also helps, as bright screens can overstimulate the brain. Over repeated cycles, these practices give your memory the best possible environment to "settle in" newly acquired information.

Reinforcing Alertness with Balanced Nutrition

1. **Steady Energy Sources**
   Complex carbohydrates—like whole grains, fruit, or legumes—release energy gradually, avoiding the sudden dips caused by sugary snacks. Coupling such foods with lean proteins (e.g., eggs, turkey, or beans) fosters sustained alertness throughout study sessions.

2. **Hydration Matters**
   Dehydration can show up as fatigue, headaches, or reduced concentration. Keeping water close at hand, especially during longer practice exams or intense reading blocks, counters these effects. A subtle but consistent intake (like sipping from a bottle regularly) ensures you don't wait until thirst is distracting you.

Finding a Supportive Mindset

Beyond sleep and diet, a well-grounded attitude can curb stress and boost motivation. Viewing each study session as a step toward mastery—rather than as a pass/fail moment—gives you space to make mistakes and refine your approach. Some learners begin daily review by acknowledging a small recent success (like mastering a certain domain or improving a quiz score), fueling positivity for the tasks ahead.

If nerves creep in, short mental resets—like a two-minute pause for mindful breathing—help break swirling anxious thoughts. Visualizing exam success can also add calm: picturing yourself reading a question, recognizing the concept, and confidently choosing the correct answer reinforces self-belief. By weaving in these low-effort mindset habits, you buffer against the worry that often accompanies high-stakes testing.

Why These Elements Matter

Study materials can only be internalized effectively if your mind is fresh and your body well-supported. Poor sleep hampers recall, erratic nutrition drains focus, and negative thought patterns sabotage confidence. In contrast, a stable daily rhythm, balanced meals, and affirming mental practices ensure that the knowledge you've worked hard to acquire stands ready at your fingertips. This synergy allows you to approach each review session and the eventual exam with clarity, composure, and the vigor needed to excel.

14.4.2 What to Expect at the Testing Center

Walking into a testing center for a high-stakes exam can feel daunting, especially if you've never been through the process before. Knowing the typical procedures and environment in advance can help you minimize anxiety and focus on performing your best. While details may differ slightly by location or exam provider, the following elements commonly appear across testing centers.

Check-In and Identification

Plan to arrive at least 30 minutes ahead of your scheduled slot. This extra buffer accommodates any unexpected traffic, last-minute form-filling, or lines at the check-in desk. Test administrators usually verify your ID—often requiring a government-issued photo document (like a driver's license or passport). Confirm beforehand which forms of ID are acceptable, as many exam providers enforce strict rules that reject expired or incomplete identification.

After verifying your credentials, the proctor may scan your fingerprints or photograph you, if the exam regulations call for biometric security. Some exams also involve a sign-in sheet where you list your arrival time or state any personal items you're carrying.

Environment and Security Measures

1. **Secure Lockers**

   Test centers typically restrict what you can bring inside—beyond ID and essential items. Phones, notes, and bulky bags often go into a locker. It's wise to double-check the exam's policy on watches or jewelry, as some require all personal items (except ID) to remain outside. Having only the bare minimum accessible prevents confusion or accusations of misconduct.

2. **Test Room Layout**

   Many centers seat candidates at individual workstations equipped with partitions for minimal distractions. A camera or proctor station monitors activity, ensuring compliance with test protocols. If you need assistance—like requesting a restroom break or dealing with a technical glitch—you raise your hand or signal a proctor quietly. Keep in mind that breaks may be timed or restricted according to exam rules.

Adhering to Testing Etiquette

While each provider's rules vary, certain norms are fairly standard. Talking or interacting with other test-takers is usually prohibited, as are unapproved materials on the desk. If you have scratch paper or earplugs, verify they're allowed. Some tests offer digital or laminated boards for note-taking. Any attempt to consult personal notes, mobile devices, or reference books mid-exam typically triggers immediate disqualification. By following guidelines respectfully, you maintain a calm atmosphere that benefits everyone.

Possible Technical or Procedural Hiccups

Now and then, the exam software might freeze or the computer could malfunction. Don't panic—alert the proctor promptly. They'll pause your time if allowed, relocate you to another workstation, or reboot the system. Keep your composure; many centers are practiced at handling minor disruptions. Once the issue is resolved, you can usually resume without penalty.

Post-Exam Steps

When time expires or you submit your exam, proctors often guide you to sign out and retrieve your belongings. Some exams give immediate pass/fail results, while others require waiting for official scoring. If you receive a preliminary score report, store it safely for reference. The staff may also remind you of confidentiality rules about not disclosing exact questions.

If your exam is one that offers immediate feedback, look for any overall performance summaries. These can clarify which domains you tackled well and where you might have struggled. That information can be especially helpful if you plan to retake the exam or continue strengthening your skills in certain areas post-certification.

14.5 Leveraging our included Member-Only E-Learning Platform

14.5.1 Unlimited Exam Simulator

A truly robust study plan demands realistic practice under timed, randomized conditions—mirroring the pressures and unpredictability of the actual exam. That's where the **unlimited exam simulator** becomes a powerful ally. Rather than relying on fixed question sets, the simulator generates new assortments of items each time, ensuring that you never grow overly familiar with a single batch. This continual freshness pushes your recall and problem-solving skills to adapt, preparing you for the dynamic nature of exam questions.

Overview

By allowing you to adjust parameters—such as the number of questions and the total time allotted—the simulator caters to varying levels of readiness. Early on, you might choose a smaller question set with extra time to review each response carefully. As confidence grows, you can ramp up to a full-length, timed simulation. This incremental approach builds exam stamina: you learn to pace yourself, handle potential information overload, and withstand the psychological impact of the ticking clock.

Crucially, after you submit a completed simulation, the platform displays which questions you missed—along with detailed explanations for why each correct choice is right. This immediate, thorough feedback helps isolate knowledge gaps or clarify misunderstood concepts. Over successive attempts, you can monitor progress on weaker areas, turning mistakes into learning moments rather than repeated pitfalls.

Usage Recommendations

1. **Start with Smaller Batches**: In the early phases of study, choose fewer questions to ease into the simulator's interface and feedback system. This helps you absorb each explanation without feeling overwhelmed.

2. **Graduate to Full-Length Attempts**: Once you're comfortable with the software and question styles, replicate a real exam session. Adhering strictly to time limits tests your ability to manage pace, especially on tricky or scenario-based items.

3. **Analyze Feedback Thoroughly**: Resist the urge to jump right into another test. Instead, review the rationales behind correct and incorrect answers. Create a short, concise note of recurring knowledge gaps—like recurring confusion about

FLSA exempt criteria—and integrate that note back into your main study materials.

4.   **Periodically Mix Domain Focus**: If the exam covers multiple domains, randomizing questions from all areas prevents you from falling into a comfort zone. Being able to switch gears between topics under exam-like constraints fosters mental agility and readiness.

App vs. Desktop

Whether you launch the simulator on your computer or mobile device, the underlying design remains consistent. You'll find the same question formats, timing controls, and feedback displays across both. Desktop usage can be beneficial for longer sessions— particularly if you want to mimic the environment of a testing center with a larger screen—while the mobile app supports quick quizzes on the go. If you want to fill idle moments productively (e.g., commuting or waiting in line), the mobile app ensures you can slip in extra practice at virtually any time.

By adjusting question sets and time constraints, the **unlimited exam simulator** keeps your preparation dynamic and responsive to emerging weaknesses. This method fosters adaptability, exam-level focus, and a nuanced grasp of both familiar and unpredictable question types. When paired with post-test reviews of detailed explanations, you'll refine your knowledge incrementally, ensuring every simulated challenge helps shape a more confident performance on exam day.

14.5.2 Digital Flashcards

Digital flashcards adapt the classic memorization tool for modern lifestyles, using on-screen "cards" that can be flipped to reveal an answer or explanation. By capitalizing on random question display and tracking features, these flashcards help ensure each session offers fresh content and immediate reinforcement. Since they're part of the e-learning platform, they integrate with your broader study data, enabling you to pinpoint which topics need more frequent review.

Question Flip: With each tap or click, you reveal the correct response and any relevant clarifications—much like physical cards but without the hassle of carrying a deck. This setup saves time otherwise spent shuffling and ensures variety in each session.

Study Techniques for Digital Cards

Short, repeated bursts of focused study often outperform marathon sessions. Glancing through 10–15 cards during a break, for instance, helps lock key terms or concepts in place without feeling overwhelming. Additionally, mixing up the difficulty levels prevents a routine where you coast on simpler questions, ensuring that each session brings a degree of challenge. If you find recurring stumbling blocks on certain cards, augment your flashcard use with the textbook's relevant sections or the platform's question explanations to reinforce understanding.

Mobile Integration

A standout convenience is the ability to practice from a phone or tablet. Waiting in a queue or commuting via public transit, you can squeeze in a quick set of flashcard flips, turning idle moments into revision opportunities. This mobility fosters a habit of mini-revisions throughout the day, rather than relying solely on larger scheduled study blocks. For some, this approach boosts retention by repeatedly activating memory recall in various contexts—an advantage paper cards or purely desktop-based methods may not match.

With digital flashcards, you blend old-school memorization power with dynamic, data-driven insights. By focusing on uncertain areas and celebrating mastery of the rest, each brief session strengthens your overall exam readiness—helping you feel more comfortable with terminology, quick facts, and any step-by-step procedures that might appear on test day.

14.5.3 Printable Full-Length Mock Exams

Although digital simulations are convenient, **printable full-length exams** can replicate the physical, time-bound atmosphere you may encounter on test day. They mirror the real question count and level of challenge, prompting you to budget your time as though you're sitting in the actual testing center. By using these printed tests alongside the e-learning platform's insights, you gain a balanced practice regimen that prepares you to manage exam logistics, refine pacing, and handle the psychological demands of a high-stakes session.

Intent and Design

Each mock exam aims to capture not only the question variety but also the structure of the real test—ensuring your familiarity with how items progress from straightforward to more complex. Because the question set is fixed in print, you won't rely on automated feedback or immediate scoring while you work through it. Instead, you proceed section by section, tracking how long you take per item or domain. This manual pacing teaches you to assess each question's difficulty and decide whether to linger or move on in the interest of finishing on time.

Suggested Approach

> ➢ **Simulate the Environment**: To get the full benefit, set aside a quiet block of time with minimal interruptions. Have a timer or a stopwatch running so you can mimic test-day constraints. If the actual exam allots, for instance, three

hours for a certain number of questions, adhere to that exact structure.

➤ **Review and Reflect**: Once finished, compare your responses against the official answer key (often located at the back of the mock exam). If you identify recurrent mistakes, note them on a separate sheet. Then, consult the e-learning platform's resources—such as question explanations or domain-specific study modules—to clarify misunderstood concepts.

Link to Feedback

While these printable exams themselves may not provide in-the-moment corrections, you can cross-reference every incorrect item with the e-learning platform's question bank or explanatory sections. This two-step feedback loop ensures that paper-based practice transforms into actionable insights. For instance, if you discover you've repeatedly erred on scenario-based questions about employee relations, you can shift focus in your next digital quiz to scenario-specific items, reinforcing the link between real-time analytics and hands-on test practice.

By merging **printable full-length exams** with the instant feedback of digital tools, you replicate the real exam's constraints while still benefiting from in-depth, platform-driven analysis afterward. Embracing this mix helps you refine pacing skills, acquaint yourself with test-day formats, and gauge readiness without relying solely on an online environment. Ultimately, that thorough preparation can reduce surprises and instill a calmer, more confident mindset when exam day arrives.

14.5.4 Integrating E-Learning Tools into Your Study Plan

Adopting the e-learning platform's components—unlimited simulators, digital flashcards, and printable mock exams—becomes most effective when built into a structured study cycle. Rather than sporadically dipping into these features, aligning them with your overarching schedule ensures that each resource complements your progress at every stage. This orchestration not only prevents content redundancy but also helps you refine your focus based on emerging strengths and weaknesses.

Scheduling Simulated Exams

One key advantage of the simulator is its flexibility in question volume and timing. Consider starting with smaller, targeted quizzes on specific domains, especially if you've recently tackled that domain in your reading. As your exam date nears, shift toward full or near-full simulations, closely mimicking the test's pacing to develop stamina and reduce exam-day stress. Some tips include:

> **Checkpoint Quizzes**: After finishing a domain review—say, compliance topics—run a mini-exam to gauge how well you retain those regulations. This approach highlights misunderstandings early.

> **Periodic Full-Length Drills**: Reserve at least one or two sessions, spaced a few weeks apart, for simulating the complete exam environment. Attempt a timed test, then spend time analyzing any missed items. If certain question types repeatedly trip you up, add more drills focusing on those formats.

Coordinating with Traditional Materials

Reviewing course chapters or class notes can feel more tangible when anchored by immediate practice. For example, an evening's reading on talent acquisition could end with 15 or 20 simulator questions specifically tied to that subject. This synergy cements newly learned details through practical application. Concurrently, if you stumble over certain items, highlight them in your notes—either by re-checking definitions or rewriting particularly challenging concepts, ensuring the link between theory and hands-on practice remains tight.

Likewise, incorporate flashcard sessions into your daily or weekly routine. After scanning a chapter, flashcards can help distill the main points—like major legislation or key frameworks—before you tackle a fresh simulator quiz. If your results consistently show confusion in a single domain, it may be worth focusing upcoming reading time on that domain to close the gap.

Tips for Balancing Digital and Offline Resources

1. **Rotate Resources to Avoid Over-Dependency**
   Use short digital quiz breaks (via the simulator or flashcards) in between longer spells of textbook reading. This variety keeps energy levels up and ensures consistent exposure to test-style questions.

2. **Track and Tweak**
   Maintain a log of your e-learning scores—like simulator quiz results. Note any trends: Do you routinely excel in People Domain questions but struggle in Strategy? Adjust your reading plan or future simulator settings accordingly.

Maintaining Steady Momentum
As you continue using e-learning alongside physical mock exams, pay attention to how each aspect complements the others. A high volume of correct answers in short simulator quizzes might point to

strong day-to-day recall, but a full printable exam check can confirm endurance and pacing under near-real conditions. By orchestrating these elements in tandem, you uphold a balanced routine—one that addresses immediate weaknesses while consistently reinforcing fundamental knowledge.

When systematically woven into your study roadmap, e-learning features like the simulator, flashcards, and full-length mocks become essential layers of exam prep. They provide immediate feedback loops, adapt to your evolving needs, and maintain engagement through varied formats. By dedicating specific times for short quiz bursts, domain-based study, and occasional full mock trials, you tap into the platform's full potential—ensuring each resource meaningfully supports your march toward exam confidence.

Chapter 15: Knowledge-Based Practice Questions

15.1 Domain-by-Domain Practice Sets

15.1.1 People

Below is a set of sample knowledge-based items centered on core concepts within the People domain. These questions target foundational vocabulary, frameworks, and processes related to talent acquisition, engagement, learning and development, and related HR activities. Refer to **Chapter 15.2** for correct answers and explanations.

Note: The questions featured in this book serve as representative samples rather than comprehensive exam simulations. In the interest of keeping the printed volume manageable, the **8 full-length mock exams** are not included here. To access these complete practice tests, simply scan the QR code below or visit www.Apex-Academic.com/shrm_exam_print.

1. Workforce Planning

An organization is experiencing an unexpected rise in voluntary turnover. Which of the following would best help forecast future staffing needs based on predicted resignations and upcoming project demands?

A. Conducting exit interviews with departing employees
B. Implementing a salary survey to benchmark current pay rates
C. Creating a skill inventory and retirement timeline analysis
D. Launching a new performance management system

2. Job Analysis

Which statement accurately describes the primary outcome of a thorough job analysis?

A. Determining the best recruitment source for each open position
B. Producing a detailed job description and specification
C. Identifying employee training budgets for the fiscal year
D. Highlighting current staff's readiness for leadership roles

3. Talent Acquisition Strategies

A mid-sized IT firm struggles to attract specialized developers in a highly competitive market. Which approach most directly addresses talent scarcity?

A. Offering internal transfers to underused employees
B. Collaborating with universities for targeted internship programs
C. Posting job openings on the company intranet
D. Conducting monthly job satisfaction surveys

4. Onboarding & Orientation

An effective onboarding program primarily aims to:

A. Provide a single day of orientation covering basic company policies

B. Ensure new hires sign all required documents within the first week

C. Integrate new employees into the culture and equip them for performance

D. Redirect all job-specific training to the employee's supervisor

---

5. Learning & Development

Which training approach typically fosters the strongest long-term skill retention?

A. One-time classroom sessions with PowerPoint slides

B. Mandated all-hands webinars repeated monthly

C. Blended programs combining interactive practice and self-paced review

D. Passive reading assignments stored in a shared drive

---

6. Employee Engagement

When analyzing engagement survey data, which metric usually offers the clearest sign of high engagement within a department?

A. The department's willingness to adopt flexible work schedules

B. High rates of internal transfers across different teams

C. Consistently strong net promoter scores from employees

D. Minimal usage of paid time off throughout the year

---

7. Performance Management

Which of the following best characterizes a constructive approach to managing underperformance?

A. Issuing immediate formal warnings without collecting detailed evidence

B. Offering a performance improvement plan with measurable milestones

C. Transferring the employee to a lower-responsibility role immediately

D. Waiting until annual reviews to discuss performance concerns

---

8. Retention Efforts

Which tactic is most closely associated with retaining top talent in a competitive industry?

A. Periodically freezing salaries and promotions for cost savings

B. Rotating employees between departments every six months

C. Providing career path clarity and individualized development plans

D. Launching a once-a-year employee satisfaction town hall

---

9. Total Rewards

A new HR manager wants to confirm that wages align with the broader market. Which step directly addresses that objective?

A. Inviting employees to negotiate salaries individually

B. Conducting an external pay survey and comparing percentile data

C. Canceling all variable pay components

D. Initiating a "spot award" program for top performers

---

10. Succession Planning

A key executive is projected to retire in 18 months. Which action best prepares for continuous leadership?

A. Asking the executive to postpone retirement

B. Assigning short-term mentorship for all employees in the department

C. Identifying high-potential individuals and developing tailored readiness plans

D. Halting external hiring to promote only from within

Note: These questions highlight various People-domain themes—like strategic hiring, employee engagement, and ongoing development. After completing this set, proceed to **Section 15.2** to review answer keys and explanations that clarify correct choices while reinforcing domain concepts.

15.1.2 Organization

Below are knowledge-based items reflecting common aspects of an **Organization** domain—covering structure, workforce management, organizational effectiveness, labor relations, and related topics. Turn to **Chapter 15.2** for the correct responses and rationales.

---

1. Organizational Structure

Which factor most strongly influences whether a company adopts a centralized or decentralized HR model?

A. Department managers' personal preferences

B. The organization's geographic dispersion and scale

C. Employee requests for varied benefit packages

D. A strict deadline for rolling out new technology

---

2. Measuring HR's Strategic Value

When HR aims to demonstrate its broader impact on achieving business goals, which metric generally conveys the clearest link to organizational performance?

A. The ratio of HR staff to total employees

B. Time to resolve employee disputes

C. Reduction in turnover among high performers

D. Number of policies introduced per quarter

---

3. Organizational Effectiveness & Development (OED)

A company experiences siloed communication between departments, hampering project handoffs. Which technique aligns best with organizational development methods to unify teams?

A. Instituting strict chain-of-command rules

B. Using cross-functional interventions or team-building sessions

C. Conducting an all-employee satisfaction survey twice a year

D. Encouraging each department to manage initiatives in isolation

---

4. Workforce Management

A significant uptick in short-term staffing is needed for a seasonal product launch. Which approach most directly tackles the short-term need without committing to long-term overhead?

A. Freezing hiring for full-time roles

B. Introducing flexible scheduling for existing employees

C. Engaging contingent or temporary workers

D. Diverting employees from other critical, busy departments

---

5. Knowledge Management

An employer wants to ensure key processes and expertise remain accessible as experienced workers retire. Which initiative best addresses this concern?

A. Rotating managers between unrelated departments every month

B. Creating an internal wiki or knowledge repository

C. Mandating daily stand-ups for all employees

D. Hiring only entry-level staff to build from the ground up

---

6. Employee & Labor Relations

A small subset of employees forms a work council to discuss wages and working conditions. If management wants to maintain constructive relations, what initial step typically supports collaboration?

A. Dismissing the work council for duplication of HR tasks

B. Scheduling periodic open forums with council representatives

C. Blocking all employee-led gatherings until official negotiation begins

D. Introducing a new top-down grievance procedure

---

7. Union Environment

Under a collective bargaining agreement, management must consult the union before altering shift schedules. Which scenario typically triggers this requirement?

A. Minor policy updates to the employee handbook
B. Annual salary adjustments aligned with standard CPI rates
C. Changes to working hours that impact contractual duties
D. Voluntary job rotation among employees

8. Change Management

Leadership decides on a reorganization that consolidates two departments. Which OED practice might minimize confusion and maintain morale during the transition?

A. Issuing a one-page memo with limited details
B. Holding cross-departmental workshops to align goals and clarify roles
C. Instructing teams to figure out new reporting lines informally
D. Postponing any discussion of changes until the final structure is locked

9. Technology Management

Which outcome best demonstrates effective deployment of a new HRIS (Human Resources Information System) in an organization?

A. Employees seldom use the self-service features for updates
B. Recruiting data remains in spreadsheets rather than the new system
C. HR processes see fewer manual errors and shortened cycle times
D. Implementation takes longer than planned but with no significant performance improvement

10. Reporting and Recordkeeping

In ensuring compliance with organizational requirements, which record management step is typically the most critical?

A. Destroying relevant files only when employees request it

B. Assigning a dedicated vendor to store all physical documents overseas

C. Reviewing statutory guidelines for retention timelines and secure disposal methods

D. Placing all records—irrespective of type—in a single, unstructured shared drive

---

Note: These questions aim to check fundamental knowledge regarding organizational structures, workforce planning, OED approaches, and technology considerations. Review your selections in **Section 15.2** for clarified answers and their corresponding rationale.

15.1.3 Workplace

Below is a set of sample knowledge-based items centered on **Workplace** topics, including compliance, safety, and risk management. These questions aim to gauge your understanding of key regulations, processes, and best practices. Refer to **Chapter 15.2** for correct answers and explanations.

---

1. Safety and Health

An organization wants to meet its "general duty" obligations under workplace safety laws. Which scenario most clearly demonstrates fulfilling that responsibility?

A. Posting one safety poster in the cafeteria and leaving it at that

B. Conducting regular checks for hazards and proactively correcting them

C. Making employees sign liability waivers upon hiring

D. Allowing departments to self-report risks only when accidents occur

---

2. Risk Management

A manufacturing firm expands to a location prone to severe weather events. Which step best exemplifies effective risk mitigation?

A. Eliminating all nonessential insurance policies

B. Relying exclusively on employees' best judgment during emergencies

C. Developing a continuity plan, including alternate supply routes and off-site data backups

D. Instructing each department to handle disasters independently without corporate guidance

---

3. Worker Protection Laws

When handling sensitive employee data—such as medical records or disciplinary files—what practice best upholds privacy and regulatory compliance?

A. Giving any manager free access to these files at any time

B. Storing them in a secure system with limited access based on defined roles

C. Uploading scanned copies to a publicly accessible folder

D. Disposing of all records every six months regardless of retention mandates

---

4. Emergency Preparedness

In designing an evacuation plan, which approach most enhances both safety and inclusivity?

A. Conducting one mandatory drill per year and assuming readiness

B. Limiting planning to a small security task force

C. Accounting for employees with disabilities and testing routes for accessibility

D. Issuing a generic memo and expecting teams to create their own procedures

---

5. Global Compliance

A multinational corporation operating in multiple countries needs to comply with various labor regulations. Which method helps the organization avoid compliance pitfalls?

A. Imposing a single, uniform policy worldwide without local adjustments

B. Allowing local offices to develop all policies in isolation

C. Maintaining a central framework but customizing key elements based on local laws

D. Strictly limiting employee oversight to corporate headquarters

6. Data Security

HR frequently processes personal information for benefits administration. Which action most directly prevents unauthorized disclosure?

A. Granting all department heads password access to the HR database
B. Using encryption and role-based access to limit who can view sensitive data
C. Keeping files unprotected on a shared network for convenience
D. Delegating record maintenance exclusively to first-line supervisors

7. Privacy and Monitoring

An employer introduces digital monitoring for productivity analytics. Which practice typically strikes a balance between organizational needs and employee privacy?

A. Running hidden software that captures all keystrokes without disclosure
B. Communicating clear monitoring policies and limiting collected data to relevant metrics
C. Encouraging employees to submit personal passwords to supervisors
D. Using random manager spot-checks on private user accounts

8. Reporting and Recordkeeping

According to common EHS (Environment, Health, and Safety) guidelines, why might an organization be required to document workplace incidents thoroughly?

A. To justify budget cuts for safety programs
B. To provide a foundation for analyzing trends and preventing recurrences
C. To hide potential liabilities from employees
D. To publicly assign blame without offering corrective measures

9. Workplace Investigations

An employee submits a complaint about potential harassment by a coworker. Which initial step aligns most with standard investigative protocols?

A. Announcing the details of the complaint in the next all-staff meeting
B. Proceeding immediately with disciplinary action against the accused
C. Ensuring confidentiality, conducting discreet interviews, and documenting findings
D. Advising the complainant to resolve it one-on-one before involving HR

---

10. Employee Well-Being

Rising health insurance costs linked to stress-related claims prompt management to address wellness. Which tactic most directly showcases a strategic response?

A. Eliminating mental health coverage to reduce costs
B. Conducting superficial check-ins only during annual reviews
C. Offering targeted programs (stress-management workshops, flexible schedules) and measuring their impact
D. Delegating well-being solely to an external vendor, with minimal internal follow-up

---

Note: Work through these items to gauge your grasp of regulations, emergency plans, privacy measures, and broader workplace policies. After you've made your selections, see **Chapter 15.2** for the answer key and explanations, which detail the rationale behind each correct choice.

15.1.4 Strategy

Here is a set of knowledge-based items designed to gauge your familiarity with **strategic concepts**—including alignment, measurement, and long-term planning. These questions address foundational strategies that underpin broader HR initiatives. For official solutions and explanatory notes, consult **Chapter 15.2**.

---

1. Strategic Alignment

A manufacturing firm wants to ensure its HR strategies fully support a new corporate goal of "expanding into high-tech production lines." Which initial HR step best reflects genuine alignment with that objective?

A. Sending out generic job postings without referencing the new direction
B. Developing skill inventories that highlight high-tech competencies
C. Focusing exclusively on existing manual-labor staff needs
D. Freezing all leadership development programs until after expansions

---

2. Metrics and KPIs

Leadership demands data proving HR's contribution to increased market share. Which metric most directly correlates HR's efforts with that strategic outcome?

A. Percentage of managers who attend monthly staff meetings
B. Ratio of HR staff to total employees
C. New-product launch speed tied to specialized talent acquisition
D. Annual payroll costs versus annual marketing budgets

---

3. Balanced Scorecard Approach

If a large organization uses a balanced scorecard, which domain typically appears alongside financial, customer, and internal process perspectives?

A. Supplier negotiation metrics
B. Learning and growth indicators
C. Mandatory volunteer hours
D. Random cultural activities

---

4. Implementing Strategic Initiatives

A multi-location retailer wants to streamline hiring processes for specialized store managers. Which action demonstrates a well-thought-out, **enterprise-level** approach?

A. Letting each store location develop its own selection criteria

B. Creating a unified competency model aligned with strategic objectives

C. Ignoring feedback from operations managers and store leads

D. Posting positions on a lesser-known local website only

---

5. Communicating Strategy to the Workforce

When rolling out a new organizational vision, which method best fosters widespread employee buy-in?

A. Announcing the strategy in a single email without further discussion

B. Holding a series of town halls that explain the rationale and invite questions

C. Requiring each department to interpret the vision independently

D. Sharing it only with senior managers, who later reveal select parts to teams

---

6. Leading Indicators vs. Lagging Indicators

Which example aligns with a **leading indicator** often tracked for strategic forecasting?

A. Annual revenue from last year

B. Employee engagement levels that hint at future retention trends

C. Customer complaints from the previous quarter

D. Final budget results posted at year-end

---

7. Mergers and Acquisitions

In the context of strategic planning, what is HR's key role during an M&A that aims for rapid market entry?

A. Imposing immediate layoffs without communication

B. Verifying cultural alignment and coordinating smooth integration plans

C. Stalling leadership announcements to avoid speculation

D. Bypassing local labor laws to expedite changes

---

8. Long-Term vs. Short-Term Balancing

A company invests heavily in R&D to future-proof its products but faces pressure from the board for near-term cost reductions. Which stance reflects strategic thinking?

A. Pulling all funds from R&D to meet quarterly cost targets
B. Maintaining a balanced approach: trimming smaller operational costs but preserving critical R&D budgets
C. Ignoring board concerns entirely in pursuit of R&D breakthroughs
D. Prioritizing short-term gains in sales departments only

---

9. Strategy Execution Barriers

When a carefully crafted strategy underperforms, which factor often emerges as the culprit?

A. Overly large training budgets for mid-level employees
B. Overemphasis on staff communication
C. Weak cross-functional collaboration that stalls execution
D. Excessive alignment with the organization's mission

---

10. Evaluating Strategic Success

In assessing whether a three-year workforce strategy boosted global market presence, which evidence offers the clearest sign of success?

A. More frequent employee social events
B. Reduced budget allocated to external consultants
C. Meaningful expansion in international sales and partnerships
D. A lower number of internal process audits

Note: Once you've worked through these 10 items, consult **Chapter 15.2** for confirmed answers and deeper explanations, detailing how each question's correct response aligns with strategic principles and best practices.

15.2 Answer Keys with Explanations

15.2.1 Rationale for Each Correct Answer

Below you'll find a concise explanation for **each correct answer** across the four domains: **People, Organization, Workplace**, and **Strategy**. The focus here is on the key logic behind why one choice best aligns with established principles or practices. For more context on the topics themselves, refer to the relevant book chapters.

People: Rationale for Correct Answers

1. **Workforce Planning**
   Correct: (C) Creating a skill inventory and retirement timeline analysis
   Why: This method helps anticipate future workforce gaps, incorporating projected resignations/retirements and upcoming skill demands.

2. **Job Analysis**
   Correct: (B) Producing a detailed job description and specification
   Why: Thorough job analysis leads directly to formal documents defining essential duties and required qualifications.

3. **Talent Acquisition Strategies**
   Correct: (B) Collaborating with universities for targeted internship programs
   Why: Partnering with academic institutions addresses talent scarcity by feeding specialized candidates into the hiring pipeline.

4. **Onboarding & Orientation**
   Correct: (C) Integrate new employees into the culture and equip them for performance
   Why: Effective onboarding goes beyond paperwork, immersing hires in organizational values and operational needs, spurring quicker effectiveness.

5. **Learning & Development**
   Correct: (C) Blended programs combining interactive practice and self-paced review
   Why: Blended learning sustains engagement while reinforcing knowledge retention through varied formats.

6. **Employee Engagement**
   Correct: (C) Consistently strong net promoter scores from employees
   Why: High eNPS typically indicates employees willing to recommend the workplace—an overarching sign of robust engagement.

7. **Performance Management**
   Correct: (B) Offering a performance improvement plan with measurable milestones
   Why: Well-defined PIPs give underperformers a structured path to correct issues, aligning with supportive yet accountable practices.

8. **Retention Efforts**
   Correct: (C) Providing career path clarity and individualized development plans
   Why: High-potential staff remain longer when they see clear advancement routes and feel their growth is prioritized.

9. **Total Rewards**
   Correct: (B) Conducting an external pay survey and comparing percentile data
   Why: Benchmarking compensation reveals whether wages align with the broader market, guiding equitable pay adjustments.

10. **Succession Planning**
    Correct: (C) Identifying high-potential individuals and developing tailored readiness plans
    Why: Targeted development ensures vital leadership roles are seamlessly filled, protecting organizational continuity.

Organization: Rationale for Correct Answers

1. **Organizational Structure**
   Correct: (B) The organization's geographic dispersion and scale
   Why: Multiple sites or global reach often necessitate a more decentralized approach, while small/regional setups may favor centralization.

2. **Measuring HR's Strategic Value**
   Correct: (C) Reduction in turnover among high performers

Why: Retaining top talent ties directly to better organizational outcomes— like higher productivity or continuity of expertise.

3. **Organizational Effectiveness & Development (OED)**
   Correct: (B) Using cross-functional interventions or team-building sessions
   Why: OED typically addresses departmental silos through collaborative methods, unifying diverse teams around shared objectives.

4. **Workforce Management**
   Correct: (C) Engaging contingent or temporary workers
   Why: Seasonal or short-term surges often call for flexible staffing, avoiding permanent hires that inflate fixed costs beyond the peak period.

5. **Knowledge Management**
   Correct: (B) Creating an internal wiki or knowledge repository
   Why: Documenting tacit expertise allows new or remaining employees to access proven processes, critical steps, and institutional know-how.

6. **Employee & Labor Relations**
   Correct: (B) Scheduling periodic open forums with council representatives
   Why: Inviting dialogue signals readiness to address wage and working condition concerns collaboratively.

7. **Union Environment**
   Correct: (C) Changes to working hours that impact contractual duties
   Why: Under many CBAs, shift alterations require union consultation to safeguard negotiated employee rights.

8. **Change Management**
   Correct: (B) Holding cross-departmental workshops to align goals and clarify roles
   Why: Facilitated sessions help employees adapt to reorganization, smoothing confusion and potential pushback.

9. **Technology Management**
   Correct: (C) HR processes see fewer manual errors and shortened cycle times
   Why: An effective HRIS demonstrates tangible improvements—like streamlined workflows and reduced errors—reflecting real ROI.

10. **Reporting and Recordkeeping**
    Correct: (C) Reviewing statutory guidelines for retention timelines and secure disposal methods
    Why: Compliance-driven archiving aligns with laws on how long to keep records and how to discard them securely.

Workplace: Rationale for Correct Answers

1. **Safety and Health**
   Correct: (B) Conducting regular checks for hazards and proactively correcting them
   Why: Ongoing hazard identification and prompt remediation fulfill a proactive stance on workplace safety.

2. **Risk Management**
   Correct: (C) Developing a continuity plan, including alternate supply routes and off-site data backups
   Why: Disaster planning and backup systems mitigate operational and employee risks in hazard-prone regions.

3. **Worker Protection Laws**
   Correct: (B) Storing them in a secure system with limited access based on defined roles
   Why: Confidential records should remain accessible only to those who truly need them, maintaining privacy standards.

4. **Emergency Preparedness**
   Correct: (C) Accounting for employees with disabilities and testing routes for accessibility
   Why: Inclusive planning acknowledges diverse employee needs, ensuring safe, feasible evacuations for everyone.

5. **Global Compliance**
   Correct: (C) Maintaining a central framework but customizing key elements based on local laws
   Why: Balancing corporate guidelines with region-specific regulatory requirements prevents compliance oversights.

6. **Data Security**
   Correct: (B) Using encryption and role-based access to limit who can view sensitive data
   Why: Controlling who sees personal or benefits information is essential for preventing unauthorized disclosure.

7. **Privacy and Monitoring**
   Correct: (B) Communicating clear monitoring policies and limiting collected data to relevant metrics
   Why: Ethical monitoring discloses the scope and rationale, ensuring employees' privacy is respected while legitimate business data is gathered.

8. **Reporting and Recordkeeping**
   Correct: (B) To provide a foundation for analyzing trends and preventing recurrences
   Why: Comprehensive incident logs help examine patterns, offering insights to reduce future hazards or problems.

9. **Workplace Investigations**
   Correct: (C) Ensuring confidentiality, conducting discreet interviews, and documenting findings
   Why: Proper investigations maintain privacy, gather facts impartially, and record outcomes systematically.

10. **Employee Well-Being**
    Correct: (C) Offering targeted programs (stress-management workshops, flexible schedules) and measuring their impact
    Why: Proactive, data-driven wellness strategies address root causes of stress rather than offering superficial fixes.

Strategy: Rationale for Correct Answers

1. **Strategic Alignment**
   Correct: (B) Developing skill inventories that highlight high-tech competencies
   Why: Linking HR efforts (e.g., specialized hiring, development) to the firm's new high-tech direction ensures direct alignment with strategic expansion goals.

2. **Metrics and KPIs**
    Correct: (C) New-product launch speed tied to specialized talent acquisition
    Why: Timely recruitment of the right expertise can shorten launch cycles—a direct link to boosting market share.

3. **Balanced Scorecard Approach**
    Correct: (B) Learning and growth indicators
    Why: The balanced scorecard typically tracks an organization's capacity to improve and innovate, reflected in staff development metrics.

4. **Implementing Strategic Initiatives**
    Correct: (B) Creating a unified competency model aligned with strategic objectives
    Why: A consistent framework ensures all store managers meet the same strategic criteria, rather than fragmented local approaches.

5. **Communicating Strategy to the Workforce**
    Correct: (B) Holding a series of town halls that explain the rationale and invite questions
    Why: Transparent sessions foster buy-in, clarifying how employees' roles connect to the overarching vision.

6. **Leading Indicators vs. Lagging Indicators**
    Correct: (B) Employee engagement levels that hint at future retention trends
    Why: Engagement often forecasts turnover or productivity changes, making it a leading indicator.

7. **Mergers and Acquisitions**
    Correct: (B) Verifying cultural alignment and coordinating smooth integration plans
    Why: Cultural due diligence and cohesive onboarding prevent friction, enabling faster, more effective synergy post-merger.

8. **Long-Term vs. Short-Term Balancing**
    Correct: (B) Maintaining a balanced approach: trimming smaller operational costs but preserving critical R&D budgets
    Why: Strategic thinking manages near-term financial demands while safeguarding long-term product development and innovation potential.

9. **Strategy Execution Barriers**
   Correct: (C) Weak cross-functional collaboration that stalls execution
   Why: Even well-crafted plans falter when departments fail to coordinate on tasks, resources, and timelines.

10. **Evaluating Strategic Success**
    Correct: (C) Meaningful expansion in international sales and partnerships
    Why: If the strategy aimed at broadening global market presence, tangible growth in those specific sales channels verifies impact.

Note: Each rationale highlights why a particular option emerges as the best match for known principles and practices—clarifying the logic that underpins correct answers. Refer back to domain chapters for deeper concept exploration.

15.2.2 References to Book Chapters

People (Questions 1–10)

1. **Workforce Planning**
   Refer to: Chapter 7.2.1 (Workforce Planning and Job Analysis). Focus on how to build skill inventories and forecast future talent needs.

2. **Job Analysis**
   Refer to: Chapter 7.2.1 (Workforce Planning and Job Analysis). Covers the creation of formal job descriptions and specifications.

3. **Talent Acquisition Strategies**
   Refer to: Chapter 7.2.2 (Recruitment Sources and Techniques). Describes partnership strategies (e.g., with universities) and recruiting in competitive markets.

4. **Onboarding & Orientation**
   Refer to: Chapter 7.2.4 (Onboarding Best Practices). Details onboarding's cultural and performance-oriented objectives.

5. **Learning & Development**
   Refer to: Chapter 7.4.2 (Training Needs Analysis and Program Design). Emphasizes approaches that blend interactive methods with self-paced review.

6. **Employee Engagement**
   Refer to: Chapter 7.3.2 (Measuring Engagement: Surveys, Focus Groups). Explores engagement metrics like net promoter scores and overall interpretation.

7. **Performance Management**
   Refer to: Chapter 7.3.4 (Performance Management Systems). Discusses performance improvement plans and constructive feedback mechanisms.

8. **Retention Efforts**
   Refer to: Chapter 7.3.3 (Retention Strategies). Explains how career path clarity fosters loyalty among high performers.

9. **Total Rewards**
   Refer to: Chapter 7.5.1 (Compensation Structures: Base Pay, Variable Pay). Guidance on external pay surveys and aligning wages with market rates.

10. **Succession Planning**
    Refer to: Chapter 7.4.4 (Career Development and Succession Planning). Addresses identifying high potentials and preparing them for critical roles.

Organization (Questions 1–10)

1. **Organizational Structure**
   Refer to: Chapter 8.1.1 (Centralized vs. Decentralized Models). Explores how geographic dispersion and scale drive HR structural choices.

2. **Measuring HR's Strategic Value**
   Refer to: Chapter 8.1.3 (Measuring and Demonstrating HR Value). Focuses on metrics (e.g., turnover among high performers) that link HR actions to organizational success.

3. **Organizational Effectiveness & Development (OED)**
   Refer to: Chapter 8.2.3 (Interventions for Improving Effectiveness). Highlights cross-functional solutions for breaking departmental silos.

4. **Workforce Management**
   Refer to: Chapter 8.3.4 (Contingent Workforce Considerations). Covers using temporary workers to handle surge periods without long-term overhead.

5. **Knowledge Management**
   Refer to: Chapter 8.3.2 (Succession Planning & Knowledge Management). Addresses internal repositories (wikis) and knowledge retention strategies.

6. **Employee & Labor Relations**
   Refer to: Chapter 8.4.4 (Non-Union Employee Relations Strategies). Discusses collaboration with employee-formed bodies or councils when unions aren't the only channel.

7. **Union Environment**
   Refer to: Chapter 8.4.3 (Union Environments: Collective Bargaining). Explains when management must confer with unions before making certain workplace changes.

8. **Change Management**
   Refer to: Chapter 8.2.3 (Interventions for Improving Effectiveness). Relates to OED's role in reorganization efforts and preserving morale.

9. **Technology Management**
   Refer to: Chapter 8.5.1 (HR Information Systems (HRIS) and Data Security). Explores how effective HRIS deployment reduces manual errors and streamlines processes.

10. **Reporting and Recordkeeping**
    Refer to: Chapter 8.5.1 (HRIS and Data Security). Touches on ensuring compliance through proper data handling and retention guidelines.

Workplace (Questions 1–10)

1. **Safety and Health**
   Refer to: Chapter 9.2.2 (Safety, Security, and Emergency Preparedness Plans). Discusses proactive hazard identification and correction as part of employer responsibilities.

2. **Risk Management**
   Refer to: Chapter 9.2.3 (Business Continuity and Disaster Recovery). Covers continuity planning for severe weather or disaster scenarios.

3. **Worker Protection Laws**
   Refer to: Chapter 4.5.1 (Protected Health Information (HIPAA)) or

Chapter 9.2.1 (Identifying and Evaluating Workplace Risks). Emphasizes secure, role-based access to sensitive records.

4. **Emergency Preparedness**
   Refer to: Chapter 9.2.2 (Safety, Security, and Emergency Preparedness Plans). Details inclusive evacuation strategies, especially for employees with special needs.

5. **Global Compliance**
   Refer to: Chapter 9.1.1 (Working Across Borders: Key Considerations) or Chapter 9.1.3 (International Assignments). Focuses on adapting corporate guidelines to local labor requirements.

6. **Data Security**
   Refer to: Chapter 9.2.2 (Safety, Security, and Emergency Preparedness Plans) or Chapter 8.5.1 (HRIS and Data Security). Stresses encryption and restricted file access for personal data.

7. **Privacy and Monitoring**
   Refer to: Chapter 9.4.3 (Handling Audits and Investigations) or Chapter 8.5.1. Spotlights transparent policies on digital monitoring.

8. **Reporting and Recordkeeping**
   Refer to: Chapter 9.2.1 (Identifying and Evaluating Workplace Risks) or Chapter 4.3.2 (Reporting and Recordkeeping). Outlines incident documentation for EHS compliance and preventing recurrence.

9. **Workplace Investigations**
   Refer to: Chapter 9.4.3 (Handling Audits and Investigations). Clarifies standard investigative protocols—maintaining confidentiality, gathering evidence, etc.

10. **Employee Well-Being**
    Refer to: Chapter 9.2.2 (Safety, Security, and Emergency Preparedness Plans) or Chapter 7.3.3 (Retention Strategies). Focuses on proactive wellness programs addressing root causes of stress.

Strategy (Questions 1–10)

1. **Strategic Alignment**
   Refer to: Chapter 10.1.2 (Strategy Formulation and Alignment). Demonstrates how HR can tailor planning (e.g., skill inventories) to new organizational goals.

2. **Metrics and KPIs**
   Refer to: Chapter 10.1.3 (Implementing and Monitoring the Strategic Plan). Discusses linking HR-driven metrics (like faster time-to-hire) to broader business outcomes.

3. **Balanced Scorecard Approach**
   Refer to: Chapter 10.2.2 (Influencing Organizational Culture and Change) or Chapter 10.1.1 (Environmental Scanning). Highlights the "learning and growth" perspective as part of a four-pronged scorecard.

4. **Implementing Strategic Initiatives**
   Refer to: Chapter 10.1.3 (Implementing and Monitoring the Strategic Plan). Explains enterprise-level interventions (like unified competency models) that reinforce overarching strategies.

5. **Communicating Strategy to the Workforce**
   Refer to: Chapter 10.2.3 (Communicating the Value of HR Initiatives). Emphasizes the importance of interactive methods (e.g., town halls) for buy-in.

6. **Leading Indicators vs. Lagging Indicators**
   Refer to: Chapter 10.1.3 (Implementing and Monitoring the Strategic Plan). Addresses how forward-looking metrics (like engagement) anticipate future changes.

7. **Mergers and Acquisitions**
   Refer to: Chapter 10.3.2 (Mergers & Acquisitions: HR's Role). Details cultural alignment and seamless workforce integration in M&A contexts.

8. **Long-Term vs. Short-Term Balancing**
   Refer to: Chapter 10.1.2 (Strategy Formulation and Alignment). Suggests sustaining crucial R&D or future-focused plans while meeting near-term pressures.

9. **Strategy Execution Barriers**
   Refer to: Chapter 10.1.3 (Implementing and Monitoring the Strategic

Plan). Explores how cross-functional collaboration or lack thereof can hinder strategic progress.

10. **Evaluating Strategic Success**
Refer to: Chapter 10.1.3 (Implementing and Monitoring the Strategic Plan). Ties global market expansion outcomes to HR strategies, verifying strategic impact.

How to Use These References

Locate each question's domain and number, then consult the corresponding chapter/subchapter. This approach ensures that if you struggled with or want to reinforce a particular concept—like knowledge management or scenario-based risk planning—you can jump straight to the precise section that covers it in depth. By pairing these references with the question's rationale, you'll solidify both the "why" and "where" behind each correct answer.

Chapter 16: Situational Judgment Practice Questions

16.1 Scenario-Based Case Studies

16.1.1 Leadership Dilemmas

Below are situational questions designed to challenge your leadership acumen in realistic workplace dilemmas. Each scenario highlights a different aspect of **Leadership & Navigation**, testing your ability to balance interpersonal, strategic, and ethical considerations. After attempting these items, refer to **Chapter 16.2** for analysis and discussion of why certain responses might be more effective.

Note: The questions featured in this book serve as representative samples rather than comprehensive exam simulations. In the interest of keeping the printed volume manageable, the **8 full-length mock exams** are not included here. To access these complete practice tests, simply scan the QR code below or visit www.Apex-Academic.com/shrm_exam_print.

Scenario 1: Team Turbulence

Context: You manage a small project team that includes two high performers and one new hire struggling with assigned tasks. Recently, tension has escalated: the high performers complain about "babysitting," while the new employee, feeling unsupported, wants more direct guidance.

Question: Which immediate step best demonstrates constructive leadership that balances each member's needs and fosters team cohesion?

A. Rotate the new hire to another team to avoid friction.
B. Ask the high performers to continue assisting until the new hire "figures it out."
C. Facilitate a meeting where everyone clarifies expectations and identify concrete ways for the new hire to develop skill proficiency.
D. Inform the new hire that performance coaching sessions will be scheduled only if work quality remains low for another month.

Scenario 2: Leadership Succession Crisis

Context: A department head announces an abrupt decision to relocate for personal reasons, providing only three weeks' notice. There's no official successor designated, and staff are anxious about losing direction on major initiatives.

Question: Which action best illustrates proactive leadership to ensure continuity?

A. Immediately appoint the most senior team member as an interim leader, regardless of skill set.
B. Freeze all major department projects until a replacement is hired.
C. Solicit short-term volunteer leads from among the team, then clarify their authority and how you'll offer support.
D. Delegate all new leadership responsibilities to an external consultant who can "bridge the gap."

Scenario 3: Strategic Shift Resistance

Context: Senior executives want a pivot toward automated systems to drive efficiency, but front-line managers worry about the potential impact on roles and morale. You've been tapped to communicate the shift and quell concerns, yet managers remain skeptical.

Question: Which approach most directly embodies an effective leadership stance when championing change?

A. Issue a memo mandating manager cooperation, warning that dissent will be noted in performance reviews.
B. Arrange small-group sessions with managers to explore specific worries, showing how upskilling and reassignments can minimize job displacement.
C. Publicly downplay the automation idea, telling staff it may never fully materialize.
D. Leave the executives to explain everything in a single company-wide email, focusing on bottom-line benefits only.

Scenario 4: Conflict Between Vision and Reality

Context: Your CEO announces a bold five-year vision to double market share. Meanwhile, budgets are tight, and multiple departments struggle to maintain existing projects. Employees sense a disconnect, leading to cynicism about "grandiose" ambitions.

Question: How can you, in a leadership capacity, reconcile the ambitious directive with current constraints to maintain credibility?

A. Consistently remind staff that top leaders "know best," expecting blind adherence.
B. Privately assure team members the new vision might not apply to them.
C. Translate the CEO's strategic aims into phased objectives, clarifying near-term steps employees can realistically achieve within budget parameters.

D. Avoid referencing the CEO's plan until finances improve, so employees won't dwell on its feasibility.

Scenario 5: Delegation vs. Micromanagement

Context: You lead a cross-functional group tasked with launching a new service line. Although the group includes seasoned professionals, you feel personally accountable for success. Consequently, you frequently revise their work, give exact directives, and demand daily updates, which is prompting frustration.

Question: Which response aligns with a balanced leadership approach that respects expertise while retaining oversight?

A. Continue daily check-ins and revise tasks to ensure zero errors, given high accountability.
B. Empower team leads to propose solutions, define how they'll track progress, and hold weekly or biweekly reviews for alignment.
C. Abandon oversight altogether, trusting the team to self-manage, and only step in at final deliverables.
D. Replace any team member who complains with individuals more tolerant of detailed supervision.

Note: For deeper insight into what makes certain responses more suitable, consult **16.2 Answer Rationales**, which highlights how each scenario's best choice aligns with effective leadership behaviors—be it fostering trust, addressing resistance, or navigating strategic complexities.

16.1.2 Ethical Conflicts

The following situational questions focus on **ethical challenges** that may arise in HR or broader organizational contexts. They test your ability to recognize dilemmas—such as conflicts of interest, misuse of confidential information, or under-the-table favors—and handle them in a way that upholds ethical standards. Refer to **16.2 Answer Rationales** for insights into the reasoning behind the preferable choices.

---

1. Conflict of Interest in Vendor Selection

Context: You serve on a committee selecting a new benefits vendor. Another committee member privately tells you their cousin owns one of the bidding companies and strongly hints that awarding the contract there could "streamline negotiations."

Question: Which response best protects organizational integrity?

A. Grant the contract to the cousin's company to expedite a deal, ignoring the personal tie.
B. Alert the rest of the committee about the cousin's involvement and establish a transparent review ensuring fair evaluation.
C. Let the member handle all vendor communication, given their "insider" connection.
D. Continue committee discussions but keep the cousin relationship secret to avoid controversy.

---

2. Gifts from a Potential Partner

Context: A staffing agency hoping to partner with your firm sends an expensive gift basket to your office. You're uncertain whether accepting the gesture violates any ethics guidelines, but it certainly feels lavish.

Question: How should you most appropriately proceed?

A. Accept the basket quietly and share with colleagues, hoping no one notices.
B. Return the gift or consult a policy that allows only nominal-value items, disclosing the interaction to your manager.
C. Use the gift basket as a raffle prize at the next employee event without

telling anyone where it came from.

D. Immediately blacklist the agency from any future collaboration, citing potential bribery.

---

3. Confidential Data Handling

Context: You discover a coworker forwarded an internal HR spreadsheet containing sensitive salary data to their personal email so they could "work from home." This action wasn't explicitly authorized.

Question: Which action best addresses the ethical breach while respecting procedural fairness?

A. Publicly reprimand the coworker so that others see the consequences of mishandling data.

B. Quietly ignore it, as they presumably needed the data for legitimate tasks.

C. Report the incident following established protocols, ensuring the coworker has a chance to explain but also reinforcing data security rules.

D. Immediately suspend the coworker without investigation, citing a zero-tolerance stance.

---

4. Nepotism Allegation

Context: A newly hired HR manager's niece recently joined the same department. Rumors circulate that the niece received preferential treatment in the selection process, overshadowing other qualified candidates.

Question: How can you address the ethical questions raised while maintaining departmental morale?

A. Warn everyone that discussing nepotism rumors is unacceptable and could lead to discipline.

B. Investigate the hire's compliance with standard procedures, verifying if the niece's qualifications match the role, then communicate that outcome to quell concerns.

C. Transfer the niece to an entirely different department, regardless of skill alignment.

D. Encourage the niece to resign, ensuring no further accusations arise.

---

5. Under-the-Table Expense Claims

Context: A long-tenured manager has been submitting expenses that appear inflated, though not egregiously so. You suspect they might be padding claims, but no official complaint has been lodged.

Question: Which step best demonstrates an ethical and investigative approach?

A. Approve the expenses routinely, given no formal complaint or proof.

B. Anonymously tip off the manager's direct supervisor to "keep an eye on it."

C. Review the expense policy thoroughly and ask for receipts or justifications in line with standard audit procedures.

D. Immediately accuse the manager of fraud during a staff meeting to see if they react defensively.

Note: These scenarios address dilemmas like conflicts of interest, gift acceptance, confidentiality lapses, nepotism, and potential financial misconduct. After selecting answers, turn to **16.2** for commentary on how an ethical framework informs the best responses.

16.1.3 Employee Relations

The following situational questions delve into **employee relations** challenges—ranging from resolving grievances to handling interpersonal disputes. Each scenario tests your skill in balancing organizational policies with a respectful, solution-driven approach. Refer to **Chapter 16.2** for commentary on why certain responses might be more effective.

---

1. Grievance Handling

Context: A long-serving team leader files a formal grievance, claiming the new department manager discriminates against senior employees by consistently assigning them more mundane tasks. Morale is dropping, and other tenured staff quietly agree something feels off.

Question: Which action best addresses the issue while maintaining fair and transparent procedures?

A. Immediately discipline the department manager for potential discrimination without investigation.
B. Encourage employees to "live with it" because reassigning tasks is standard management prerogative.
C. Initiate a structured review of the work allocation process, conducting interviews and documenting findings before drawing conclusions.
D. Transfer all senior employees to a different department to remove potential conflict.

---

2. Manager-Employee Dispute

Context: A line manager accuses an employee of insubordination. The employee counters that the manager routinely belittles them in front of peers. Tensions escalate—both sides threaten to escalate to HR or even legal channels.

Question: Which approach best demonstrates constructive resolution steps in line with employee relations best practices?

A. Suggest they resolve it outside of work hours to keep HR out of internal fights.

B. Escalate the matter directly to senior executives, bypassing all standard steps.

C. Arrange a mediated meeting (e.g., with an HR representative) to clarify behaviors, collect evidence, and define mutual respect guidelines going forward.

D. Document the employee's alleged insubordination and proceed with discipline, ignoring the belittling claims.

---

3. Handling Anonymous Complaints

Context: The anonymous tip line receives multiple messages indicating favoritism in performance evaluations for a particular manager's "in-group." No specific employee steps forward publicly, so management questions whether it's worth investigating.

Question: Which action aligns most closely with employee relations protocols?

A. Disregard all anonymous tips on principle, requiring named complaints only.

B. Conduct a quick chat with the accused manager, then close the file if they deny wrongdoing.

C. Compare performance ratings across this manager's team versus similar teams, looking for unusual patterns and verifying evaluation criteria.

D. Share the tip-line messages with the entire department, urging self-policing.

---

4. Cross-Functional Team Conflict

Context: Members from two different departments are at odds over project deadlines. Each side blames the other for delays. Complaints of hostile email exchanges and undermining each other's work have reached HR.

Question: What step demonstrates a balanced approach to employee relations that prioritizes collaboration?

A. Reassign one department's members to a new project, letting the other handle deadlines alone.
B. Email both groups urging them to "stop the blame game" and figure it out.
C. Bring representatives from each department together, reviewing roles and clarifying shared goals, then agree on mutual deadlines and escalation procedures.
D. Ignore the conflict, expecting that competitive tension leads to better productivity eventually.

---

5. Addressing Cultural Misunderstandings

Context: An employee from a different cultural background reports feeling alienated by casual jokes referencing stereotypes. Coworkers claim it's "harmless banter" that never intended to offend. Tensions quietly rise as the employee contemplates resigning.

Question: Which response best aligns with respectful, inclusive employee relations?

A. Advise the employee to "lighten up" since no malicious intent was meant.
B. Launch a formal harassment investigation accusing the entire team of discrimination.
C. Call a brief department meeting to clarify respectful communication norms, reaffirm zero tolerance for stereotyping, and create an avenue for follow-up if issues persist.
D. Offer the employee a transfer, thus preserving the team's existing dynamic.

Note: These scenarios emphasize problem-solving, neutral investigation, and the need for open dialogue in addressing employee concerns. After selecting answers, consult **Section 16.2** for deeper explanations of each scenario's recommended resolution path.

16.2 Answer Rationales

16.2.1 Why Certain Responses Are Stronger

Below are concise explanations clarifying why a particular response represents the strongest choice in each scenario. This section builds on the details from **16.1**, so these rationales assume familiarity with the original situations. The focus here is simply to highlight the unique reasoning behind each preferred solution.

16.1.1 Leadership Dilemmas

Scenario 1 (Team Turbulence)

Best Answer: **C**

Why It's Stronger: It tackles both the new hire's need for support and the high performers' frustration by promoting structured dialogue, shared expectations, and a clear plan to develop the newcomer's skills—rather than ignoring tensions or forcing a quick shuffle.

Scenario 2 (Leadership Succession Crisis)

Best Answer: **C**

Why It's Stronger: Soliciting volunteers for interim leadership and clarifying support signals transparency and encourages capable, motivated individuals to step forward. It avoids hasty appointments or freezing projects, ensuring continuity while a permanent solution is found.

Scenario 3 (Strategic Shift Resistance)

Best Answer: **B**

Why It's Stronger: Proactively involving managers in small-group sessions demonstrates empathy for their concerns about automation and outlines how training or role adjustments may mitigate any negative impact, reinforcing trust and buy-in.

Scenario 4 (Conflict Between Vision and Reality)

Best Answer: **C**

Why It's Stronger: Translating lofty ambitions into phased steps acknowledges current constraints. This approach preserves credibility by presenting a practical roadmap, rather than brushing aside resource limitations or demanding blind adherence.

Scenario 5 (Delegation vs. Micromanagement)

Best Answer: **B**

Why It's Stronger: Empowering experienced team members to propose solutions and meet at regular intervals balances accountability with respect for expertise—reducing overreach while still upholding leadership oversight.

16.1.2 Ethical Conflicts

1. Conflict of Interest in Vendor Selection

Best Answer: **B**

Why It's Stronger: Disclosing the personal connection and ensuring a fair, transparent review process upholds integrity, preventing silent favoritism or hidden biases.

2. Gifts from a Potential Partner

Best Answer: **B**

Why It's Stronger: Consulting guidelines on gift value and notifying a manager displays caution and openness, ensuring no perceived or actual conflict of interest in forging business relationships.

3. Confidential Data Handling

Best Answer: **C**

Why It's Stronger: Following established protocols to report the incident and clarifying expectations highlights data security as a serious concern, while giving the coworker due process.

4. Nepotism Allegation

Best Answer: **B**

Why It's Stronger: Conducting a compliance check of the niece's qualifications and the hiring steps, then communicating findings, demonstrates fairness—addressing rumors rather than shutting them down or taking abrupt measures.

5. Under-the-Table Expense Claims

Best Answer: **C**

Why It's Stronger: Reviewing the expense policy and seeking proper documentation is both measured and respectful of due process—balancing the need to verify integrity without making premature accusations.

16.1.3 Employee Relations

1. Grievance Handling

Best Answer: **C**

Why It's Stronger: Investigating the work allocation process, collecting feedback, and documenting findings maintains neutrality, ensuring decisions are based on evidence rather than swift assumptions.

2. Manager-Employee Dispute

Best Answer: **C**

Why It's Stronger: Arranging a mediation underscores the organization's commitment to fairness and clarity, letting both parties present their perspectives and collaborate on respectful solutions.

3. Handling Anonymous Complaints

Best Answer: **C**

Why It's Stronger: Comparing performance ratings for unusual patterns addresses potential favoritism systematically, rather than dismissing or acting on unsubstantiated claims without analysis.

4. Cross-Functional Team Conflict

Best Answer: **C**

Why It's Stronger: Bringing representatives together fosters a cooperative environment to define roles, deadlines, and escalation paths—resolving tension and enhancing collaboration instead of ignoring or isolating teams.

5. Addressing Cultural Misunderstandings
Best Answer: **C**
Why It's Stronger: Directly discussing respectful communication norms in a brief meeting, reaffirming zero tolerance for stereotyping, and offering follow-up avenues shows both responsiveness and inclusivity without labeling the entire team as guilty.

Note: Each best answer stands out by aligning with proven leadership, ethical, or collaborative principles—reflecting mindful problem-solving rather than quick fixes or dismissive actions.

16.2.2 Links to Specific Competencies

Below are concise references connecting each scenario from **16.1** to relevant behavioral competencies in **Part IV**. Rather than repeating the scenario details or rationales, this list simply highlights which chapters/sub-chapters illuminate the underpinnings of each chosen response.

16.1.1 Leadership Dilemmas

Scenario 1 (Team Turbulence)
Relates to: Chapter 11.1.2 (Core Proficiency Indicators in Leadership & Navigation), focusing on balancing team needs, and Chapter 12.1.2 (Conflict Resolution Techniques) for managing tension between seasoned employees and a new hire.

Scenario 2 (Leadership Succession Crisis)
Relates to: Chapter 11.1.1 (Key Concepts and Definitions in Leadership & Navigation), demonstrating adaptability when a leader departs abruptly, and Chapter 13.2.1 (Internal Consulting Models) if interim leadership solutions require broader consultation.

Scenario 3 (Strategic Shift Resistance)

Relates to: Chapter 10.1.2 (Strategy Formulation and Alignment), covering communication of strategic pivots, and Chapter 11.1.4 (Practical Scenarios: Leading Teams, Influencing Stakeholders), emphasizing stakeholder engagement amid resistance.

Scenario 4 (Conflict Between Vision and Reality)

Relates to: Chapter 10.2.3 (Communicating the Value of HR Initiatives), focusing on bridging ambitious goals with limited resources, and Chapter 11.1.3 (Senior-Level Indicators in Leadership & Navigation) for advanced leadership in reconciling constraints.

Scenario 5 (Delegation vs. Micromanagement)

Relates to: Chapter 11.2.1 (Ethical Frameworks in HR) for respecting autonomy, though it's primarily leadership-focused; also Chapter 12.1.1 (Establishing Trust and Credibility), emphasizing empowerment of skilled teams over micromanagement.

16.1.2 Ethical Conflicts

Conflict of Interest in Vendor Selection

Relates to: Chapter 11.2.3 (Handling Ethical Dilemmas) for transparency in personal ties, and Chapter 12.2.2 (Listening and Feedback Mechanisms) if clarifications with the committee are needed.

Gifts from a Potential Partner

Relates to: Chapter 11.2.2 (Code of Conduct Development) on gift acceptance guidelines, and Chapter 12.1.1 (Establishing Trust and Credibility) to avoid perceived bribery.

Confidential Data Handling

Relates to: Chapter 11.2.3 (Handling Ethical Dilemmas) concerning data privacy, and Chapter 8.5.1 (HR Information Systems and Data Security) for procedural references.

Nepotism Allegation
Relates to: Chapter 11.2.1 (Ethical Frameworks in HR) on fairness in hiring, and Chapter 8.4.4 (Non-Union Employee Relations Strategies) for ensuring transparency within the department.

Under-the-Table Expense Claims
Relates to: Chapter 11.2.3 (Handling Ethical Dilemmas) for investigating potential financial misconduct, and Chapter 13.3.2 (Evidence-Based Decision Making) to gather proof before concluding wrongdoing.

16.1.3 Employee Relations

Grievance Handling
Relates to: Chapter 8.4.2 (Managing Grievances and Disciplinary Actions) on structured processes, and Chapter 12.1.2 (Conflict Resolution Techniques) regarding evidence-based resolution.

Manager-Employee Dispute
Relates to: Chapter 12.1.2 (Conflict Resolution Techniques) for mediating heated disagreements, and Chapter 8.4.4 (Non-Union Employee Relations Strategies) if no union channels exist.

Handling Anonymous Complaints
Relates to: Chapter 12.2.2 (Listening and Feedback Mechanisms) to address anonymous feedback methodically, and Chapter 8.4.4 (Non-Union Employee Relations Strategies) for neutral fact-finding.

Cross-Functional Team Conflict
Relates to: Chapter 12.1.2 (Conflict Resolution Techniques) again for bridging departmental standoffs, and Chapter 8.2.3 (Interventions for Improving Effectiveness) if organizational development solutions are necessary.

Addressing Cultural Misunderstandings
Relates to: Chapter 12.3.1 (Cultural Intelligence (CQ)) for respecting diverse

backgrounds, and Chapter 8.4.4 (Non-Union Employee Relations Strategies) when building an inclusive climate without formal union intervention.

How to Use These Links:

Match each scenario's primary challenge to the corresponding competency references here. By revisiting those chapters, you'll see how day-to-day situational judgment aligns with the broader behavioral and ethical frameworks underpinning effective HR practice.

Chapter 17: Access to Digital Content

Your success doesn't end with this book. To further support your preparation and mastery of the material, we've included powerful digital tools designed to enhance your study process. These resources are accessible on both mobile and desktop devices, providing flexibility and convenience.

Unlimited Exam Simulator

The unlimited exam simulator is your ultimate tool for practicing and perfecting your test-taking skills. This feature generates an unlimited number of practice exams tailored to your preferences, ensuring you always have fresh material to work with.

Key Features:
- ✓ Choose the number of questions and set the time limit.
- ✓ Randomized questions ensure no two tests are ever the same.

How It Helps:
- ✓ Builds confidence by simulating actual test conditions.
- ✓ Identifies weak areas by tracking performance over multiple attempts.

Scan the QR Code or go to:

www.apex-academic.com/shrm_exam_sim

Access Code can be found on page 472 of this book.

Digital Flashcards

Our flashcard set is a convenient way to review critical concepts and memorize key terms, concepts, and requirements.

Key Features:
- ✓ Includes People Domain, Organization Domain, Workplace Domain, and more.
- ✓ Flip between terms and definitions with a single click.

How It Helps:
- ✓ Reinforces understanding through repetition.
- ✓ Quick and efficient for on-the-go study sessions.

Scan the QR Code or go to:

www.apex-academic.com/shrm_flashcard

Access Code can be found on page 472 of this book

Printable Full-Length Exams

For those who prefer a physical study option, we've included printable full-length exams. These are formatted to match the real exam, offering an authentic test experience offline.

Key Features:

- Downloadable PDFs of complete practice exams.
- Includes answer keys for self-assessment.
- Matches the format, question count, and difficulty of the actual test.

How It Helps:

- Allows for focused practice without screen distractions.
- Provides a realistic testing environment when paired with a timer.

Scan the QR Code or go to:

www.apex-academic.com/shrm_exam_print

Access Code can be found on page 472 of this book

A Message From Apex Academic Resources

Dear Reader,

Bringing a comprehensive resource like *SHRM-CP/SCP Exam Success* to life requires a substantial commitment from a dedicated team. Authors, subject matter experts, editors, and designers all contribute their skills to create a guide that aims to support your progress toward mastering the material.

If this book has informed you, guided you, or benefited you in any way, we would greatly appreciate your honest feedback on Amazon. Your reviews not only help us refine our approach for future publications but also assist other readers in discovering tools that fit their own professional needs. Whether your thoughts take the form of a brief note or a detailed evaluation, your input is genuinely important to us.

Thank you for choosing our resource and for placing your trust in our work. We hope this material has been a valuable step forward, and we wish you all the best as you continue to move ahead with your goals.

With gratitude,
The Apex Academic Resources Team

Made in the USA
Las Vegas, NV
28 May 2025

22716694R00302